LEARN ITALIAN (ITALIANO) THE FAST AND FUN WAY

by Marcel Danesi, Ph.D.
Professor of Italian
Professor of Methodology
University of Toronto

Heywood Wald, Coordinating Editor
Chairman, Department of Foreign Languages
Martin Van Buren High School, New York

To help you pace your learning, we've included stopwatches *like the one above* throughout the book to mark each 15-minute interval. You can read one of these units each day or pace yourself according to your needs.

CONTENTS

Cover and Book Design Milton Glaser, Inc.
Illustrations Juan Suarez

All inquiries should be addressed to:
Barron's Educational Series, Inc.
250 Wireless Boulevard
Hauppauge, New York 11788

Library of Congress Catalog Card No. 83-26641

International Standard Book No. 0-8120-2854-6

PRINTED IN THE UNITED STATES OF AMERICA
23 880 98

Library of Congress Cataloging-in-Publication Data

Danesi, Marcel, 1946-
Learn Italian the fast and fun way.

1. Italian language—Conversation and phrase books—English. I. Title.
PC1121.D36 1985 458.3′421 83-26641
ISBN 0-8120-2854-6

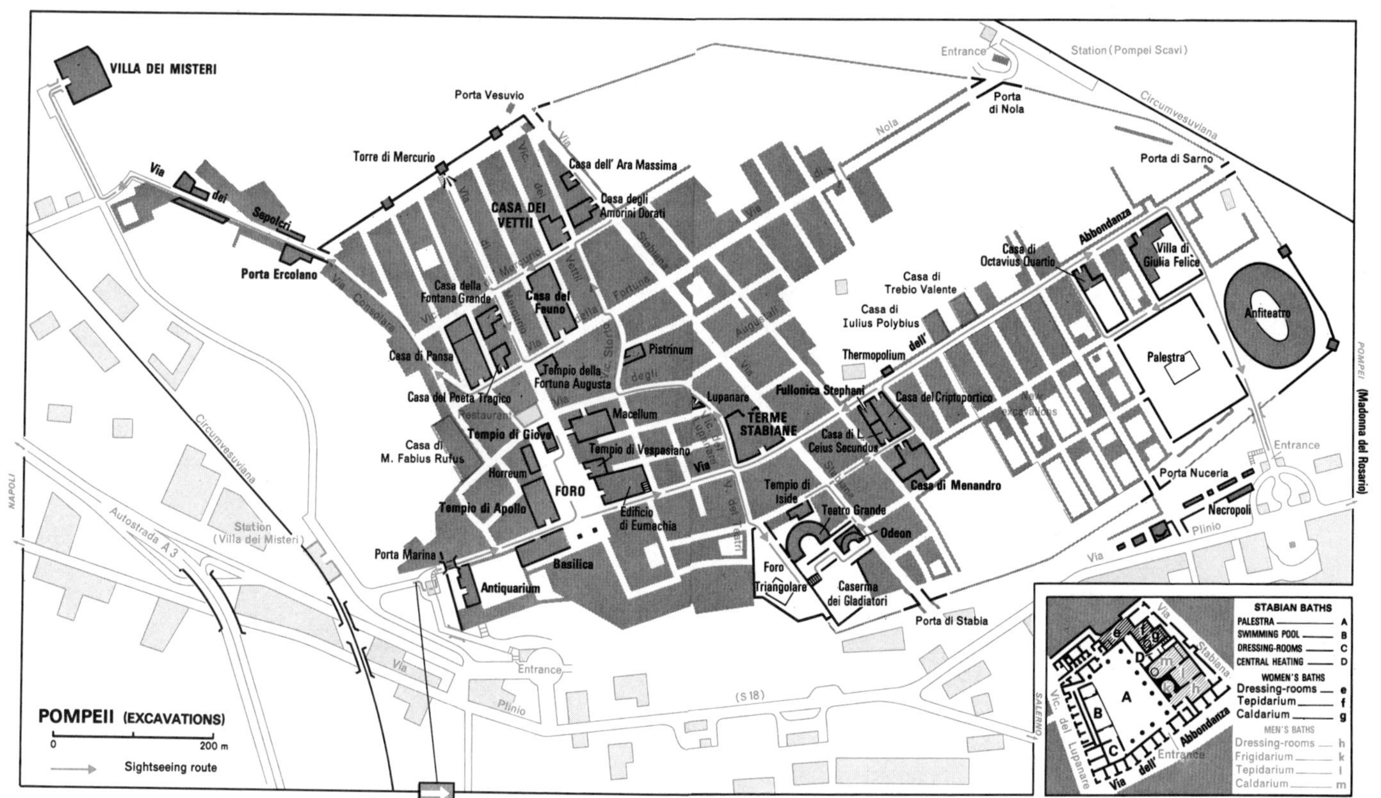

(Courtesy of Michelin Guide, Italy, *10th Edition—reprinted with permission)*

Italian is a "Romance" language, along with French, Spanish, Portuguese, and Rumanian, to mention the most widely spoken ones. This is because they all derive directly from the language of Rome—Latin. Most of the approximately 56 million inhabitants of Italy speak Italian. There are also many immigrants of Italian origin in North America who continue to speak Italian, especially in the home.

Italy is a peninsula in the shape of a "boot." There are also two islands on its western coast: Sardinia **(Sardegna)** and Sicily **(Sicilia)**. It is surrounded by the Mediterranean Sea **(Mar Mediterraneo)**, which takes on different names, as you can see on the map. The Alps **(le Alpi)** and the Apennines **(gli Appennini)** are the two main mountain chains in Italy. Politically, the country is divided into twenty regions—each with its own dialect and local traditions. The capital of Italy is Rome **(Roma)**. You will enjoy visiting many interesting spots.

You might, for example, want to see Venice's famous San Marco church and square, Florence's breathtaking Piazza del Duomo, Rome's immortal Colosseum, Naples' famous San Carlo theater. You might also want to shop in Milan's world-famous Galleria. Or, you might want to enjoy the tranquil surroundings on the island of Capri. Other famous cities you might want to visit are Trieste, Turin **(Torino)**, Genoa **(Genova)**, Bologna, Pisa, and Palermo—to mention but a few.

Italian painting, sculpture, literature, and music are famous all over the world. Who has not heard of the great Renaissance artist Michelangelo or of the great scientist Galileo? The names Dante, Boccaccio, Petrarch **(Petrarca)**, Leonardo da Vinci, Verdi, Puccini, Rossini, Paganini, Marconi are forged into history, as, of course, is that of Christopher Columbus **(Cristoforo Colombo).** Today, Italy is famous for its artisanship and design, especially in the fields of clothing, furniture, and automobiles. Its cinematography is internationally acclaimed. Italy's cuisine also enjoys a worldwide reputation, notably with spaghetti, ravioli, lasagna **(lasagne),** gnocchi, and macaroni **(maccheroni).**

By learning the language of Italy, you will acquire a valuable key to many of its cultural treasures. Just put in 15 minutes a day at a pace comfortable for you. Some days you'll cover many pages, some not so many. Now, let's get started.

PRONUNCIATION

It is thought by many that Italian is an easy language to speak, that it is written as it is spoken. This is generally true. The following charts will help you with the troublesome letters and sounds. First we give you the vowels, then the consonants. You'll need to familiarize yourself with these sounds, even though each time a new phrase is introduced in this book, the pronunciation is also shown.

VOWELS

ITALIAN VOWELS	ENGLISH EQUIVALENT	SYMBOL
c*a*s*a*	**h*a*rd**	**ah**
b*e*n*e*	**b*e*t**	**eh**
p*i*acere	***ea*se, p*i*ano**	**ee, y**
v*o*l*o*	**b*o*ne**	**oh**
sc*u*si	**r*u*le, g*u*ava**	**oo, w**

NOTE: Speakers in different parts of Italy will pronounce *e* and *o* slightly differently, but not enough to make a substantial difference. The *i* and *u* may stand for "y" and "w" sounds respectively. This has to do with syllable considerations. For your own practical purposes, just follow the pronunciation aids provided throughout the book.

CONSONANTS

ITALIAN LETTERS	SYMBOLS	PRONUNCIATION/EXAMPLES
c	k	Before *a, o, u,* and all consonants, pronounce with a hard "c." Example: *come* (KOH-meh) how.
c	ch	Before *e* and *i,* use the "ch" sound, as in "church." Example: *arrivederci* (ah-rree-veh-DEHR-chee) good-bye.
ch	k	Before *e* and *i,* pronounce with a hard "k" sound. Example: *che* (keh) what.
ci	ch	Before *a, o,* and *u,* use the "ch" sound, as in "church." Example: *ciao* (CHAH-oh) hi or bye.
g	g	Before *a, o, u,* and all consonants, pronounce with a hard "g" as in "gas." Example: *gatto* (GAH-ttoh) cat.
g	j	Before *e* and *i,* pronounce the "j" sound as in "just." Example: *gita* (JEE-tah) trip.
gh	g	Before *e* and *i,* use the hard "g" sound. Example: *spaghetti* (spah-GEH-ttee).
gi	j	Before *a, o,* and *u,* pronounce with a "j" sound. Example: giorno (JOHR-noh) day.
gli	lly	Pronounce like the "lli" in "million." Example: *figlia* (FEE-llyah) daughter.
gn	ny	Pronounce like the "ny" in "canyon." Example: *gnocchi* (NYOH-kkee) dumplings.

CONSONANTS (continued)

ITALIAN LETTERS	SYMBOLS	PRONUNCIATION/EXAMPLES
qu	kw	Pronounce like the English "quick." Example: *quando* (KWAHN-doh) when.
s	s, z	Might be pronounced "s" as in "sit" or "z" as in "zoo." Examples: *sorella* (soh-REH-llah) sister and *sbaglio* (ZBAH-llyoh) mistake.
sc, sch	sk	For letters "sc" before *a, o, u,* and consonants, and for letters "sch" before *e* and *i*. Both of these combinations are pronounced "sk" as in "ski." Examples: *scusi* (SKOO-see) excuse me and *scherzo* (SKEHR-tsoh) prank.
sc	sh	Before *e* and *i*, use the English "sh" sound. Example: *scendere* (SHEHN-deh-reh) to get off.
z	ts, dz	Sometimes pronounced "ts" and sometimes "dz." Examples: *zio* (TSEE-oh) uncle and *zucchero* (DZOO-kkeh-roh) sugar.

Most consonants can be doubled, and these are represented by double letters. In this book, doubled consonants are indicated phonetically by a doubled symbol ("kk," "gg," and so on). Simply double, or lengthen, your articulation.

The remaining Italian sounds and letters correspond, more or less, to English ones. For example:

(boh-LOH-nyah)
B**ologna**

(sahr-DEH-nyah)
Sar***d*****egna**

(fee-REHN-tseh)
Firenze

(pah-LEHR-moh)
P**a*****l*****ermo**

(MAH-reh)
m**are**

(NAH-poh-lee)
N**apoli**

(PEE-sah)
P**isa**

(ROH-mah)
R**oma**
(rolled)

(toh-REE-noh)
T**orino**
(touching the upper teeth)

(VEE-noh)
v**ino**

Now write these words, along with the English translation, and pronounce them, using the pronunciation rules just given.

arrivederci ______________________________

figlia ______________________________

figlio ______________________________

valige ______________________________

volo ______________________________

HOW ENGLISH AND ITALIAN ARE SIMILAR

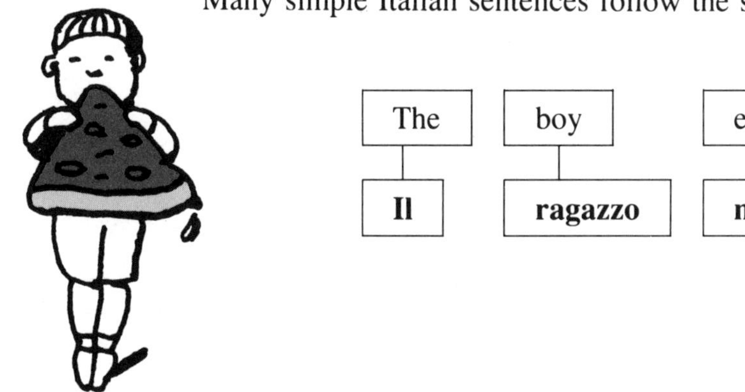

Many simple Italian sentences follow the same arrangement as English ones:

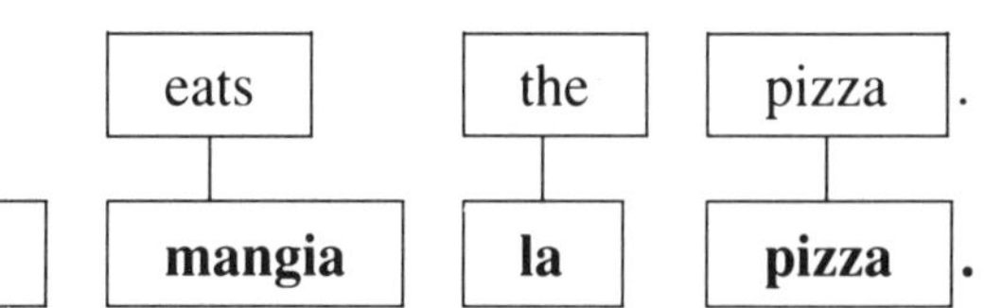
The
boy
eats
the
pizza.
Il
ragazzo
mangia
la
pizza.

The differences that exist between the two languages will come out as you study this book. For example, you will learn that adjectives usually follow nouns in Italian:

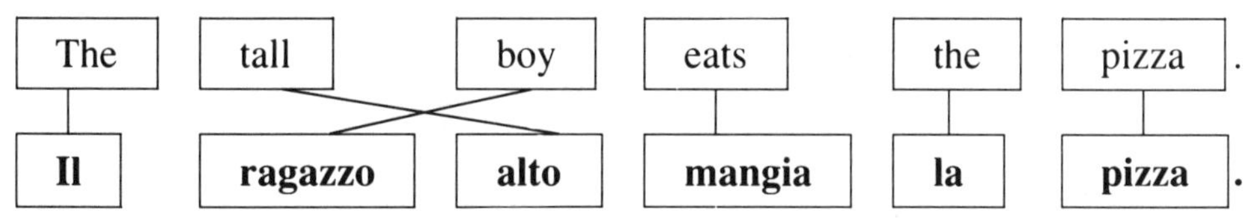
The
tall
boy
eats
the
pizza.
Il
ragazzo
alto
mangia
la
pizza.

Many Italian words can be learned simply by recognizing patterns such as the following:

ENGLISH WORDS ENDING IN:	ITALIAN WORDS ENDING IN:
-ION	**-IONE**
correction	**correzione**
occasion	**occasione**
nation	**nazione**
station	**stazione**
function	**funzione**
-TY	**-TÀ**
city	**città**
ability	**abilità**
parity	**parità**
sociability	**sociabilità**
sincerity	**sincerità**
-IST	**-ISTA**
dentist	**dentista**
violinist	**violinista**
pianist	**pianista**
artist	**artista**
-OR	**-ORE**
actor	**attore**
sculptor	**scultore**
vigor	**vigore**
color	**colore**

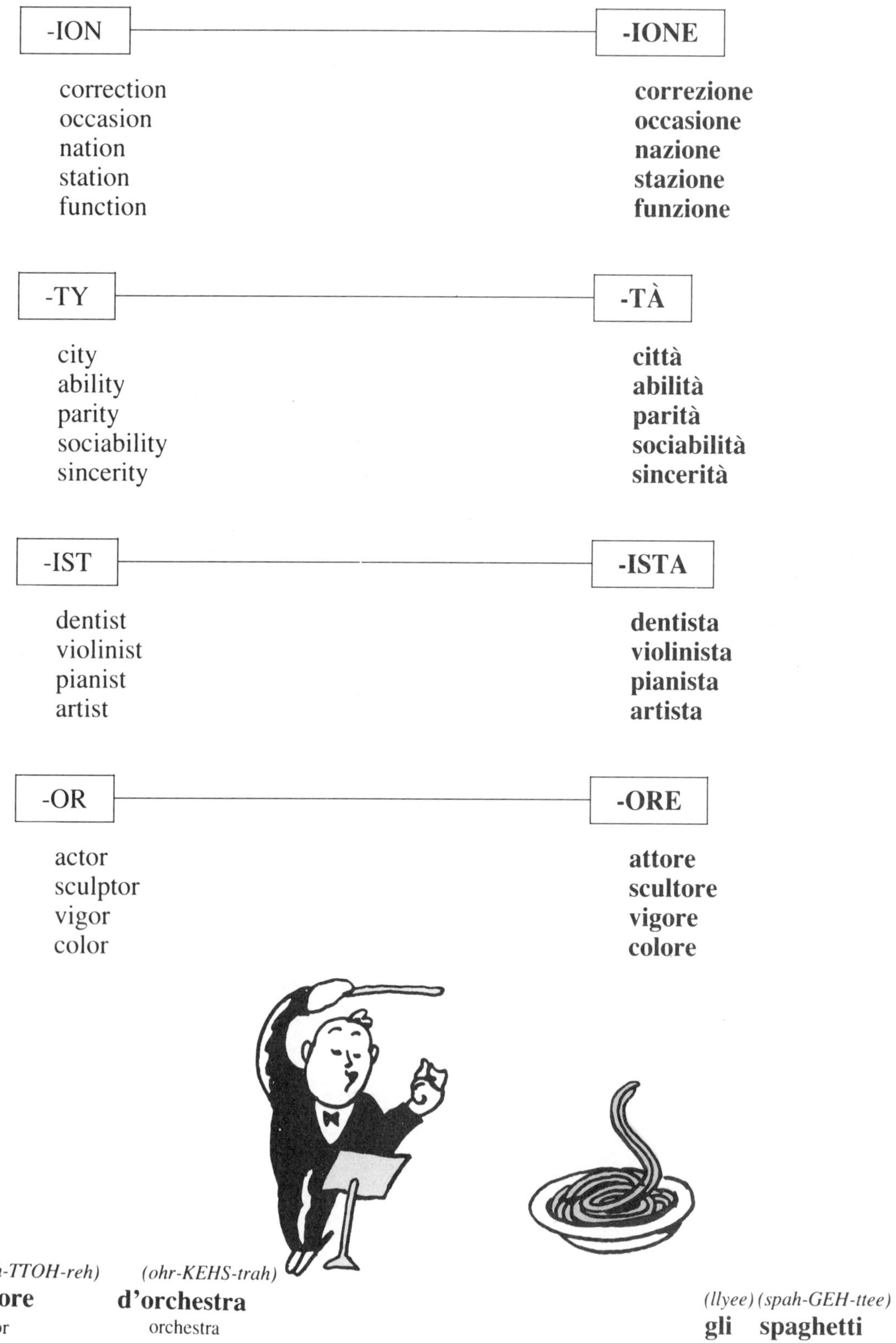

(dee-reh-TTOH-reh) *(ohr-KEHS-trah)*
il direttore d'orchestra
conductor orchestra

(llyee) (spah-GEH-ttee)
gli spaghetti

As you learn the language, you will discover many other similar patterns.

This book will attempt to make it as easy and as enjoyable as possible for you to learn to speak and understand basic Italian. For your purposes, you will need a few important grammatical skills and a basic vocabulary of about one thousand words.

(MAH-kkee-nah)
la macchina
car

(mee-keh-LAHN-jeh-loh)
il "David" di Michelangelo
Michelangelo's David

You will learn only the present and imperative tenses, which is really all you will need in order to communicate your needs and intentions. Some of the dialogues may seem to be somewhat unrealistic—this is because they are deliberately written in the present tense.

You will have opportunities to check your progress throughout the book. If you forget something, or feel that you need some reinforcement, go over the appropriate parts.

By working through this book for about 15 minutes a day, you will develop the ability to ask for a hotel room, to exchange money, to order food, and so on. Do not overdo it! In the 15 minutes you will spend each day on learning Italian, work only through the pages that you can cover comfortably. Have fun!

GETTING TO KNOW PEOPLE

(FAH-reh) (koh-noh-SHEHN-tsah) (JEHN-teh)
Fare la conoscenza della gente

1 Come si inizia una conversazione

(KOH-meh) (see) (ee-NEE-tsee-ah) (kohn-vehr-sa-TSYOH-neh)

Starting a Conversation

When you go to Italy, and we hope you will soon, one of the first things you will want to do is to meet people and strike up a friendly conversation. To do this you will need some handy expressions for conversation openers. You'll find several of them you can use in these easy conversations. Underline them so you can remember them better.

Read over the following dialogue several times, pronouncing each line carefully out loud. Try to "act out" each role. The dialogue contains some basic words and expressions that will be useful to you.

(Mark Smith and his wife, Mary, their daughter Anne, and their son John have just arrived at the Rome airport and are looking for their luggage. Mark approaches an airline employee.)

(BWOHN) (JOHR-noh) (see-NYOH-reh) MARK **Buon giorno, signore.**	Hello (or Good day/Good morning), sir.
(deh-SEE-deh-rah) COMMESSO **Buon giorno. Desidera** *(kwahl-KOH-sah)* **qualcosa?**	Hello. May I help you? (*literally*, do you want something)
(CHEHR-koh)(MEE-eh) (vah-LEE-jeh) MARK **Sì. Cerco le mie valige.**	Yes. I am looking for my suitcases.
(BEH-neh) (KYAH-mah) COMMESSO **Bene. Come si chiama,** *(LEH-ee)* **lei?**	Well (or Fine/Okay). What is your name? (*literally,* what do you call yourself)
(KYAH-moh) MARK **Mi chiamo (il signor) Mark Smith.**	My name is (Mr.) Mark Smith.
(DOH-veh) (AH-bee-tah) COMMESSO **Dove abita?**	Where do you live?
(AH-bee-toh) (NEH-llyee) MARK **Abito negli Stati Uniti, a Chicago.**	I live in the United States, in Chicago.

(NOO-meh-roh) (SOO-oh)
COMMESSO **Il numero del suo volo?** — Your flight number?

(treh-chehn-toh-TREH)
MARK **Trecentotré da New York.** — 303 from New York.

(moh-MEHN-toh) (fah-VOH-reh)
COMMESSO **Un momento, per favore.** — One moment, please.

(joh-VAH-nnee)
(As the clerk looks through some papers on his desk, Giovanni, an Italian business friend, runs into Mark.)

(CHAH-oh) (STAH-ee)
GIOVANNI **Ciao, Mark. Come stai?** — Hi, Mark. How are you?

MARK **Giovanni! Sto bene, e tu?** — John! I am well, and you?

(MOHL-toh) (SEH-ee) (kwee) (vah-KAHN-tsah)
GIOVANNI **Molto bene. Sei qui per una vacanza?** — Very well. Are you here for a holiday?

(preh-ZEHN-toh) (MEE-ah) (fah-MEE-llyah) (MOH-llyeh) (FEE-llyah) (FEE-llyoh)
MARK **Sì. Ti presento la mia famiglia. Mia moglie Mary, mia figlia Anne, e mio figlio John.** — Yes. Let me introduce my family to you. My wife Mary, my daughter Anne, and my son John.

(pyah-CHEH-reh)
GIOVANNI **Piacere.** — A pleasure.

(SKOO-see) (ah-RREE-vah-noh) (PROH-ssee-moh)
COMMESSO **Scusi, signore, le valige arrivano con il prossimo volo.** — Excuse me, sir, the suitcases are arriving with the next flight.

(ah-chee-DEHN-tee)
MARK **Accidenti!** — Darn it!

(pah-TSYEHN-tsah)
GIOVANNI **Pazienza, Mark. Sei in Italia.** — Patience, Mark. You're in Italy.

MARK *(to the clerk)* **Grazie** *(GRAH-tsee-eh)* **e arrivederla.** *(ah-rree-veh-DEHR-lah)*	Thank you and good-bye *(polite)*.
COMMESSO **Prego, signore.** *(PREH-goh)*	You're welcome, sir.
MARK *(to Giovanni)* **Ciao.**	Good-bye *(familiar)*.
GIOVANNI **Arrivederci a tutti.** *(TOO-ttee)*	Good-bye to all.
TUTTI **Arrivederci.** *(ah-rree-veh-DEHR-chee)*	Good-bye *(familiar)*.

Now without looking back try to fill in the missing dialogue parts. Check your answers from the dialogue only *after* attempting to fill in the parts from memory.

Buon giorno, signore.

B________ g________. Desidera qualcosa?

Sì. Cerco le mie v________.

Bene. Come si c________, lei?

M_____ c________ (il signor) Mark Smith.

Il n________ del suo v________?

Trecentotré d_____ New York.

Un momento, p________ f________.

By rearranging the following words you will get sentences from the dialogue.

mia / la / presento / Ti / famiglia

____

arrivano / valige / le / prossimo / volo / il / con / Scusi / signore

____

tutti / a / Arrivederci

____

ANSWERS

Sentences Ti presento la mia famiglia. Scusi, signore, le valige arrivano con il prossimo volo. Arrivederci a tutti.

(pehr-SOH-neh) (KOH-seh)

LE PERSONE E LE COSE

People and Things

One of the first things you will need to know how to do in Italian is naming people and things. Look carefully at the following:

(seen-goh-LAH-reh) (ploo-RAH-leh)

Singolare e plurale

singular plural

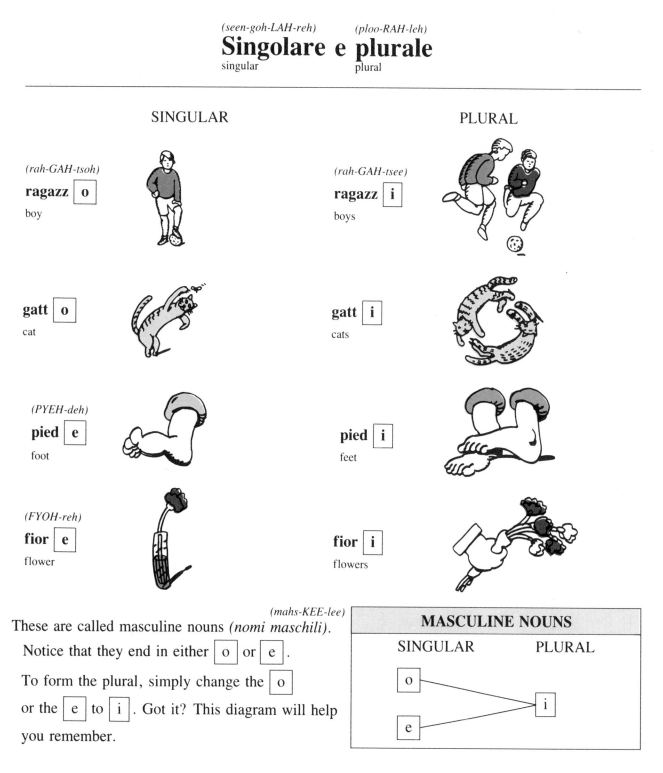

SINGULAR	PLURAL
(rah-GAH-tsoh) **ragazz** [o] boy	 *(rah-GAH-tsee)* **ragazz** [i] boys 
gatt [o] cat	 **gatt** [i] cats 
(PYEH-deh) **pied** [e] foot	 **pied** [i] feet 
(FYOH-reh) **fior** [e] flower	 **fior** [i] flowers 

These are called masculine nouns *(nomi maschili)*. *(mahs-KEE-lee)*

Notice that they end in either [o] or [e].

To form the plural, simply change the [o] or the [e] to [i]. Got it? This diagram will help you remember.

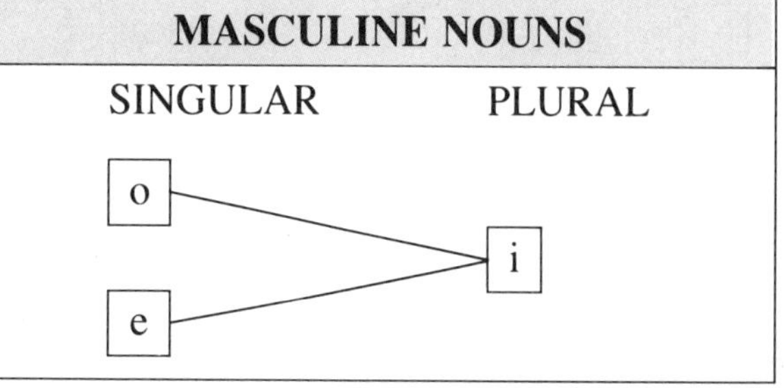

Now look at the following additional nouns.

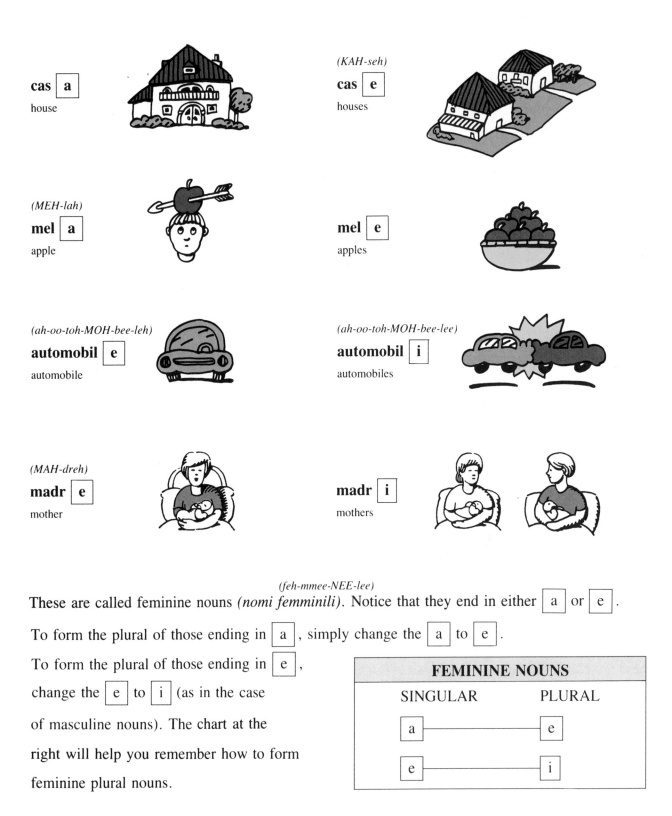

SINGULAR		PLURAL	
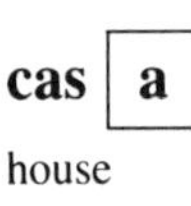 **cas** **a** house		*(KAH-seh)* **cas** **e** houses	
(MEH-lah) **mel** **a** apple		**mel** **e** apples	
(ah-oo-toh-MOH-bee-leh)  **automobil** **e** automobile		*(ah-oo-toh-MOH-bee-lee)* **automobil** **i** automobiles	
(MAH-dreh) **madr** **e** mother		**madr** **i** mothers	 

These are called feminine nouns *(nomi femminili)* *(feh-mmee-NEE-lee)*. Notice that they end in either a or e. To form the plural of those ending in a, simply change the a to e.

To form the plural of those ending in e, change the e to i (as in the case of masculine nouns). The chart at the right will help you remember how to form feminine plural nouns.

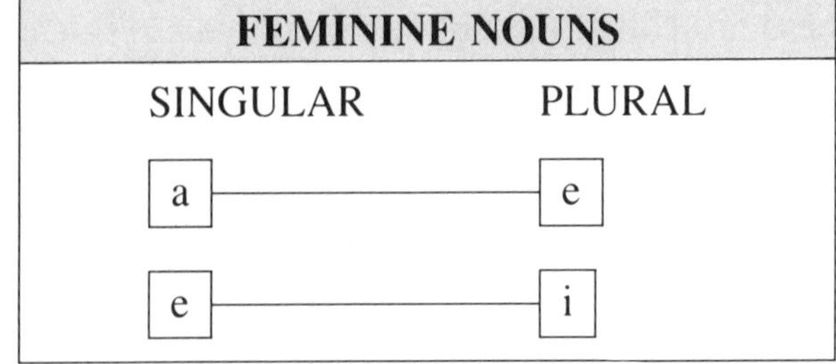

FEMININE NOUNS

SINGULAR	PLURAL
a	e
e	i

An even easier way to remember how to form the plural of any noun is seen in this chart, which simply combines the previous two.

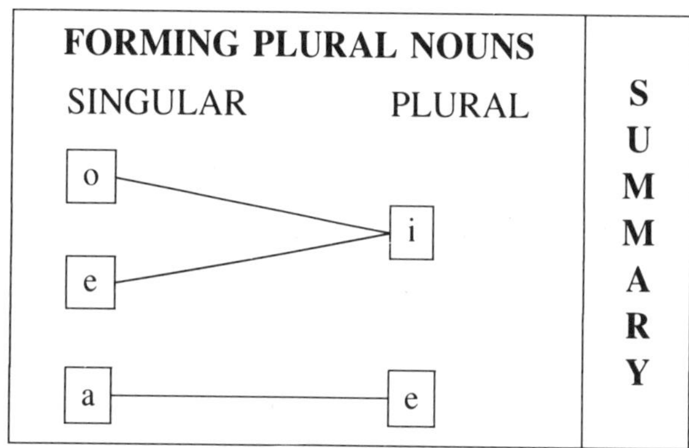

Got it? Now test yourself by trying to put the following nouns into the plural.

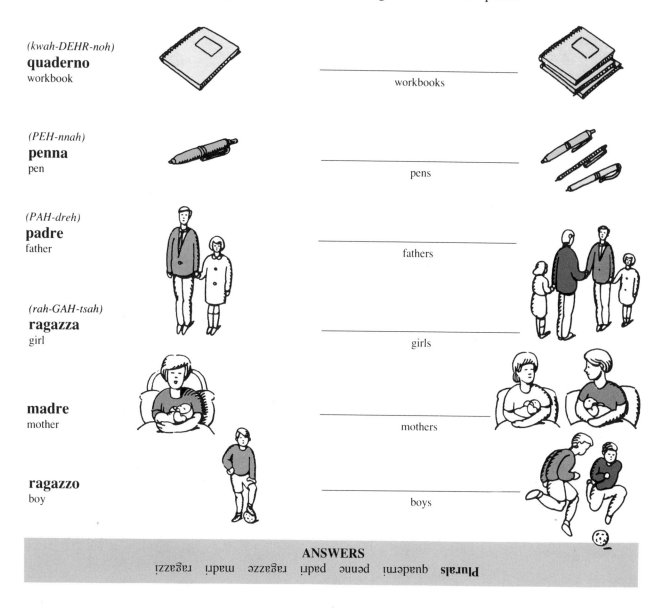

(kwah-DEHR-noh)
quaderno
workbook

____
workbooks

(PEH-nnah)
penna
pen

____
pens

(PAH-dreh)
padre
father

____
fathers

(rah-GAH-tsah)
ragazza
girl

____
girls

madre
mother

____
mothers

ragazzo
boy

____
boys

ANSWERS

Plurals quaderni penne padri ragazze madri ragazzi

Una, un', uno, un

A and *An*

When we name something (that is, use a noun) in English, we often precede the noun with "a" or "an." The same is true in Italian. Here is how we say these words, depending on whether the noun is masculine or feminine.

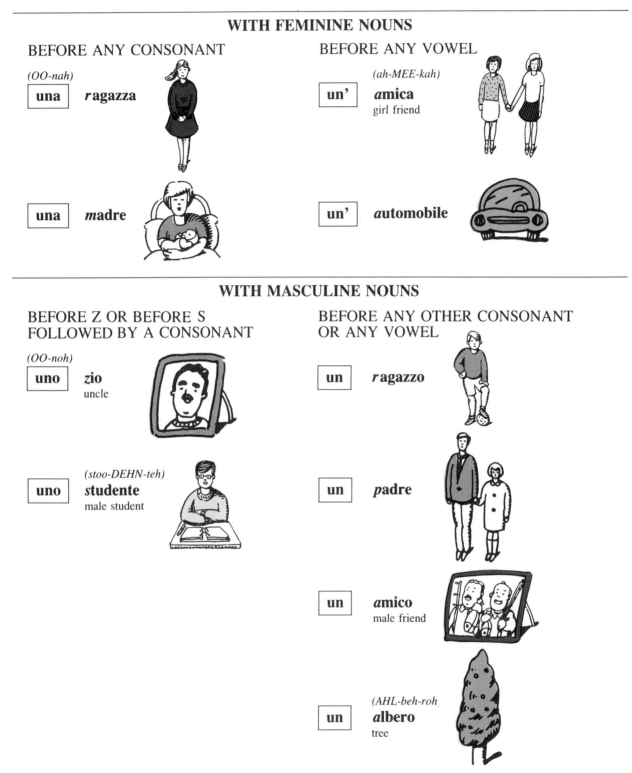

WITH FEMININE NOUNS

BEFORE ANY CONSONANT

(OO-nah)
una ***r*agazza**

BEFORE ANY VOWEL

(ah-MEE-kah)
un' ***a*mica**
girl friend

una ***m*adre**

un' ***a*utomobile**

WITH MASCULINE NOUNS

BEFORE Z OR BEFORE S FOLLOWED BY A CONSONANT

(OO-noh)
uno ***z*io**
uncle

(stoo-DEHN-teh)
uno ***s*tudente**
male student

BEFORE ANY OTHER CONSONANT OR ANY VOWEL

un ***r*agazzo**

un ***p*adre**

un ***a*mico**
male friend

(AHL-beh-roh)
un ***a*lbero**
tree

As you can see, in front of feminine nouns, "a" or "an" is **una** if the noun begins with a consonant, and **un'** if it begins with a vowel. In front of masculine nouns, **uno** is used if the noun begins with *z* or with *s* plus a consonant (*sp, st, sm,* etc.); otherwise **un** is used. Notice that **un** does not have an apostrophe in the masculine. The following chart is a handy summary to which you might refer if you run into any difficulties.

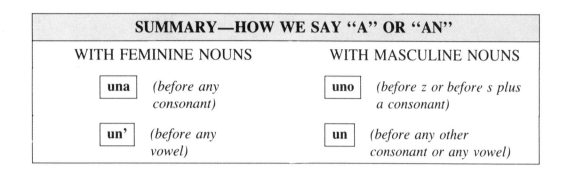

SUMMARY—HOW WE SAY "A" OR "AN"			
WITH FEMININE NOUNS		WITH MASCULINE NOUNS	
una	*(before any consonant)*	**uno**	*(before z or before s plus a consonant)*
un'	*(before any vowel)*	**un**	*(before any other consonant or any vowel)*

Now give this a try. Fill in the appropriate form of "a" or "an" in the space provided for each of the following nouns.

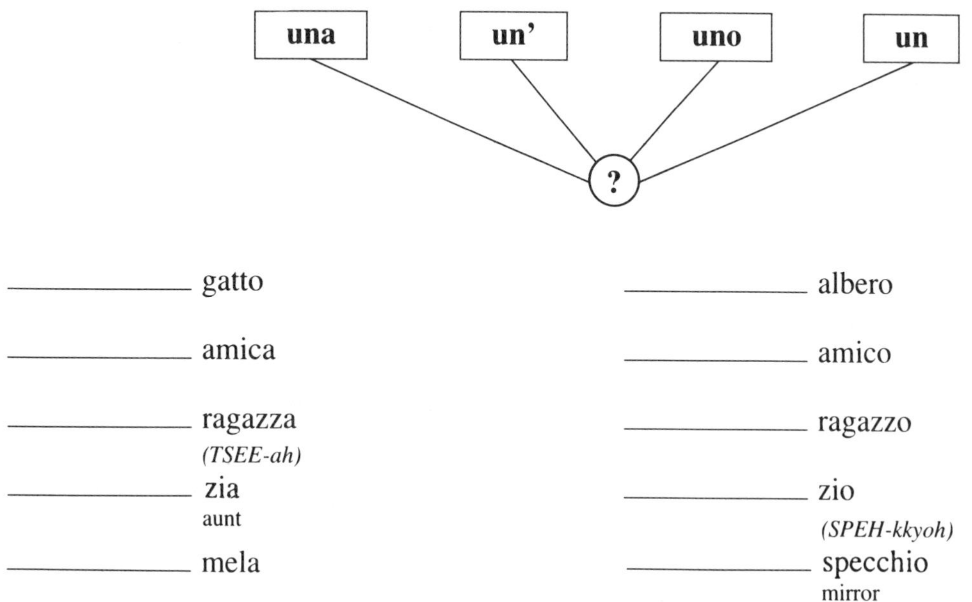

ANSWERS

Articles un (gatto) un' (amica) una (ragazza) una (zia) una (mela) un (albero) un (amico) un (ragazzo) uno (zio) uno (specchio)

How did you do? Let's try another, this time filling in both the "a" or "an" and the Italian word for what is shown.

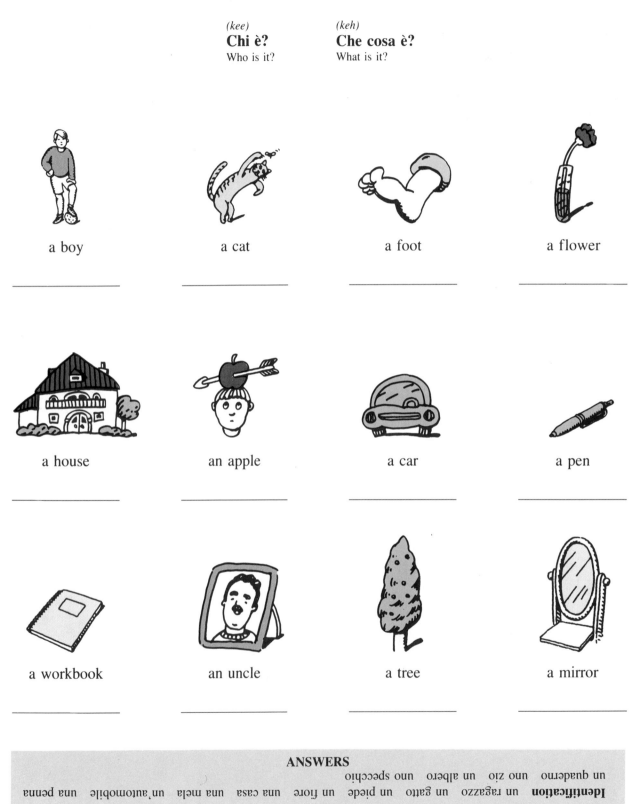

(kee)	*(keh)*
Chi è?	**Che cosa è?**
Who is it?	What is it?

a boy

____

a cat

____

a foot

____

a flower

____

a house

____

an apple

____

a car

____

a pen

____

a workbook

____

an uncle

____

a tree

____

a mirror

____

ANSWERS

Identification un ragazzo un gatto un piede un fiore una casa una mela un'automobile una penna un quaderno uno zio un albero uno specchio

Io, tu, lei e voi

I and You

In Italian, ''I'' is translated to *(EE-oh)* io. This word is not capitalized as in English, unless it is the first word in a sentence.

''You'' is represented in several ways:

tu	—When addressing friends or family members in the singular (familiar address).
lei	—When addressing any stranger or superior in the singular (polite address). May also be capitalized when written **(Lei)**.
voi	—As the plural of both tu and lei in current spoken Italian. (Although there is a more formal way of addressing more than one person **(loro)**, it is seldom used in the spoken language.)

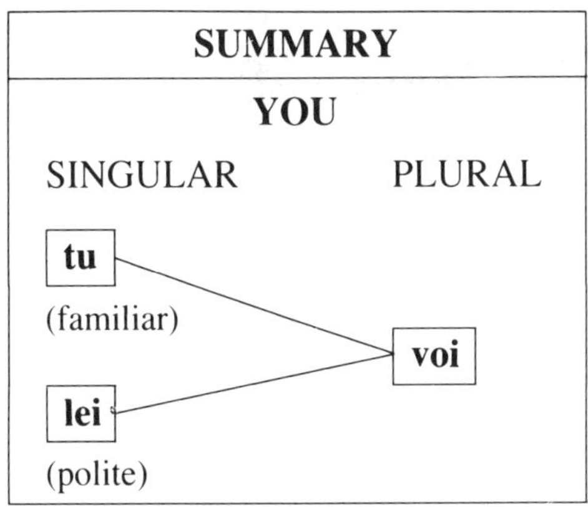

The chart at the left will help you remember how to say ''you'' in Italian.

(pahr-LYAH-moh) PARLIAMO DEI *(pah-REHN-tee)* PARENTI

Talking About Relatives

Here is Giorgio's family.

And here is Giorgio's family tree. Fill in the blanks to practice the words that tell the different family relationships.

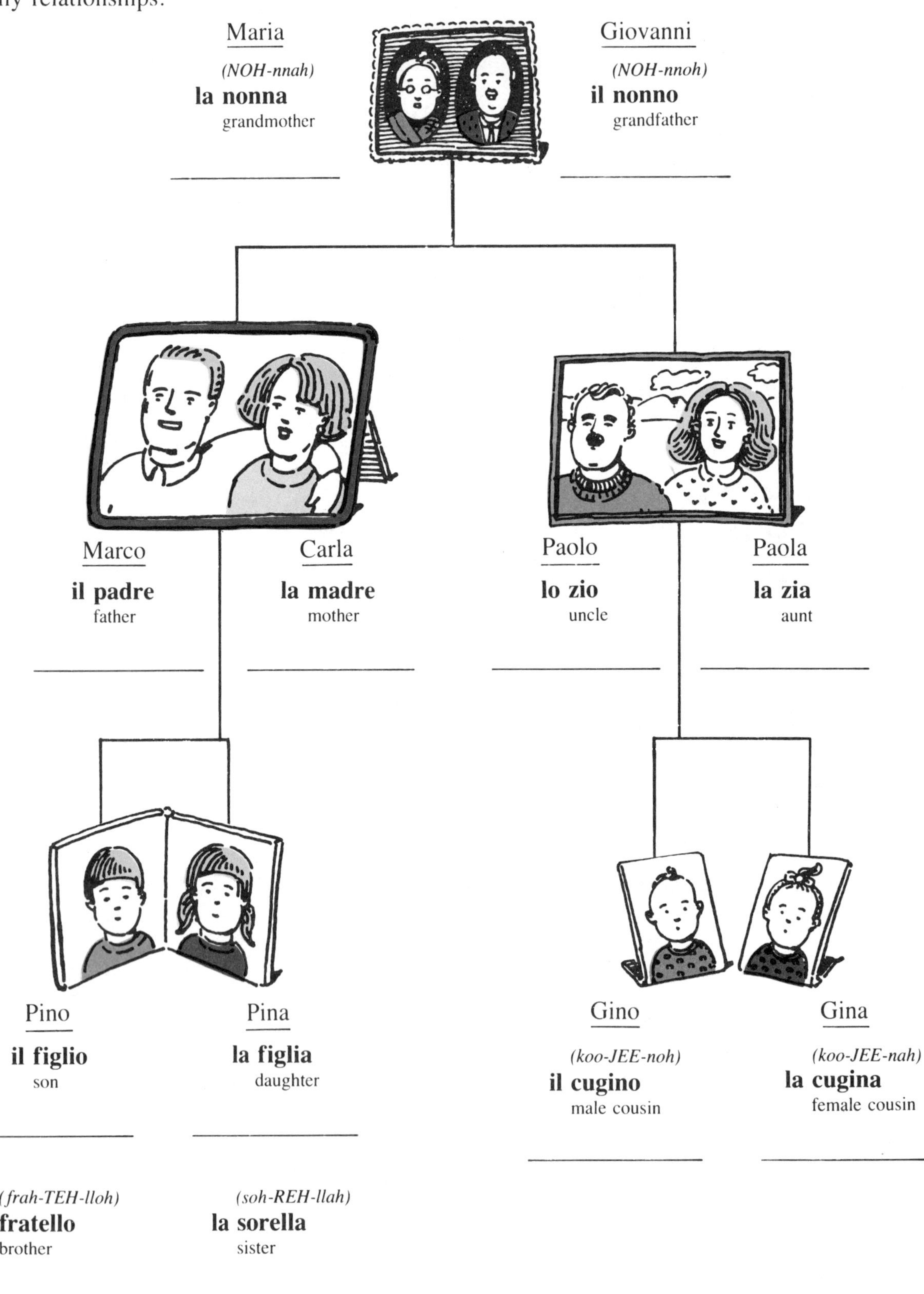

Look carefully at the family tree and then fill in the following blanks. We've done one as an example. *Be careful to copy the forms of "the"* **(il, la, lo)** *correctly*. Don't forget that **il marito** is the husband and **la moglie** is the wife. Good luck!

Model: Pino è ___il figlio___ di Marco.

1. Gino è ____________ di Gina.
2. Giovanni è ____________ di Carla.
3. Paola è ____________ di Pino.
4. Maria è ____________ di Pina.
5. Pino è ____________ di Gina.
6. Giovanni è ____________ di Maria.
7. Paola è ____________ di Paolo.
8. Pina è ____________ di Pino.
9. Giovanni è ____________ di Pina.
10. Carla è ____________ di Pino.
11. Gino è ____________ di Paola.
12. Paolo è ____________ di Pina.
13. Pina è ____________ di Gina.

Not so hard, right? Practice your knowledge of family names by finding the plurals of these nouns that are hidden in the puzzle, and then writing them out for additional practice.

cugino ____________

cugina ____________

zio ____________

zia ____________

fratello ____________

nonna ____________

sorella ____________

figlio ____________

figlia ____________

madre ____________

padre ____________

nonno ____________

c u g i n i x x x x x x x x x x x x x x x z
x x x x x x x c u g i n e x x x x x x x x i
x x x x z x x x x x x x x x x f r a t e l l i
x x x x i x x n x x x x x x x x x x x x x x
x x x x e x x x o x x x x x x x x x x x x x
x x x x x x x x x n o n n e x x x x x x x x
m a d r i x x x x x n x x x p a d r i x x x
x x x x x x x x x x f i g l i x x x x x x x
f i g l i e x x x x x x x s o r e l l e x x

ANSWERS

Fill-ins **1.** il fratello **2.** il padre **3.** la zia **4.** la nonna **5.** il cugino **6.** il marito **7.** la moglie **8.** la sorella **9.** il nonno **10.** la madre **11.** il figlio **12.** lo zio **13.** la cugina

Plurals cugini cugine zii zie fratelli nonne sorelle figli figlie madri padri nonni

Now you're really moving! If you're a puzzle fan, give this a try—in Italian, of course.

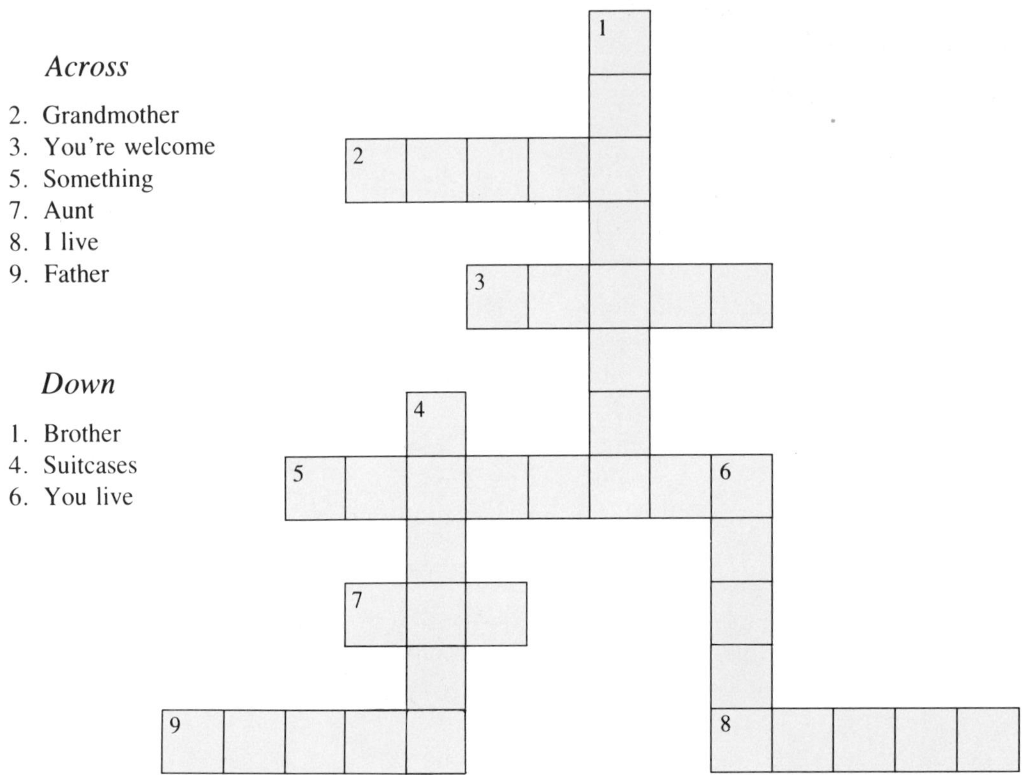

Across

2. Grandmother
3. You're welcome
5. Something
7. Aunt
8. I live
9. Father

Down

1. Brother
4. Suitcases
6. You live

It is time to return to the Smiths, just beginning their trip to Italy. See if you understand what the following paragraph is all about. Read the selection, then answer the questions that follow.

Il signor Smith e la sua famiglia *(fah-MEE-llyah)* family **arrivano in Italia con il volo trecentotré da New York. Il signor Smith dice** *(DEE-cheh)* says **«Buon giorno» al commesso** *(koh-MMEH-ssoh)* clerk**.**

Il signor Smith dice «Grazie» e il commesso dice «Prego». Infine, *(een-FEE-neh)* finally **il signor Smith dice «Arrivederla».**

ANSWERS

Crossword Across: 2. nonna **3.** prego **5.** qualcosa **7.** zia **8.** abito **9.** padre

Down: 1. fratello **4.** valigie **6.** abita

(kee)
Chi arriva da New York?
Who

- ☐ Il commesso arriva da New York.
- ☐ Il signor Smith e la sua famiglia arrivano da New York.

(keh)
Che dice il signor Smith?
What

- ☐ Il signor Smith dice «Buon giorno».
- ☐ Il signor Smith dice «Ciao».

Che dice il commesso?

- ☐ Il commesso dice «Accidenti!»
- ☐ Il commesso dice «Prego».

Now study and say aloud these parts of Giorgio's house.

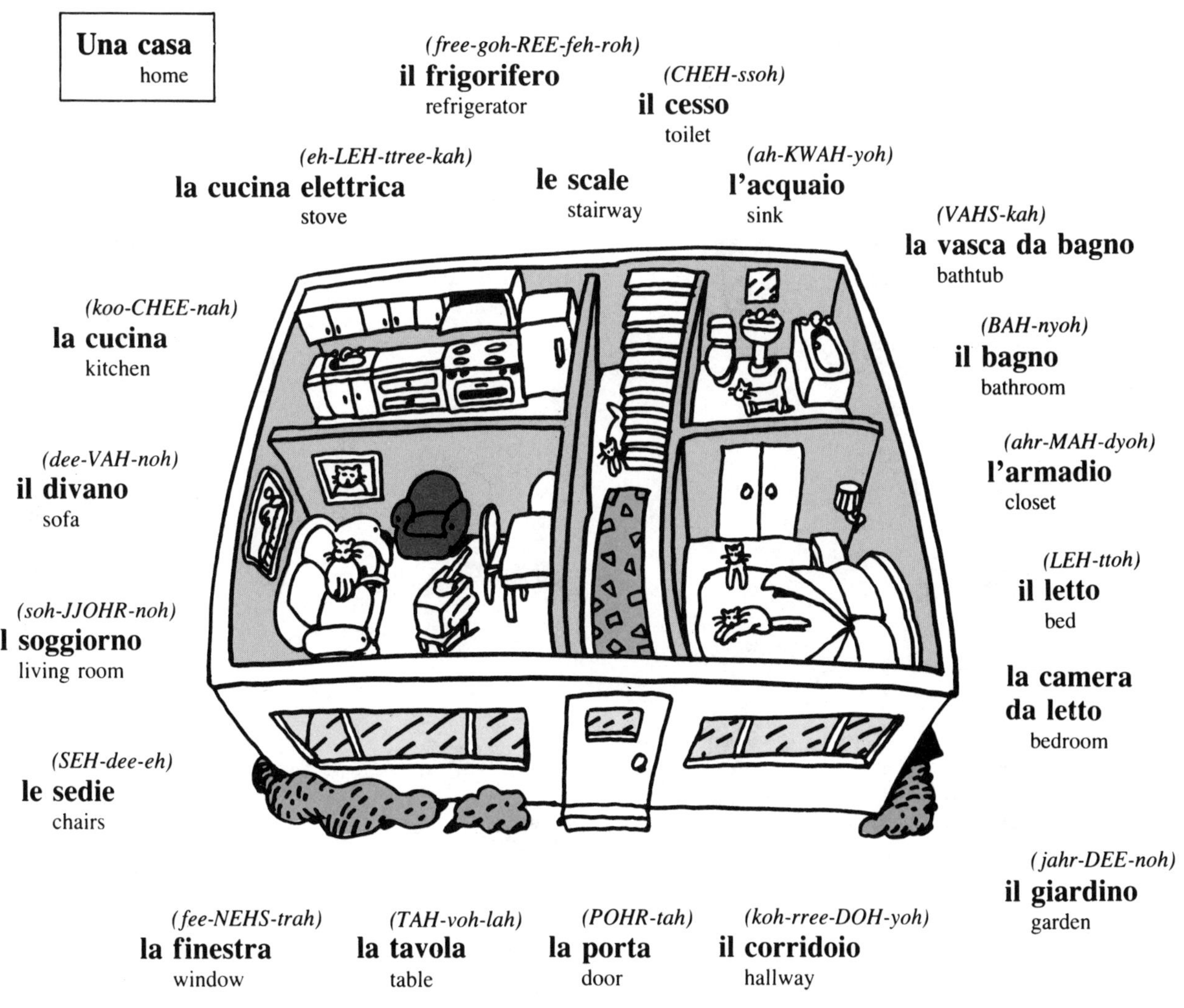

ANSWERS

Comprehension Il signor Smith e la sua famiglia arrivano da New York. Il signor Smith dice ,,Buon giorno.'' Il commesso dice ,,Prego.''

ARRIVAL

(ah-RREE-voh)
L' arrivo

2 In cerca di un posto per passare la notte

(CHEHR-kah) *(pah-SSAH-reh)* *(NOH-teh)*

Finding a Place to Spend the Night

You'll probably book your hotel room from home—at least for your first night—but whether you have a reservation or not, you'll want to know some basic words that describe the services and facilities you expect to find at your hotel. Learn these words first, and notice how they are used in the dialogue you will read later.

(ahl-BEHR-goh)
l'albergo
hotel

(preh-noh-tah-TSYOH-neh)
la prenotazione
reservation

(PREH-tsoh)
il prezzo
price

(pah-ssah-POHR-toh)
il passaporto
passport

(KAH-meh-rah)
la camera
room

(BAH-nyoh)
il bagno
bathroom

(preh-noh-TAH-reh)
prenotare
to reserve

(koh-MMEH-ssah)
la commessa
female clerk

(kah-meh-RYEH-rah)
la cameriera
maid/waitress

(POHR-tah)
la porta
door

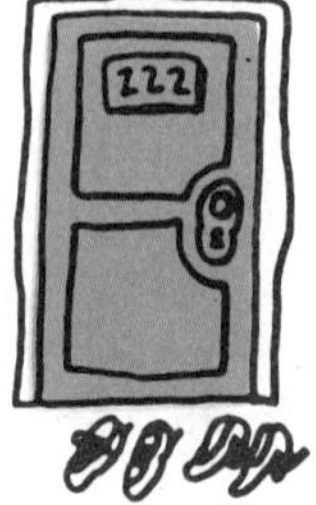

(fee-NEHS-trah)
la finestra
window

I molti modi di dire «the» in italiano

The Many Ways of Saying "The" in Italian

WITH FEMININE NOUNS

SINGULAR | PLURAL

Before Any Consonant

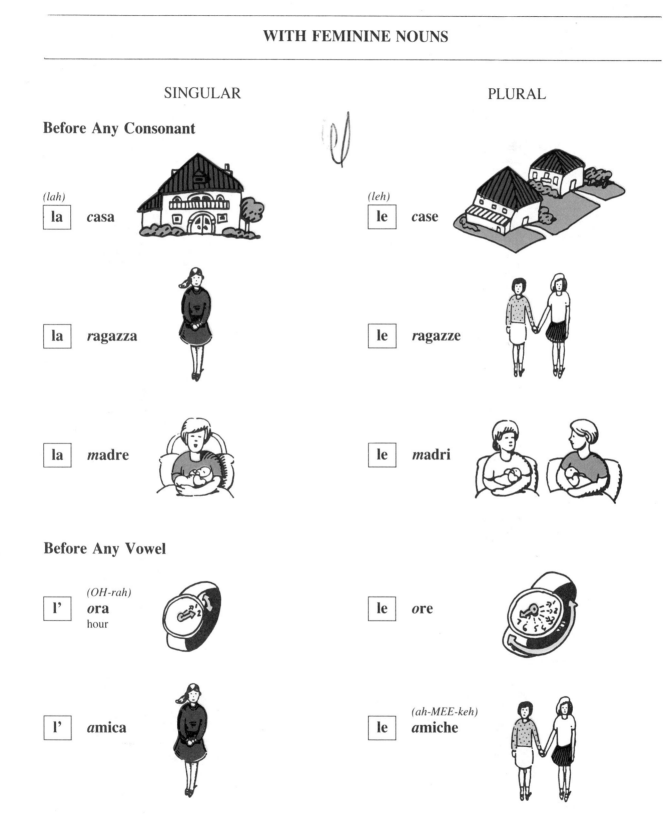

(*lah*)

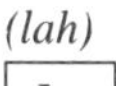

la ***c*asa**

(*leh*)

le ***c*ase**

la ***r*agazza**

le ***r*agazze**

la ***m*adre**

le ***m*adri**

Before Any Vowel

l' (*OH-rah*) ***o*ra** hour

le ***o*re**

l' ***a*mica**

le (*ah-MEE-keh*) ***a*miche**

WITH MASCULINE NOUNS

SINGULAR			PLURAL		
Before z or Before s Plus a Consonant					
(loh) **lo**	*z*io		*(llyee)* **gli**	*z*ii	
lo	*st*udente		**gli**	*st*udenti	
Before Any Other Consonant					
(eel) **il**	*r*agazzo		*(ee)* **i**	*r*agazzi	
il	*p*adre		**i**	*p*adri	
Before Any Vowel					
l'	*a*lbero		*(llyee)* **gli**	*a*lberi	

Got it? This chart will help you remember.

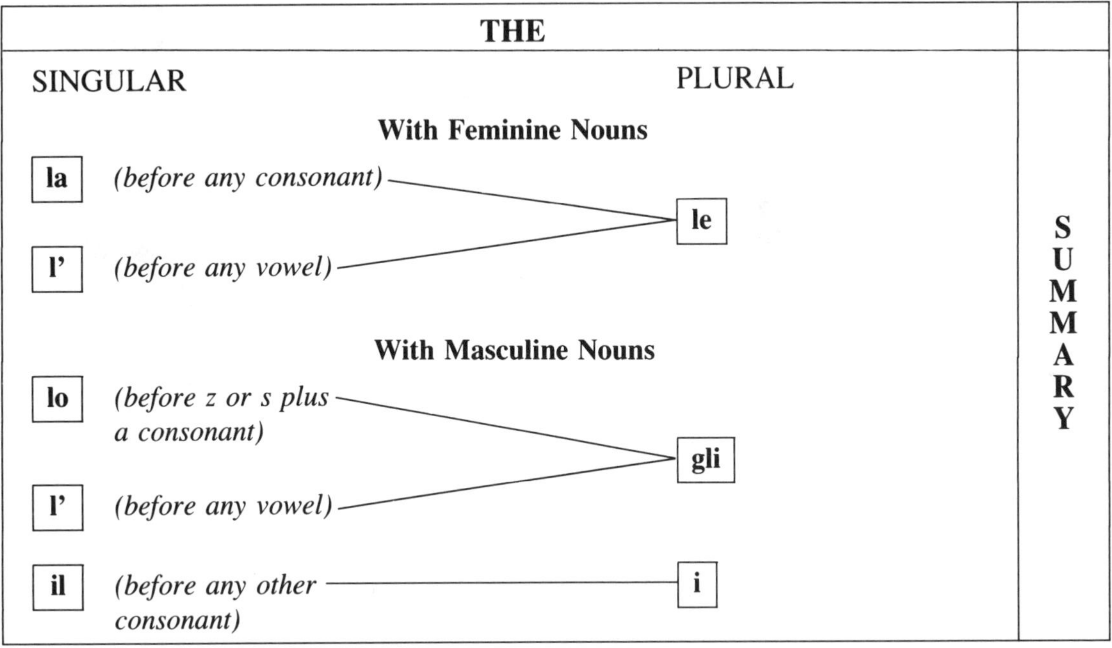

THE
SINGULAR
PLURAL
With Feminine Nouns
la (before any consonant)
l' (before any vowel)
le
With Masculine Nouns
lo (before z or s plus a consonant)
l' (before any vowel)
gli
il (before any other consonant)
i
SUMMARY

That's it! Now test yourself and your familiarity with "the." Choose the appropriate way of saying "the" in front of the following singular nouns.

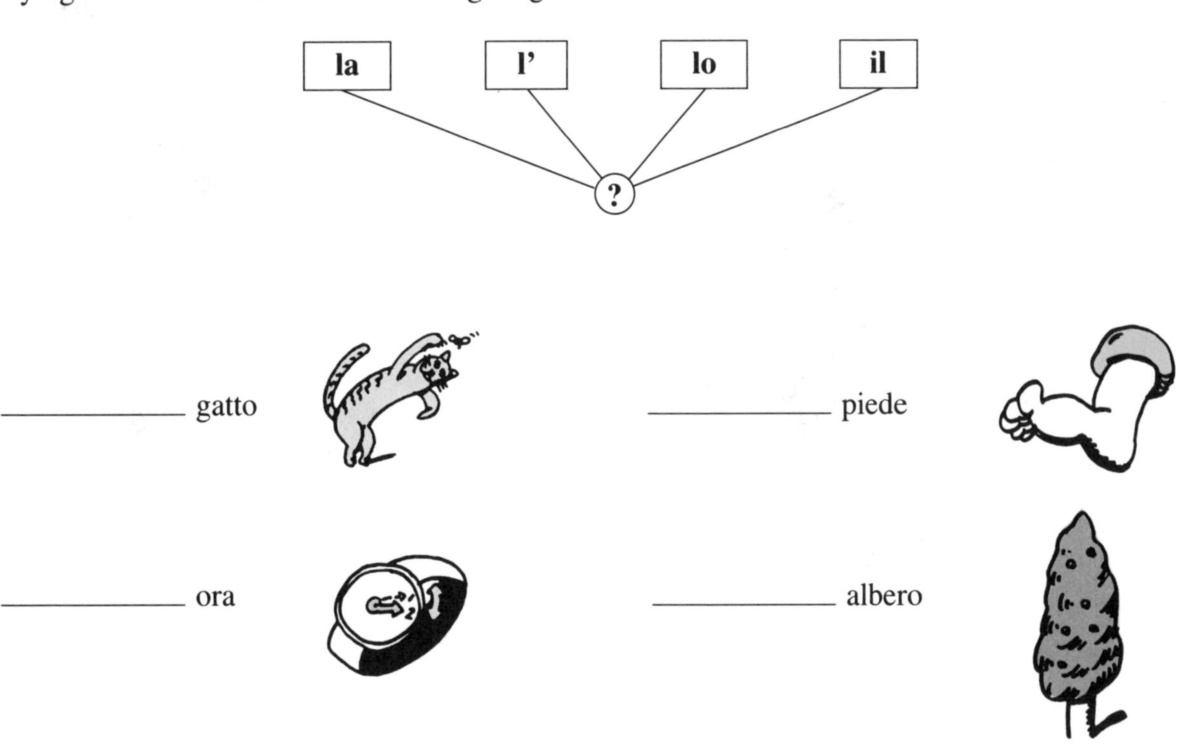

__________ gatto

__________ piede

__________ ora

__________ albero

ANSWERS

Singular nouns il (gatto) l' (ora) il (piede) l' (albero)

_____ fiore

_____ amica

_____ mela

_____ penna

Magnifico! Now choose the correct form of "the" in Italian for the same nouns in the plural.

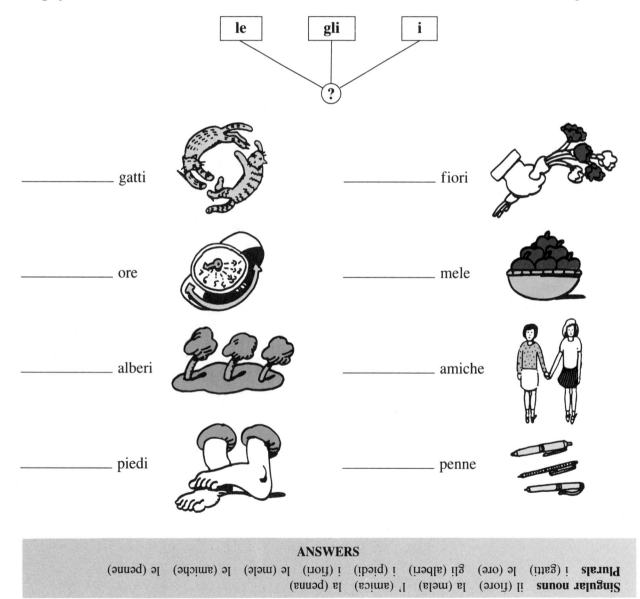

le **gli** **i**

?

_____ gatti

_____ fiori

_____ ore

_____ mele

_____ alberi

_____ amiche

_____ piedi

_____ penne

ANSWERS

Singular nouns il (fiore) la (mela) l' (amica) la (penna)

Plurals i (gatti) le (ore) gli (alberi) i (piedi) i (fiori) le (mele) le (amiche) le (penne)

(seh) (VWOH-EE) (KYEH-deh-reh) (kwal-KOH-sah)

SE VUOI CHIEDERE QUALCOSA

If You Want To Ask For Something

You'll find yourself asking questions every day of your trip—of hotel clerks, tour guides, waiters, and taxi drivers. To form a question, become familiar with these key words.

(keh) **che** *or* **cosa** *or* **che cosa** — WHAT?

(kee) **chi** — WHO?

(DOH-veh) **dove** — WHERE?

(KOH-meh) **come** — HOW?

(pehr-KEH) **perché** — WHY?

(KWAHN-doh) **quando** — WHEN?

(KWAHN-toh) **quanto** — HOW MUCH/ HOW MANY?

(KWAH-leh) **quale** — WHICH?

Notice that when quanto is followed by a noun, it *agrees* with the noun by changing in the following way.

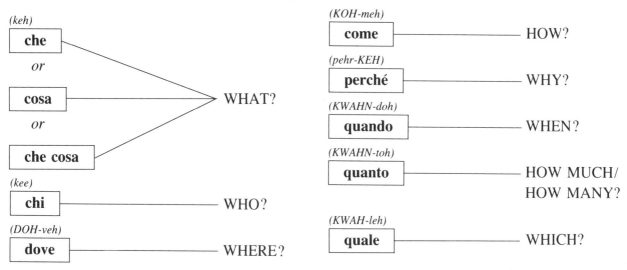

quant o (deh-NAH-roh) **denaro** money

quant i **ragazzi**

quant a **pizza**

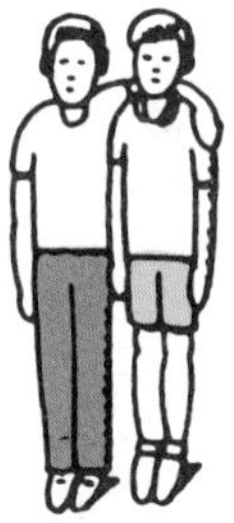

quant e **ragazze**

There are times when you don't even need to use these words to ask a question. Often you can turn a statement into a question by either of these two methods:

(1) raise your voice intonation in the normal way for questions:

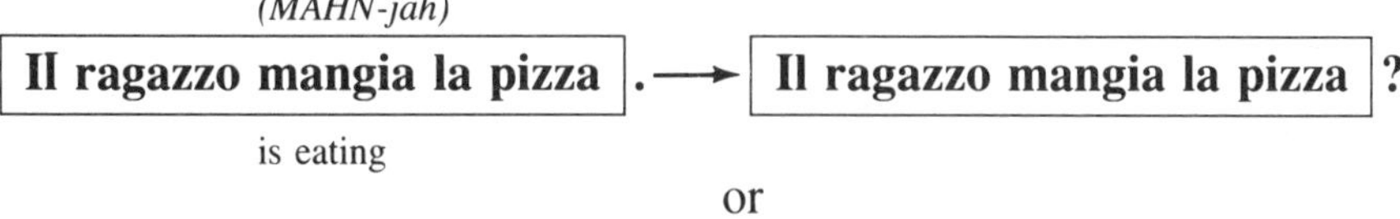

(MAHN-jah)

Il ragazzo mangia la pizza. → **Il ragazzo mangia la pizza**?

is eating

or

(2) put the *subject* at the end of the sentence:

Il ragazzo **mangia la pizza**. → **Mangia la pizza**, **il ragazzo**?

Now match up each question with its answer.

1. **Che cosa mangia Maria?**
2. **Parla italiano Giovanni?**
   does speak
3. **Perché canti?**
   do you sing
4. **Quando arrivano?**
   do they arrive
5. **Dove arrivano?**
6. **Dov'è la penna?**
   is
7. **Chi è?**
   Who is it?

a. *(EH-kkoh)* **Ecco la penna.**
   Here is

b. **Maria mangia la pizza.**

c. **È il padre di Maria.**
   of

d. **Sì, Giovanni parla italiano**
   speaks

e. *(PYAH-cheh)* **Canto perché mi piace.**
   I sing because I like it

f. **Arrivano domani.**
   tomorrow

g. *(ah-eh-roh-POHR-toh)* **Arrivano all' aeroporto.**
   at the airport

Now some more adventures of the Smith family. (We don't recommend that you go to a strange city without a reservation; let's see how our friends make out.)

Read each line carefully several times out loud. *Role-play* the dialogue.

MARK **Scusi, signore, ci** *(chee)* **può** *(pwoh)* **dare una camera** *(KAH-meh-rah)* **per una settimana** *(seh-ttee-MAH-nah)***? Non ho** *(oh)* **una prenotazione.**	Excuse me, sir, can you give us a room for a week? I do not have a reservation.
COMMESSO **Impossibile** *(eem-poh-SSEE-bee-leh)***, signore.**	Impossible, sir.
MARK **Perché?**	Why?
COMMESSO **Perchè l'albergo** *(ahl-BEHR-goh)* **e molto pieno** *(PYEH-noh)***.**	Because the hotel is very full.

ANSWERS

Matching 1-b, 2-d, 3-e, 4-f, 5-g, 6-a, 7-c

MARK **Senta, io e la mia famiglia** — Listen, my family and I

(ah-BBYAH-moh) (bee-ZOH-nyoh) (oor-JEHN-teh)
abbiamo bisogno urgente di — urgently need

(SYAH-moh) (ah-meh-ree-KAH-nee)
una camera. Siamo americani. — a room. We are Americans.

(cheh) (PEE-kkoh-lah)
COMMESSO **Va bene. C'è una piccola** — Okay. There is a small room on the third floor (fourth floor in North American terms).

(TEHR-tsoh) (PYAH-noh)
camera al terzo piano.

(KOHS-tah)
MARK **Quanto costa?** — How much does it cost?

(cheen-kwahn-tah-MEE-lah) (LEE-reh)
COMMESSO **Cinquantamila lire.** — 50.000 lira. *(See unit 25 on banking for information on money.)*

MARK **D'accordo.** — Okay.

COMMESSO **Come si chiama?** — What's your name?

(KWEHS-tah)
MARK **Sono Mark Smith. Questa è mia** — I am Mark Smith. This is my wife, Mrs. Mary

(see-NYOH-rah)
moglie, la signora Mary Smith. Ecco — Smith. Here are our passports.

i nostri passaporti.

COMMESSO **Camera numero trentacinque.** — Room number 35. Here is the key.

(KYAH-veh)
Ecco la chiave.

(MEE-lleh)
MARK **Grazie mille!** — Thanks a million! (*literally*, a thousand thanks)

COMMESSO **Prego.** — You're welcome.

Now, without looking back, try to complete the missing dialogue parts. Check your answers only *after* attempting to fill in the missing parts from memory.

Scusi, signore, ci può dare una c____________ per una s____________?

Non ho una p____________.

Impossibile, signore.

Perché?

P ____________ è molto pieno.

Senta, io e la mia famiglia abbiamo b____________ urgente di una camera. Siamo americani.

Va b______________. C'è una p______________ camera al terzo p______________.

Q______________ costa?

Cinquantamila l______________.

Can you make sentences found in the dialogue out of the following scrambled words?

chiave / Ecco / la

____

signora / la / Questa / moglie / mia / è / Mary Smith

____

chiama / si / Come

____

Study and repeat aloud these parts of a hotel room. Then write the Italian word and draw a line to the appropriate item in the picture.

lo specchio
mirror
____

(LAHM-pah-dah)
la lampada
lamp
____

(ah-KWAH-yoh)
l'acquaio
sink
____

(ah-shoo-gah-MAH-noh)
l'asciugamano
towel
____

(kah-sseh-TTOH-neh)
il cassettone
chest of drawers
____

(DOH-chah)
la doccia
shower
____

la vasca
bathtub
____

(koo-SHEE-noh)
il cuscino
pillow
____

(CHEH-ssoh)
il cesso
toilet
____

il letto
bed
____

il divano
sofa
____

la porta
door
____

ANSWERS

Sentences Ecco la chiave. Questa è mia moglie, la signora Anne Smith. Come si chiama?

Pronomi e verbi

Pronouns and Verbs

You've already learned how to say "I" and "you" in Italian. Now it's time to move on to the forms for "he," "she," "we," and "they." Here are your new words:

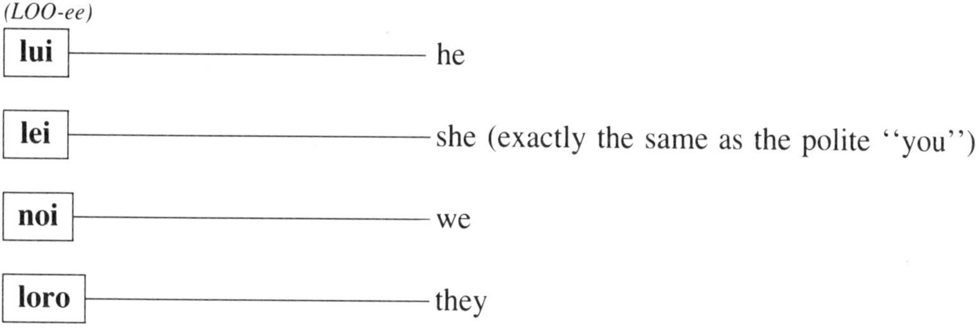

(LOO-ee)
lui — he
lei — she (exactly the same as the polite "you")
noi — we
loro — they

Use this table to help you remember the Italian pronouns.

PRONOUNS				SUMMARY
io	I	**noi**	we	
tu	you (familiar)	**voi**	you (plural)	
lui	he	**loro**	they (masculine/feminine)	
lei	she/you (formal)			

Now, here are three common Italian verbs:

(pahr-LAH-reh)	*(kahn-TAH-reh)*	*(ah-rree-VAH-reh)*
parl*are*	**cant*are***	**arriv*are***
to speak	to sing	to arrive

Notice that they end in are . So do many other verbs. Watch how they are conjugated.

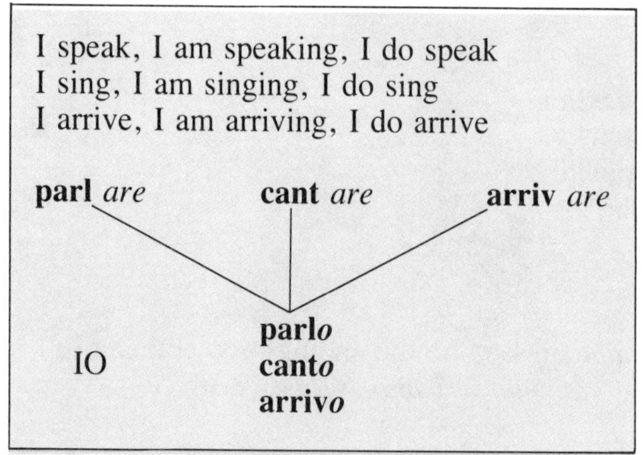

I speak, I am speaking, I do speak
I sing, I am singing, I do sing
I arrive, I am arriving, I do arrive
parl are
cant are
arriv are
IO
parlo
canto
arrivo

We speak, we are speaking, we do speak
We sing, we are singing, we do sing
We arrive, we are arriving, we do arrive
parl are
cant are
arriv are
NOI
parliamo
cantiamo
arriviamo

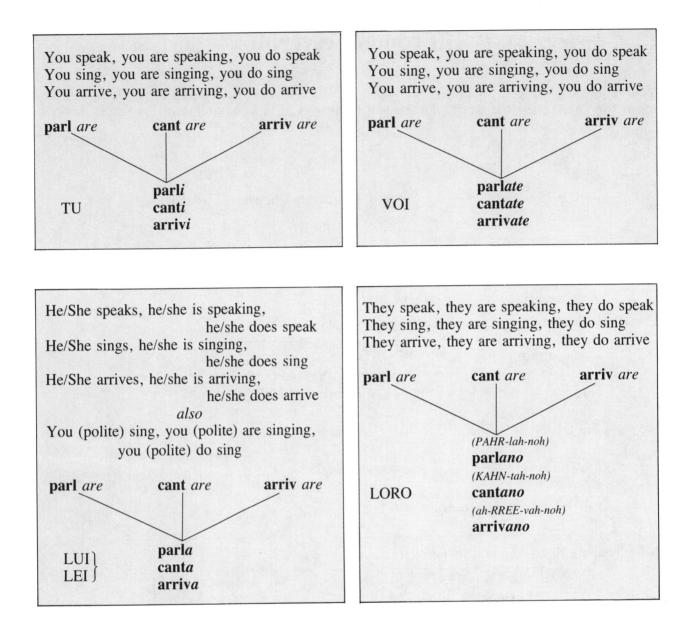

You speak, you are speaking, you do speak
You sing, you are singing, you do sing
You arrive, you are arriving, you do arrive

parl *are* **cant** *are* **arriv** *are*

TU **parl*i***
cant*i*
arriv*i*

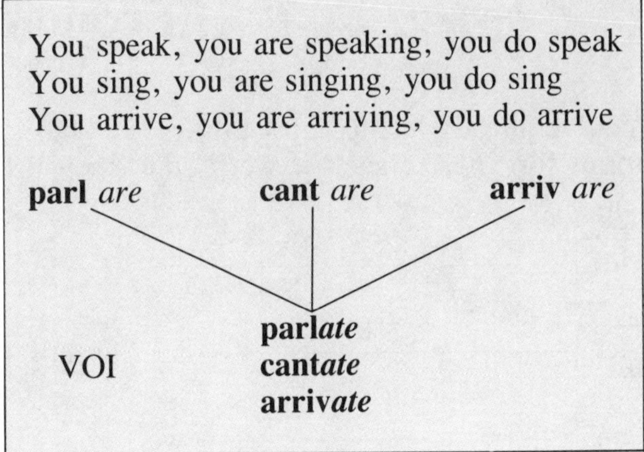

He/She speaks, he/she is speaking, he/she does speak
He/She sings, he/she is singing, he/she does sing
He/She arrives, he/she is arriving, he/she does arrive

also

You (polite) sing, you (polite) are singing, you (polite) do sing

parl *are* **cant** *are* **arriv** *are*

LUI
LEI } **parl*a***
cant*a*
arriv*a*

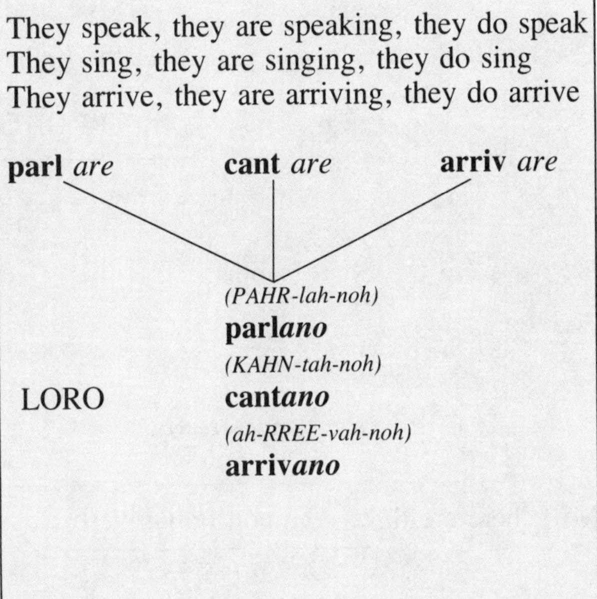

They speak, they are speaking, they do speak
They sing, they are singing, they do sing
They arrive, they are arriving, they do arrive
parl are
cant are
arriv are
LORO
(PAHR-lah-noh)
parlano
(KAHN-tah-noh)
cantano
(ah-RREE-vah-noh)
arrivano

Got it? Note that the pronouns are not necessary because the endings specify which person is involved. The pronouns are, in general, optional.

io parl*o* or **parl*o***	**noi parl*iamo*** or **parl*iamo***
tu parl*i* or **parl*i***	**voi parl*ate*** or **parl*ate***
lui / **lei** } **parl*a*** or **parl*a***	**loro parl*ano*** or **parl*ano***

Notice as well that *parlano, cantano, arrivano* are *not* stressed on the ending *-ano*. Be careful! Note that the forms *parla/canta/arriva* and *parlano/cantano/arrivano* are used with corresponding non-pronoun subjects:

Il ragazzo **parl*a* italiano.**
The boy speaks Italian.

Le zie **cant*ano* bene.**
The aunts sing well.

Maria **arriv*a* domani.**
Mary is arriving tomorrow.

I ragazzi **parl*ano* italiano.**
The boys speak Italian.

La zia **cant*a* bene.**
The aunt sings well.

Maria e Carla **arriv*ano* domani.**
Mary and Carla are arriving tomorrow.

Here's a chart of "are" verb endings to help you remember.

VERB ENDINGS				
"ARE" VERBS				**SUMMARY**
io	**-o**	**noi**	**-iamo**	
tu	**-i**	**voi**	**-ate**	
lui / lei	**-a**	**loro**	**-ano**	

Now test yourself. Add the correct endings on the verb *abitare,* (to live in a place) which you have already encountered.

1. (io) abit ______________
2. (tu) abit ______________
3. (lui) abit ______________
4. (lei) abit ______________
5. (noi) abit ______________
6. (voi) abit ______________
7. (loro) abit ______________
8. il ragazzo abit ______________
9. i ragazzi abit ______________

Bene! See if you can put the correct endings on the following verbs, and if you understand the sentence.

La ragazza parl____________ italiano.

Gli zii arriv____________ domani.

Tu parl____________ e io cant____________.

Noi cant____________ e voi parl____________.

Note: To make any verb negative, just add non before it.

parlo—I speak — non parlo—I do not speak

cantano—they sing — non cantano—they do not sing

ANSWERS

Verbs **1.** (abit)o **2.** (abit)i **3.** (abit)a **4.** (abit)a **5.** (abit)iamo **6.** (abit)ate **7.** (abit)ano **8.** (abit)a **9.** (abit)ano

Verbs (parl)a (arriv)ano (parl)i / (cant)o (cant)iamo / (parl)ate

Slow down! If you are getting confused, just ease up your pace and review what you've learned so far. *Capisci?* (Do you understand?) See how much Italian you already know by doing the following "verb" crossword puzzle.

Across
1. You (familiar) speak
2. She arrives
4. We speak
6. They arrive
7. I live
8. They sing

Down
1. I speak
3. He sings
5. You (plural) sing

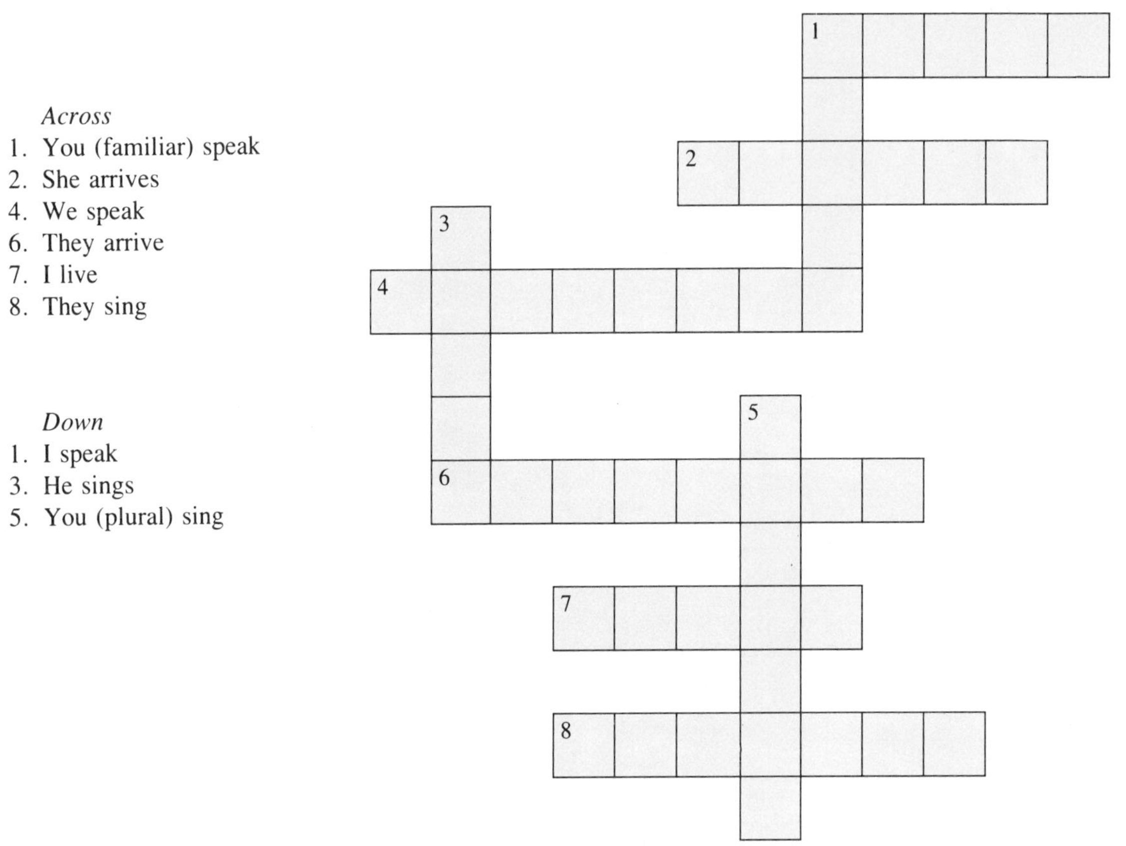

Now see if you remember what you have learned about forming questions by matching up the answers on the right to the questions on the left.

1. Che cosa è?	a. Abito a Roma.
2. Chi non parla italiano?	b. È un albergo.
3. Dove abita lei?	c. Mi chiamo Giovanni Spina.
4. Come si chiama lei?	d. Io non parlo italiano.
5. Quando arrivano le valige?	e. Costa 50.000 lire.
6. Quanto costa la camera?	f. Arrivano domani.

ANSWERS

Crossword Across: 1. parli **2.** arriva **4.** parliamo **6.** arrivano **7.** abito **8.** cantano
Down: 1. parlo **3.** canta **5.** cantate
Comprehension 1-b, 2-d, 3-a, 4-c, 5-f, 6-e

Test yourself on the many ways to say "the" by matching up the nouns on the right with the appropriate forms of "the" on the left.

1. l'	a. finestra
2. lo	b. porta
3. la	c. albergo
4. lo	d. camera
5. la	e. amica
6. la	f. amico
7. l'	g. specchio
8. il	h. zio
9. il	i. passaporto
10. l'	j. bagno

Now try to put the correct plural form (*le, gli,* or *i*) in front of the preceding nouns that are now plural.

________ finestre	________ amici
________ porte	________ specchi
________ alberghi	________ zii
________ camere	________ passaporti
________ amiche	________ bagni

The following brief passage will allow you to test your comprehension of what you have learned so far. Read it several times, then try to choose the correct answer to each question.

Il signor Jones non ha una prenotazione all'albergo. Non ci sono più camere. Allora, la signora Jones dice al commesso che sono americani. Il commesso dice che (that) **c'è una piccola camera al terzo piano. La camera non ha il bagno e costa cinquantamila lire.**

Chi non ha la prenotazione?

- ☐ Il signor Jones non ha la prenotazione.
- ☐ Il commesso non ha la prenotazione.

Che cosa dice la signora Jones?

- ☐ Dice "Buon giorno."
- ☐ Dice che sono americani.

Ha il bagno?

- ☐ Sì.
- ☐ No.

Ci sono camere?

- ☐ Sì.
- ☐ No.

Dov'è la piccola camera?

- ☐ Al terzo piano.
- ☐ A Chicago.

Quanto costa?

- ☐ 45.000 lire.
- ☐ 50.000 lire.

ANSWERS

Matching **1**-c, **2**-g, **3**-a, **4**-h, **5**-b, **6**-d, **7**-e, **8**-i, **9**-j, **10**-f

Plurals le (finestre) le (porte) gli (alberghi) le (camere) le (amiche) gli (amici) gli (specchi) gli (zii) i (passaporti) i (bagni)

Comprehension Il signor Jones non ha la prenotazione. Dice che sono americani. No. No. Al terzo piano. 50.000 lire.

SEEING THE SIGHTS

(POON-tee) (een-teh-REH-sseh)
I punti d'interesse

3 In giro a piedi

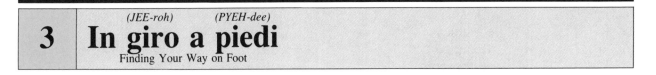

(JEE-roh) (PYEH-dee)

Finding Your Way on Foot

"How do I get to . . . ?" "Where is the nearest subway?" "Is the museum straight ahead?" You'll be asking directions and getting answers wherever you travel. Acquaint yourself with the words and phrases that will make getting around easier. Don't forget to read each line out loud several times to practice your pronunciation, and act out each part to be certain you understand these new words.

(John and Anne set out on their first day to visit a museum.)

(kyeh-DYAH-moh) (VEE-jee-leh) (moo-ZEH-oh) ANNE **John, chiediamo al vigile dove si trova il museo.**	John, let's ask the policeman how to find the museum.
JOHN *(to the policeman)* **Scusi, signore, ci sa dire dove si trova il museo?**	Excuse me, sir, can you tell us how to find the museum?
(CHER-toh) (DREE-ttee) (see-NEES-trah) VIGILE **Certo. Andate dritti fino a Via Verdi; poi a sinistra a Via Rossini; e**	Certainly. Go straight to Verdi Street, then to the left at Rossini Street, and then to the right

(DEHS-trah)
poi a destra a Via Dante, dove c'è il at Dante Street, where the traffic lights are.
(seh-MAH-foh-roh)
semaforo. Il museo si trova a due The museum can be found two blocks after the
(ee-zoh-LAH-tee)
isolati dopo il semaforo. traffic lights.

JOHN **Grazie mille.** Thanks a million.

(cheh) (keh)
VIGILE **Non c'è di che.** Don't mention it.

(after having followed the directions)

(KWEHS-toh)
ANNE **Questo non è il museo.** This is not the museum.

(oo-FFEE-choh) (pohs-TAH-leh)
È l'ufficio postale. It's the post office.

(TAHR-dee)
JOHN **Pazienza. È tardi. Torniamo all'albergo.** Patience. It's late. Let's go back to the hotel.

Now see if you can fill in the missing dialogue parts without looking back. Check your answers only after attempting to complete the missing parts from memory.

John, c____________ al vigile dove si trova il m____________.

Scusi, signore, ci sa d____________ dove si t____________ il museo?

C____________. Andate d____________ fino a Via Verdi; poi a s____________

a Via Rossini, e poi a d____________ a Via Dante, dove c'è il s____________.

Il museo si trova a due i____________ dopo il semaforo.

Grazie m____________.

Non c'è di c____________.

(*KOH-meh*) (*ahn-DAH-reh*)

COME SI FA PER ANDARE A . . .?

How Do I Get to . . .?

La ragazza va [**a**] **Roma.**
goes

The girl goes *to* Rome.

Il signor Smith abita [**in**] **America.**

Mr. Smith lives *in* America.

La ragazza viene [**da**] **Roma.**
comes

The girl comes *from* Rome.

Odore [**di**] **piedi!**
smell

Smell *of* feet!

Il gatto è [**su**] **un tetto.**

The cat is *on* a roof.

Il museo è [**lontano**] **dal semaforo.**

The museum is *far* from the traffic lights.

Il gatto è [**vicino a**] **un fiore.**

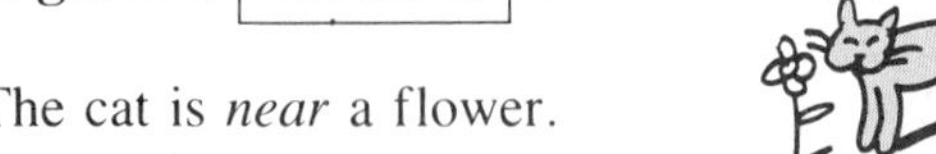

The cat is *near* a flower.

La porta è [**a destra**] **e la finestra è** [**a sinistra**].

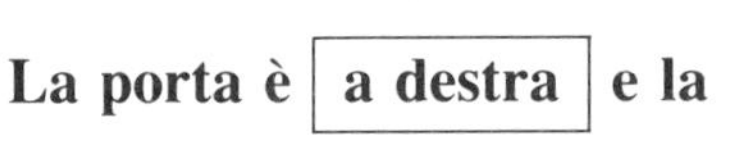

The door is *to the right* and the window is *to the left*.

La pizza è [**per**] **lo zio.**

The pizza is *for* the uncle.

(*fohr-MAH-jjoh*)
Gli spaghetti [**con**] **il formaggio.**

Spaghetti *with* cheese.

Maria arriva [**dopo**] **sua madre.**

Mary arrives *after* her mother.

L'uomo è [**su**] **un tetto.**

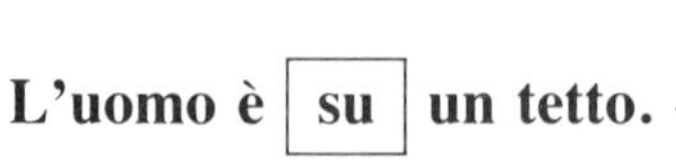

The man is *on* a roof.

Il gatto è [**accanto a**] **una gatta.**

The male cat is *next to* a female cat.

Can you match up the following?

1.	con il formaggio	a.	after her mother
2.	accanto a una gatta	b.	with cheese
3.	dopo sua madre	c.	next to a female cat
4.	a destra	d.	to the left
5.	a sinistra	e.	to the right
6.	a Roma	f.	the smell of feet
7.	da Roma	g.	for the uncle
8.	odore di piedi	h.	from Rome
9.	per lo zio	i.	to Rome
10.	vicino a un fiore	j.	in America
11.	su un tetto	k.	far from the traffic lights
12.	lontano dal semaforo	l.	on a roof
13.	in America	m.	near a flower

I verbi ancora una volta

Verbs Once Again

In the previous unit you learned about "are" verbs. Now you will learn about "ere" verbs.

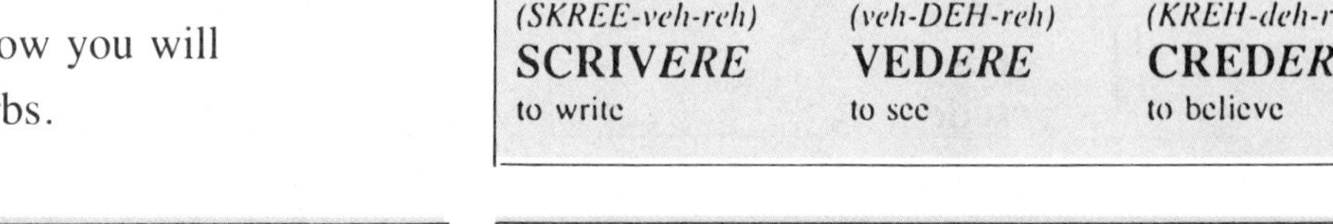

(SKREE-veh-reh)
SCRIVERE
to write
(veh-DEH-reh)
VEDERE
to see
(KREH-deh-reh)
CREDERE
to believe

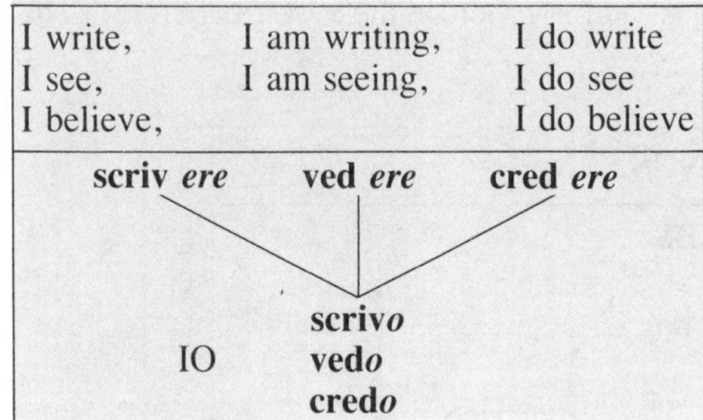

I write, I am writing, I do write
I see, I am seeing, I do see
I believe, I do believe
scriv ere
ved ere
cred ere
IO
scrivo
vedo
credo

We write, we are writing, we do write
We see, we are seeing, we do see
We believe, we do believe
scrive ere

ANSWERS

Matching 1-b, 2-c, 3-a, 4-e, 5-d, 6-i, 7-h, 8-f, 9-g, 10-m, 11-l, 12-k, 13-j

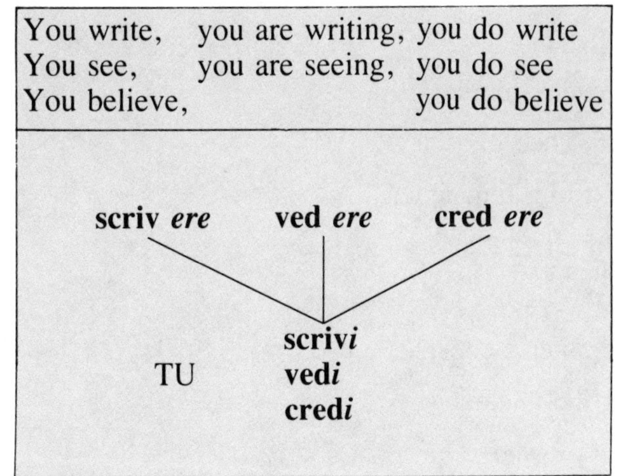

You write, you are writing, you do write
You see, you are seeing, you do see
You believe, you do believe
scriv ere
ved ere
cred ere
TU
scrivi
vedi
credi

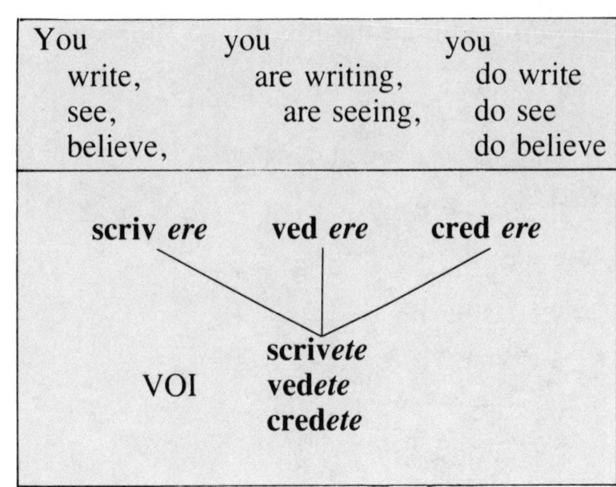

You write, you are writing, you do write
see, are seeing, do see
believe, do believe
scriv ere
ved ere
cred ere
VOI
scrivete
vedete
credete

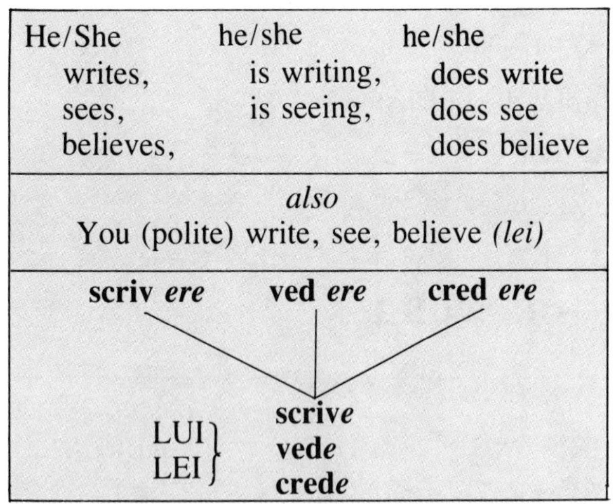

He/She writes, he/she is writing, he/she does write
sees, is seeing, does see
believes, does believe
also
You (polite) write, see, believe (lei)
scriv ere
ved ere
cred ere
LUI
LEI
scrive
vede
crede

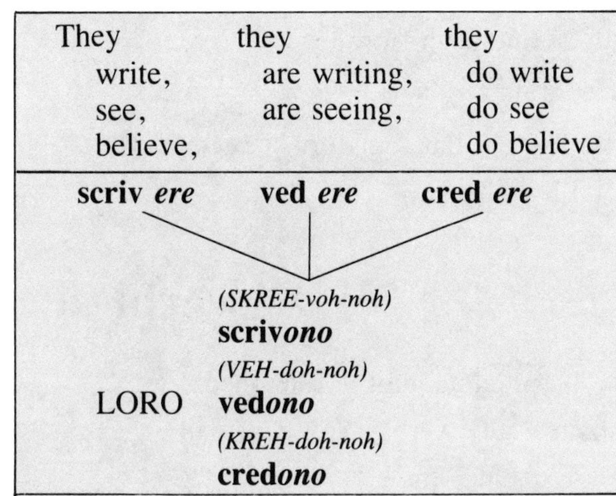

They write, they are writing, they do write
see, are seeing, do see
believe, do believe
scriv ere
ved ere
cred ere
LORO
(SKREE-voh-noh)
scrivono
(VEH-doh-noh)
vedono
(KREH-doh-noh)
credono

Once again, notice that the pronouns are optional and that *scrivono, vedono, credono* are not stressed on the ending *-ono*. To form the negative, just add *non* before the verb (as before). The following chart is a summary of "ere" verbs.

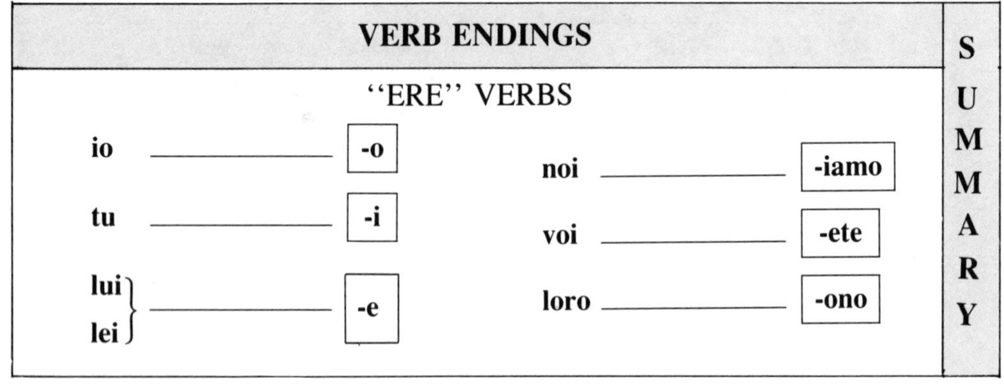

VERB ENDINGS — SUMMARY

"ERE" VERBS

io	**-o**	**noi**	**-iamo**
tu	**-i**	**voi**	**-ete**
lui / lei	**-e**	**loro**	**-ono**

Now test your learning of these verbs in the following phrases, to get the correct form of an "ere" verb.

Il commesso *scriv*______. Io non *cred*______ a Maria. Tu non *ved*______ il semaforo.

Io *scriv*______ a Maria.   I gatti non *scriv*______.   I ragazzi non *ved*______ il semaforo.

Noi *cred*______ a Maria.   Voi *ved*______ il vigile.

Alcune parole utili

Some Useful Words

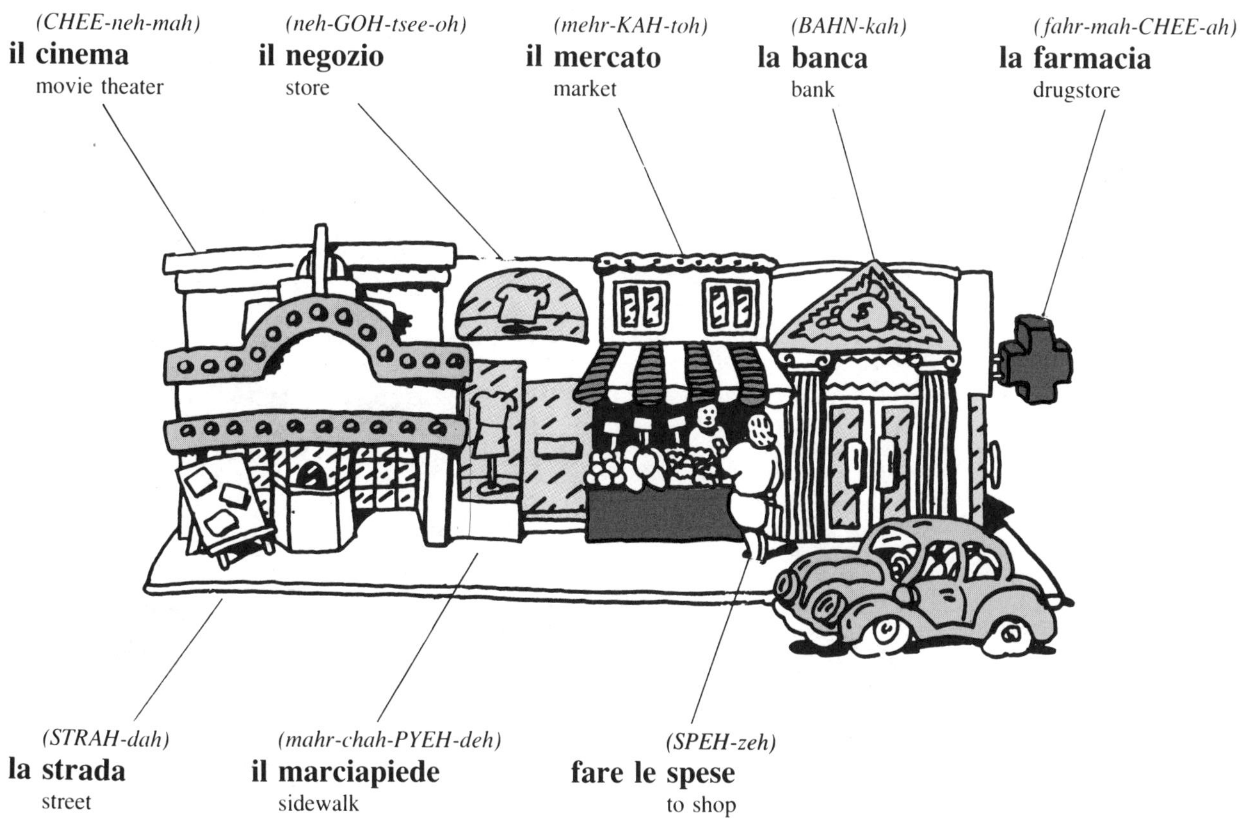

ANSWERS

Verbs (scriv) e (cred) o (ved) i (scriv) o (scriv) ono (ved) ono (cred) iamo (ved) ete

Come si indicano le cose in italiano

How to Point Out Things in Italian

Words like "this" and "that" are important to know, particularly when you go shopping and want to buy that good-looking pair of gloves in the shop window. The Italian forms of these verbs vary, depending on whether the item is masculine or feminine, and whether you are pointing to one item or to many.

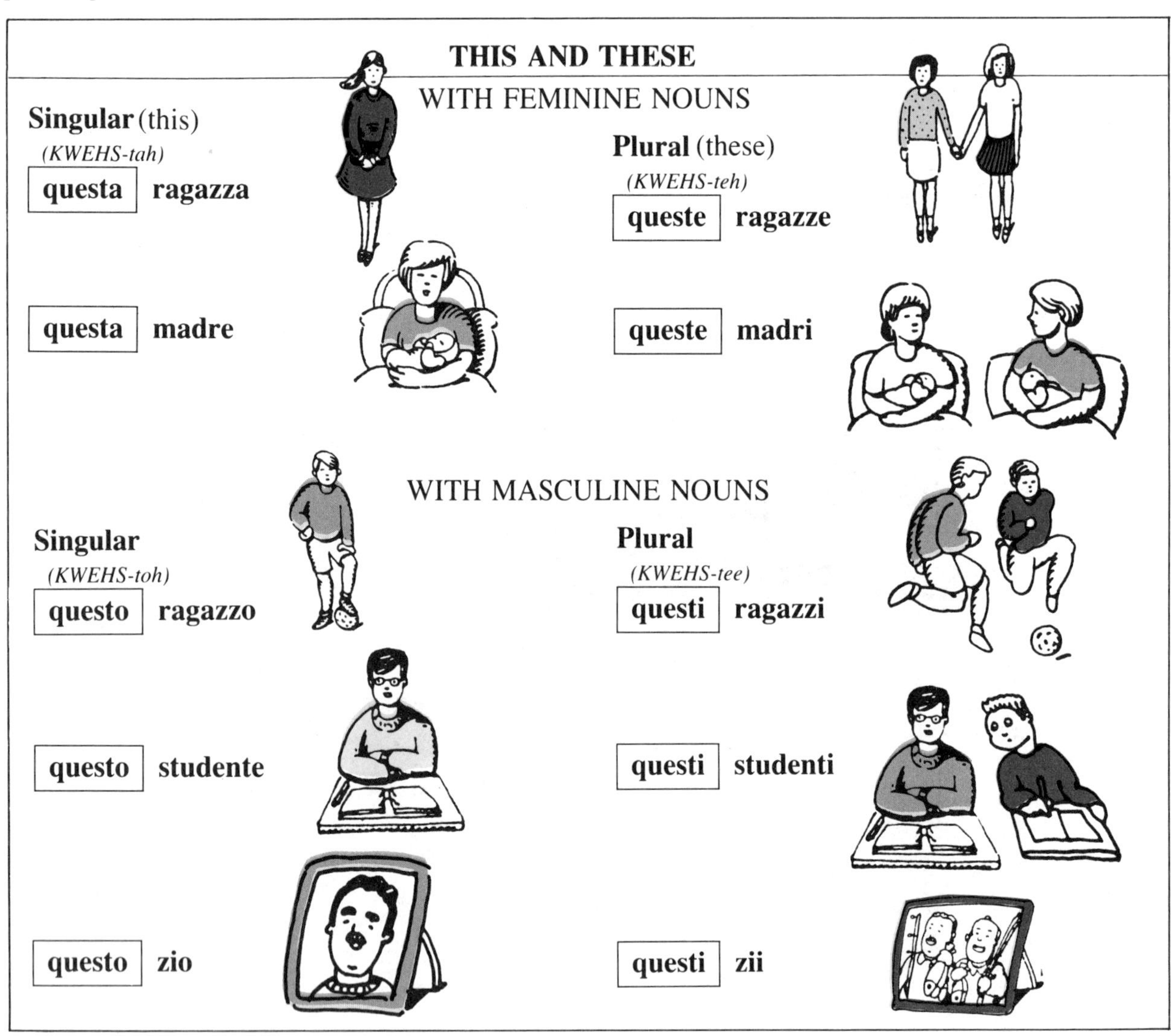

THIS AND THESE

WITH FEMININE NOUNS

Singular (this) *(KWEHS-tah)*	**Plural** (these) *(KWEHS-teh)*
questa ragazza	**queste ragazze**
questa madre	**queste madri**

WITH MASCULINE NOUNS

Singular *(KWEHS-toh)*	**Plural** *(KWEHS-tee)*
questo ragazzo	**questi ragazzi**
questo studente	**questi studenti**
questo zio	**questi zii**

In front of vowels, you may drop the vowel *in the singular* if you wish:

questa amica	*or*	quest'amica
questo amico	*or*	quest'amico

THAT AND THOSE

WITH FEMININE NOUNS

Singular (that)	**Plural** (those)
Before Any Consonant	
(KWEH-llah) **quella ragazza**	*(KWEH-lleh)* **quelle ragazze**
Before Any Vowel	
quell' amica	**quelle amiche**

WITH MASCULINE NOUNS

Singular	**Plural**
Before z or Before s Plus a Consonant	
(KWEH-lloh) **quello zio**	*(KWEH-lyee)* **quegli zii**
quello studente	**quegli studenti**
Before Any Vowel	
quell' amico	**quegli amici**
Before Any Other Consonant	
(kwehl) **quel ragazzo**	*(KWEH-ee)* **quei ragazzi**

This table will help you remember these words.

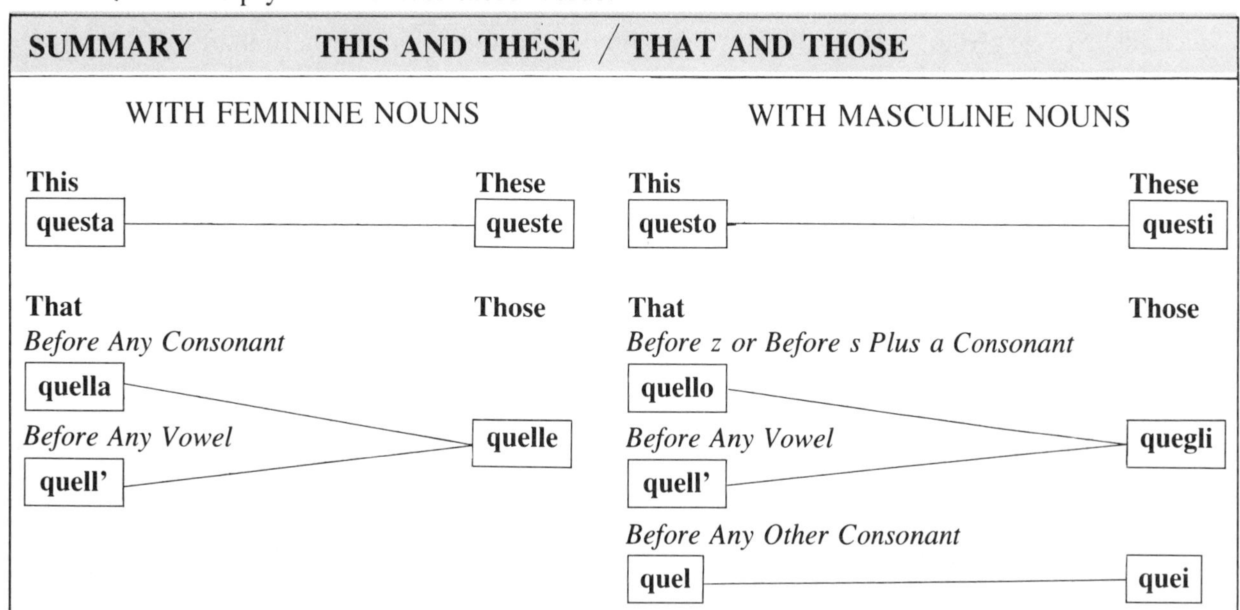

SUMMARY THIS AND THESE / THAT AND THOSE
WITH FEMININE NOUNS
This
questa
These
queste
That
Those
Before Any Consonant
quella
Before Any Vowel
quell'
quelle
WITH MASCULINE NOUNS
This
questo
These
questi
That
Those
Before z or Before s Plus a Consonant
quello
Before Any Vowel
quell'
quegli
Before Any Other Consonant
quel
quei

Now practice what you have learned. Fill in the appropriate form of "this" or "that" for each of these singular nouns.

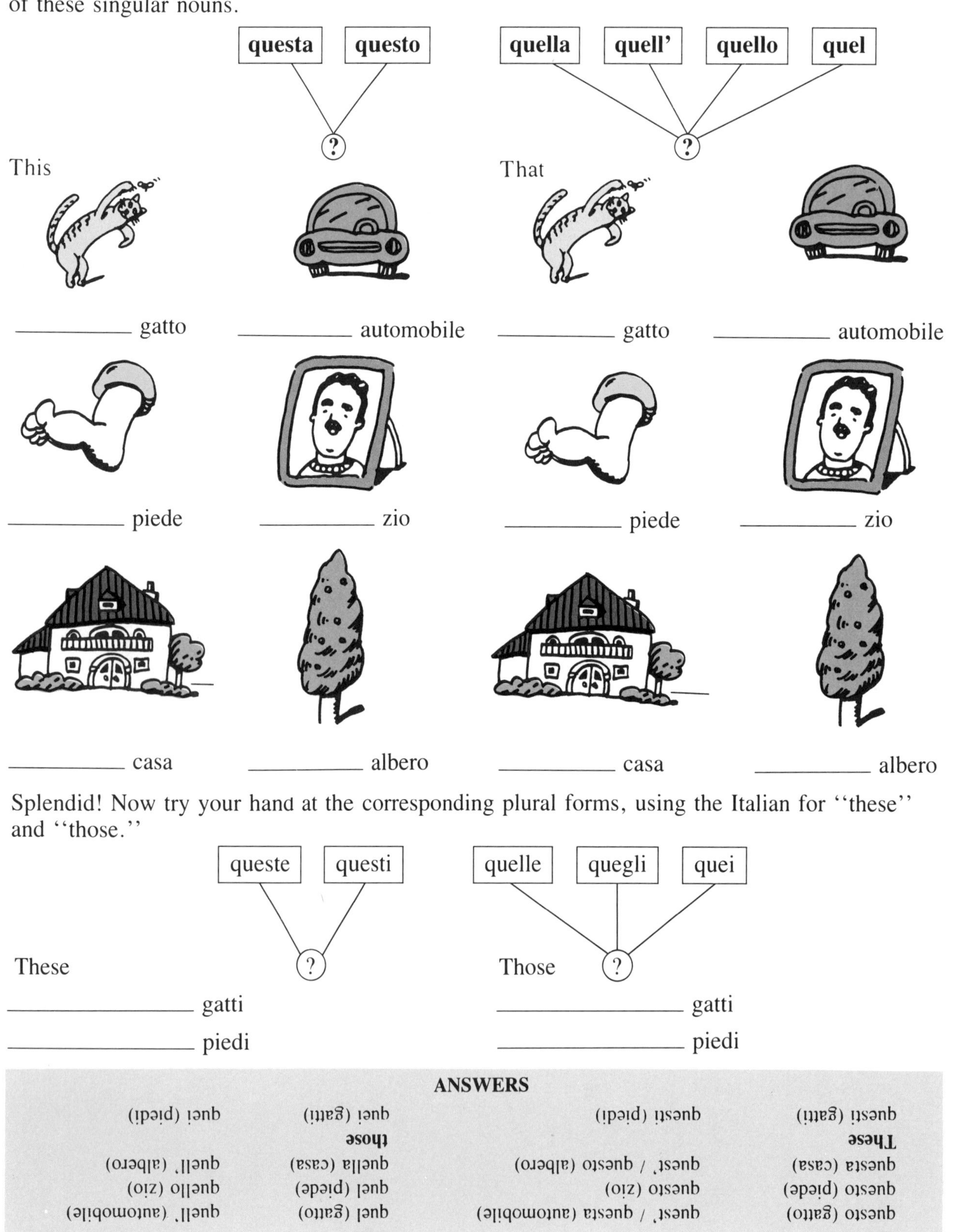

This

_________ gatto

_________ automobile

_________ piede

_________ zio

_________ casa

_________ albero

That

_________ gatto

_________ automobile

_________ piede

_________ zio

_________ casa

_________ albero

Splendid! Now try your hand at the corresponding plural forms, using the Italian for "these" and "those."

queste | questi | quelle | quegli | quei

These

_________ gatti

_________ piedi

Those

_________ gatti

_________ piedi

ANSWERS

This
questo (gatto)
quest' / questa (automobile)
questo (piede)
questo (zio)
questa (casa)
quest' / questo (albero)

These
questi (gatti)
questi (piedi)

that
quel (gatto)
quell' (automobile)
quel (piede)
quello (zio)
quella (casa)
quell' (albero)

those
quei (gatti)
quei (piedi)

_______________ case | _______________ case

_______________ automobili | _______________ automobili

_______________ zii | _______________ zii

_______________ alberi | _______________ alberi

Now you really have it. Can you change the following "this/these" forms to their corresponding "that/those" forms? Good luck!

questo marciapiede	_______________	marciapiede	questi alberghi	_______________	alberghi
questi marciapiedi	_______________	marciapiedi	quest'amica	_______________	amica
questa strada	_______________	strada	queste amiche	_______________	amiche
queste strade	_______________	strade	questo zio	_______________	zio
quest'albergo	_______________	albergo	questi zii	_______________	zii

For a quick refresher, complete the endings for these "ere" verbs, too.

1. Maria non ved__________ Carlo.

2. Noi ved__________ la zia di Maria.

3. I ragazzi ved__________ i fiori.

4. Io non ved__________ i fiori.

5. Tu ved__________ lo zio di Carlo.

ANSWERS

queste (case) quelle (case) questi (zii) quegli (zii)
queste (automobili) quelle (automobili) questi (alberi) quegli (alberi)

That / those
quel (marciapiede) quelle (strade) quell' (amica) quello (zio)
quei (marciapiedi) quell' (albergo) quelle (amiche) quegli (zii)
quella (strada) quegli (alberghi)

Verbs 1. (ved) e **2.** (ved)iamo **3.** (ved) ono **4.** (ved) o **5.** (ved) i

Now fill in the blanks with one of the following: a | da | di | vicino | accanto

Maria va __________ Roma.

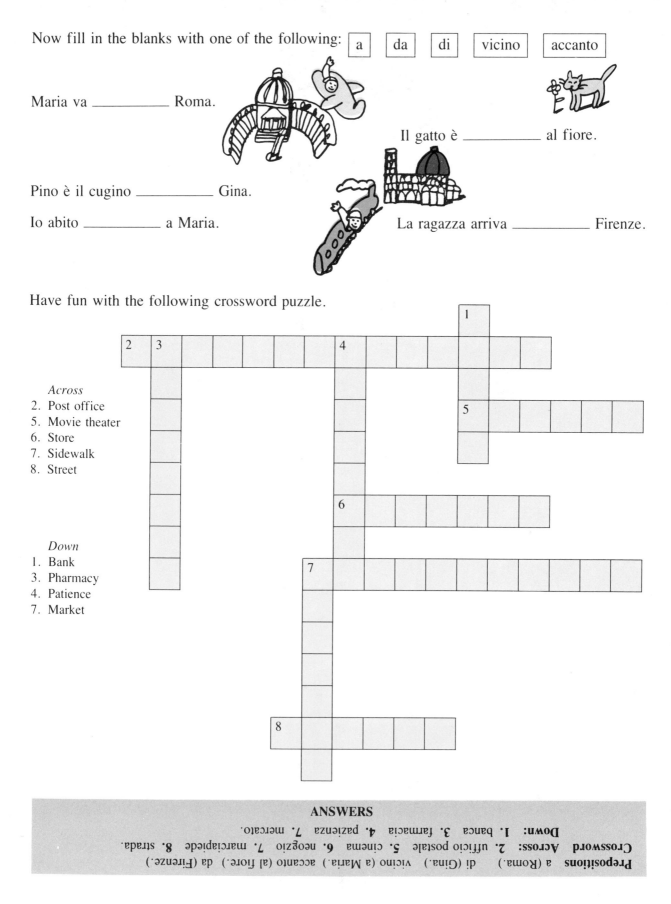

Il gatto è __________ al fiore.

Pino è il cugino __________ Gina.

Io abito __________ a Maria.

La ragazza arriva __________ Firenze.

Have fun with the following crossword puzzle.

Across

2. Post office
5. Movie theater
6. Store
7. Sidewalk
8. Street

Down

1. Bank
3. Pharmacy
4. Patience
7. Market

ANSWERS

Prepositions a (Roma.) di (Gina.) vicino (a Maria.) accanto (al fiore.) da (Firenze.)

Crossword Across: 2. ufficio postale **5.** cinema **6.** negozio **7.** marciapiede **8.** strada.

Down: 1. banca **3.** farmacia **4.** pazienza **7.** mercato.

What's happening to Maria? Read the passage to review your words for directions, then answer the following questions.

Maria chiede al vigile dove si trova la banca. Il vigile dice di andare a destra e poi a sinistra.

Maria arriva al semaforo e non vede la banca, ma vede l'ufficio postale. Allora torna
but

all'albergo.

Now, select the appropriate answers.

Chi chiede al vigile dove si trova la banca?	☐ L'ufficio postale. ☐ Il museo. ☐ Maria.
Che cosa dice il vigile?	☐ Dice di andare a destra e poi a sinistra. ☐ Dice di tornare all'albergo. ☐ Dice «Buon giorno».
Dove arriva Maria?	☐ Maria arriva all'aeroporto. ☐ Maria arriva a Roma. ☐ Maria arriva al semaforo.
Che cosa vede?	☐ Vede l'albergo. ☐ Vede l'ufficio postale. ☐ Vede il vigile.
Dove torna?	☐ Torna in America. ☐ Torna a Roma. ☐ Torna all'albergo.

ANSWERS

Comprehension Maria. Dice di andare a destra e poi a sinistra.
Maria arriva al semaforo. Vede l'ufficio postale. Torna all'albergo.

4 (MEH-tsee) Mezzi di (trahs-POHR-toh) trasporto (POO-bblee-chee) pubblici

Public Transportation

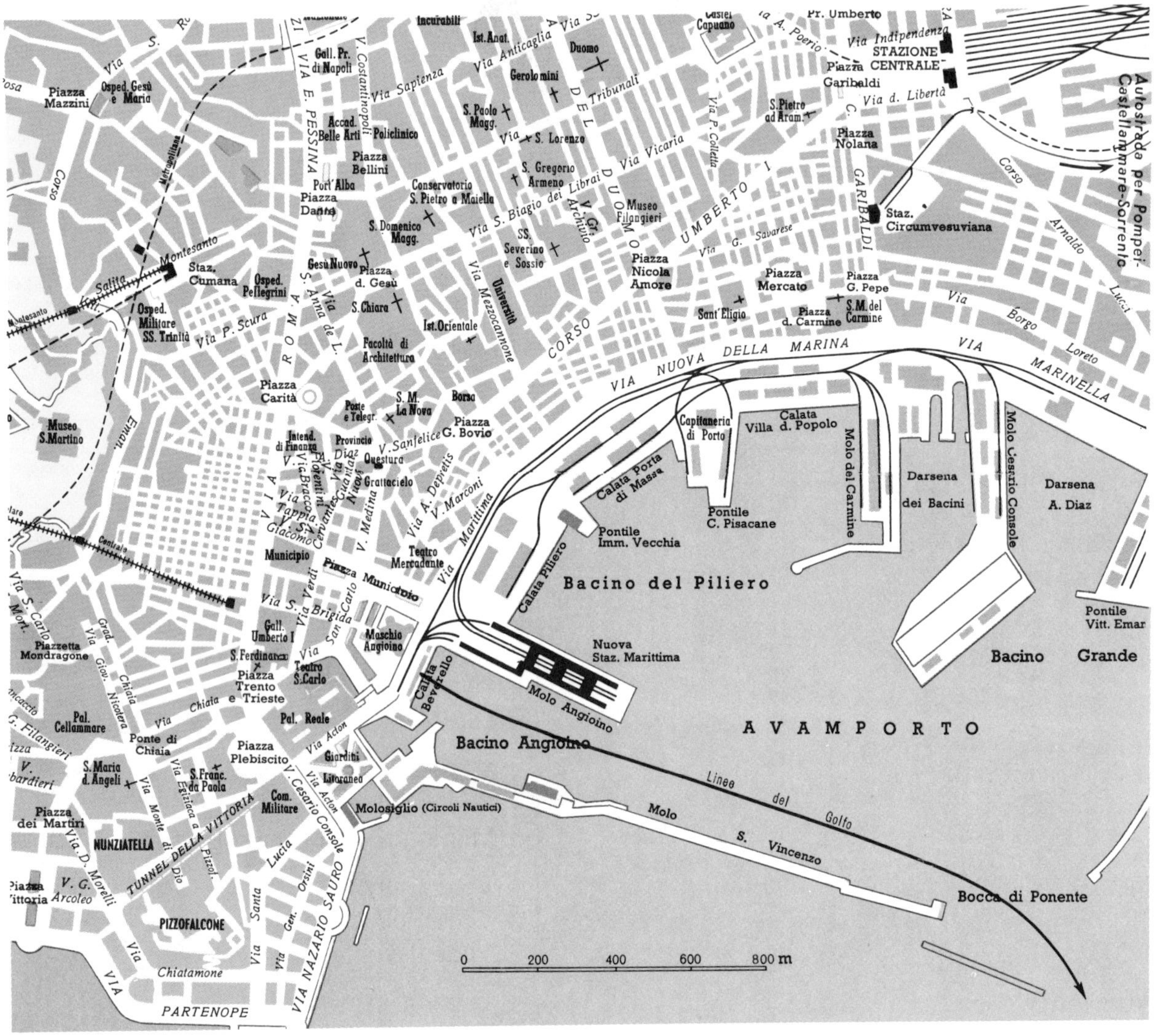

Bus Map of Naples *(Courtesy of Bonechi Publishers, Florence)*

The following dialogue contains some useful words and expressions that you might find helpful when you will need to use public means of transportation.

Remember to read each line out loud several times and to act out each part.

	(prehn-DYAH-moh) (tah-SSEE)	
MARY	**Prendiamo il tassì per andare al cinema?**	Shall we take the taxi to go to the movies?
MARK	**Quanto lontano è?**	How far is it?

MARY	**Si trova in Via Verdi.**	It's on Verdi Street.
MARK	**No. Costa troppo.**	No. It costs too much.
MARY	**Allora prendiamo la** *(meh-troh-poh-lee-TAH-nah)* **metropolitana.**	Then let's take the subway.
MARK	**Penso che non ce ne sia una.**	I don't think there is one.
MARY	**Allora prendiamo l'autobus.**	Then let's take the bus.
MARK	**Va bene.**	Okay.

(They get on a bus.)

MARK	**Scusi, signore, questo autobus va a Via Verdi?**	Excuse me, sir, does this bus go to Verdi Street?
CONDUTTORE	**Sì, ma dove va?**	Yes, but where are you going?
MARK	*(shehn-DYAH-moh)* **Scendiamo al cinema. Quanto costa** *(bee-LLYEH-ttoh)* **un biglietto?**	We are getting off at the movie theater. How much does a ticket cost?
CONDUTTORE	**Trecento lire, signore, e** *(dee-vehr-tee-MEHN-toh)* **buon divertimento.**	300 lira *(see unit 25)*, sir, and enjoy yourself.
MARK	**Che conduttore** *(kohn-doo-TTOH-reh)* **simpatico!** *(seem-PAH-tee-koh)* **Come sono cortesi** *(kohr-TEH-zee)* **gli italiani!**	What a nice driver! How courteous the Italians are!

Che cosa è?

_______________ _______________ _______________ _______________

ANSWERS

Identification (È) un tassì (È) un autobus (È) una metropolitana (È) un'automobile

Altre parole che esprimono l'azione

More Action Words

Now you will learn about "ire" verbs.

(dohr-MEE-reh)	*(pahr-TEE-reh)*	*(sehn-TEE-reh)*
dorm*ire*	**part*ire***	**sent*ire***
to sleep	to leave/depart	to hear

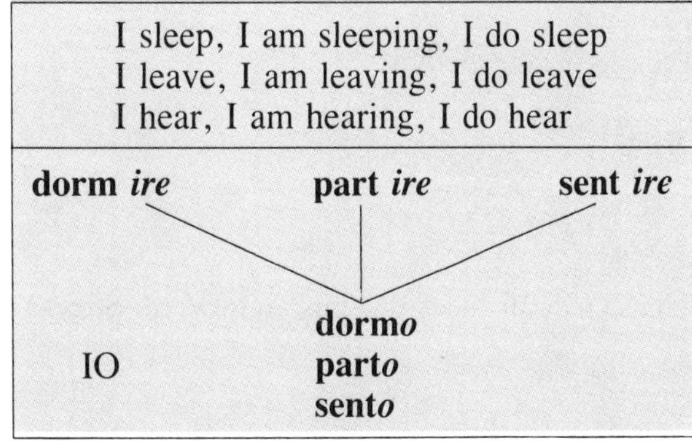

I sleep, I am sleeping, I do sleep
I leave, I am leaving, I do leave
I hear, I am hearing, I do hear
dorm ire
part ire
sent ire
IO
dormo
parto
sento

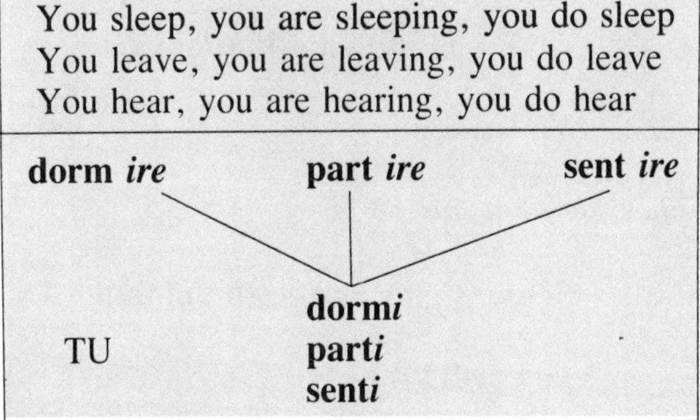

You sleep, you are sleeping, you do sleep
You leave, you are leaving, you do leave
You hear, you are hearing, you do hear
dorm ire
part ire
sent ire
TU
dormi
parti
senti

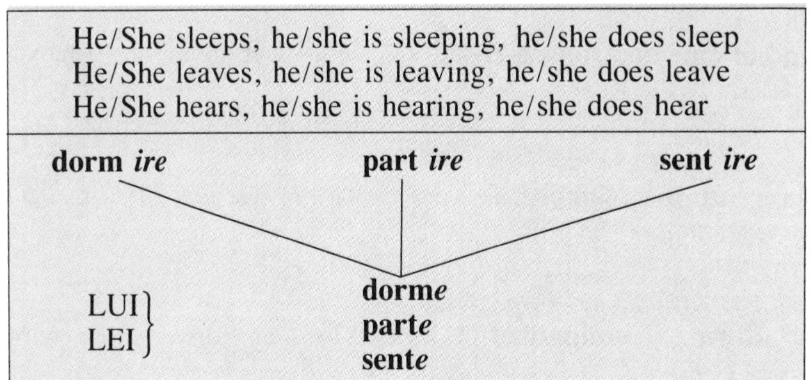

He/She sleeps, he/she is sleeping, he/she does sleep
He/She leaves, he/she is leaving, he/she does leave
He/She hears, he/she is hearing, he/she does hear
dorm ire
part ire
sent ire
LUI
LEI
dorme
parte
sente

We sleep, we are sleeping, we do sleep
We leave, we are leaving, we do leave
We hear, we are hearing, we do hear
dorm ire
part ire
sent ire
NOI
dormiamo
partiamo
sentiamo

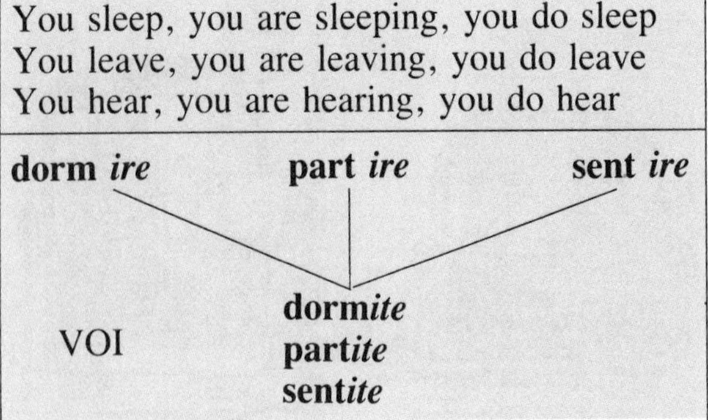

You sleep, you are sleeping, you do sleep
You leave, you are leaving, you do leave
You hear, you are hearing, you do hear
dorm ire
part ire
sent ire
VOI
dormite
partite
sentite

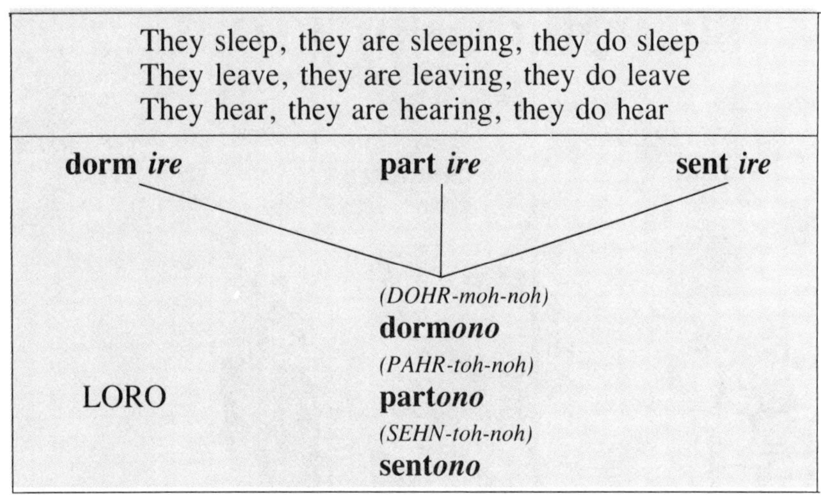

They sleep, they are sleeping, they do sleep
They leave, they are leaving, they do leave
They hear, they are hearing, they do hear
dorm *ire*
part *ire*
sent *ire*
LORO
(*DOHR-moh-noh*)
dorm*ono*
(*PAHR-toh-noh*)
part*ono*
(*SEHN-toh-noh*)
sent*ono*

As in the case of "are" and "ere" verbs, notice that the pronouns are optional and that *dormono, partono, sentono* are not stressed on the ending *-ono*. Remember that to form the negative you just put *non* before the verb. The following chart will help you remember the ending for "ire" verbs.

VERB ENDINGS

"IRE" VERBS

io ________	**-o**	**noi** ________	**-iamo**
tu ________	**-i**	**voi** ________	**-ite**
lui / **lei** ________	**-e**	**loro** ________	**-ono**

SUMMARY

Practice your technique in forming "ire" verbs by adding the correct ending in these sentences.

L'autista sent________ la voce (*VOH-cheh*) (voice) del signor Smith.

Il signor Smith e sua moglie dorm________ tutto (all) il giorno.

Io part________ domani.

Tu non part________ domani.

Voi dorm________ tutto il giorno.

Noi sent________ la voce della signora Smith.

ANSWERS

Verbs (sent) e (dorm) ono (part) o (part) i (dorm) ite (sent) iamo

SIGNOR CONDUTTORE . . .

How to Tell the Conductor

(sah-LEE-reh) **salire** to get on	*(ah-oo-TEES-tah)* **l'autista** driver	*(kohm-PRAH-reh)* **comprare** to buy	*(SHEHN-deh-reh)* **scendere** to get off	*(fehr-MAH-tah)* **la fermata** stop

(bee-LLYEH-ttoh)
il biglietto
ticket

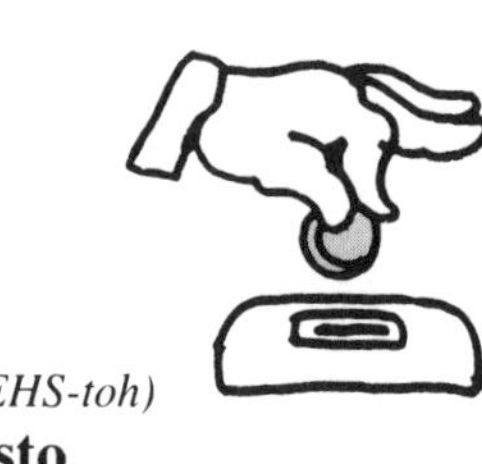

(REHS-toh)
il resto
change

Here are some verbs that don't follow the rules. You've learned how to use common verbs that end in "are," "ere," and "ire." Unfortunately, using verbs isn't that simple! *Naturalmente!* There are exceptions to the rules, and we call them "irregular verbs." These are some common irregular verbs—notice how they take on different forms, depending upon the subject. It is hard work, but you just have to learn these well, 'cause you will want to use them often.

	IRREGULAR VERBS				
	ANDARE to go	VENIRE to come	FARE to do/make	DARE to give	DIRE to say/tell
IO	**vado**	*(VEHN-goh)* **vengo**	*(FAH-choh)* **faccio**	**do**	*(DEE-koh)* **dico**
TU	*(VAH-ee)* **vai**	*(VYEH-nee)* **vieni**	*(FAH-ee)* **fai**	*(DAH-ee)* **dai**	*(DEE-chee)* **dici**
LUI / LEI	**va**	*(VYEH-neh)* **viene**	**fa**	**dà**	*(DEE-cheh)* **dice**
NOI	**andiamo**	**veniamo**	*(fah-CHAH-moh)* **facciamo**	**diamo**	*(dee-CHAH-moh)* **diciamo**
VOI	**andate**	**venite**	**fate**	**date**	**dite**
LORO	**vanno**	*(VEHN-goh-noh)* **vengono**	**fanno**	**danno**	*(DEE-koh-noh)* **dicono**

Now fill in the blanks with the appropriate verb forms. How many can you complete without looking back?

Io *vado* a Roma e tu ________ a Firenze. Il ragazzo *va* al negozio (store) e loro ________ al cinema.

Noi *andiamo* a Venezia e voi ________ a Pisa. Io *vengo* da Napoli e tu ________ da Milano.

Il signore *viene* da Bologna e loro ________ da Torino.

Voi *venite* da Palermo e noi ________ da Trieste.

Tu *fai* le spese (shop) e **anche** (also) *(AHN-keh)* io ________ le spese.

Il ragazzo non *fa* le spese, ma voi ________ le spese **sempre** (always).

Noi *facciamo* le spese e anche voi ________ le spese.

Io *dico* «buon giorno» e tu ________ **«buona sera»** (good evening/good afternoon).

Have some fun finding the Italian translations for the following verbs in the word search puzzle. To reinforce your memory, write each one in the space provided.

x	x	v	a	n	n	o	x	x	x	x	x	x	x	v	x	x	x	x	x	x	x	x	x	x
x	x	x	x	x	x	x	x	x	x	x	x	x	x	e	x	x	x	d	x	x	x	x	x	f
x	d	x	x	x	x	v	i	e	n	e	x	x	x	n	x	x	x	a	x	x	x	x	x	a
x	x	i	x	x	x	x	x	x	x	x	x	x	x	g	x	x	x	n	x	x	x	x	x	c
x	x	x	c	x	x	x	x	x	x	x	x	x	x	o	x	x	x	n	x	x	x	x	x	c
x	x	x	x	o	x	x	x	x	x	x	x	x	x	x	x	x	x	o	x	x	x	x	x	i
x	x	f	a	n	n	o	x	x	x	x	x	x	x	x	x	x	x	x	x	x	x	x	x	o
x	x	x	x	x	x	o	x	d	i	c	o	x	x	x	d	i	a	m	o	x	x	x	x	x
v	a	d	o	x	x	x	x	x	x	x	x	x	x	x	x	x	x	x	x	x	x	x	x	x

1. they go ________ 2. she comes ________ 3. I come ________

4. I do ________ 5. they give ________ 6. I say ________

7. they say ________ 8. we give ________ 9. they do ________

10. I go ________

ANSWERS

Word search **1.** vanno **2.** viene **3.** vengo **4.** faccio **5.** danno **6.** dico **7.** dicono **8.** diamo **9.** fanno **10.** vado

Irregular verbs vai (a Firenze.) vanno (al cinema.) andate (a Pisa.) vieni (da Milano.) vengono (da Torino.) veniamo (da Trieste.) faccio (le spese.) fate (le spese sempre.) fate (le spese.) dici («buona sera»)

Le preposizioni ancora una volta

Getting Back to Prepositions

Do you remember the Italian for those little words "of," "to," and "from"? (They are called *preposizioni*.) When *a, in, di, da,* and *su* occur right before "the," they "contract"; that is, they become one word with the various forms of "the."

di + il	su + il
È il libro [del] ragazzo.	**Il gatto è [sul] tetto.**
of the	on the
(It is the book *of the* boy.)	(The cat is *on the* roof.)

The contractions are summarized for you in the following chart.

	WORDS THAT CAN BE CONTRACTED						
+	LA	LE	L'	LO	GLI	IL	I
A	**alla**	**alle**	**all'**	**allo**	**agli**	**al**	**ai**
IN	**nella**	**nelle**	**nell'**	**nello**	**negli**	**nel**	**nei**
DI	**della**	**delle**	**dell'**	**dello**	**degli**	**del**	**dei**
DA	**dalla**	**dalle**	**dall'**	**dallo**	**dagli**	**dal**	**dai**
SU	**sulla**	**sulle**	**sull'**	**sullo**	**sugli**	**sul**	**sui**

Now try to use some of these in the following.

La ragazza arriva __________ aeroporto domani.
at the

Il gatto è __________ albero.
on the

Quei libri **sono** __________ amiche di Pino.
are of the

Quelle penne sono __________ amici di Maria.
of the

Lo zio è __________ banca.
in the

Quel signore è __________ farmacia.
in the

Maria va __________ mercato.
to the

Giovanni fa le spese __________ negozi di Roma.
in the

Marco scende __________ autobus.
from the

ANSWERS

Prepositions All' (aeroporto) nella (farmacia.) sull' (albero) al (mercato.) delle (amiche) nei (negozi) degli (amici) dall' (autobus) nella (banca)

Di

Some

ian is expressed by using *di* plus *the* (see also the previous chart).

SOME

di + i

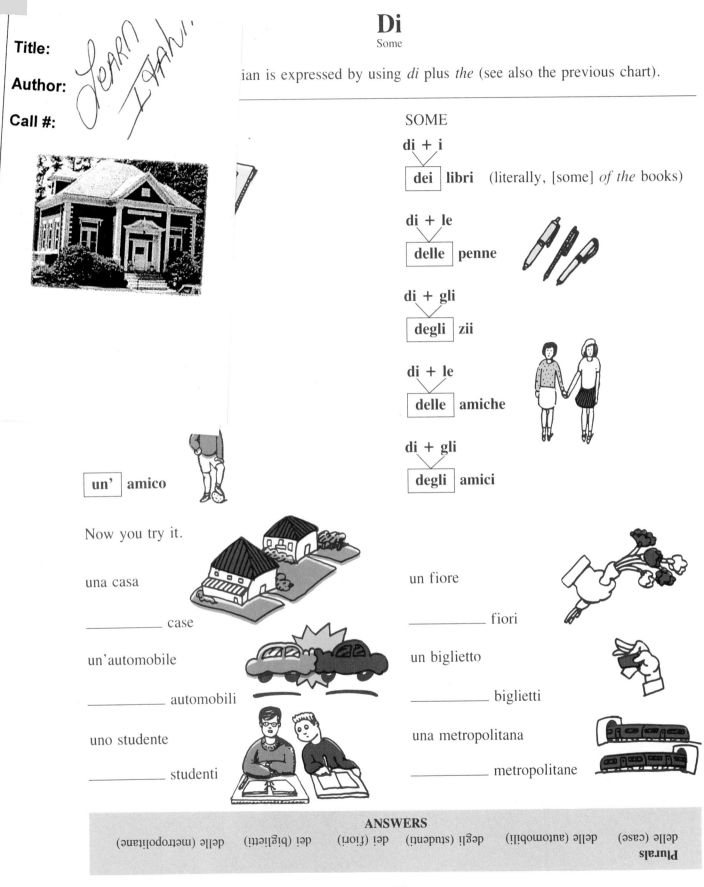

dei **libri** (literally, [some] *of the* books)

di + le

delle **penne**

di + gli

degli **zii**

di + le

delle **amiche**

di + gli

degli **amici**

un' **amico**

Now you try it.

una casa

__________ case

un'automobile

__________ automobili

uno studente

__________ studenti

un fiore

__________ fiori

un biglietto

__________ biglietti

una metropolitana

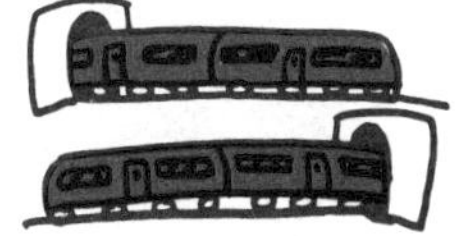

__________ metropolitane

ANSWERS

Plurals
delle (case) delle (automobili) degli (studenti) dei (fiori) dei (biglietti) delle (metropolitane)

Read the following brief passage and see what you have learned to help you get where you are going. Then, select the appropriate answer to each question.

Il signor Rossi e sua moglie prendono l'autobus per due fermate. Poi prendono la metropolitana. Loro scendono in Via Verdi. Arrivano al mercato e comprano molte cose.

due: two; cose *(KOH-zeh)*: things

Che cosa prendono il signor Rossi e sua moglie per due fermate?
- ☐ Prendono la metropolitana.
- ☐ Prendono il tassì.
- ☐ Prendono l'autobus.

Poi che cosa prendono?
- ☐ Prendono la metropolitana.
- ☐ Prendono il tassì.
- ☐ Prendono l'autobus.

Dove scendono?
- ☐ Scendono in Via Rossini.
- ☐ Scendono in Via Verdi.
- ☐ Scendono in Via Dante.

Che cosa comprano?
- ☐ Comprano un libro.
- ☐ Comprano molte cose.
- ☐ Comprano una penna.

Now for review, fill in the missing verb endings.

1. Maria part__________ domani.
2. Loro dorm__________ tutto il giorno.
3. Io non dorm__________ al cinema!
4. Io part__________ domani e tu part __________ questa **sera** (evening).
5. Tu dorm__________ sull'autobus.
6. Noi part__________ questa sera.
7. Voi non dorm__________ in quell'albergo.

Now let's see if you remember your prepositions.

Maria va __________ (to the) negozio.

Io vengo __________ (from the) farmacia.

Ecco la penna __________ (of the) amico di Maria.

Maria **sale** (gets on) __________ (the) autobus.

Giovanni è __________ (in the) banca.

ANSWERS

Comprehension Prendono l'autobus. Prendono la metropolitana. Scendono in Via Verdi. Comprano molte cose.

Verbs **1.** (part) e **2.** (dorm) ono **3.** (dorm) o **4.** (part) o / (part) i **5.** (dorm) i **6.** (part) iamo **7.** (dorm) ite

Prepositions al (negozi) dalla (farmacia.) dell' (amico) sull' (autobus.) nella (banca.)

5

(NOO-meh-ree)

L'ora e i numeri

All About Time and Numbers

CHE ORA È / CHE ORE SONO?

What Time Is It?

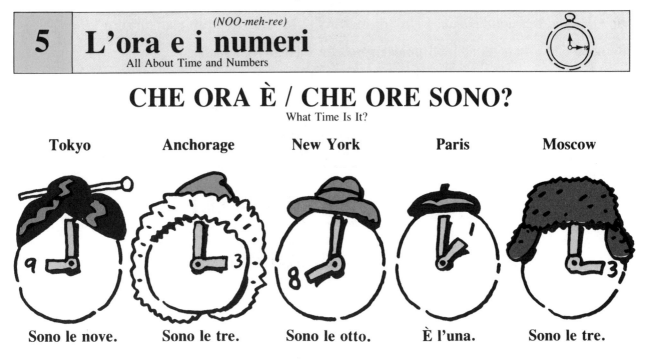

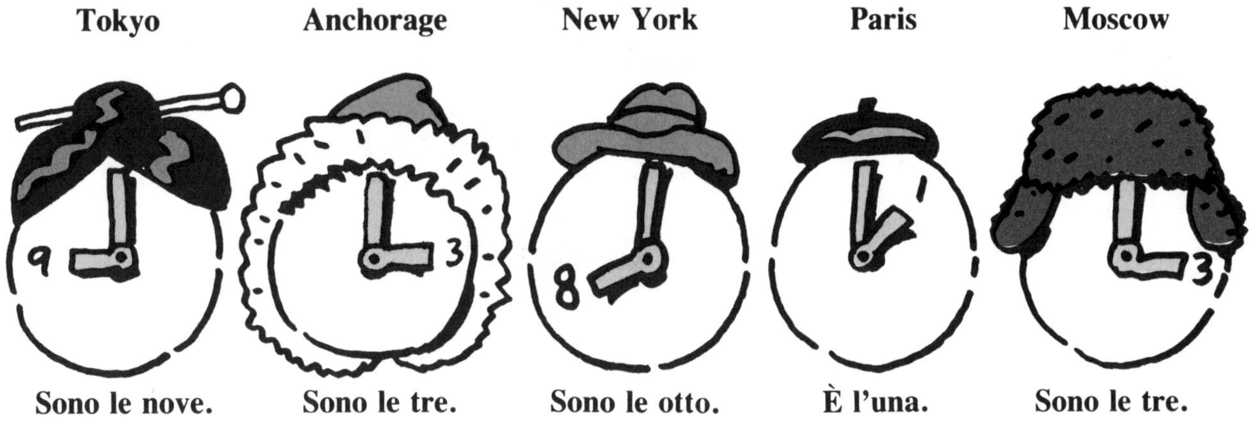

Sono le nove. **Sono le tre.** **Sono le otto.** **È l'una.** **Sono le tre.**

Expressing time is easy. Simply state the hour preceded by *le*. This is true for all hours except for one o'clock, for which you use *l'*.

To add the minutes, just use *e* (''and'').

Sono le sei e dieci (6:10).

Sono le sette e venti (7:20).

Sono le nove e trentanova (9:39).

If the minute hand is close to the next hour, you can also tell time by quoting the next hour **meno** (minus) the number of minutes to go.

Sono le dieci e cinquanta. =
Sono le undici meno dieci (10:50).

Sono le undici e cinquantacinque. =
Sono le dodici meno cinque (11:55).

You can replace the quarter hours and the half-hours with the following expressions.

2:15 = le due e quindici = le due e **un quarto**

3:30 = le tre e trenta = le tre e **mezzo** / **mezza**

4:45 = le quattro e quarantacinque = le quattro e **tre quarti** **=**
le cinque meno **un quarto**

For A.M. you can use the expression **di mattina** ; for P.M. you can use **di sera** for the late afternoon and evening, and **del pomeriggio** for the early afternoon.

For official time, Italian uses the "24-hour clock."

Mario arriva al*le tredici e venti* = 13:20 = 1:20 P.M.
Giovanni parte al*le diciotto e dieci* = 18:10 = 6:10 P.M.
Il signor Smith fa la prenotazione al*le venti e mezzo* = 20:30 = 8:30 P.M.

COME SI CONTA IN ITALIANO

How to Count in Italian

I numeri cardinali

Cardinal Numbers

1 uno

2 due

3 tre

(KWAH-ttroh)
4 quattro

(CHEEN-kweh)
5 cinque

(SEH-ee)
6 sei

7 sette

8 otto

9 nove

(DYEH chee)
10 dieci

(OOHN-dee-chee)
11 undici

(DOH-dee-chee)
12 dodici

(TREH-dee-chee)
13 tredici

(kwah-TTOHR-dee-chee)
14 quattordici

(KWEEN-dee-chee)
15 quindici

(SEH-dee-chee)
16 sedici

(dee-chah-SSEH-tteh)
17 diciassette

(dee-CHOH-ttoh)
18 diciotto

(dee-chah-NNOH-veh)
19 diciannove

(VEHN-tee)
20 venti

---

21 ventuno

22 ventidue

23 ventitré

24 ventiquattro

25 venticinque

26 ventisei

27 ventisette

28 ventotto

29 ventinove

30 trenta

---

31 trentuno

32 trentadue

. . .

(kwah-RAHN-tah)
40 quaranta

41 quarantuno

42 quarantadue

. . .

(cheen-KWAHN-tah)
50 cinquanta

51 cinquantuno

52 cinquantadue

. . .

60 sessanta

61 sessantuno

62 sessantadue

. . .

70 settanta

71 settantuno

72 settantadue

. . .

80 ottanta

81 ottantuno

82 ottantadue

. . .

90 novanta

91 novantuno

92 novantadue

. . .

(*CHEHN-toh*) **100 cento**	**1,000 mille**	**1,002 milledue**	**3,000 tremila**
	1,001 milleuno	**2,000 duemila**	**10,000 diecimila**

Now try to write out in words the following prices.

La pizza costa ______________ (95) **lire. Gli spaghetti costano** ______________ (100) **lire.**

Il libro costa ______________ (88) **lire. La penna costa** ______________ (67) **lire.**

Il biglietto costa ______________ (74) **lire. Maria ha** (has) ______________ (23) **dollari** (*DOH-llah-ree*) (dollars) **americani; Marco ha** ______________ (32) **dollari; Giovanni ha** ______________ (29) **dollari. Quanti dollari?** ______________ (23 + 32 + 29) 84 **dollari.**

Un momento. Now give the following times in words.

2:24	______________	4:12	______________
6:15	______________	8:20	______________
9:17	______________	11:01	______________
3:58	______________	5:30	______________
7:45	______________	1:10	______________
10:35	______________	12:47	______________

ANSWERS

Numbers novantacinque (95) cento (100) ottantotto (88) sessantasette (67) settantaquattro (74) ventitré (23) trentadue (32) ventinove (29) ottantaquattro (84)

Time

le due e ventiquattro (2:24)
le sei e quindici / le sei e un quarto (6:15)
le nove e diciassette (9:17)
le tre e cinquantotto / le quattro meno due (3:58)
le sette e quarantacinque / le sette e tre quarti / le otto meno un quarto (7:45)
le dieci e trentacinque (10:35)

le quattro e dodici (4:12)
le otto e venti (8:20)
le undici e uno (11:01)
le cinque e mezzo / le cinque e trenta (5:30)
l'una e dieci (1:10)
le dodici e quarantasette / l'una meno tredici (12:47)

(meh-tsoh-JOHR-noh)	*(meh-tsah-NOH-tteh)*
mezzogiorno	**mezzanotte**
noon	midnight

The following dialogue contains some useful words and expressions related to the telling of time.

Don't forget to read each line out loud several times and to act out each part.

(A stranger approaches Mark on the street.)

STRANIERO	**Scusi, signore, che ora è?**	Excuse me, sir, what time is it?
MARK	**È mezzanotte.**	It's midnight.
STRANIERO	**Ma come, è ancora giorno?** *(ahn-KOH-rah)*	How can that be? It is still daytime?
MARK	**Scusi, allora è mezzogiorno.**	Excuse me, then it's noon.
STRANIERO	**Ma lei scherza?** *(SKEHR-tsah)*	Are you joking?
MARK	**No. Non ho l'orologio.** *(oh-roh-LOH-joh)*	No. I don't have a watch.
STRANIERO	**Lei è un turista?** *(too-REES-tah)*	Are you a tourist?
MARK	**Sì.**	Yes.
STRANIERO	**Vuole comprare un orologio? Centomila lire.** *(VWOH-leh)*	Do you want to buy a watch? 100.000 lira.
MARK	**È troppo!**	That is too much!
STRANIERO	**Diecimila lire.**	10.000 lira.
MARK	**No, grazie.**	No, thanks.
STRANIERO	**Ecco il suo orologio. Io sono un borsaiolo onesto!** *(bohr-sah-YOH-loh)*	Here is your watch. I am an honest pickpocket!

Now fill in the missing dialogue parts. Check your answers only after you have attempted to fill in the parts from memory.

Scusi signore, che o__________ è?

È m__________.

Ma come, è ancora g__________.

Scusi, allora è m__________.

Ma lei s__________?

No. Non ho l'o__________.

Lei è un t__________?

Sì.

Vuole c__________ un orologio?

Centomila lire.

È troppo!

Diecimila l__________.

No, g__________.

Ecco il suo orologio. Io sono un b__________ onesto!

I numeri ordinali 1–10

Ordinal Numbers 1–10

First:	**primo**	Fourth:	*(KWAHR-toh)* **quarto**	Seventh:	*(SEH-ttee-moh)* **settimo**	Tenth:	*(DEH-chee-moh)* **decimo**
Second:	*(seh-KOHN-doh)* **secondo**	Fifth:	*(KWEEN-toh)* **quinto**	Eighth:	*(oh-TTAH-voh)* **ottavo**		
Third:	*(TEHR-tsoh)* **terzo**	Sixth:	**sesto**	Ninth:	*(NOH-noh)* **nono**		

Repeat aloud and write the floor designations in the appropriate blanks next to this control panel.

__________ __________

__________ __________

__________ __________

__________ __________

__________ __________

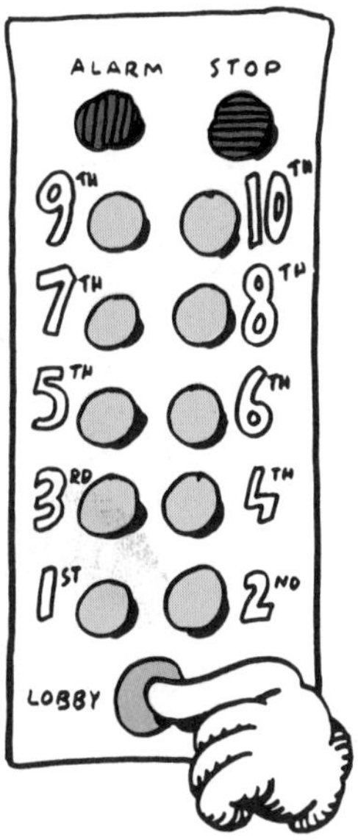

Ricordati
Remember

(YEH-ree)
ieri Londra
yesterday

(OH-jjee) (pah-REE-jee)
oggi Parigi
today

(doh-MAH-nee)
domani Roma
tomorrow

(AHN-keh)
anche Pisa
also/too

(DOH-poh)
dopo Madrid
later

By now, you should be able to make sense out of the following sentences.

(kwee)
Tu vieni **qui**.
here

Io vado **là (lì).**
there

(MOHL-toh)
Mia moglie non ha **molto** denaro.
much money

Mio marito ha **poco** denaro.
little

Adesso/ora andiamo a Bologna.
Now

Andiamo **almeno** fino a Palermo.
at least

Giovanni non sta **bene**. (John does not feel well.)
well

(MEH-lyee-oh)
Ora sta **meglio**. (Now he is better.)
better

(POH-ee)
Poi andiamo al cinema.
Then

Questo biglietto costa **troppo**.
too much

(voh-lehn-TYEH-ree)
Io vado a Milano **volentieri**.
gladly

Mia moglie **non** va **mai** al cinema.
never

Io **non** sento **niente/nulla**.
nothing

Io **non** vedo **nessuno**.
no one

See if you remember the meaning of these useful words by matching them with their English equivalents.

1. nessuno	a. yesterday
2. bene	b. today
3. meglio	c. tomorrow
4. niente	d. again
5. poi	e. also/too
6. troppo	f. already
7. mai	g. here
8. volentieri	h. much
9. ieri	i. little
10. anche	j. now
11. oggi	k. at least
12. domani	l. well
13. ancora	m. better
14. già	n. then
15. adesso/ora	o. too much
16. almeno	p. gladly
17. molto	q. never
18. poco	r. nothing
19. qui	s. no one

Now choose from the following eight words and put the appropriate words in the blanks below.

domani **oggi** **anche** **qui** **molto** **mai** **niente** **nessuno**

?

Maria abita ________________ a Roma.

Quando arriva Giovanni, ________________ o ________________?
or

Domani arriva ________________ la zia di Gina.

Lui non scrive ________________ a suo zio.

Marisa non sa ________________.
knows

Io non vedo ________________.

Luisa ha ________________ denaro.
has

ANSWERS

Matching **1**-s, **2**-l, **3**-m, **4**-r, **5**-n, **6**-o, **7**-q, **8**-p, **9**-a, **10**-e, **11**-b **12**-c, **13**-d **14**-f, **15**-j, **16**-k, **17**-h, **18**-i, **19**-g

Fill-ins qui (a Roma.) oggi / domani? anche (la zia) mai (a suo zio.) niente. nessuno. molto

I verbi!

Verbs!

Previously, you learned about "ire" verbs. Now you will learn about a different kind of "ire" verb. These verbs take an "isc" in the *io, tu, lui / lei,* and *loro* forms. We've shown you how it is done.

(fee-NEE-reh)	*(kah-PEE-reh)*	*(preh-feh-REE-reh)*
fin*ire*	**cap*ire***	**prefer*ire***
to finish	to understand	to prefer

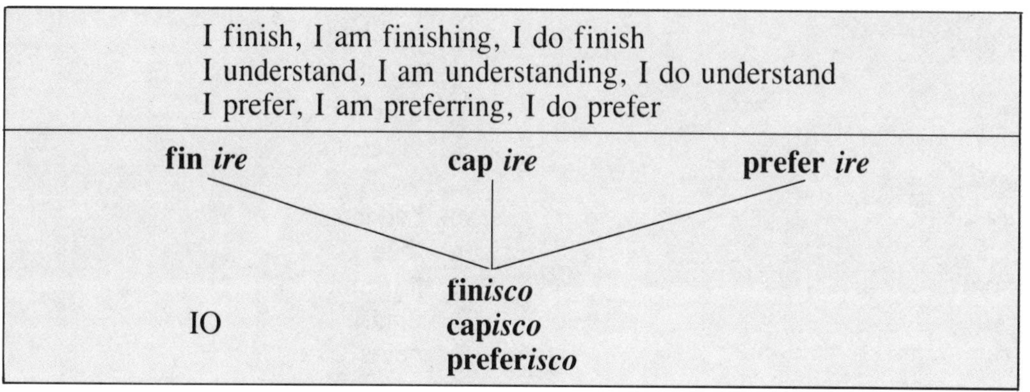

I finish, I am finishing, I do finish
I understand, I am understanding, I do understand
I prefer, I am preferring, I do prefer
fin ire
cap ire
prefer ire
IO
finisco
capisco
preferisco

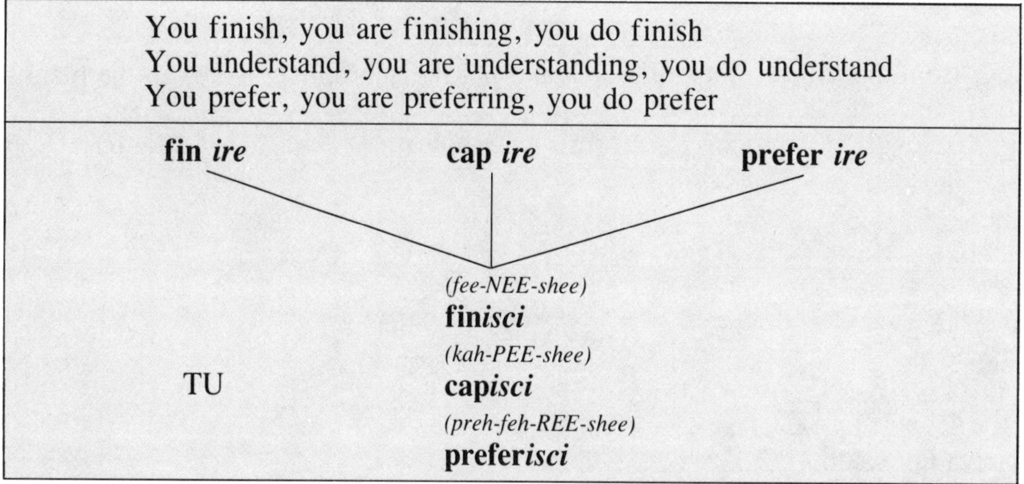

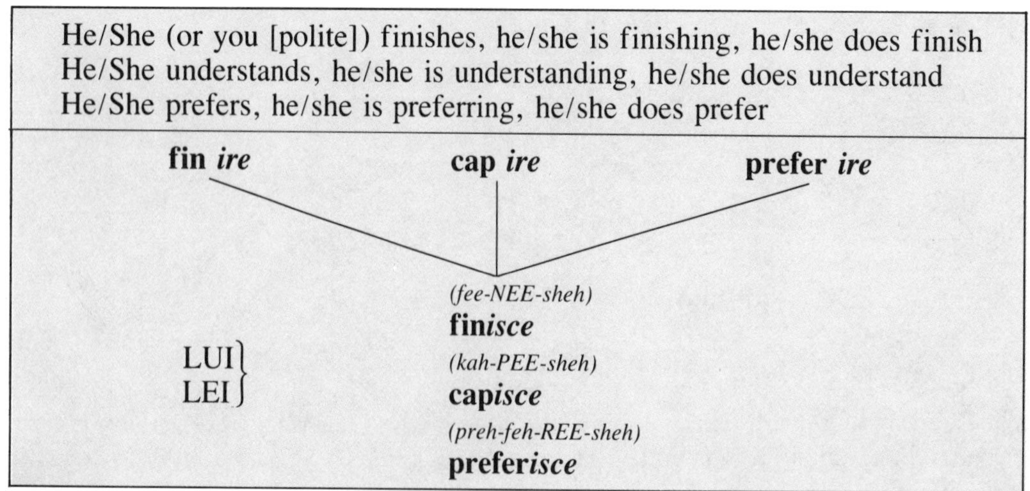

He/She (or you [polite]) finishes, he/she is finishing, he/she does finish
He/She understands, he/she is understanding, he/she does understand
He/She prefers, he/she is preferring, he/she does prefer
fin ire
cap ire
prefer ire
LUI
LEI
(fee-NEE-sheh)
finisce
(kah-PEE-sheh)
capisce
(preh-feh-REE-sheh)
preferisce

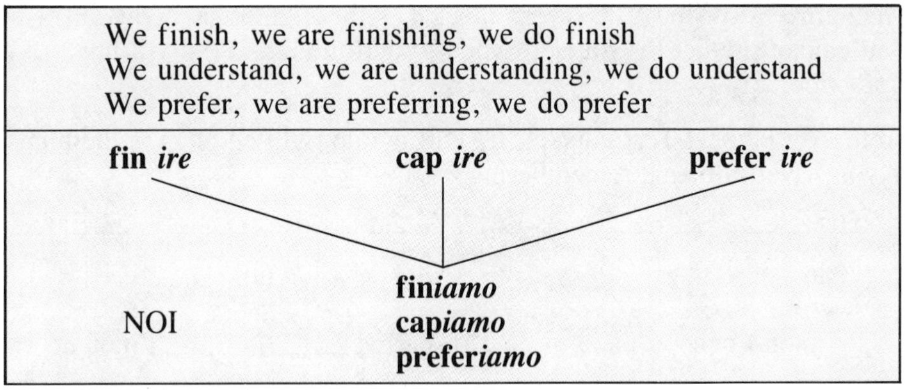

We finish, we are finishing, we do finish
We understand, we are understanding, we do understand
We prefer, we are preferring, we do prefer

fin ***ire*** **cap** ***ire*** **prefer** ***ire***

NOI **fin*iamo*** **cap*iamo*** **prefer*iamo***

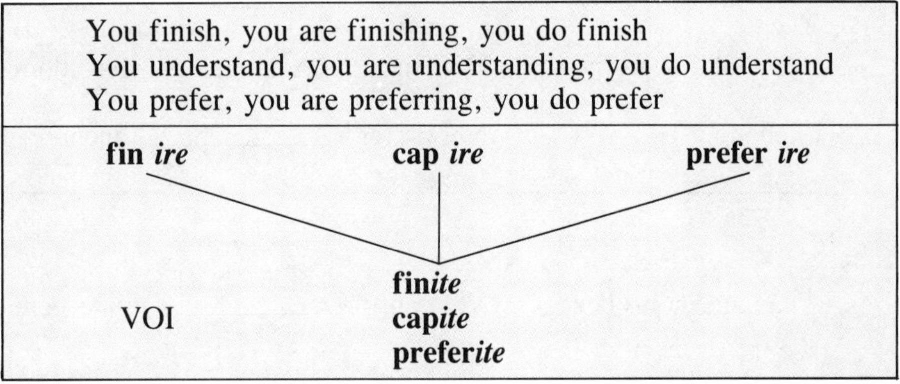

You finish, you are finishing, you do finish
You understand, you are understanding, you do understand
You prefer, you are preferring, you do prefer

fin ***ire*** **cap** ***ire*** **prefer** ***ire***

VOI **fin*ite*** **cap*ite*** **prefer*ite***

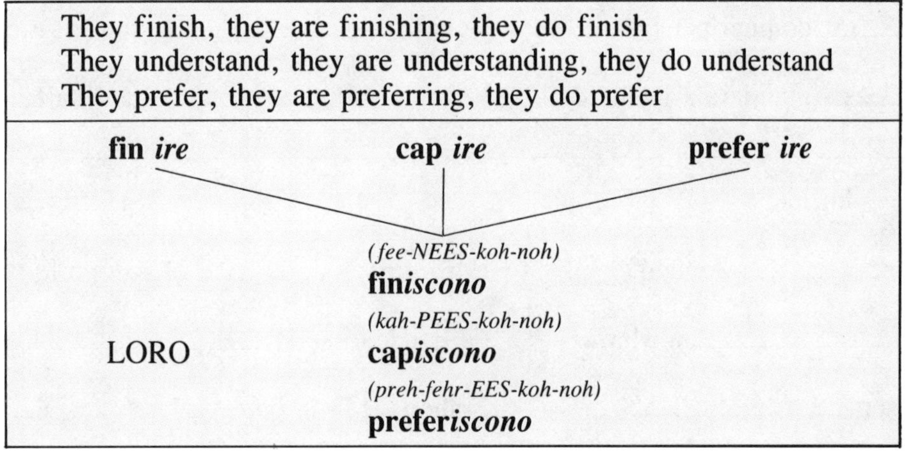

They finish, they are finishing, they do finish
They understand, they are understanding, they do understand
They prefer, they are preferring, they do prefer

fin ***ire*** **cap** ***ire*** **prefer** ***ire***

LORO

(fee-NEES-koh-noh)
fin*iscono*
(kah-PEES-koh-noh)
cap*iscono*
(preh-fehr-EES-koh-noh)
prefer*iscono*

The table at the right will help you remember these special "ire" verb endings.

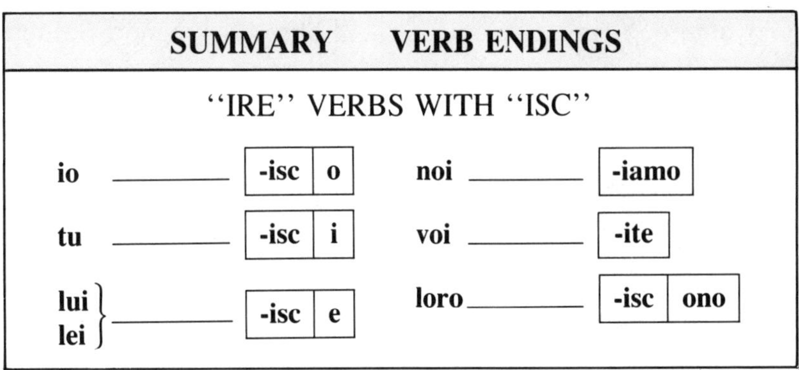

SUMMARY VERB ENDINGS

"IRE" VERBS WITH "ISC"

io ______	**-isc o**	**noi** ______	**-iamo**
tu ______	**-isc i**	**voi** ______	**-ite**
lui / lei ______	**-isc e**	**loro** ______	**-isc ono**

How can you recognize a special "ire" verb that takes these endings? You can't. *Mi dispiace*! (I'm sorry!) You cannot predict by yourself when to add the *isc*. You will have to learn the *isc* verbs through practice.

Let's review all the verb types! Test yourself by putting the right endings in the blanks. Look back at the charts if you have problems remembering.

---

io

Io cant__________ molto bene.

Io non scriv__________ mai a mio zio.

Io non dorm__________ tutto il giorno.

Io cap__________ l'italiano.

noi

Noi parl______________ l'italiano **come** gli italiani.
like

Noi ved______________ Giovanni **stasera**.
tonight

Noi fin______________ il libro domani.

Noi prefer______________ andare a Bologna.

---

tu

Tu parl__________ l'italiano molto bene.

Tu non ved__________ nessuno.

Tu part__________ domani per l'Italia.

Tu prefer__________ andare a Roma.

voi

Voi cant______________ molto bene.

Voi scriv______________ molto bene.

Voi dorm______________ tutto il giorno.

Voi non cap______________ l'italiano.

---

lui/lei

Lui arriv______________ domani.

Lei non cred______________ a Maria.

Il turista non sent______________ la voce del vigile.

Giovanni non fin______________ il libro.

loro

Loro arriv______________ dopo le sei.

Gli studenti scriv______________ l'**esame**.
exam

Franco e Maria part______________ domani per l'Italia.

I signori Smith non cap______________ l'italiano.

ANSWERS

Verb review

io	**tu**	**lui / lei**	**noi**	**voi**	**loro**
(cant) o	(parl) i	(arriv) a	(parl) iamo	(cant) ate	(arriv) ano
(scriv) o	(ved) i	(cred) e	(ved) iamo	(scriv) ete	(scriv) ono
(dorm) o	(part) i	(sent) e	(fin) iamo	(dorm) ite	(part) ono
(cap) isco	(prefer) isci	(fin) isce	(prefer) iamo	(cap) ite	(cap) iscono

Il mio e il tuo

Mine and Yours

What's mine and what's yours? Here's how to tell in Italian. Notice that the forms of these words change, depending on the noun.

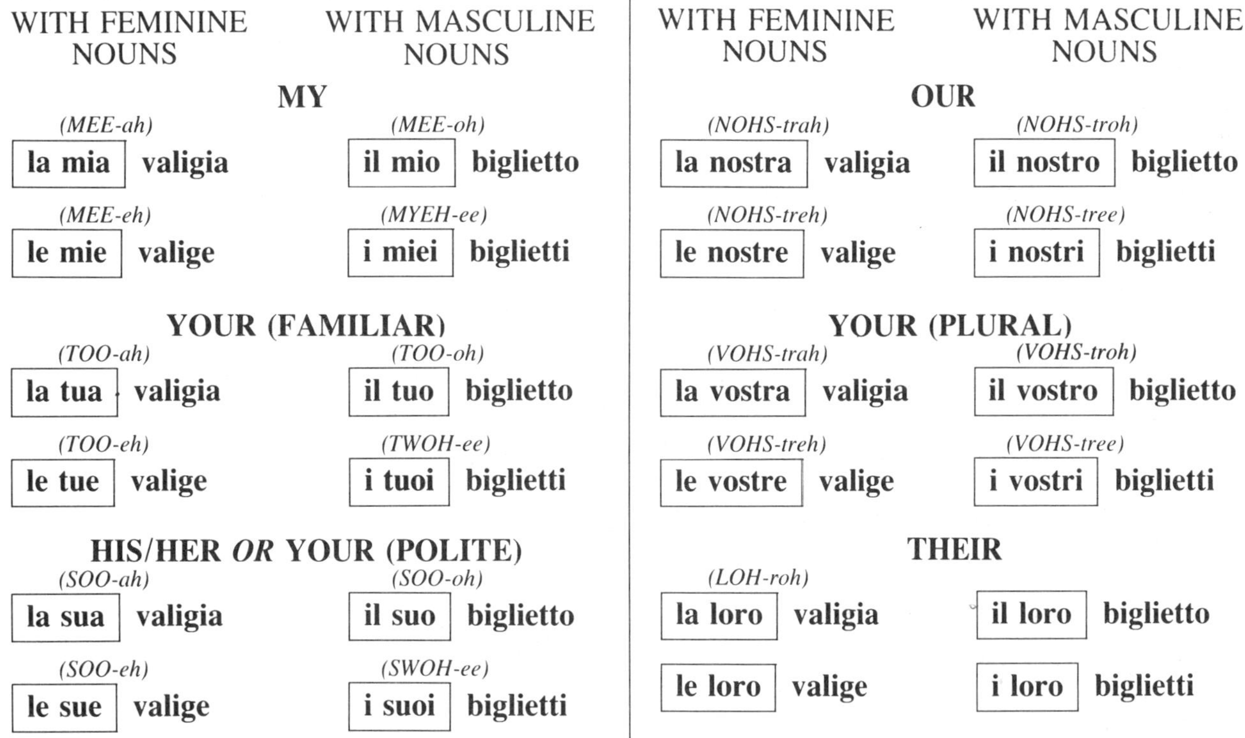

	WITH FEMININE NOUNS	WITH MASCULINE NOUNS
MY	*(MEE-ah)* **la mia valigia**	*(MEE-oh)* **il mio biglietto**
	(MEE-eh) **le mie valige**	*(MYEH-ee)* **i miei biglietti**
YOUR (FAMILIAR)	*(TOO-ah)* **la tua valigia**	*(TOO-oh)* **il tuo biglietto**
	(TOO-eh) **le tue valige**	*(TWOH-ee)* **i tuoi biglietti**
HIS/HER *OR* YOUR (POLITE)	*(SOO-ah)* **la sua valigia**	*(SOO-oh)* **il suo biglietto**
	(SOO-eh) **le sue valige**	*(SWOH-ee)* **i suoi biglietti**
OUR	*(NOHS-trah)* **la nostra valigia**	*(NOHS-troh)* **il nostro biglietto**
	(NOHS-treh) **le nostre valige**	*(NOHS-tree)* **i nostri biglietti**
YOUR (PLURAL)	*(VOHS-trah)* **la vostra valigia**	*(VOHS-troh)* **il vostro biglietto**
	(VOHS-treh) **le vostre valige**	*(VOHS-tree)* **i vostri biglietti**
THEIR	*(LOH-roh)* **la loro valigia**	**il loro biglietto**
	le loro valige	**i loro biglietti**

Notice that "my," "your," and other possessive pronouns are preceded by the appropriate forms of "the." These are dropped only when the noun refers to a singular and unmodified family member (except for "their," which *always* retains the article "the"). For example:

mio zio	*but* **i** miei zii
tua sorella	*but* **la** tua sorella **piccola** (small)
nostro padre	*but* **il loro** padre

Notice, as well, that the forms *la sua, le sue, il suo,* and *i suoi* mean "his," "her," or "you" (polite).

Now test your knowledge by putting the appropriate possessive adjective in front of the following nouns.

________________ (my)	fiore	________________ (my (be careful!))	zia
________________ (my)	fiori	________________ (my (be careful again!))	zie
________________ (your (familiar))	casa	________________ (his)	penna
________________ (your (familiar))	case	________________ (his)	penne
________________ (his)	gatto	________________ (her)	orologio
________________ (his)	gatti	________________ (her)	orologi
________________ (her (be careful!))	gatto	________________ (their)	biglietto
________________ (her)	gatti	________________ (their)	biglietti
________________ (our)	amico	________________ (their)	lira
________________ (our)	amici	________________ (their)	lire

If someone asks you, can you give the time in Italian? Read the passage and then answer the questions that follow.

Che ore sono? **chiede il padre a sua figlia.** **Sono le tre e mezzo,** **dice la figlia.**

A che ora parti per l'Italia? **chiede il padre.** **Alle cinque e venti,** **risponde la figlia.**
(rees-POHN-deh) answers

Ciao e buon viaggio. (have a good trip) **Ciao papà.** (dad)

Che cosa chiede il padre a sua figlia?
- ☐ Come stai?
- ☐ Che ore sono?
- ☐ Che fai?

Che ore sono?
- ☐ Sono le tre e un quarto.
- ☐ Sono le tre e venticinque.
- ☐ Sono le tre e mezzo.

A che ora parte la figlia?
- ☐ Alle cinque e venti.
- ☐ Alle cinque e un quarto.
- ☐ A mezziogiorno.

ANSWERS

Possessives il mio (fiore) il suo (gatto) il nostro (amico) la sua (penna) il loro (biglietto)
i miei (fiori) i suoi (gatti) i nostri (amici) le sue (penne) i loro (biglietti)
la tua (casa) il suo (gatto) mia (zia) il suo (orologio) la loro (lira)
le tue (case) i suoi (gatti) le mie (zie) i suoi (orologi) le loro (lire)

Comprehension Che ore sono? Sono le tre e mezzo. Alle cinque e venti.

6

(TREH-nee)

I treni

Trains

If you will be taking the train, the words and expressions in the following dialogue might prove to be useful to you.

Don't forget to read each line out loud several times and to act out each part.

(EH-kkoh-chee) (stah-TSYOH-neh) MARY **Eccoci alla stazione** *(feh-rroh-vee-AH-ree-ah)* **ferroviaria.**	Here we are at the train station.
(RAH-pee-doh) ANNE **Papà, prendiamo il rapido per andare a Firenze?**	Dad, are we taking the luxury train to go to Florence?
MARK **No. Costa troppo.**	No. It costs too much.
ANNE **Allora prendiamo il** *(dee-reh-TTEE-ssee-moh)* **direttissimo?**	Then are we taking the fast train?
MARK **Sì.** *(to a ticket clerk)* **Scusi, quanto costa un biglietto di andata e ritorno per quattro persone a Firenze?**	Yes. Excuse me, how much does a round-trip ticket to Florence for four persons cost?

COMMESSO **Il direttissimo?** — The fast train?

MARK **Sì.** — Yes.

COMMESSO *(skohm-pahr-tee-MEHN-toh)* **Scompartimento per** *(foo-mah-TOH-ree)* **fumatori o per non fumatori?** — Smoking or no smoking compartment?

MARK **Non fumatori.** — No smoking.

COMMESSO **Centomila lire. Ecco i biglietti.** — 100,000 lira. Here are the tickets.

MARK **Grazie. Quando parte il treno?** — Thank you. When does the train leave?

COMMESSO **Il treno parte alle quindici a trenta.** — The train leaves at 15:30 (3:30 PM).

Now try to complete the missing dialogue parts. Check your answers only after you have attempted to fill in the missing parts from memory.

Eccoci alla s______________ ferroviaria.

Papà, prendiamo il r______________ per andare a Firenze?

No. C______________ troppo.

Allora prendiamo il d______________?

Sì. Scusi quanto costa un biglietto di a______________

e r______________ per quattro persone a Firenze?

(oh-RAH-ree-oh)

L'orario

Train Schedule

Remember that train schedules use official time, based on a 24-hour clock:

1:00 p.m. = 13:00 hours = **le tredici**
2:00 p.m. = 14:00 hours = **le quattordici**
12:00 midnight = 24:00 hours = **le ventiquattro**

Note that the name of the city of departure *(Bologna)* is at the top of the schedule. Each city served by this line follows, with the departure time (from Bologna) for each train listed in the column on the left, followed by the arrival time at the right. Additional information regarding the type of each train is also given.

Firenze

	ar an	Observations Bemerkungen
19 04	20 32	✕
19 33	20 55	
21 13	22 39	
22 01	23 20	✕
22 23	23 30	Rapido
23 23	0 50	

Milano

	ar an	Observations Bemerkungen
5 20	8 22	
6 12	9 00	
6 44	9 12	
6 58	9 20	
7 20	9 50	
8 01	9 55	Rapido
8 18	1)11 24	
10 36	13 00	
10 54	13 40	✕
11 00	13 50	✕
12 00	13 55	[R] TEE ✕
12 30	15 20	✕
13 12	15 25	✕
13 23	16 00	✕
14 05	16 40	✕
15 02	17 10	
15 42	17 30	[R] TEE ✕
16 07	19 00	
17 15	19 05	[R] TEE ✕
18 20	20 30	Rapido ✕
18 49	1)21 25	
19 58	22 45	
20 44	23 07	
21 44	23 35	[R] TEE ✕
21 50	23 40	[R] TEE ✕
22 00	0 45	

1) Milano P.G.

Napoli

	ar an	Observations Bemerkungen
1 09	9 20	🛏 ⊢⊣
3 58	11 35	
8 44	17 22	✕
10 23	19 48	✕
13 47	1)20 10	[R] TEE ✕
14 55	21 52	Rapido ✕
15 10	2)22 08	✕
18 00	2) 1 46	🛏 ⊢⊣
19 24	3 01	🛏 ⊢⊣
22 01	2) 5 10	🛏 ⊢⊣
22 40	2) 5 36	🛏 ⊢⊣

1) Napoli Merg.
2) Napoli C.F.

Palermo

	ar an	Observations Bemerkungen
5 35	23 22	[X] Roma [R] ✕
13 05	8 25	[R] ✕ [X] Roma 🛏 ⊢⊣
15 10	10 58	🛏 ⊢⊣
18 15	13 20	🛏 ⊢⊣
22 01	17 35	🛏 ⊢⊣
22 40	17 57	🛏 ⊢⊣

Pisa

	ar an	Observations Bemerkungen
6 18	10 00	[X] Firenze
8 05	10 36	✕ [X] Firenze
9 09	12 30	✕ [X] Firenze
9 56	12 30	Rapido [X] Firenze
10 16	13 10	[X] Firenze
△10 30	13 10	
13 05	15 32	[R] ✕ [X] Firenze
13 47	16 22	[R] TEE ✕ [X] Firenze
△14 55	17 14	Rapido ✕ [X] Firenze

△ 29 V - 24 IX 83

Pisa

	ar an	Observations Bemerkungen
16 24	19 02	✕ [X] Firenze
17 17	19 57	✕ [X] Firenze
18 53	22 10	[R] TEE ✕ [X] Firenze
19 04	22 10	✕ [X] Firenze
19 33	23 23	✕ [X] Firenze
21 13	23 48	

Roma

	ar an	Observations Bemerkungen
1 09	1) 6 30	🛏 ⊢⊣
1 34	7 15	🛏 ⊢⊣
5 35	10 40	
6 18	12 05	
8 05	12 55	✕
8 17	13 15	✕
8 44	14 42	✕
9 09	13 45	✕
10 04	14 05	[R] TEE ✕
10 16	14 50	✕
10 23	1)15 50	✕
13 05	17 10	[R] ✕
13 12	18 50	✕
13 47	17 45	[R] TEE ✕
14 10	19 48	✕
14 55	19 13	Rapido ✕
15 10	1)19 46	✕
15 17	20 07	✕
16 24	17 40	✕
17 17	22 50	✕
18 15	1)23 09	✕
18 53	23 00	[R] TEE ✕
19 04	23 50	✕
19 24	1) 0 13	

1) Roma Tib.na

Torino

	ar an	Observations Bemerkungen
3 30	8 15	🛏 ⊢⊣
4 05	8 48	
6 20	10 45	
15 10	19 15	
18 37	22 50	
19 52	0 10	

Venezia

	ar an	Observations Bemerkungen
5 12	7 40	
5 58	8 15	
8 11	10 30	
11 13	12 48	✕
11 25	13 37	✕
12 25	13 31	✕
13 28	15 40	
14 49	16 37	[R] ✕
16 35	18 54	✕
17 22	19 14	✕
18 13	20 28	✕
21 01	23 08	
22 01	0 04	
22 25	0 38	

Verona

	ar an	Observations Bemerkungen
6 21	8 06	
8 19	10 00	
11 14	13 14	
△12 20	13 46	
12 55	14 33	
16 10	17 50	
△16 25	18 15	
17 46	19 10	
18 59	20 49	
22 10	23 42	

△ 29 V - 24 IX 83

(courtesy of Italian State Railways)

Il rapido is a luxury train that stops only at main railway stations. *Il direttissimo* is a fast train that stops at more railway stations. *Il diretto* is a "through" train that stops at many more railway stations.

Now fill in the following blanks, writing out the numbers in words, using the timetable.

From **Bologna** to **Venezia** is less than ________ hours.

From **Bologna** to **Milano** con il **rapido** is almost ________ hours.

From **Bologna** to **Torino** is more than ________ hours.

From **Bologna** to **Pisa** con il **rapido** is about ________ e ________ hours.

Voglio / Vorrei

I Want / I Would Like

"To want" is a very useful verb when requesting or asking for things. The Italian **volere** *(voh-LEH-reh)* is irregular.

VOLERE

io	**voglio** *(VOH-llyee-oh)*	I want	**noi**	**vogliamo** *(voh-LLYAH-moh)*	we want
tu	**vuoi** *(VWOH-ee)*	you [familiar] want	**voi**	**volete** *(voh-LEH-teh)*	you [plural] want
lui / **lei**	**vuole** *(VWOH-leh)*	he/she wants you (polite) want	**loro**	**vogliono** *(VOH-llyoh-noh)*	they want

If you want to be polite, then you should use the following form.

Vorrei *(voh-RREH-ee)* — I would like

Now try your hand at these. Fill in the blanks below with the appropriate form of *volere*.

La figlia del signor Smith ______________ (wants) un biglietto di andata e ritorno.

Quelle persone ______________ (want) andare a piedi.

Io ______________ (want) andare con il direttissimo, ma tu ______________ (want) andare con il rapido.

Noi ______________ (want) un biglietto per lo scompartimento per non fumatori.

ANSWERS

Numbers tre due quattro due e mezzo

Voi ______________ due biglietti di andata e ritorno.
want

Io ______________ un orario per favore.
would like

Io ______________ anche un biglietto per Roma.
would like

(kah-RROH-tsah)
IN CARROZZA!
All Aboard!

(vyah-JJAH-reh)
viaggiare
to travel

il treno
train

(pah-sseh-JJEH-roh)
il passeggero
passenger

(seh-DEHR-see)
sedersi
to sit down

(ahl-TSAHR-see)
alzarsi
to get up

ANSWERS

Verbs
vuole (un biglietto)
vogliono (andare)
(Io) voglio / vuoi (andare)
vogliamo (un biglietto)
volete (due biglietti)
vorrei (un orario)
vorrei (anche)

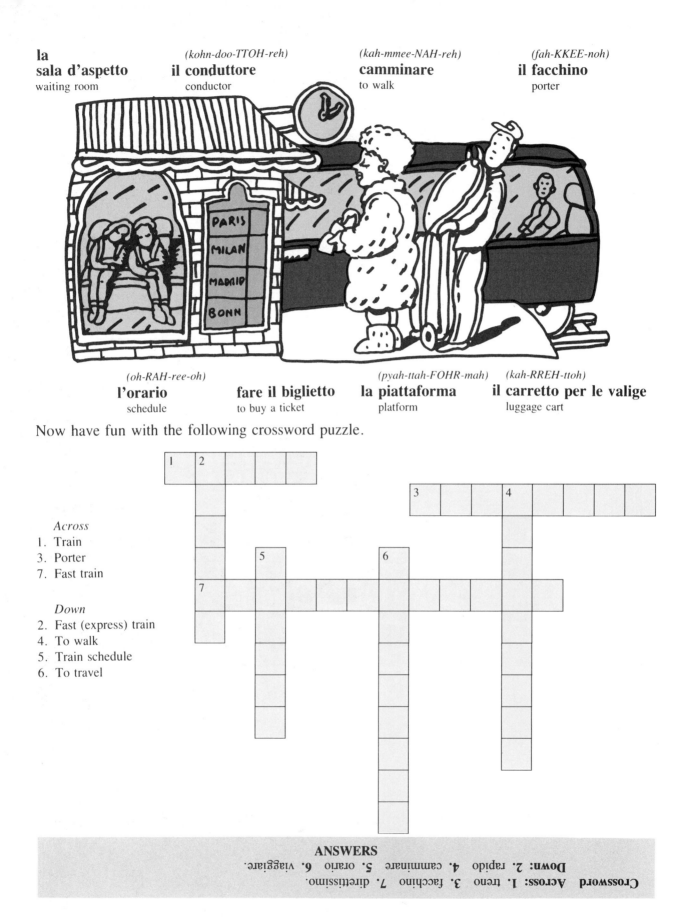

Now have fun with the following crossword puzzle.

Across
1. Train
3. Porter
7. Fast train

Down
2. Fast (express) train
4. To walk
5. Train schedule
6. To travel

ANSWERS

Crossword Across: 1. treno **3.** facchino **7.** direttissimo.
Down: 2. rapido **4.** camminare **5.** orario **6.** viaggiare.

Voi _______________ due biglietti di andata e ritorno.
want

Io _______________ un orario per favore.
would like

Io _______________ anche un biglietto per Roma.
would like

(kah-RROH-tsah)

IN CARROZZA!

All Aboard!

(vyah-JJAH-reh)
viaggiare
to travel

il treno
train

(pah-sseh-JJEH-roh)
il passeggero
passenger

(seh-DEHR-see)
sedersi
to sit down

(ahl-TSAHR-see)
alzarsi
to get up

ANSWERS

Verbs

vuole (un biglietto) (Io) voglio / vuoi (andare) volete (due biglietti) vorrei (anche)
vogliono (andare) vogliamo (un biglietto) vorrei (un orario)

la sala d'aspetto
waiting room

(kohn-doo-TTOH-reh)
il conduttore
conductor

(kah-mmee-NAH-reh)
camminare
to walk

(fah-KKEE-noh)
il facchino
porter

(oh-RAH-ree-oh)
l'orario
schedule

fare il biglietto
to buy a ticket

(pyah-ttah-FOHR-mah)
la piattaforma
platform

(kah-RREH-ttoh)
il carretto per le valige
luggage cart

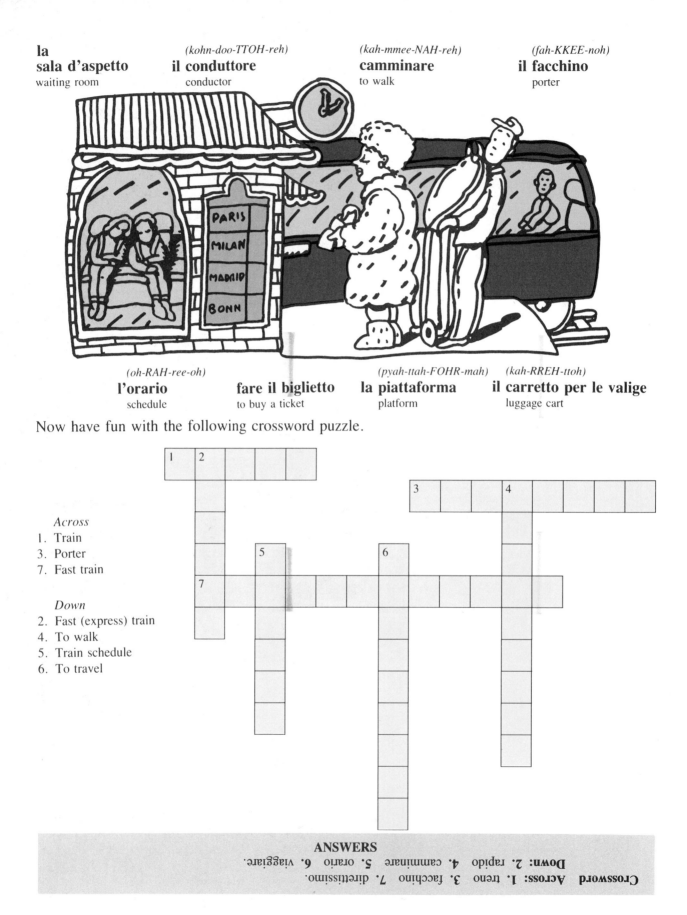

Now have fun with the following crossword puzzle.

Across
1. Train
3. Porter
7. Fast train

Down
2. Fast (express) train
4. To walk
5. Train schedule
6. To travel

ANSWERS

Crossword **Across: 1.** treno **3.** facchino **7.** direttissimo.
Down: 2. rapido **4.** camminare **5.** orario **6.** viaggiare.

I pronomi riflessivi

Reflexive Pronouns

A reflexive verb refers or "reflects" the action back to the subject. For example, "to wash" is a reflexive verb because you wash yourself, or "reflect back" the action of the verb upon yourself. This is done by means of reflexive pronouns, like "myself" and "yourself." Here are the reflexive pronouns in Italian.

REFLEXIVE PRONOUNS			
mi	myself	(chee) **ci**	ourselves
ti	yourself (familiar)	**vi**	yourselves
si	himself/herself/yourself (polite)/ itself/oneself	**si**	themselves

Now let's conjugate a reflexive verb. To do this, just conjugate the verb as you would normally and simply put the reflexive pronouns *right before* the verb (even in the negative). For example:

io — **mi lavo** (I wash myself)
tu — **ti lavi** (you wash yourself)
lui/**lei** — **si lava** (he/she washes himself/herself)
noi — **ci laviamo** (we wash ourselves)
voi — **vi lavate** (you wash yourselves)
loro — **si lavano** (they wash themselves)

NEGATIVE

io — **non mi lavo**
tu — **non ti lavi**
lui/lei — **non si lava**
noi — **non ci laviamo**
voi — **non vi lavate**
loro — **non si lavano**

Notice that the reflexive form for "oneself" is attached to the infinitive form: *(lah-VAHR-see)* **lavarsi**. (to wash oneself)

Here are three more useful reflexive verbs.

(ahl-TSAHR-see)	*(seh-DEHR-see)*	*(dee-vehr-TEER-see)*
alzarsi	**sedersi**	**divertirsi**
to get up	to sit down	to enjoy oneself

But the verb *sedersi* is irregular, so this is how you form the reflexive.

SEDERSI

io	**mi siedo**	**noi**	**ci sediamo**
tu	**ti siedi**	**voi**	**vi sedete**
lui / lei	**si siede**	**loro**	**si siedono**

Now try your hand at the following. Fill in the blanks with the correct reflexive pronoun and verb form.

Il signor Smith ________________ nello scompartimento.
(sits down)

La signora Smith ________________ alle sette e mezzo.
(gets up)

Io ________________ alle sei e tu ________________ alle sette.
(get up) (get up)

Noi ________________ molto quando andiamo a Roma.
(enjoy ourselves)

Voi non ________________ mai quando andate in Italia.
(enjoy yourselves)

I passeggeri ________________ nello scompartimento.
(sit down)

Io non ________________ nello scompartimento per fumatori.
(sit down)

Tu ________________ nello scompartimento numero tre.
(sit down)

The following passage is about train travel. Read it and then answer the questions that follow.

Marco e Maria vanno alla stazione ferroviaria. Fanno il biglietto di andata e ritorno per Venezia. Viaggiano con il rapido fino a Bologna. E poi da Bologna a Venezia vanno con il direttissimo. Arrivano alle sedici.

ANSWERS

Verbs
si siede (nello)
si alza (alle)
(Io) mi alzo / ti alzi (alle)
ci divertiamo (molto)
vi divertite (mai)
si siedono (nello)
mi siedo (nello)
ti siedi (nello)

Dove vanno Marco e Maria?	☐ Vanno a Roma. ☐ Vanno a Bologna. ☐ Vanno a Venezia.
Che cosa fanno?	☐ Fanno le spese. ☐ Fanno il biglietto. ☐ Non fanno niente.
Come viaggiano fino a Bologna?	☐ Viaggiano con il diretto. ☐ Viaggiano con il rapido. ☐ Viaggiano con il direttissimo.
E da Bologna a Venezia?	☐ Con il diretto. ☐ Con il rapido. ☐ Con il direttissimo.
A che ora arrivano?	☐ Arrivano alle due. ☐ Arrivano alle sedici. ☐ Arrivano alle diciotto.

ANSWERS

Comprehension

Vanno a Venezia.
Fanno il biglietto.
Viaggiano con il rapido.
Con il direttissimo.
Arrivano alle sedici.

7 Paesi e lingue

(LEEN-gweh)

Countries and Languages

Parlo un po' d'etaliano. (I speak a little Italian.) And so quick! By now you've learned quite a bit of Italian. Take a look at the rest of the world, too, and learn how to say the names of other countries—in Italian, of course.

COUNTRY	CITY
(ah-oos-TRAH-lee-ah) **l'Australia**	**Sydney**
il Canada	**Ottawa**
la Cina China	*(peh-KEE-noh)* **Pechino** Peking
(FRAHN-chah) **la Francia**	**Parigi**
(jehr-MAH-nee-ah) **la Germania**	**Berlino**
(een-geel-TEH-rrah) **l'Inghilterra** England	**Londra**
l'Italia	**Roma**
(jah-PPOH-neh) **il Giappone**	**Tokyo**
il Messico	*(chee-TTAH)* **la città del Messico**
la Russia	**Mosca**
(SPAH-nyah) **la Spagna**	**Madrid**
(SVEE-tseh-rah) **la Svizzera**	*(jee-NEH-vrah)* **Ginevra**
(STAH-tee-oo-NEE-tee) **gli Stati Uniti**	**Washington**

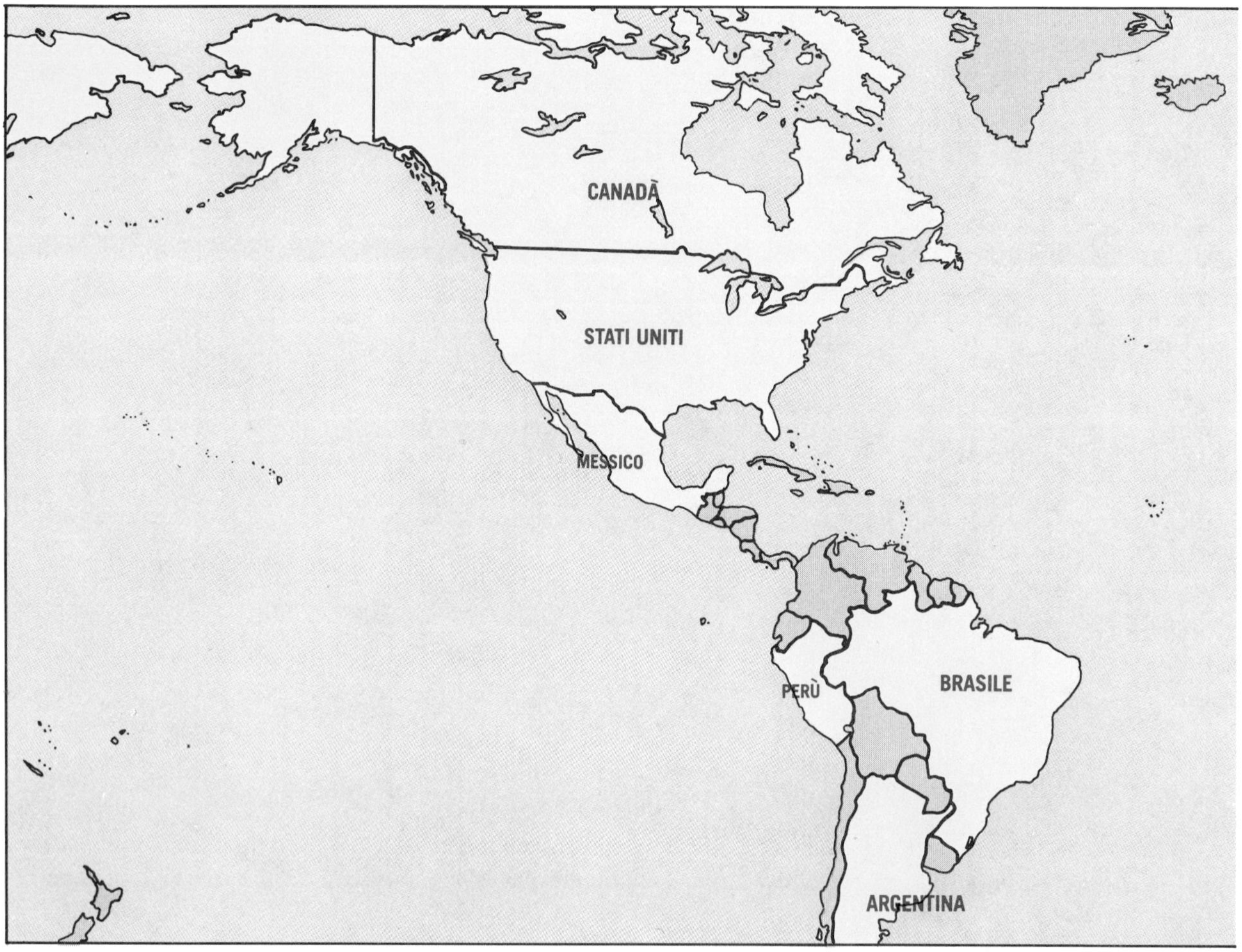

CANADÀ
STATI UNITI
MESSICO
BRASILE
PERÙ
ARGENTINA

Parlo
I Speak

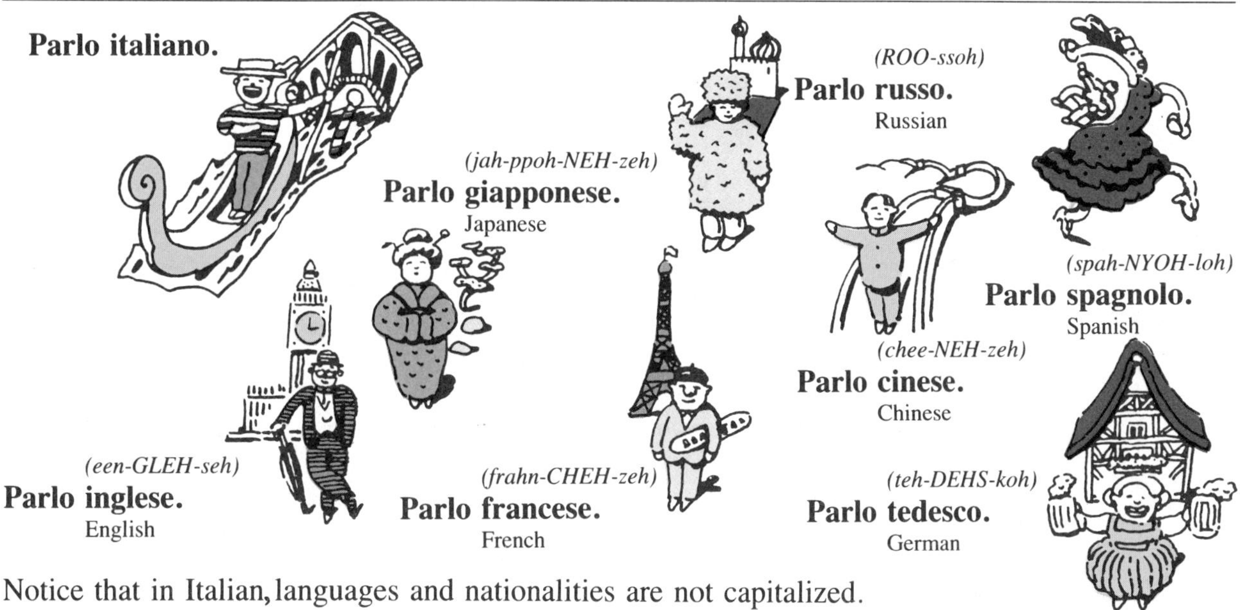

Parlo italiano.

(jah-ppoh-NEH-zeh)
Parlo giapponese.
Japanese

(ROO-ssoh)
Parlo russo.
Russian

(spah-NYOH-loh)
Parlo spagnolo.
Spanish

(chee-NEH-zeh)
Parlo cinese.
Chinese

(een-GLEH-seh)
Parlo inglese.
English

(frahn-CHEH-zeh)
Parlo francese.
French

(teh-DEHS-koh)
Parlo tedesco.
German

Notice that in Italian, languages and nationalities are not capitalized.

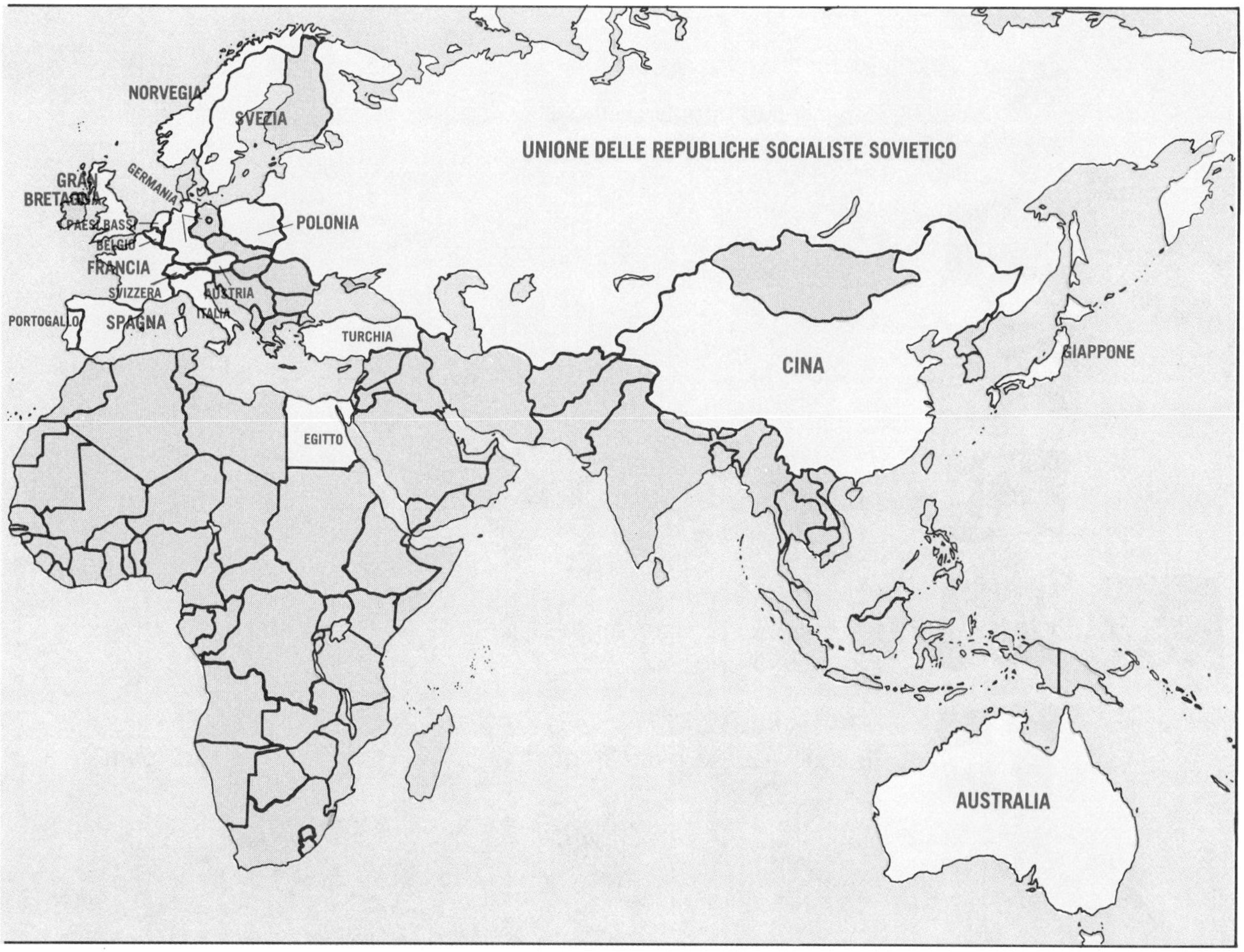

NORVEGIA
SVEZIA
UNIONE DELLE REPUBLICHE SOCIALISTE SOVIETICO
GRAN BRETAGNA
GERMANIA
PAESI BASSI
BELGIO
POLONIA
FRANCIA
SVIZZERA
AUSTRIA
PORTOGALLO
SPAGNA
ITALIA
TURCHIA
CINA
GIAPPONE
EGITTO
AUSTRALIA

Sono

I Am

(EH-sseh-reh)
The verb *essere* is irregular.
to be

ESSERE

io	**sono**	**noi**	**siamo**
tu	**sei**	**voi**	**siete**
lui / **lei**	**è**	**loro**	**sono**

Now let's use this verb with nationalities.

1. Io sono americano e anche tu ________________ americano.

2. Io sono austriaco *(aoos-TREE-ah-koh)* Austrian e anche lui ________________ austriaco.

3. Io sono australiano Australian e anche lei ________________ australiana.

4. Io sono belga *(BEHL-gah)* Belgian e anche noi ________________ belgi *(BEHL-jee)*.

5. Io sono inglese *(een-GLEH-seh)* English e anche voi ________________ inglesi.

6. Io sono canadese *(kah-nah-DEH-zeh)* Canadian e anche loro ________________ canadesi.

7. Io sono cinese *(chee-NEH-zeh)* Chinese e anche tu ________________ cinese.

8. Io sono danese *(dah-NEH-zeh)* Danish e anche quel signore ________________ danese.

ANSWERS

Verbs **1.** sei **2.** è **3.** è **4.** siamo **5.** siete **6.** sono **7.** sei **8.** è

(oh-lahn-DEH-zeh)
9. Io sono olandese e anche mia moglie ______________ olandese.
Dutch

(frahn-CHEH-zeh)
10. Io sono francese e anche noi ______________ francesi.
French

(teh-DEHS-koh) *(teh-DEHS-kee)*
11. Io sono tedesco e anche voi ______________ tedeschi.
German

(ee-tah-LYAH-noh)
12. Io sono italiano e anche i passeggeri ______________ italiani.
Italian

(jah-ppoh-NEH-zeh)
13. Io sono giapponese e anche tu ______________ giapponese.
Japanese

(meh-ssee-KAH-noh)
14. Io sono messicano e anche il mio amico ______________ messicano.
Mexican

(nohr-veh-JEH-zeh)
15. Io sono norvegese e anche noi ______________ norvegesi.
Norwegian

(poh-LAH-kkoh)
16. Io sono polacco e anche voi ______________ polacchi.
Polish

(ROO-ssoh)
17. Io sono russo e anche i miei amici ______________ russi.
Russian

(spah-NYOH-loh)
18. Io sono spagnolo e anche tu ______________ spagnolo.
Spanish

(sveh-DEH-zeh)
19. Io sono svedese e anche la sua amica ______________ svedese.
Swedish

(SVEE-tseh-roh)
20. Io sono svizzero e anche voi ______________ svizzeri.
Swiss

(TOOR-koh)
21. Io sono turco e anche gli studenti ______________ turchi.
Turkish

ANSWERS

9. è **10.** siamo **11.** siete **12.** sono **13.** sei **14.** è **15.** siamo **16.** siete **17.** sono **18.** sei **19.** è **20.** siete **21.** sono

Be careful with "is." Notice that it has an accent, whereas "and" does not. Also, you may recall from previous dialogues that "there is" is *c'è* with the plural form *(ci sono)* "there are." Remember that *ecco* is used to point out something. This table will help you remember the difference.

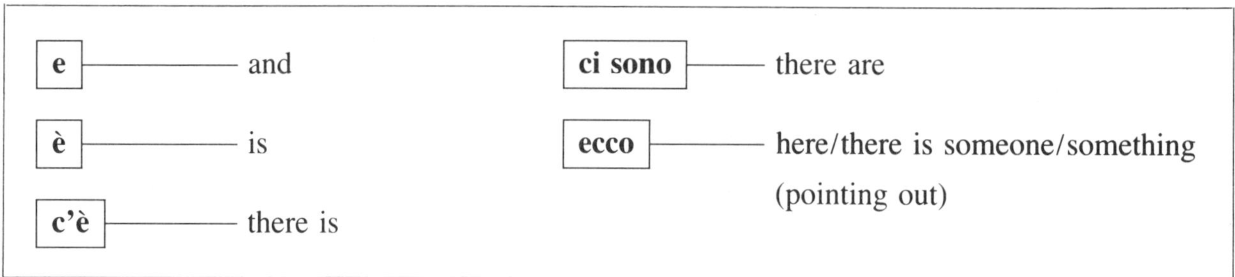

e	and	**ci sono**	there are
è	is	**ecco**	here/there is someone/something (pointing out)
c'è	there is		

Notice that with *quale* (which) the final *e* is dropped with è ("is").

Qual è il tuo biglietto? (Which is your ticket?)

Qual è la tua chiave? (Which is your key?)

Try this now with the following sentences.

__________ il tuo orologio? __________ la tua automobile? __________ il tuo passaporto?

Vado a . . .

I Am Going to . . .

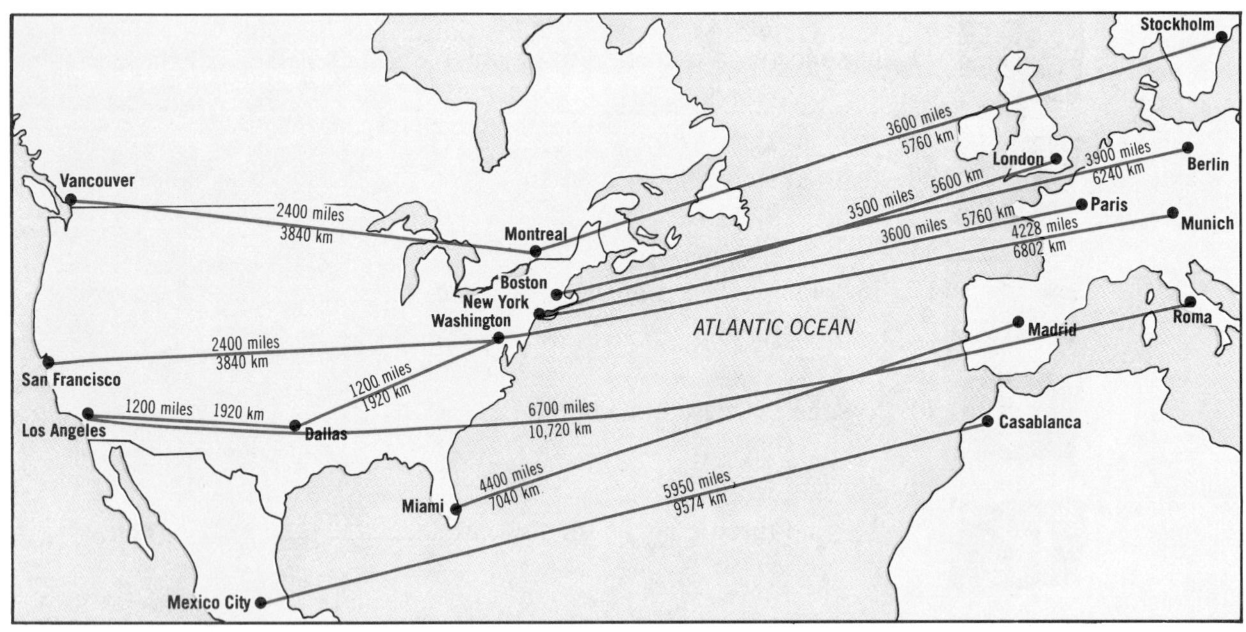

To say that something is "in" a **country**, use the corresponding preposition *in*. For example:

Dov'è Mosca? È *in* Russia. (Where is Moscow? It is in Russia.)

However, for the United States you have to use *negli Stati Uniti*. With any **city** *a* is used.

Dov'è la Statua della Libertà? È *a* New York.
Statue of Liberty

You continue, using *in* or *a* in these sentences.

Dov'è la Torre Eiffel? È ________________ Parigi.

Dov'è New York? È ________________ Stati Uniti.

Dov'è Acapulco? È ________________ Messico.

Dov'è Berlino? È ________________ Germania.

Dov'è il Colosseo? È ________________ Roma, ________________ Italia.

Dov'è il Prado? È ________________ Madrid, ________________ Spagna.

Now try your skill with what you have just learned. Fill in the blanks as shown.

________________ ________________ Firenze. I fiorentini ________________ molto simpatici.
I am — in — Florentines — are

________________ Italia, si parla ________________. Roma ________________ ________________
In — one — Italian — is — the

capitale d'Italia, Parigi ________________ ________________ capitale della ________________
is — the — France

________________ Madrid ________________ ________________ capitale della ________________.
and — is — the — Spain

Capisco
I Understand

Look back to the section on "ire" verbs, if you have forgotten how to conjugate *capire*. Now try the following.

Io *capisco* l'italiano, ma tu non *capisci* l'italiano.
but

ANSWERS

Prepositions a (Parigi.) negli (Stati Uniti.) in (Messico.) in (Germania.) a (Roma), in (Italia.) a (Madrid), in (Spagna.)

Fill-ins
Io sono a (Firenze) sono (molto) In (Italia) italiano (Roma) è la (capitale) (Parigi) è la (capitale) (della) Francia e (Madrid) è la (capitale) Spagna

You continue.

1. Io _______________ il tedesco, ma tu non _______________ il tedesco.
2. Lui _______________ lo spagnolo, ma loro non _______________ lo spagnolo.
3. Maria _______________ l'inglese, ma noi non _______________ l'inglese.
4. I passeggeri _______________ l'italiano, ma voi non _______________ l'italiano.

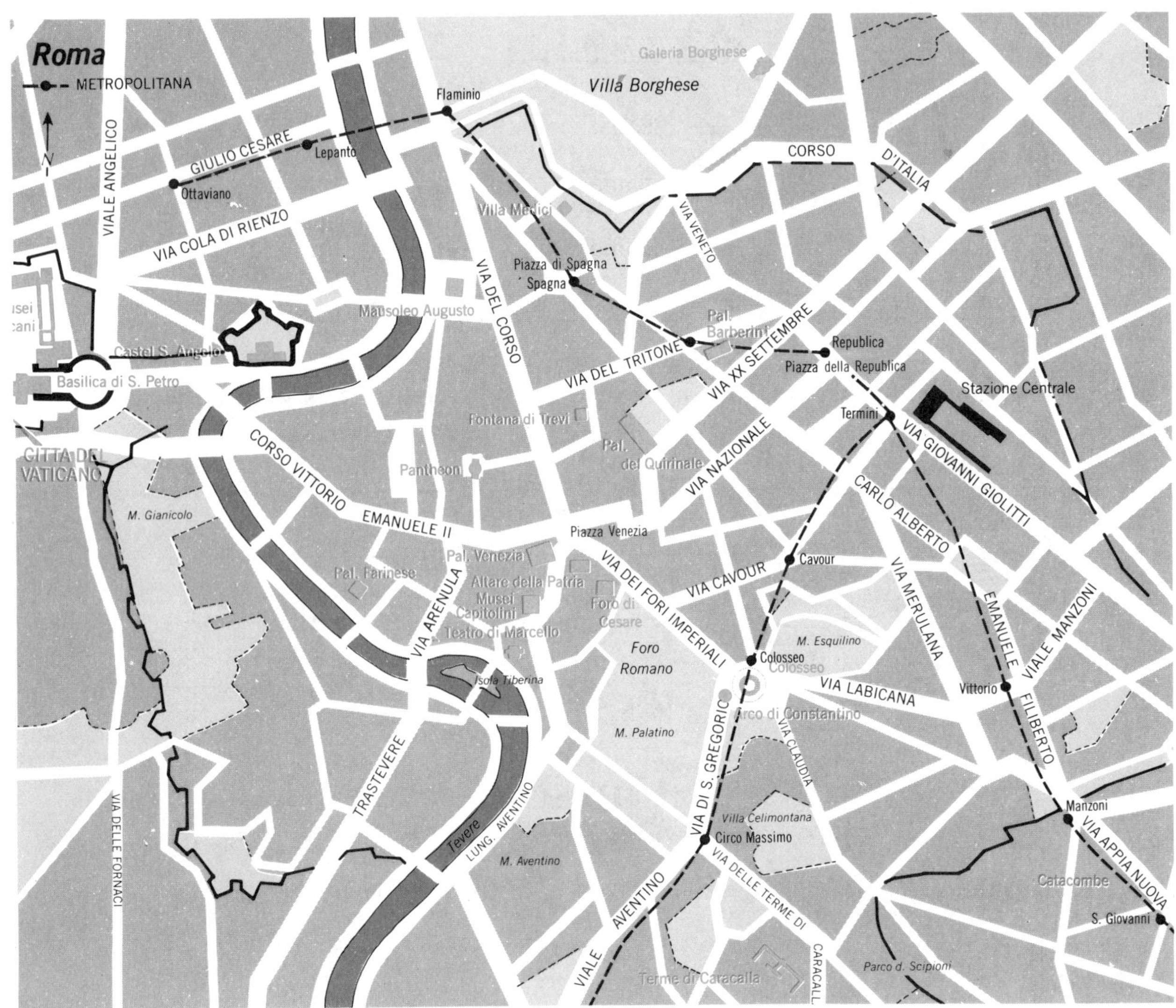

Subway Map of Rome

ANSWERS

Verbs **1.** (Io) capisco / capisci (il) **2.** (Lui) capisce / capiscono (lo)
3. (Maria) capisce / capiamo (l'inglese.) **4.** (passeggeria) capiscono / capite (l'italiano.)

Read the following dialogue, repeating each line out loud several times. Don't forget to act out each part.

(Knowing the frustration of not being understood, can you imagine how Anne felt when her wallet was stolen?)

ANNE	**Scusi, signore, lei parla inglese?**	Excuse me, sir, do you speak English?
VIGILE	**No. Solo italiano.**	No. Only Italian.
ANNE	**Qualcuno ha rubato il mio** *(pohr-tah-FOH-llyoh)* **portafoglio nella metropolitana.**	Someone stole my wallet in the subway.
VIGILE	*(preh-OH-kkoo-pee)* **Non si preoccupi, signorina! Compili questo modulo.**	Don't worry, Miss! Fill out this form.
ANNE	**Parli più lentamente, per favore.**	Speak more slowly, please.
VIGILE	**Va bene. Scriva il suo nome e il** *(een-dee-REE-tsoh)* **suo indirizzo, e anche il numero di** *(teh-LEH-foh-noh)* **telefono del suo albergo.**	Okay. Write your name and your address, and also the phone number of your hotel.
ANNE	**Non ho più soldi, carte di** *(KREH-dee-toh)* **credito, o passaporto.** *(fah-ROH)* **Cosa farò?**	I have no more money, credit cards, or passport. What am I going to do?
VIGILE	**Per il passaporto, lei deve andare** *(ahm-bah-SHAH-tah)* **alla sua ambasciata.**	For the passport, you have to go to your embassy.
ANNE	**Lei non mi** *(pwoh)* **può** *(ah-yoo-TAH-reh)* **aiutare?**	Can't you help me?
VIGILE	*(preh-OH-koo-pee)* **Non si preoccupi.** *(koh-MEEN-choh)* **Comincio a** *(chehr-KAH-reh)* **cercare il ladro** *(SOO-bee-toh)* **subito.**	Please don't worry. I am starting the search for the thief right now.
ANNE	**Grazie mille.**	Thank you very much.

Now try to complete the missing dialogue parts without looking back. Check your answers after you have attempted this exercise from memory.

Scusi, signore, lei parla i ______________?

No. Solo i ______________.

Qualcuno ha rubato il mio p______________ nella metropolitana.

Non si preoccupi, signorina! Compili questo m______________.

Parli più l______________, per favore.

Va bene. Scriva il suo n______________ e il suo i______________, e anche il numero di t______________ del suo albergo.

Non ho più s______________, carte di c______________, o passaporto. Cosa farò?

By rearranging the following words, you will get sentences found in the dialogue.

passaporto / Per / il / ambasciata / alla / deve / sua / lei / andare

____

non / Lei / aiutare / può / mi

____

The following brief passage reflects what you have learned about countries, languages, and nationalities. After you have read it, choose the appropriate ending to each sentence.

La signorina Smith è americana. Lei non parla l'italiano molto bene. Vuole andare in Svizzera, in Francia e in Germania, ma qualcuno ha rubato il suo portafoglio. Adesso parla a un vigile. Il vigile non parla inglese, ma capisce il francese. Allora, la signorina e il vigile parlano in francese.

La signorina Smith . . .
- ☐ parla italiano molto bene.
- ☐ non parla inglese.
- ☐ è americana.

Lei vuole andare . . .
- ☐ in Russia.
- ☐ in Francia.
- ☐ in Italia.

ANSWERS

Sentences Per il passaporto, lei deve andare alla sua ambasciata. Lei non mi può aiutare?

Comprehension è americana. in Francia.

Qualcuno ha rubato . . .

- ☐ il suo portafoglio.
- ☐ il suo passaporto.
- ☐ i suoi soldi.

Adesso parla a . . .

- ☐ suo padre.
- ☐ sua madre.
- ☐ un vigile.

Il vigile capisce . . .

- ☐ il tedesco.
- ☐ il francese.
- ☐ lo spagnolo.

Now have fun with the following crossword puzzle.

Across

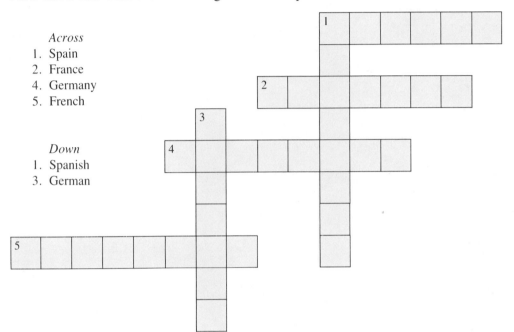

1. Spain
2. France
4. Germany
5. French

Down

1. Spanish
3. German

ANSWERS

il suo portafoglio. un vigile. il francese.

Crossword Across: 1. Spagna **2.** Francia **4.** Germania **5.** francese.
Down: 1. spagnolo **3.** tedesco.

8 Automobili, furgoni e pulmini / La segnaletica

Cars and Vans/Road Signs

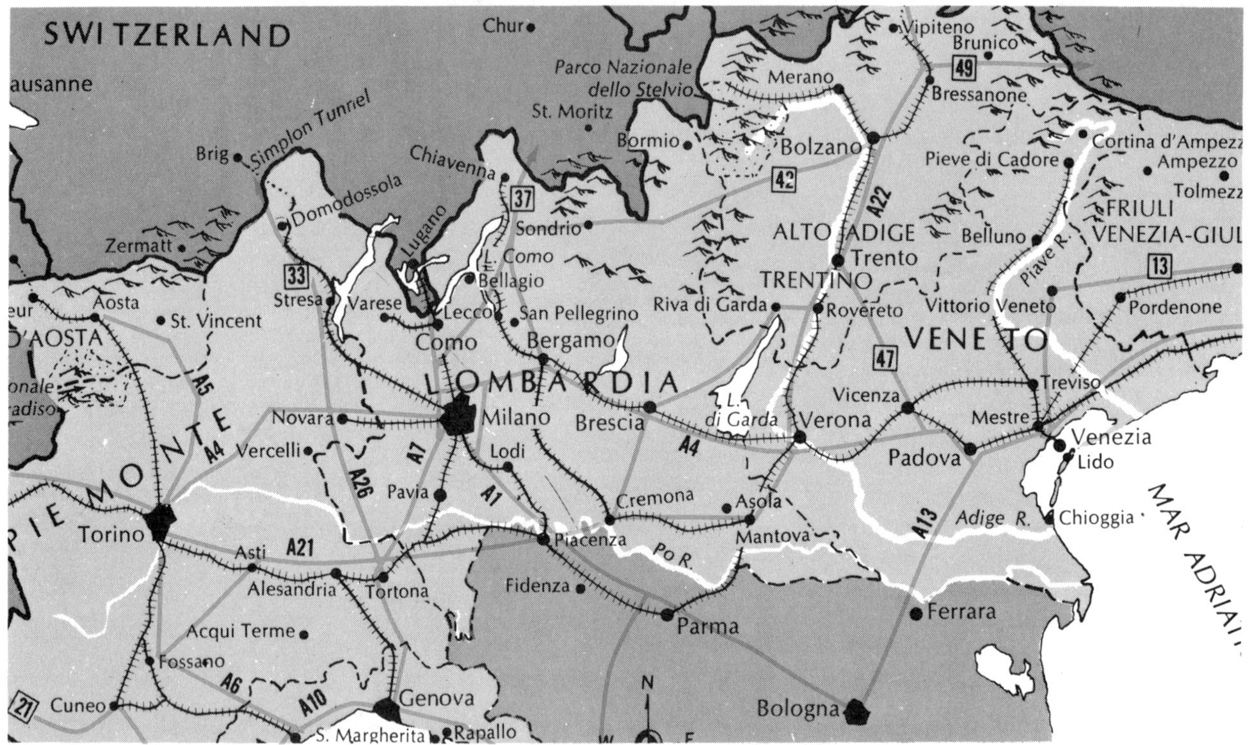

Northern Italy *(Courtesy of Fisher Annotated Travel Guides ©—reprinted with permission)*

ALL'AGENZIA DI AUTOMOBILI DA NOLEGGIO

At the Car Rental Office

You may want to see the country close up. As you read the following dialogue, make sure that you repeat each line out loud several times. The words and expressions in it will prove useful if you want to rent a car.

(Mark has decided to rent a car and take his family for an excursion into the Italian countryside.)

MARK	**Buon giorno. Vorrei noleggiare** *(noh-leh-JJAH-reh)* **una macchina.** *(MAH-kkee-nah)*	Good day. I would like to rent a car.
COMMESSO	**Per quanto tempo?**	For how long?
MARK	**Per due settimane.**	For two weeks.
COMMESSO	**Vediamo. Abbiamo una Lancia e una FIAT.**	Let's see. We have a Lancia and a FIAT.

MARK **Prendo la FIAT. Sono incluse** *(MEE-llyah)* **anche le miglia nel prezzo?**

I'll take the FIAT. Is the mileage included in the price?

COMMESSO **Sì, ma la benzina** *(behn-DZEE-nah)* **no. La sua patente di guida** *(GWEE-dah)* **e la sua carta di credito, per favore.**

Yes, but it does not include the gas. Your driver's license and credit card, please.

MARK **Mi fa vedere come funziona** *(foon-TSYOH-nah)* **il cambo di marcia** *(MAHR-chah)* **e come funzionano i fari?**

Can you show me how the gearshift and the headlights work?

COMMESSO **Certo. Ecco la chiave e i documenti.** *(doh-koo-MEHN-tee)* **Stia** *(STEE-ah)* **attento! Gli autisti italiani sono pazzi!** *(PAH-tsee)*

Certainly. Here are the key and the papers. Be careful! Italian drivers are crazy!

Now try to complete the missing dialogue parts without looking back. Check your answers after attempting the exercise from memory.

Buon giorno. V__________ n__________ una macchina.

Per q__________ t__________?

Per due s__________.

Vediamo. A__________ una Lancia e una FIAT.

Prendo la FIAT. Sono incluse anche le m__________ nel p__________?

Sì, ma la b__________ no. La sua p__________ di g__________

e la sua carta di credito, per favore.

Mi fa vedere come f__________ il cambio di m__________

e come funzionano i f__________?

Certo. Ecco la chiave e i d__________. S__________ a__________!

Gli a__________ italiani sono pazzi!

Cose essenziali

Some Essentials

Here are some more words that you should know before you hit the road.

(ah-SSEE-koo-rah-tsyoh-neh) **l'assicurazione**	insurance	**nord-sud-est-ovest**	north-south-east-west
(ah-FFAH-reh) **un buon affare**	a good deal/bargain	*(POON-tah)* **l'ora di punta**	rush hour
(oo-tee-lee-TAH-ree-ah) **l'utilitaria**	compact car	*(stah-TSYOH-neh) (sehr-VEE-tsyoh)* **la stazione di servizio**	service station
una macchina grande	a large car	*(PYEH-noh)* **fare il pieno**	to fill up
(foor-GOH-neh) (pool-MEE-noh) **furgone / pulmino**	van	*(TRAH-ffee-koh)* **il traffico**	traffic
(eh-CHEH-ssoh) **multa per eccesso** *(veh-loh-chee-TAH)* **di velocità**	speeding ticket	*(jee-RAH-reh)* **girare**	to turn
(pahr-KEH-jjoh) **il parcheggio**	parking	*(rah-JOH-neh)* **avere ragione**	to be right
		(TOHR-toh) **avere torto**	to be wrong

Now choose one of the above words or expressions according to the meaning of each sentence. Don't forget to make necessary verb changes. *Buona fortuna!*

1. C'è molto t_______________ durante (during) l'ora di p_______________.
2. Maria ha r_______________, la stazione di s_______________ si trova a n_______________, non a s_______________, del semaforo.
3. Preferisco l'u_______________, non la macchina g_______________.
4. Alla stazione di servizio faccio sempre il p_______________.
5. Hai t_______________. Il f_______________ costa poco. È un buon a_______________.
6. Il vigile dà una m_______________ per eccesso di v_______________ al signor Smith.
7. Giovanni non g_______________ a destra, lui g_______________ a sinistra.
8. Va a est, non a o_______________.
9. Qui non c'è il p_______________.

ANSWERS

Fill-ins

1. traffico / punta **2.** ragione / servizio/nord / sud **3.** utilitaria / grande **4.** pieno **5.** torto / furgone / affare **6.** multa / velocità **7.** gira / gira **8.** ovest **9.** parcheggio

(seh-nyah-LEH-tee-kah)

LA SEGNALETICA / SEGNALI STRADALI

Road Signs

If you're planning to drive while you're abroad, spend some time remembering the meanings of these signs.

Dangerous Intersection

Danger!

Stop

Speed Limit (in km/hr)

Minimum Speed

End of Limited Speed

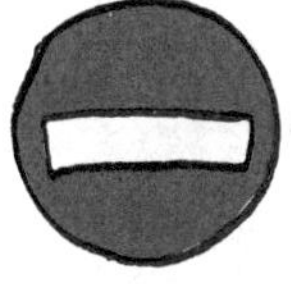

No Entrance

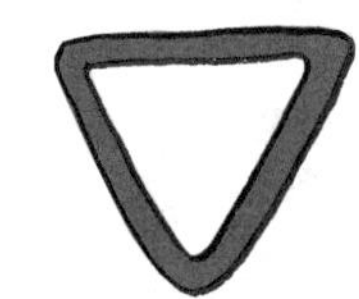

Yield Right-of-way

Two-way Traffic

Dangerous Curve

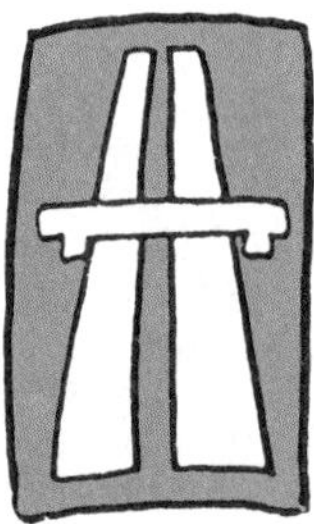

Entrance to Expressway

Expressway Exit
(road narrows)

Customs

No Passing

End of No Passing Zone

One-way Street

Detour

Road Closed

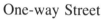

Parking

Roundabout

No Parking

No Parking (or waiting)

No Cyclists

Pedestrian Crossing

Railroad Crossing (no gate)

Guarded Railroad Crossing

(sehr-VEE-tsee-oh)

ALLA STAZIONE DI SERVIZIO

At the Service Station

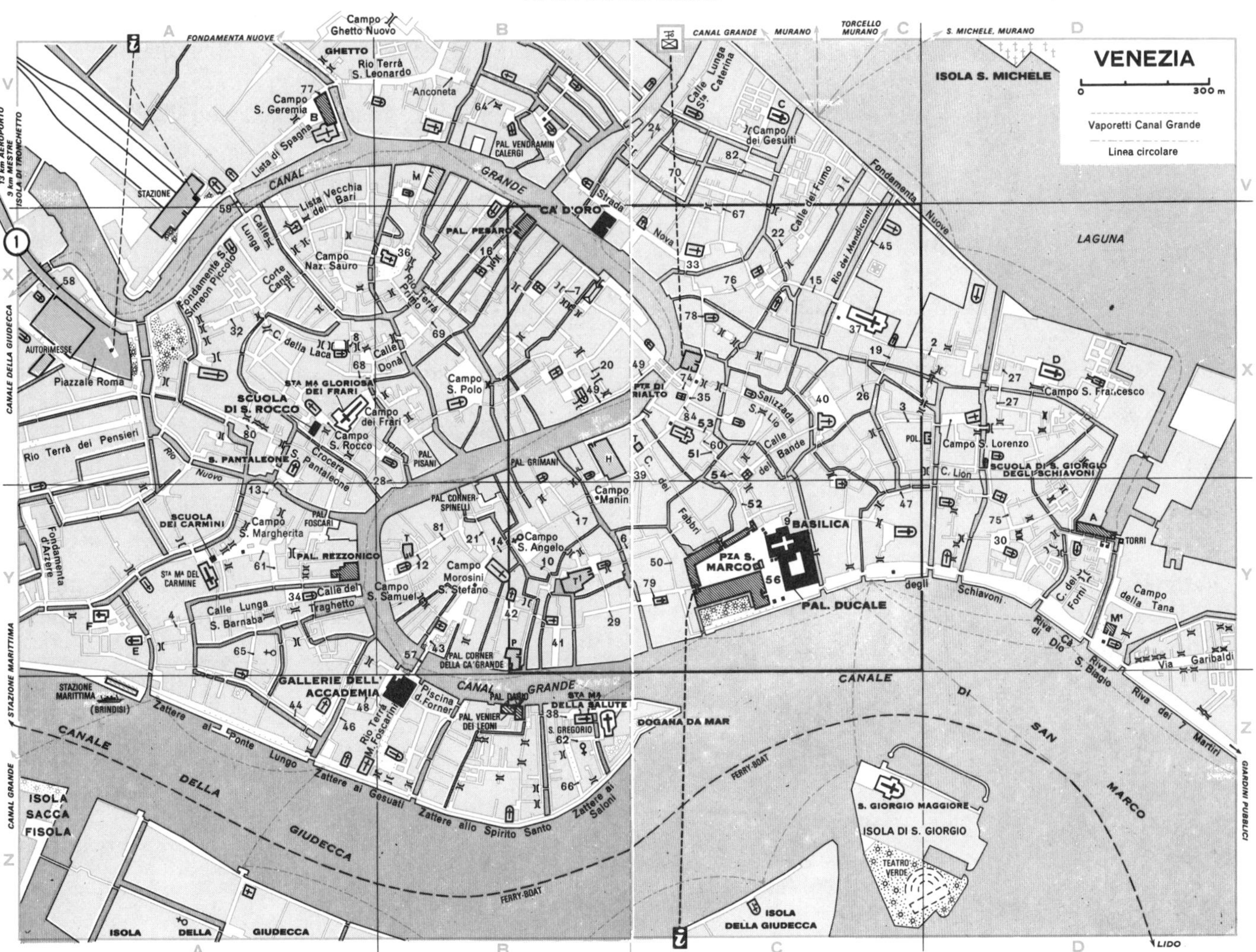

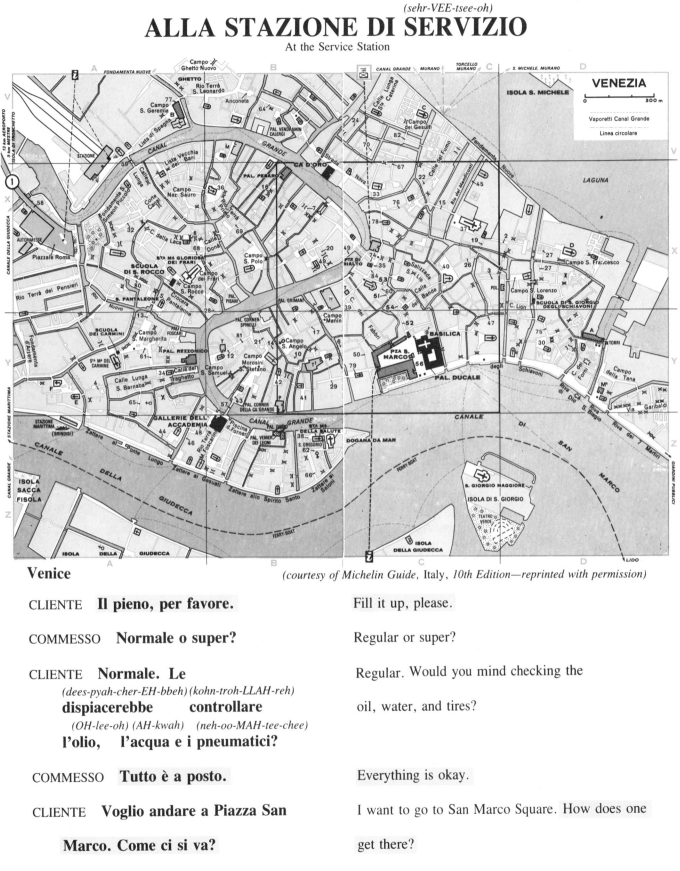

Venice

(courtesy of Michelin Guide, Italy, *10th Edition—reprinted with permission)*

CLIENTE **Il pieno, per favore.** — Fill it up, please.

COMMESSO **Normale o super?** — Regular or super?

CLIENTE **Normale. Le** *(dees-pyah-cher-EH-bbeh)* **dispiacerebbe** *(kohn-troh-LLAH-reh)* **controllare** *(OH-lee-oh)* **l'olio,** *(AH-kwah)* **l'acqua e i** *(neh-oo-MAH-tee-chee)* **pneumatici?** — Regular. Would you mind checking the oil, water, and tires?

COMMESSO **Tutto è a posto.** — Everything is okay.

CLIENTE **Voglio andare a Piazza San Marco. Come ci si va?** — I want to go to San Marco Square. How does one get there?

COMMESSO *(points to map)* **Guardi. Lei si trova qui alla Stazione di Santa Lucia. Prenda la strada che va intorno al Canal Grande. Questa strada la porta** *(dee-reh-ttah-MEHN-teh)* **direttamente alla piazza.**	Look. You are here at Santa Lucia Railroad Station. Take the road that goes all around the Grand Canal. This road will take you directly to the square.
(TRAH-ffee-koh) CLIENTE **C'è molto traffico?**	Is there a lot of traffic?
COMMESSO **No. Non c'è affatto traffico, perché Venezia ha solo canali!**	No. There is no traffic at all, because Venice has only canals!

Read over this dialogue several times and then test your memory by completing the missing dialogue parts. Check your answers only after you have attempted to complete the missing parts from memory.

CLIENTE ________________________________.

COMMESSO **Normale o super?**

CLIENTE __________. **Le dispiacerebbe controllare** ____________________?

COMMESSO **Tutto è a posto.**

CLIENTE **Voglio andare a Piazza San Marco.** ____________________?

COMMESSO **Guardi. Lei si trova qui** ____________________

____________________. **Prenda la strada che va**

____________________. **Questa strada**

la porta ____________________.

CLIENTE **C'è** ____________________?

COMMESSO **No. Non c'è** ____________________ **perché**

Venezia ____________________!

L'AUTOMOBILE / LA MACCHINA

The Car

(voh-LAHN-teh)
il volante
steering wheel

(KLAHK-sohn)
il clacson
horn

(peh-DAH-leh)
il pedale del freno
brake pedal

(tehr-jee-krees-TAH-llee)
i tergicristalli
windshield wipers

(KAHM-byoh)
la leva del cambio
gear shift

(kroos-KOH-ttoh)
il cruscotto
dashboard

(ah-cheh-leh-rah-TOH-reh)
l'acceleratore
accelerator

(free-TSYOH-neh)
il pedale della frizione
clutch pedal

(bah-OO-leh)(pohr-tah-bah-GAH-llyee)
il baule / il portabagagli
trunk

(TAHR-gah)
la targa
plate

(pah-rah-OOR-tee)
il paraurti
bumper

(KOH-fah-noh)
il cofano
hood

(FAH-ree) (proh-yeh-TTOH-ree)
i fari / i proiettori
headlights

(bah-tteh-REE-ah)
la batteria
battery

(rah-dee-ah-TOH-reh)
il radiatore
radiator

(moh-TOH-reh)
il motore
motor

(pah-rah-BREH-tsah)
il parabrezza
windshield

(sehr-bah-TOH-yoh)
il serbatoio
gas tank

(kah-rroh-tseh-REE-ah)
la carrozzeria
body (of the car)

(TEH-ttoh) (pah-dee-LLYOH-neh)
il tetto / il padiglione
roof

(pohr-TYEH-rah) (spohr-TEH-lloh)
la portiera / lo sportello
door

(POHM-pah)
la pompa
gas pump

(pah-rah-FAHN-goh)
il parafango
fender

(neh-oo-MAH-tee-chee)
i pneumatici
tires

Now fill in the names for the following auto parts.

(ree-pah-RAH-reh) (ah-jjoos-TAH-reh)

Per riparare / aggiustare la macchina

Some Essentials for Repair

The following words and expressions will be useful to you if your car breaks down in Italy.

Mi può aiutare?	Can you help me?
(ZGOHN-fee-oh) **Il mio pneumatico è sgonfio.**	My tire is flat.

La mia macchina non parte.	My car doesn't start.
I freni non funzionano.	The brakes don't work.
Ho bisogno di benzina.	I need gas.
(Mi faccia) il pieno, per favore.	Fill 'er up, please.

Come si fa per chiedere

How to Ask for . . .

In order to get people to do things for you, you will have to know how to use verbs in a "command" or "imperative" way. Look at the following chart. This shows you how to form the imperative of regular verbs.

THE IMPERATIVE			
	PARL*ARE* CAMMIN*ARE*	SCRIV*ERE* RISPOND*ERE*	DORM*IRE* FIN*IRE*
Singular Familiar Command:	**Parl*a*!** Speak! **Cammin*a*!** Walk!	**Scriv*i*!** Write! **Rispond*i*!** Answer!	**Dorm*i*!** Sleep! **Fin*isci*!** Finish!
Singular Polite Command:	**Parl*i*!** **Cammin*i*!**	**Scriv*a*!** **Rispond*a*!**	**Dorm*a*!** **Finisc*a*!**
Plural Command:	**Parl*ate*!** **Cammin*ate*!**	**Scriv*ete*!** **Rispond*ete*!**	**Dorm*ite*!** **Fin*ite*!**

The command "Let's speak, walk," and so on, is given by a form you already know.

Parl*iamo*! ________	Let's speak!
Scriv*iamo*! ________	Let's write!
Fin*iamo*! ________	Let's finish!
Dorm*iamo*! ________	Let's sleep!

Notice that, as in English, pronouns are not used with the imperative. Also notice that verbs like *finire*, which take the extra *isc* (remember?), also take it in the imperative singular command form.

To make reflexive verbs imperative, add on the reflexive pronouns in the familiar and plural forms.

REFLEXIVE IMPERATIVES		
	ALZ*ARSI*	DIVERT*IRSI*
Singular Familiar Command:	*(AHL-tsah-tee)* **Alza*ti*!**	*(dee-VEHR-tee-tee)* **Diverti*ti*!**
Singular Polite Command:	***Si* alzi!**	***Si* diverta!**
Plural Command:	*(ahl-TSAH-teh-vee)* **Alzate*vi*!**	*(dee-vehr-TEE-teh-vee)* **Divertite*vi*!**
	and	
	(ahl-TSYAH-moh-chee) **Alziamo*ci*!** Let's get up!	*(dee-vehr-TYAH-moh-chee)* **Divertiamo*ci*!** Let's enjoy ourselves!

One more thing about imperatives: don't get discouraged! With a little practice, you will become familiar and quite proficient with these verb forms. To make any verb negative, you have learned to put *non* just before it. So too with imperative verbs. But there is one change you must make. For the singular familiar command in the negative, use the infinitive (*parlare, scrivere*).

NEGATIVE IMPERATIVES		
Singular Familiar Command:	**Non parlare!** Don't speak!	**Non scrivere!** Don't write!
Other Command Forms:	**Non parli! Non scriva! Non parlate! Non scrivete!** (Just put *non* before the appropriate imperative form.)	

Now try the following.

You are speaking to your friend. Tell him to do as you wish, by filling in the blanks as indicated.

1. Giovanni, __________ (speak) italiano! *(LEH-tteh-rah)*
2. Giovanni, __________ (finish) la pizza!
3. Giovanni, __________ (write) la **lettera!**
4. Giovanni, non __________ (walk) (be careful!) lentamente!
5. Giovanni, __________ (get up) domani alle sei!

ANSWERS

Familiar commands 1. parla (italiano!) 2. finisci (la pizza!) 3. scrivi (la lettera!) 4. camminare (lentamente!) 5. alzati (domani)

Now say the polite forms, because you are speaking to a stranger.

Now use the corresponding singular polite forms.

Signora Smith, ______________ italiano! (speak)   Signora Smith, ______________ la pizza! (finish)

Signora Smith, ______________ la lettera! (write)   Signora Smith, non ______________ lentamente! (walk)

Signora Smith, ______________ domani alle sei! (get up)

Finally, try giving a command to a group of people.

Ragazzi, ______________ italiano! (speak)   Ragazzi, ______________ la pizza! (finish)

Ragazzi, ______________ la lettera! (write)   Ragazzi, non ______________ lentamente! (walk)

Ragazzi, ______________ domani alle sei! (get up)

The imperatives of the irregular verbs you have learned so far are as follows.

	ANDARE	VENIRE	FARE	DARE	DIRE	SEDERSI	ESSERE
Singular Familiar Command:	**Va'!**	*(VYEH-nee)* **Vieni!**	**Fa'!**	**Da'!**	**Di'!**	*(SYEH-dee-tee)* **Siediti!**	*(SEE-ee)* **Sii!**
Singular Polite Command:	**Vada!**	*(VEHN-gah)* **Venga!**	*(FAH-chah)* **Faccia!**	*(DEE-ah)* **Dia!**	**Dica!**	**Si sieda!**	*(SEE-ah)* **Sia!**
Plural Command:	**Andate!**	**Venite!**	**Fate!**	**Date!**	**Dite!**	*(seh-DEH-teh-vee)* **Sedetevi!**	*(SYAH-teh)* **Siate!**

For the negative of an irregular verb, use the infinitive (*Non andare! Non venire!* etc.).

Now choose the familiar or polite command forms of these verbs. *Stia attento!* (Be careful!)

1. Marco, ______________ a casa! (go home)
2. Anna, ______________ qui! (come)
3. Signor Smith, ______________ a casa! (go)
4. Signora Smith, ______________ questo! (do)
5. Signorina Rossi, ______________ qui! (come)
6. Maria, ______________ questo! (do)

ANSWERS

Singular commands parli (italiano!) finisca (la pizza!) scriva (la lettera!) cammini (lentamente!) si alzi (domani)

Plural commands parlate (italiano!) finite (la'pizza!) scrivete (la lettera!) camminate (lentamente!) alzatevi (domani)

Familiar or polite commands **1.** va' (a casa!) **2.** vieni (qui!) **3.** vada (a casa!) **4.** faccia (questo!) **5.** venga (qui!) **6.** fa' (questo!)

7. Gíovanni, ________________ la penna a Maria!
give

8. Signor Verdi, ________________ la penna alla signorina Smith!
give

9. Signora Rossi, ________________ la verità! (veh-ree-TAH) truth
say/tell

10. Gina, ________________ la verità!
say/tell

11. Pina, ________________ qui!
sit

12. Signorina Verdi, ________________ qui!
sit

13. Signor Smith, ________________ gentile!
be

14. Gino, ________________ gentile!
be

Using the command form does not always mean you are giving orders. When someone asks for directions, your response will be "go to the right." That's a command, too, in a way. Giving directions in Italian is an essential communicative skill. Try your hand at giving directions to the **autorimessa** (ah-oo-toh-ree-MEH-ssah) garage in the diagram. Here are the verbs and expressions you will need.

(jee-RAH-reh)
girare
to turn

a destra

andare dritto
straight ahead

a sinistra

Avere
To Have

Like "to be," *avere* is an essential verb for communicating in your new language. Notice that the "h" is not pronounced.

AVERE to have			
io ________________	*(oh)* **ho**	**noi** ________________	*(ah-BBYAH-moh)* **abbiamo**
tu ________________	*(AH-ee)* **hai**	**voi** ________________	*(ah-VEH-teh)* **avete**
lui / **lei** ________________	*(ah)* **ha**	**loro** ________________	*(AH-nnoh)* **hanno**

Singular Familiar Command: *(AH-bbee)* **Abbi!** *Singular Polite Command:* *(AH-bbyah)* **Abbia!** *Plural Command:* *(ah-BBYAH-teh)* **Abbiate!**

ANSWERS

7. da' (la penna) **8.** dia (la penna alla) **9.** dica (la verità!) **10.** di' (la verità!) **11.** siediti (qui!) **12.** si sieda (qui!) **13.** sia (gentile!) **14.** sii (gentile!)

Directions
Va' / Vada dritto, gira / giri a destra. Gira / Giri a destra poi a destra ancora.
Gira / Giri a sinistra, poi a destra, poi a sinistra ancora.

Capisci? Put the right form of *avere* in the spaces provided.

Quell'uomo _______________ due furgoni.

Io non _______________ la patente di guida.

Noi _______________ una Lancia da noleggiare.

Voi _______________ un'utilitaria.

Tu _______________ sempre ragione.

Loro _______________ torto.

Le macchine americane _______________ una carrozzeria grande.

Here are two more verbs that are useful, but first, review the verb *volere* in chapter 6.

(poh-TEH-reh) **POTERE** to be able to			*(doh-VEH-reh)* **DOVERE** to have to	
io	*(POH-ssoh)* **posso**	*(poh-SSYAH-moh)* **noi possiamo**	*(DEH-voh)* **devo**	*(doh-BBYAH-moh)* **dobbiamo**
tu	*(PWOH-ee)* **puoi**	*(poh-TEH-teh)* **voi potete**	*(DEH-vee)* **devi**	*(doh-VEH-teh)* **dovete**
lui / **lei**	*(pwoh)* **può**	*(POH-ssoh-noh)* **loro possono**	*(DEH-veh)* **deve**	*(DEH-voh-noh)* **devono**

Now use the right form of *potere* or *dovere* in the following sentences.

Io non _______________ (potere) andare in Italia quest'**anno** (year).

I passeggeri _______________ (dovere) scendere a Bologna.

Voi _______________ (dovere) comprare l'assicurazione per la macchina!

I turisti _______________ (potere) noleggiare quella macchina.

Io _______________ (dovere) portare la mia macchina alla stazione di servizio.

Tu _______________ (potere) portare la tua macchina a quella stazione di servizio.

Il signor Smith non _______________ (potere) guidare in Italia perché ha lasciato *(lah-SHAH-toh)* (he left) la sua patente in America.

ANSWERS

Verbs (avere) ha (due) hai (sempre) ho (la) hanno (torto.) abbiamo (una) hanno (una) avete (un'utilitaria.)

More verbs (potere/dovere) posso (andare) devono (scendere) dovete (comprare) possono (noleggiare) devo (portare) puoi (portare) può (guidare)

Attenzione! (Watch out!) Driving in a foreign country means watching the road even when the scenery is breathtaking.

Che bella veduta! Yes, how beautiful! Read the passage that follows and determine what happened on this trip. Answer the questions that follow.

(een-chee-DEHN-teh)
Un autista americano e un autista italiano hanno avuto un piccolo incidente. L'autista
had Accident

(soo-CHEH-ssoh) (DAH-nnoh) (GRAH-veh)
italiano chiede come è successo. Il danno non è grave, ma la macchina dell'italiano è
it happened damage serious

(NWOH-vah) (deh-CHEE-deh) (BREH-veh) (dees-koo-SYOH-neh)
nuova. L'autista italiano decide di chiamare un vigile. Dopo una breve discussione, i due
new decided brief discussion

(ah-jjoos-TAH-reh) (oh-NYOO-noh) (PROH-pree-ah)
autisti decidono di farsi aggiustare ognuno la propria macchina. Il vigile dice ai due
fix each one own

autisti che bisogna stare attenti quando si guida.
be careful one

Chi ha avuto un incidente?

- ☐ Due turisti americani.
- ☐ Un autista americano e un autista italiano.
- ☐ Un autista e un vigile.

Chi chiede come è successo?

- ☐ L'autista americano.
- ☐ Il vigile.
- ☐ L'autista italiano.

Com'è il danno?

- ☐ È grave.
- ☐ Non è grave.
- ☐ È molto grave.

Chi decide di chiamare il vigile?

- ☐ L'autista italiano.
- ☐ L'autista americano.
- ☐ Nessuno.

Che cosa decidono di fare, gli autisti?

- ☐ Decidono di andare insieme a Roma.
- ☐ Decidono di andare alla stazione di servizio.
- ☐ Decidono di farsi aggiustare ognuno la propria macchina.

Che cosa dice il vigile?

- ☐ Dice che bisogna guidare solo le macchine nuove.
- ☐ Dice che bisogna stare attenti quando si guida.
- ☐ Dice che non bisogna fare un incidente.

ANSWERS

Comprehension Un autista americano e un autista italiano. L'autista italiano. Non è grave. L'autista italiano. Decidono di farsi aggiustare ognuno la propria macchina. Dice che bisogna stare attenti quando si guida.

Now see how many of the following words and expressions you remember by matching them up with their English meanings.

1. incidente	a. No Left Turn
2. danno	b. One-Way
3. aggiustare	c. No Parking
4. girare	d. rush hour
5. guidare	e. west
6. benzina	f. east
7. clacson	g. south
8. cruscotto	h. (car) horn
9. pneumatici	i. No Passing
10. volante	j. gas
11. Divieto di sorpasso	k. to drive
12. Divieto di svolta a sinistra	l. to turn
13. Senso unico	m. steering wheel
14. Divieto di sosta	n. dashboard
15. ora di punta	o. to fix
16. nord	p. accident
17. sud	q. tires
18. est	r. damage
19. ovest	s. north

ANSWERS

Matching **1**-p, **2**-r, **3**-o, **4**-l, **5**-k, **6**-j, **7**-h, **8**-n, **9**-q, **10**-m, **11**-i, **12**-a, **13**-b, **14**-c, **15**-d, **16**-s, **17**-g, **18**-f, **19**-e

9 Il campeggio

(kahm-PEH-jjoh)

Il campeggio

Camping

These words will be useful to you if you go camping in any of the many mountain spots throughout Italy. You will be able to buy equipment in most of the resort villages found in the Italian mountains.

(mah-teh-RAH-ssoh)(pneh-oo-MAH-tee-koh)
il materasso pneumatico
air mattress

(KAH-pee)(vehs-tee-AH-ree-oh)
il capi di vestiario
articles of clothing

(pah-GAH-yeh)
le pagaie
paddles

(koh-PEHR-tah)
la coperta
blanket

(PEE-lah)(tahs-KAH-bee-leh)
la pila tascabile
flashlight

(kah-NEHS-troh)
il canestro
basket

(roo-SHEH-lloh)
il ruscello
brook

(TEHN-dah)
la tenda
tent

(AHL-beh-roh)
l'albero
tree

(SOH-leh)
il sole
sun

(kah-NOH-ah)
la canoa
canoe

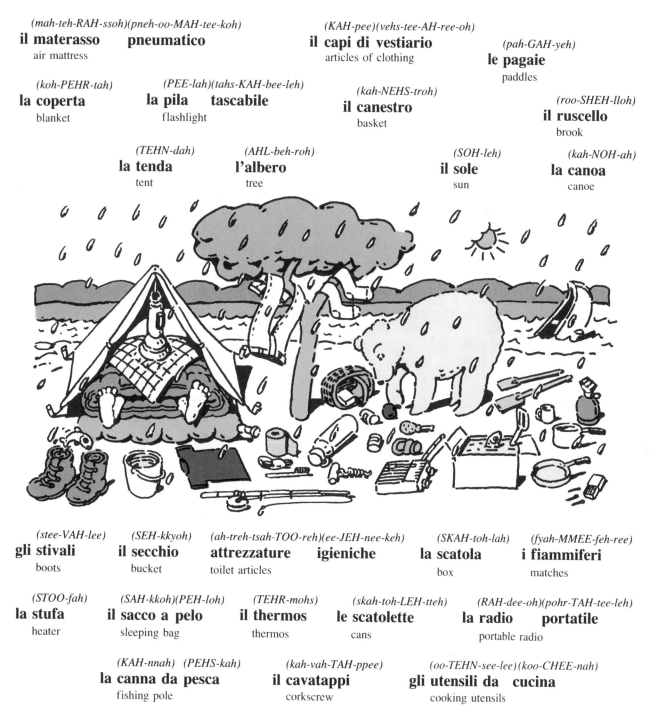

(stee-VAH-lee)
gli stivali
boots

(SEH-kkyoh)
il secchio
bucket

(ah-treh-tsah-TOO-reh)(ee-JEH-nee-keh)
attrezzature igieniche
toilet articles

(SKAH-toh-lah)
la scatola
box

(fyah-MMEE-feh-ree)
i fiammiferi
matches

(STOO-fah)
la stufa
heater

(SAH-kkoh)(PEH-loh)
il sacco a pelo
sleeping bag

(TEHR-mohs)
il thermos
thermos

(skah-toh-LEH-tteh)
le scatolette
cans

(RAH-dee-oh)(pohr-TAH-tee-leh)
la radio portatile
portable radio

(KAH-nnah) (PEHS-kah)
la canna da pesca
fishing pole

(kah-vah-TAH-ppee)
il cavatappi
corkscrew

(oo-TEHN-see-lee)(koo-CHEE-nah)
gli utensili da cucina
cooking utensils

Practice your "outdoor" Italian. Find the camping words and expressions in the following puzzle and circle them. When you locate each one, write it down and pronounce it aloud. We've found the first one for you, as an example.

materasso pneumatico

q	m	a	t	e	r	a	s	s	o	p	n	e	u	m	a	t	i	c	o	a	z	w	s	p	x	e	d	c
r	f	v	t	g	b	y	h	n	u	i	j	m	k	q	l	a	s	o	l	e	p	o	l	a	i	j	n	u
h	r	b	y	g	v	t	f	c	r	l	d	x	e	s	b	z	a	p	q	x	s	w	c	g	d	e	v	f
r	u	b	g	t	n	h	y	m	j	a	u	k	o	p	e	q	a	e	z	w	c	s	x	a	e	d	c	r
m	s	k	s	c	a	t	o	l	e	t	t	e	n	j	r	i	b	r	h	u	a	v	g	i	y	c	f	t
x	c	d	r	z	s	e	q	a	z	a	w	s	x	e	o	d	c	t	r	f	p	m	k	e	i	n	j	u
z	e	a	q	t	h	e	r	m	o	s	x	c	c	a	v	a	t	a	p	p	i	d	e	v	f	r	b	g
t	l	n	h	y	m	j	u	k	l	c	o	p	q	a	z	w	s	x	e	d	d	c	r	f	v	t	y	h
z	l	a	q	x	s	w	c	d	s	a	c	c	o	a	p	e	l	o	v	f	i	r	b	g	t	n	z	a
p	o	l	n	y	q	a	z	w	x	b	e	d	r	f	v	i	j	n	b	r	v	p	m	q	z	x	c	v
y	h	n	u	t	e	n	s	i	l	i	d	a	c	u	c	i	n	a	t	g	e	b	r	f	v	f	w	s
q	a	z	w	s	x	e	d	c	r	l	f	v	y	h	n	z	a	q	x	w	s	e	c	c	h	i	o	d
x	s	c	a	n	n	a	d	a	p	e	s	c	a	w	c	d	e	v	f	s	t	u	f	a	r	a	e	w
z	a	q	x	s	w	c	d	e	b	f	r	g	h	y	h	u	n	k	i	j	i	l	o	n	q	m	a	c
i	r	a	d	i	o	p	o	r	t	a	t	i	l	e	w	c	s	d	f	g	a	h	b	o	v	m	p	o
m	k	o	n	j	u	b	h	y	v	g	t	c	f	r	x	a	d	w	x	f	r	q	w	a	t	i	e	a
a	t	t	r	e	z	z	a	t	u	r	e	i	g	i	e	n	i	c	h	e	i	p	o	u	y	f	t	r
z	x	e	c	v	b	n	m	a	s	d	f	g	h	q	w	e	e	r	t	y	o	u	i	z	x	e	w	t
q	w	n	e	r	t	y	u	i	o	p	a	s	d	f	g	s	h	j	k	l	z	x	c	v	b	r	n	m
p	o	d	i	u	r	w	q	a	l	k	s	j	s	c	a	t	o	l	a	d	h	f	g	m	z	i	b	y
z	m	a	x	n	c	b	v	l	a	p	q	o	w	i	e	r	r	u	t	y	z	q	w	e	r	t	c	p
p	z	o	c	s	t	i	v	a	l	i	i	v	u	b	y	o	d	q	p	w	o	b	n	v	m	c	l	z

ANSWERS

Word search

materasso pneumatico
coperta
pila tascabile
sacco a pelo
scatolette
thermos
utensili da cucina
cavatappi
capi di vestiario
attrezzature igieniche
radio portatile
albero
stufa
canna da pesca
canestro
stivali
canoa
pagaie
secchio
scatola
fiammiferi
tenda
sole
ruscello

9 Il campeggio

(kahm-PEH-jjoh)

Il campeggio
Camping

These words will be useful to you if you go camping in any of the many mountain spots throughout Italy. You will be able to buy equipment in most of the resort villages found in the Italian mountains.

(mah-teh-RAH-ssoh)(pneh-oo-MAH-tee-koh)
il materasso pneumatico
air mattress

(KAH-pee)(vehs-tee-AH-ree-oh)
il capi di vestiario
articles of clothing

(pah-GAH-yeh)
le pagaie
paddles

(koh-PEHR-tah)
la coperta
blanket

(PEE-lah)(tahs-KAH-bee-leh)
la pila tascabile
flashlight

(kah-NEHS-troh)
il canestro
basket

(roo-SHEH-lloh)
il ruscello
brook

(TEHN-dah)
la tenda
tent

(AHL-beh-roh)
l'albero
tree

(SOH-leh)
il sole
sun

(kah-NOH-ah)
la canoa
canoe

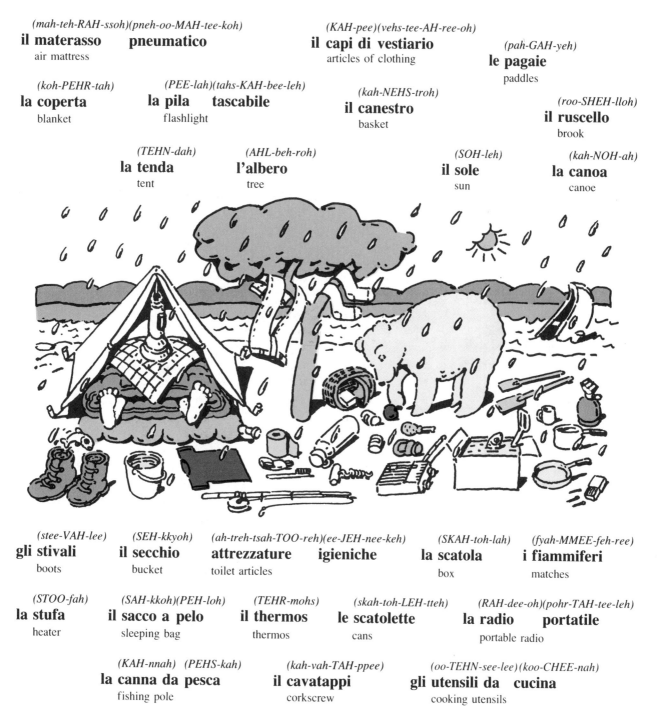

(stee-VAH-lee)
gli stivali
boots

(SEH-kkyoh)
il secchio
bucket

(ah-treh-tsah-TOO-reh)(ee-JEH-nee-keh)
attrezzature igieniche
toilet articles

(SKAH-toh-lah)
la scatola
box

(fyah-MMEE-feh-ree)
i fiammiferi
matches

(STOO-fah)
la stufa
heater

(SAH-kkoh)(PEH-loh)
il sacco a pelo
sleeping bag

(TEHR-mohs)
il thermos
thermos

(skah-toh-LEH-tteh)
le scatolette
cans

(RAH-dee-oh)(pohr-TAH-tee-leh)
la radio portatile
portable radio

(KAH-nnah) (PEHS-kah)
la canna da pesca
fishing pole

(kah-vah-TAH-ppee)
il cavatappi
corkscrew

(oo-TEHN-see-lee)(koo-CHEE-nah)
gli utensili da cucina
cooking utensils

Practice your "outdoor" Italian. Find the camping words and expressions in the following puzzle and circle them. When you locate each one, write it down and pronounce it aloud. We've found the first one for you, as an example.

materasso pneumatico

```
q m a t e r a s s o p n e u m a t i c o a z w s p x e d c
r f v t g b y h n u i j m k q l a s o l e p o l a i j n u
h r b y g v t f c r l d x e s b z a p q x s w c g d e v f
r u b g t n h y m j a u k o p e q a e z w c s x a e d c r
m s k s c a t o l e t t e n j r i b r h u a v g i y c f t
x c d r z s e q a z a w s x e o d c t r f p m k e i n j u
z e a q t h e r m o s x c c a v a t a p p i d e v f r b g
t l n h y m j u k l c o p q a z w s x e d d c r f v t y h
z l a q x s w c d s a c c o a p e l o v f i r b g t n z a
p o l n y q a z w x b e d r f v i j n b r v p m q z x c v
y h n u t e n s i l i d a c u c i n a t g e b r f v f w s
q a z w s x e d c r l f v y h n z a q x w s e c c h i o d
x s c a n n a d a p e s c a w c d e v f s t u f a r a e w
z a q x s w c d e b f r g h y h u n k i j i l o n q m a c
i r a d i o p o r t a t i l e w c s d f g a h b o v m p o
m k o n j u b h y v g t c f r x a d w x f r q w a t i e a
a t t r e z z a t u r e i g i e n i c h e i p o u y f t r
z x e c v b n m a s d f g h q w e e r t y o u i z x e w t
q w n e r t y u i o p a s d f g s h j k l z x c v b r n m
p o d i u r w q a l k s j s c a t o l a d h f g m z i b y
z m a x n c b v l a p q o w i e r r u t y z q w e r t c p
p z o c s t i v a l i i v u b y o d q p w o b n v m c l z
```

ANSWERS

Word search

materasso pneumatico	scatolette	attrezzature igieniche	canestro	scatola
coperta	thermos	radio portatile	stivali	fiammiferi
pila tascabile	utensili da cucina	albero	canoa	tenda
sacco a pelo	cavatappi	stufa	pagaie	sole
	capi di vestiario	canna da pesca	secchio	ruscello

AL CAMPEGGIO

To the Campground

Now read the following two dialogues, which contain some useful words, expressions, and information on camping. Read them aloud, repeating each line several times, until you can pronounce them easily.

(Mark calls his friend Giovanni on the phone to ask for some camping information.)

GIOVANNI **Pronto. Chi parla?**

Hello. Who is it?

MARK **Ciao, Giovanni. Sono Mark. Mi sai dire se c'è un campeggio qui**
(vee-CHEE-noh)
vicino?

Hi, Giovanni. It's Mark. Can you tell me if there is a campground near here?

GIOVANNI **Sì, volentieri. Prendi**
(ah-oo-toh-STRAH-dah) (kee-LOH-meh-tree)
l'autostrada per venti chilometri, e
(CHEHR-kah) (kahr-TEH-lloh) (strah-DAH-leh)
cerca un cartello stradale che
(EEN-dee-kah)
indica il campeggio.

Yes, gladly. Take the highway for 20 kilometers, and look for a road sign that indicates where the campground is.

(koh-NOH-shee)
MARK **Lo conosci?**

Are you familiar with it?

(preh-oh-kkoo-PAH-reh)
GIOVANNI **Sì. Non ti preoccupare! È**
(FAH-chee-leh)
facile trovarlo. Tutti i campeggi
(pah-EH-zee)
italiani sono vicini a piccoli paesi.

Yes. Don't worry! It's easy to find. All Italian campgrounds are near small towns.

(BAH-nyee)
MARK **Ci sono i bagni?**

Are there any bathrooms?

GIOVANNI **Penso di sì.**

I think so.

(poh-TAH-bee-leh)
MARK **C'è acqua potabile?**

Is there drinking water?

(preh-feh-REE-bee-leh)
GIOVANNI **In Italia è preferibile bere**
(eem-boh-ttee-LLYAH-tah)
acqua imbottigliata o,
(nah-toor-ahl-MEHN-teh) (VEE-noh)
naturalmente, vino!

In Italy it is preferable to drink bottled water or, naturally, wine!

(eh-leh-ttree-chee-TAH)
MARK **C'è l'elettricità?**

Is there any electricity?

GIOVANNI **Non credo.**

I don't believe so.

MARK **Costa molto?**

Does it cost a lot?

GIOVANNI **Costa molto poco.** It costs very little.

(fahn-TAHS-tee-koh)

MARK **Fantastico! Il campeggio italiano fa** *(PROH-pree-oh)* **proprio per me!** Fantastic! Italian camping is truly for me!

(neh-GOH-tsee-oh) (JEH-neh-ree) (ah-lee-mehn-TAH-ree)

AL NEGOZIO DI GENERI ALIMENTARI

At the Grocery Store

(Mark Smith and his family enter a grocery store near the campground.)

(deh-SEE-deh-rah)

COMMESSA **Buona sera. Desidera, signora?** Good evening. Can I help you, madam?

(PAH-kkoh)

MARY **Sì. Vorrei un pacco di spaghetti,** *(BOO-rroh) (LEE-troh)* **cento grammi di burro, un litro di** *(LAH-tteh) (SAH-leh) (boh-TTEE-llyah)* **latte, un po' di sale, e una bottiglia di vino.** Yes. I would like a package of spaghetti, 100 grams (about ¼-pound) of butter, a liter of milk, a bit of salt, and a bottle of wine.

COMMESSA **Trentamila lire.** 30,000 lira.

(POH-lloh)

MARK **Vogliamo anche quel pollo e quella scatola di fiammiferi, va bene?** We also want that chicken and that box of matches, okay?

COMMESSA	**Lei è un turista americano?**	Are you an American tourist?
MARK	**Sì.**	Yes.
COMMESSA	**Va bene.** *(She takes their money.)* **Dove va, al campeggio?**	Okay. Where are you going, to the campground?
MARK	**Sì. Grazie e arrivederci.**	Yes. Thank you and good-bye.
COMMESSA	**Arrivederci.**	Good-bye.

Now without looking back, match the following to form lines from the first dialogue.

Pronto. Chi . . .	italiani sono vicini a piccoli paesi.
Mi sai dire se . . .	acqua potabile?
Prendi . . .	preferibile bere acqua imbottigliata o, naturalmente, vino!
Non ti . . .	di sì.
Tutti i campeggi . . .	italiano fa proprio per me!
Ci sono . . .	preoccupare!
Penso . . .	parla?
C'è . . .	c'è un campeggio qui vicino?
In Italia è . . .	l'autostrada per venti chilometri.
Il campeggio . . .	i bagni?

Check your answers only after you have attempted to match up these items from memory. Now try to complete the missing parts from the second dialogue. Check your answers only after you have attempted to do this exercise from memory.

Buona s________________. D________________, signora?

Sì. Vorrei un p________________ di spaghetti, cento g________________

di b________________, un litro di l________________, un po' di s________________,

e una b________________ di v________________.

Trentamila l________________.

Vogliamo anche quel p__________ e quella s__________ di f__________,

va bene?

Lei è un t__________ a__________?

Sì.

Va bene. Dove va, al c__________?

Sì. Grazie e a__________.

Arrivederci.

In the first dialogue above you were introduced to the verb *bere*, "to drink." This is conjugated as follows.

BERE To Drink					
Io	***bevo***	**il vino.**	**Noi**	***beviamo***	*(kah-FFEH)* **il caffè.** coffee
Tu	***bevi***	**il vino.**	**Voi**	***bevete***	**il caffè con latte.**
Lei	***beve***	**il latte.**	**Loro**	*(BEH-voh-noh* ***bevono***	**solo il vino.**

Come si dice . . .?

How Do You Say . . .?

Here are some expressions that might come in handy on your camping excursion.

(bee-ZOH-nyoh) **Ho bisogno di . . .**	I need	**avere fame**	to be hungry
Lo so	I know it	**avere sonno**	to be sleepy
Non lo so	I do not know it	**avere sete**	to be thirsty
avere caldo	to be hot	*(pah-OO-rah)* **avere paura**	to be afraid
avere freddo	to be cold		

Now try to match each sentence with a picture.

1.

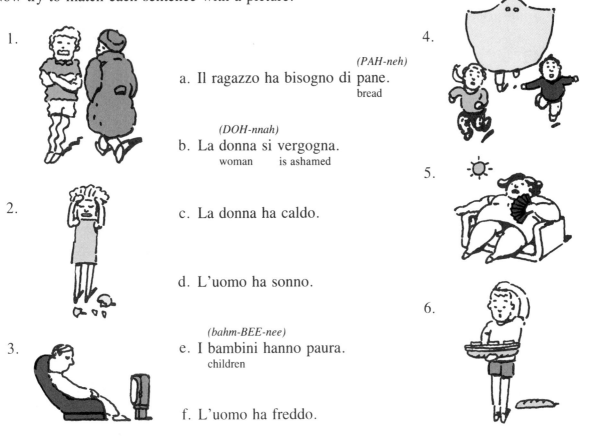

2.

3.

4.

5.

6.

a. Il ragazzo ha bisogno di pane. (PAH-neh) bread

b. La donna si vergogna. (DOH-nnah) woman; is ashamed

c. La donna ha caldo.

d. L'uomo ha sonno.

e. I bambini hanno paura. (bahm-BEE-nee) children

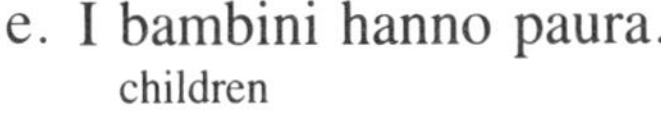

f. L'uomo ha freddo.

Camping is fun as long as the weather holds out. See how the Smith family fared on their trip. Test your readiness for camping by selecting the appropriate answers to the questions, based on the following passage.

La famiglia Smith è al campeggio vicino a Roma.

Fa molto caldo e allora decidono di andare alla spiaggia. (SPYAH-jjah) beach

Ma l'acqua è fredda e allora solo Anne va nell'acqua.

ANSWERS

Matching 1-f, 2-b, 3-d, 4-e, 5-c, 6-a

(jeh-LAH-toh) (KAHM-pehr)

John prende un gelato dal camper, ma la madre non vuole.

ice cream / camper

(nahs-KOHN-deh) (KAH-neh)

John nasconde il gelato e il cane lo mangia.

hides / dog / eats it

Dov'è il campeggio?
- ☐ È vicino a Roma.
- ☐ È vicino a Piazza San Marco.
- ☐ È vicino a Firenze.

Dove decidono di andare?
- ☐ A Roma.
- ☐ Nel camper.
- ☐ Alla spiaggia.

Com'è l'acqua?
- ☐ È calda.
- ☐ È fredda.
- ☐ È piena di vino.

Chi mangia il gelato?
- ☐ La madre.
- ☐ Il cane.
- ☐ John.

Che cosa prende, John?
- ☐ Prende una bottiglia di vino.
- ☐ Prende un gelato.
- ☐ Prende una scatola di fiammiferi.

Now have fun with the following crossword puzzle.

Across

3. Vorrei cento grammi di . . .
4. Loro . . . solo il vino.
5. Il sacco a . . .
6. Vorrei un litro di . . .

Down

1. L'uomo non ha caldo, ha . . .
2. L'uomo va a dormire perché ha . . .
3. Vorrei una . . . di vino.
5. La canna da . . .

ANSWERS

Comprehension È vicino a Roma. Alla spiaggia. È fredda. Il cane. Prende un gelato.

Crossword Across: 3. burro **4.** bevono **5.** pelo **6.** latte.

Down: 1. freddo **2.** sonno **3.** bottiglia **4.** pesca.

10 Il tempo / Le stagioni / I giorni della settimana / I mesi

(stah-JOH-nee) (MEH-zee)

Weather / Seasons / Days of the Week / Months

Italian months are very similar to English. Say them aloud a few times, until you are familiar with the Italian pronunciation.

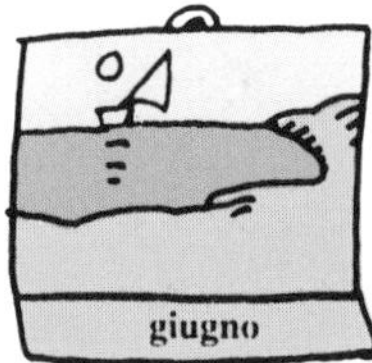

(jeh-NNAH-yoh)
gennaio
January

(feh-BBRAH-yoh)
febbraio
February

(MAHR-tsoh)
marzo
March

(ah-PREE-leh)
aprile
April

(MAH-jjoh)
maggio
May

(JOO-nyoh)
giugno
June

(LOO-llyoh)
luglio
July

(ah-GOHS-toh)
agosto
August

(seh-TTEHM-breh)
settembre
September

(oh-TTOH-breh)
ottobre
October

(noh-VEHM-breh)
novembre
November

(dee-CHEHM-breh)
dicembre
December

Now do the same with these expressions relating to the seasons.

(een-VEHR-noh)
—È inverno
Winter

Fa molto freddo.
It's very cold.

(NEH-vee-kah)
Nevica.
It's snowing.

(JEH-lee-doh)
Fa un freddo gelido.
It's freezing.

(ehs-TAH-teh)
—È estate
Summer

Fa caldo.
It is hot.

(OO-mee-doh)
È umido.
It is humid.

(ah-FOH-zoh)
È afoso.
It is muggy.

(boo-rahs-KOH-soh)
Il tempo è burrascoso.
It's stormy.

(PYOH-veh)
Piove.
It's raining.

(TWOH-nah)
Tuona.
It's thundering.

(ah-oo-TOO-nnoh)
—È autunno
Fall

Fa fresco.
It's chilly.

(dee-ROH-ttoh)
Piove a dirotto.
It's raining cats and dogs.

(NEH-bbyah)
C'è la nebbia.
It's foggy.

(pree-mah-VEH-rah)
—È primavera
Spring

Fa fresco.
It is cool.

C'è il sole.
It is sunny.

CHE TEMPO FA?

How Is the Weather?

If you look carefully at the seasons you will see that many expressions connected with the weather use the verb form *fa* . . .

Che tempo fa?	How is the weather?	**Fa caldo.**	It is hot.
Fa fresco.	It is cool/chilly.	**Fa molto freddo.**	It is very cold.
Fa freddo.	It is cold.	**Fa un freddo gelido.**	It is freezing.

Here are some other useful weather expressions.

C'è il sole.	It is sunny.	**Tuona.**	It is thundering.
È umido.	It is humid.	**Piove a dirotto.**	It is raining cats and dogs.
È afoso.	It is muggy.	**Nevica.**	It is snowing.
È burrascoso.	It is stormy.	**C'è la nebbia.**	It is foggy.
Piove.	It is raining.		

In general, if you want to say the weather is beautiful or bad, use the following expressions.

Fa bel tempo.	The weather is beautiful.	**Fa brutto tempo.**	The weather is bad/awful.

If you have learned the weather phrases well, you should be able to choose the appropriate expression to describe each picture.

1. ____________________ 2. ____________________ 3. ____________________

4. ____________________ 5. ____________________ 6. ____________________

7. ____________________ 8. ____________________

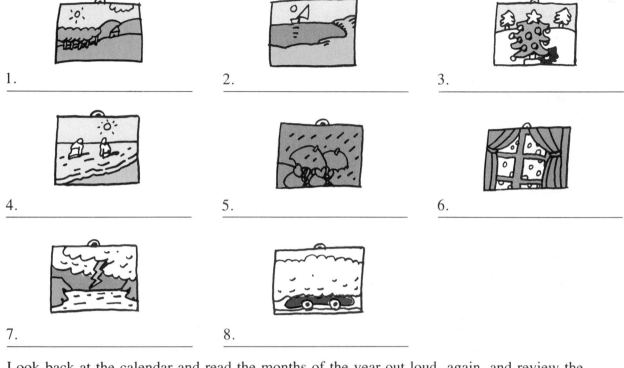

Look back at the calendar and read the months of the year out loud, again, and review the ordinal numbers in chapter 5. Then try the following. Be careful not to capitalize the months.

Il terzo mese ____________________

Il quinto mese ____________________

Il primo mese ____________________

Il quarto mese ____________________

Il secondo mese ____________________

Il sesto mese ____________________

Il decimo mese ____________________

Il settimo mese ____________________

Il nono mese ____________________

l'ottavo mese ____________________

Il mese dopo ottobre ____________________
after

(OOL-tee-moh)
l'ultimo mese ____________________
last

ANSWERS

Identification
1. Fa bel tempo. **2.** C'è il sole. **3.** Fa freddo. **4.** Fa caldo. **5.** Piove. **6.** Nevica. **7.** Fa brutto tempo. **8.** C'è la nebbia.

Months
(Il terzo mese) è marzo. (Il decimo mese) è ottobre. (Il quinto mese) è maggio. (Il settimo mese) è luglio. (Il primo mese) è gennaio. (Il nono mese) è settembre. (Il quarto mese) è aprile. (L'ottavo mese) è agosto. (Il secondo mese) è febbraio. (Il mese dopo ottobre) è novembre. (Il sesto mese) è giugno. (L'ultimo mese) è dicembre.

To say a date in Italian, just use the cardinal numbers in the following formula.

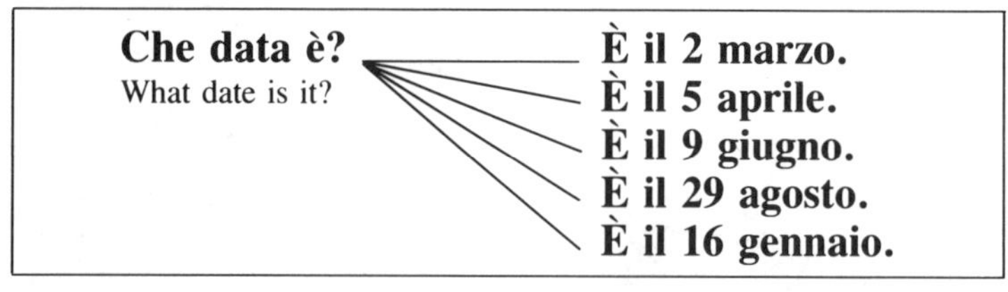

Che data è?
What date is it?
È il 2 marzo.
È il 5 aprile.
È il 9 giugno.
È il 29 agosto.
È il 16 gennaio.

The only exception is for the first day of each month, for which you use the ordinal number.

Che data è? — **È il primo ottobre.** / **È il primo luglio.**

Now you should be able to write out the following dates in Italian.

Che data è?

______________ January 4	______________ July 30
______________ February 7	______________ August 24
______________ March 11	______________ September 8
______________ April 19	______________ October 15
______________ May 28	______________ November 20
______________ June 1 (Be careful!)	______________ December 10

Here are the days of the week in Italian. Read them out loud several times; then see if you can figure out each of the logic puzzles that follow. Once again, remember that you do not capitalize the days of the week.

(loo-neh-DEE)
lunedì ________ Monday

(mahr-teh-DEE)
martedì ________ Tuesday

(mehr-koh-leh-DEE)
mercoledì ________ Wednesday

(joh-veh-DEE)
giovedì ________ Thursday

(veh-nehr-DEE)
venerdì ________ Friday

(SAH-bah-toh)
sabato ________ Saturday

(doh-MEH-nee-kah)
domenica ________ Sunday

ANSWERS

Dates

È il quattro gennaio. (January 4) È il trenta luglio. (July 30) È il sette febbraio. (February 7) È il ventiquattro agosto. (August 24) È l'undici marzo. (March 11) È l'otto settembre. (September 8) È il diciannove aprile. (April 19) È il quindici ottobre. (October 15) È il ventotto maggio. (May 28) È il venti novembre. (November 20) È il primo giugno. (June 1) È il dieci dicembre. (December 10)

1. il giorno **dopo** lunedì: ________________
after

2. il giorno dopo domenica: ________________

3. il giorno **prima** di domenica: ________________
before

4. il giorno prima di venerdì: ________________

5. il giorno dopo martedì: ________________

6. il giorno dopo sabato: ________________

7. il giorno prima di sabato: ________________

(ah-jjeh-TTEE-vee)

Aggettivi

Adjectives

There are two main kinds of adjectives in Italian: one that ends in **-o** and another that ends in **-e**. Adjectives usually follow the noun they modify and agree with its gender (masculine or feminine) and its number (singular or plural). Confused? Don't worry! Just look at the following examples and then try your hand at the activities that follow.

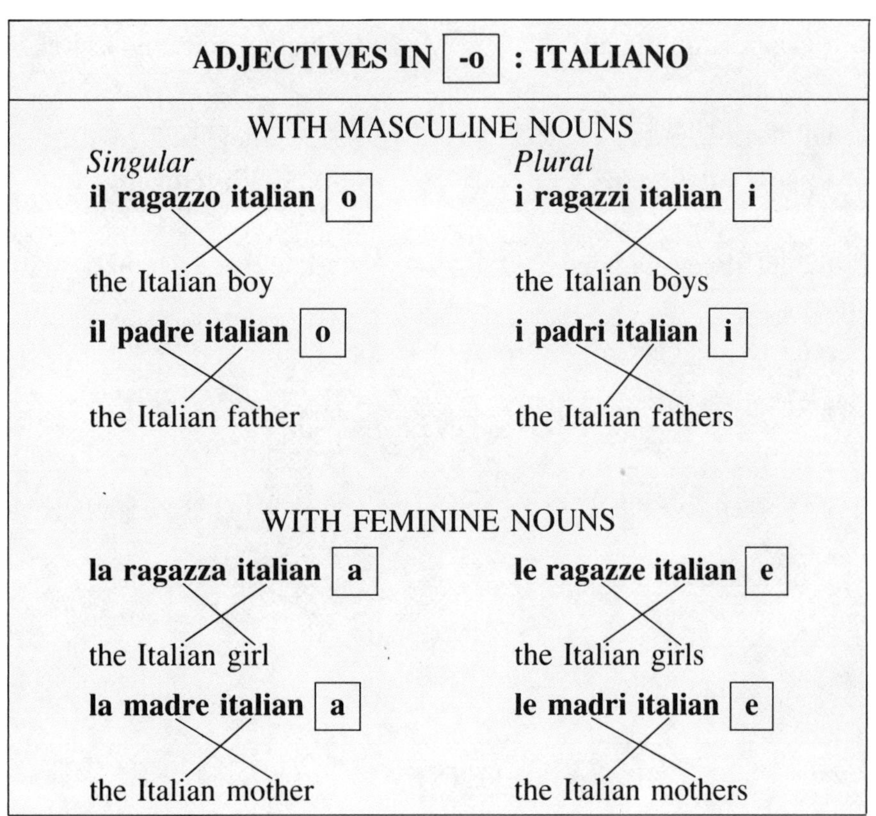

ADJECTIVES IN -o : ITALIANO

WITH MASCULINE NOUNS

Singular	*Plural*
il ragazzo italian o	**i ragazzi italian i**
the Italian boy	the Italian boys
il padre italian o	**i padri italian i**
the Italian father	the Italian fathers

WITH FEMININE NOUNS

Singular	*Plural*
la ragazza italian a	**le ragazze italian e**
the Italian girl	the Italian girls
la madre italian a	**le madri italian e**
the Italian mother	the Italian mothers

ANSWERS

Days
1. martedì (Tuesday) **2.** lunedì (Monday) **3.** sabato (Saturday) **4.** giovedì (Thursday) **5.** mercoledì (Wednesday) **6.** domenica (Sunday) **7.** venerdì (Friday)

Get it? Adjectives that end in -e are even simpler. Simply use -e with any singular noun (masculine or feminine) and -i with any plural noun (masculine or feminine).

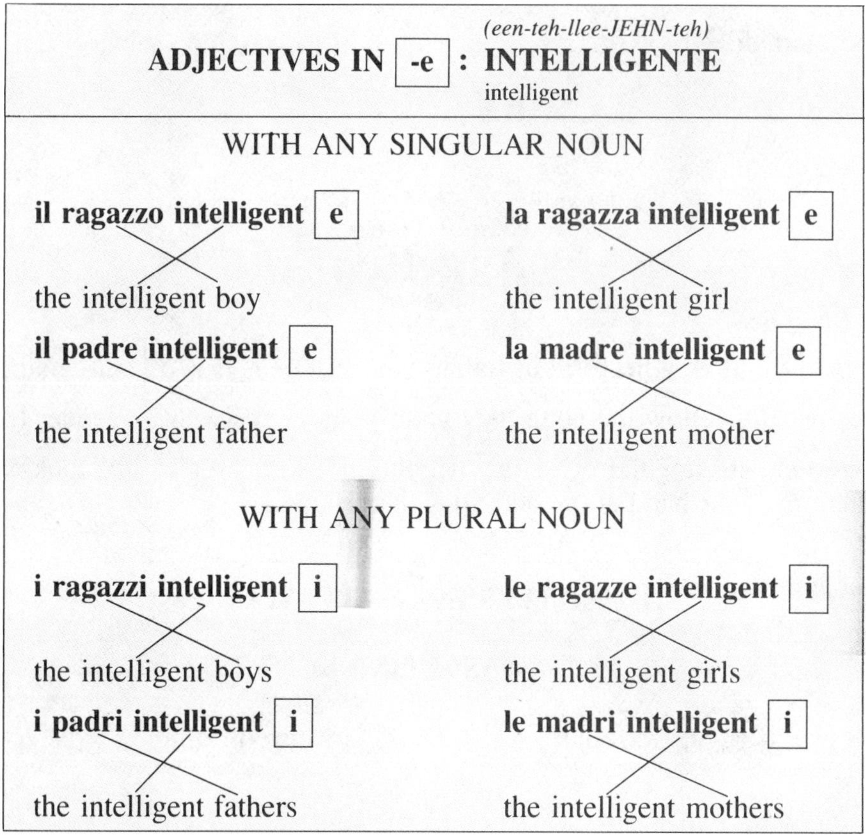

You can always refer to this chart if you forget later on.

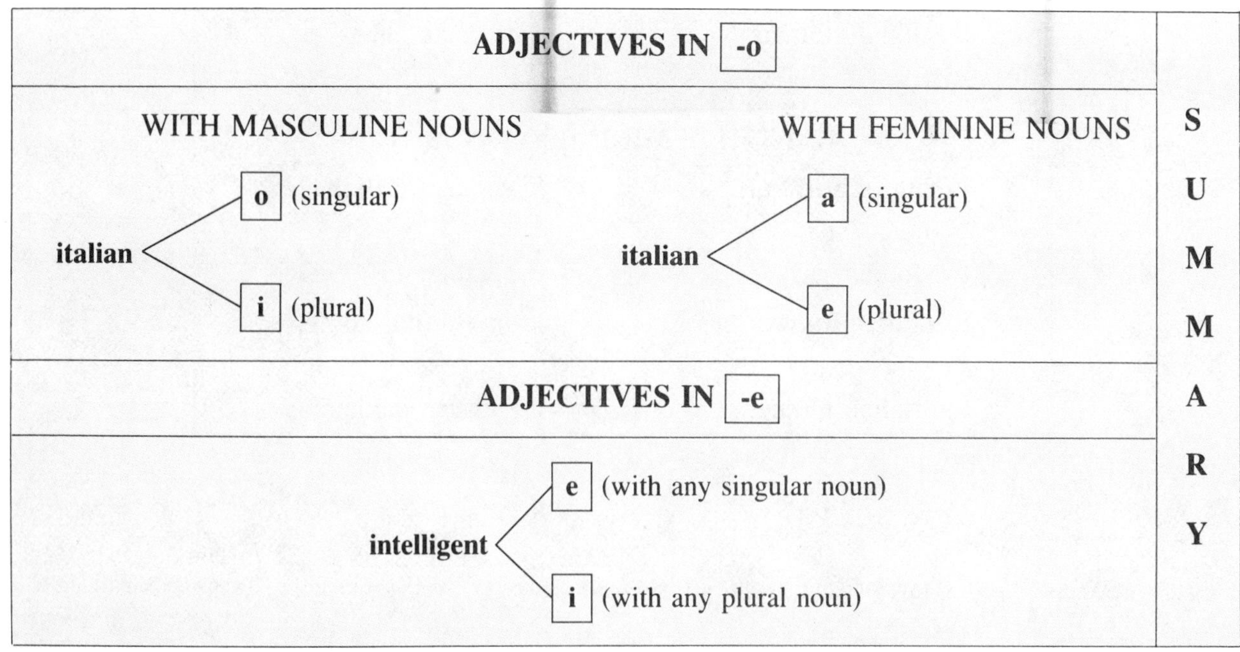

Adjectives normally follow the noun in Italian. Some are also used in front of the noun.

il ragazzo simpatico *or* **il simpatico ragazzo**

the nice boy — the nice boy

A few adjectives, like the ordinal numbers you learned in chapter 5, are used only in front of the noun.

il primo ragazzo

the first boy

As in English, an adjective can be separated from the noun by certain verbs like "to be." However, the agreement patterns in the charts still apply, as you see in these examples.

Il ragazzo è simpatico.
The boy is nice.

La ragazza è bella.
The girl is beautiful.

I ragazzi sono simpatici.
The boys are nice.

Le ragazze sono simpatiche.
The girls are nice.

Io sono alta e tu sei bassa.
I am tall and you are short.

(joh-VAH-neh)
Io sono giovane e
I am young and
(VEH-kkyoh)
tu sei vecchio.
you are old.

(CHEH-nah) (BWOH-nah)
La cena è buona.
The dinner is good.

La cena è pronta.
The dinner is ready.

La mia stanza è grande.
My room is big.

La mia stanza è piccola.
My room is small.

(KOH-moh-dah)
La mia stanza è comoda.
My room is comfortable.

La mia stanza
My room
(roo-moh-ROH-zah)
è rumorosa.
is noisy.

Here is a list of the adjectives just used. Match them to their English equivalents.

1. intelligente	a. short
2. italiano	b. tall
3. simpatico	c. beautiful
4. bello	d. Italian
5. alto	e. intelligent
6. basso	f. nice
7. giovane	g. comfortable
8. vecchio	h. noisy
9. buono	i. big
10. pronto	j. small
11. grande	k. good
12. piccolo	l. ready
13. comodo	m. young
14. rumoroso	n. old

It should be easy for you to put the correct ending on each of these adjectives.

Quelle ragazze sono intelligent________.

Il passeggero italian________ è simpatic________.

Quella ragazza è bell________, alt________ e giovan________.

I miei due zii sono bass________ e vecch________.

Questa pizza non è buon________.

La cena è pront________.

La mia stanza è piccol________ ma comod________.

The following dialogue contains various words and expressions connected with the weather. Read it aloud several times and role-play each part.

(Anne has made an Italian friend, Gina. Anne has spent the night at Gina's house. It is now the morning after.)

ANNE	**Buon giorno, Gina. Sono le otto. C'è un bel sole e fa bel tempo.**	Good morning, Gina. It's eight o'clock. It's sunny and the weather is beautiful.

ANSWERS

Matching **1**-e, **2**-d, **3**-f, **4**-c, **5**-b, **6**-a, **7**-m, **8**-n, **9**-k, **10**-l, **11**-i, **12**-j, **13**-g, **14**-h

Fill-ins

(intelligent) i (buon) a (italian) o, (simpatic) o (pront) a (bell) a, (alt) a, (giovan) e (piccol) a, (comod) a (bass) i, (vecch) i

GINA	*(ahn-KOH-rah)* **Ho ancora sonno.** *(VOH-llyoh) (ahn-KOH-rah)* **Voglio dormire ancora un'altra ora.**	I'm still sleepy. I want to sleep another hour.

ANNE	*(eem-poh-SEE-bee-leh) (preh-vee-ZYOH-nee)* **Impossibile! Le previsioni** *(meh-teh-oh-roh-LOH-jee-keh) (EEN-dee-kah-noh)* **meteorologiche indicano che** *(stah-SEH-rah)* **forse piove stasera. I due ragazzi con** *(KOO-ee)* **cui abbiamo un appuntamento ci** *(ahs-PEH-ttah-noh) (doh-BBYAH-moh) (oo-SHEE-reh)* **aspettano. Dobbiamo uscire** *(mah-TTEE-nah)* **questa mattina!**	No way! (*literally,* Impossible!) The weather forecast indicates that it may rain tonight. The two boys with whom we have a date are waiting for us. We have to go out this morning!
GINA	**Solo un'altra mezz'ora?**	Only another half-hour?
ANNE	**No. Adesso!**	No. Now!

(She starts exercising and making noise so that Gina is forced to get up from bed.)

ANNE	**Finalmente! Com'è il mio ragazzo?**	Finally! How is my date?
GINA	**È molto simpatico.**	He is very nice.
ANNE	**Bene!**	Good!
GINA	*(REE-kkoh)* **È anche molto ricco.**	He is also very rich.
ANNE	*(eem-POHR-tah)* **Non importa!**	It doesn't matter!
GINA	**Su! Andiamo!** *(to herself)* **Ho *ancora* sonno.**	Come on! Let's go! I'm *still* sleepy.

Now try to complete the missing dialogue parts from memory. Check your answers after you have finished.

Buon giorno, Gina. S________________ le otto. C'è un bel s________________ e fa b________________ t________________.

Ho ancora s________________. Voglio dormire ancora un'altra o________________.

Impossibile! Le p________________ m________________ indicano che forse p________________ stasera. I due ragazzi con cui abbiamo un a________________ ci aspettano. Dobbiamo uscire questa m________________!

Solo un'altra mezz'ora?

No. A________________! Finalmente. Com'è il mio ragazzo?

È molto s________________.

Bene!

È anche molto r________________.

Non i________________.

Here are words describing the various times of the day:

(mah-TTEE-nah)	*(poh-meh-REE-jjoh)*	*(SEH-rah)*	*(NOH-tteh)*
la mattina	**il pomeriggio**	**la sera**	**la notte**
morning	afternoon	evening	night

And here are two expressions using these words:

Buona sera.	Good evening./Good afternoon.
Buona notte. (can be used only when departing, not arriving)	Good night.

Now match these words with the pictures and write the Italian in the blanks.

____
night

____
evening

____
afternoon

____
morning

IL LUNEDÌ

On Mondays

Il lunedì vado sempre a scuola. (On Mondays I always go to school.)

Il martedì mangio sempre la pizza.

Il mercoledì vado sempre al cinema.

Notice that to say "on Mondays, on Tuesdays, . . ." all you have to do is use the masculine article **il**.
The only time you use the **la** form is for Sunday.

La domenica dormo tanto. (On Sundays I sleep a lot.)

ANSWERS

Identification
notte sera pomeriggio mattina

See if you can read the following brief passage and then select the appropriate answer to each question.

Oggi è il quattro novembre.
today

(SOH-lee-toh)
Di solito il sabato faccio le spese.
usually — I do my shopping

Sono nato il quattordici febbraio e ho trentadue anni.
I was born — I am thirty-two years old

(kah-lehn-DAH-ree-oh) *(seh-nyeh-ROH)*
Oggi voglio comprare un calendario per il nuovo anno. Su questo calendario segnerò
calendar — I will mark down

(eem-pohr-TAHN-tee) *(nah-TAH-leh)* *(PAHS-kwah)*
tre date importanti: Natale, Pasqua,
important — Christmas — Easter

(kohm-pleh-AH-nnoh)
e il mio compleanno.
birthday

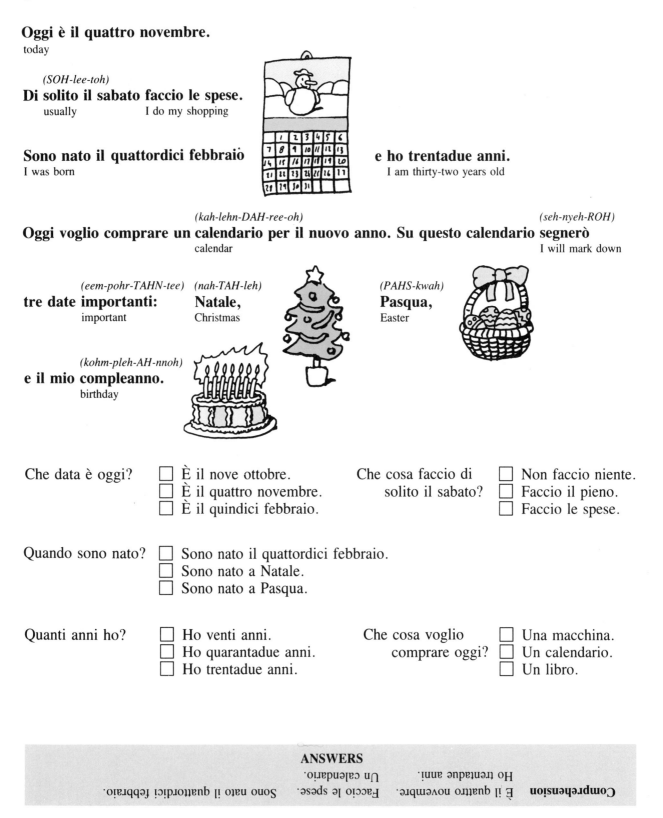

Che data è oggi?
- ☐ È il nove ottobre.
- ☐ È il quattro novembre.
- ☐ È il quindici febbraio.

Che cosa faccio di solito il sabato?
- ☐ Non faccio niente.
- ☐ Faccio il pieno.
- ☐ Faccio le spese.

Quando sono nato?
- ☐ Sono nato il quattordici febbraio.
- ☐ Sono nato a Natale.
- ☐ Sono nato a Pasqua.

Quanti anni ho?
- ☐ Ho venti anni.
- ☐ Ho quarantadue anni.
- ☐ Ho trentadue anni.

Che cosa voglio comprare oggi?
- ☐ Una macchina.
- ☐ Un calendario.
- ☐ Un libro.

ANSWERS

Comprehension È il quattro novembre. Faccio le spese. Sono nato il quattordici febbraio. Ho trentadue anni. Un calendario.

11 Gli aerei / In giro . . .

(ah-EH-reh-ee)

Planes / Sightseeing

Can you find these items in the picture? Say each one aloud as you locate it.

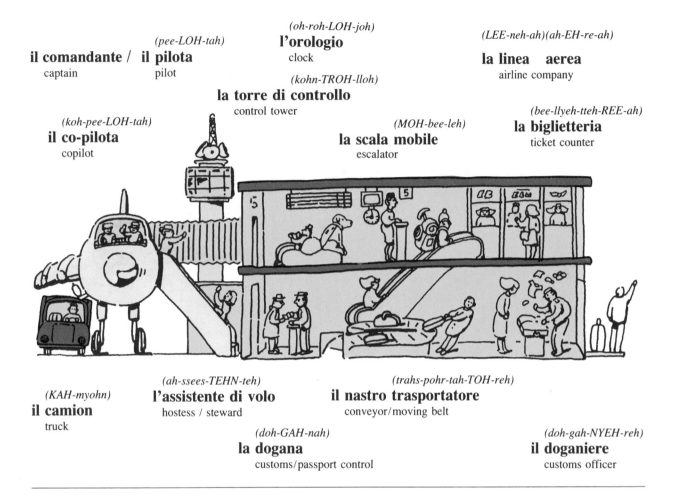

il comandante / il pilota (pee-LOH-tah)
captain / pilot

l'orologio (oh-roh-LOH-joh)
clock

la linea aerea (LEE-neh-ah)(ah-EH-re-ah)
airline company

la torre di controllo (kohn-TROH-lloh)
control tower

il co-pilota (koh-pee-LOH-tah)
copilot

la scala mobile (MOH-bee-leh)
escalator

la biglietteria (bee-llyeh-tteh-REE-ah)
ticket counter

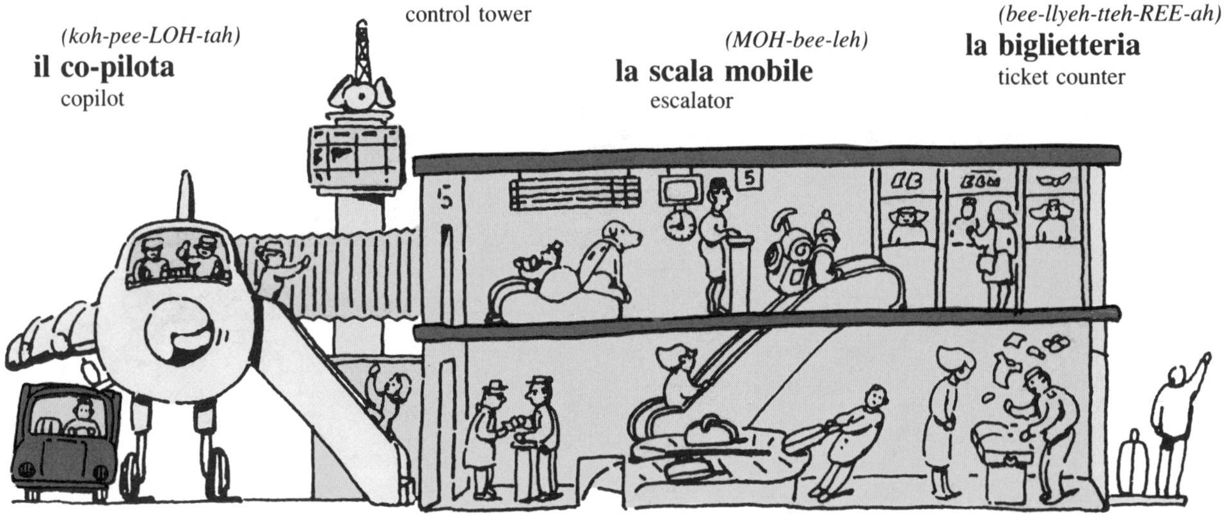

il camion (KAH-myohn)
truck

l'assistente di volo (ah-ssees-TEHN-teh)
hostess / steward

il nastro trasportatore (trahs-pohr-tah-TOH-reh)
conveyor/moving belt

la dogana (doh-GAH-nah)
customs/passport control

il doganiere (doh-gah-NYEH-reh)
customs officer

L'AEREO

(ah-EH-reh-oh)

The Plane

When you reach Italy you wil' land at either the Rome or Milan airport. Domestic flights are available to major cities within Italy.

Read the following words and expressions out loud several times. They might come in handy on an Italian airplane.

(eh-kwee-PAH-jjoh)
l'equipaggio
crew

(oo-SHEE-tah) (see-koo-REH-tsah)
l'uscita di sicurezza
emergency exit

(scohm-pahr-tee-MEHN-toh) (foo-mah-TOH-ree)
lo scompartimento per fumatori
smoking section

lo scompartimento per non-fumatori
no-smoking section

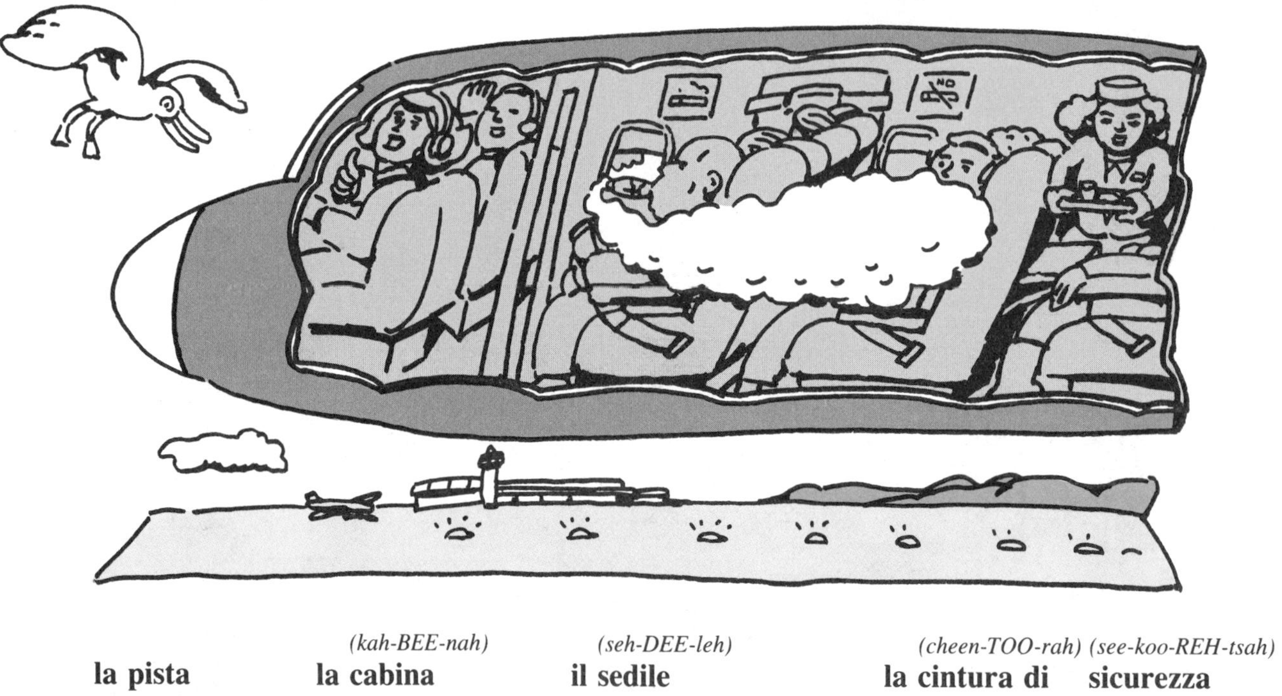

la pista
runway

(kah-BEE-nah)
la cabina
cabin

(seh-DEE-leh)
il sedile
seat

(cheen-TOO-rah) (see-koo-REH-tsah)
la cintura di sicurezza
seat belt

il passeggero
passenger

(vah-SSOH-yoh)
il vassoio
tray

There are certain words and expressions in this dialogue that you might hear or need on a plane. Read each line out loud several times and act out each part.

ASSISTENTE	**La carta d'imbarco** *(eem-BAHR-koh)*, **per favore.**	Boarding pass, please.
MARK	**Eccola.** *(EH-kkoh-lah)*	Here it is.

(The Smiths take their seats on the plane.)

PILOTA	**Il decollo** *(deh-KOH-lloh)* **è previsto tra qualche** *(KWAHL-keh)* **minuto.** *(mee-NOO-toh)* **I passeggeri sono pregati** *(preh-GAH-tee)* **di**	The takeoff is expected in a few minutes. All passengers are requested to fasten their

(ah-lah-CHAH-reh)
allacciare le cinture di sicurezza e di non fumare. — seat belts and to refrain from smoking.

(pehr-FEH-ttoh)
MARY **Ah, che decollo perfetto! I piloti italiani sono proprio bravi.** — Ah, what a perfect takeoff! Italian pilots are really great.

MARK *(to the hostess)* **Signorina, quando si mangia?** — Miss, when do we eat?

ASSISTENTE **Tra qualche minuto, signore.** — In a few minutes, sir.

MARK **Vorrei un cocktail, per favore.** — I would like a cocktail, please.

(SOO-bee-toh)
ASSISTENTE **Sì, subito.** — Yes, right away.

(An hour later the plane is about to land.)

(ah-tteh-RRAH-jjoh) *(preh-VEES-toh)*
PILOTA **Signore e signori, l'atterraggio è previsto tra qualche minuto.** — Ladies and gentlemen, we will be landing in a few minutes.

(STOH-mah-koh)
MARK **Meno male! Mi fa male lo stomaco.** — Thank goodness! My stomach hurts.

(SOH-lee-toh) (mahn-JAH-toh)
MARY **Come al solito, hai mangiato troppo!** — As usual, you ate too much!

By matching the items in the left column to those in the right column, you will get dialogue lines. Check your answers only after you have attempted to do this exercise from memory.

La carta . . .	è previsto tra qualche minuto.
Il decollo . . .	sono proprio bravi.
I passeggeri . . .	si mangia?
I piloti italiani . . .	hai mangiato troppo!
Signorina, quando . . .	l'atterraggio è previsto tra qualche minuto.
Signore e signori . . .	male lo stomaco.
Mi fa . . .	d'imbarco, per favore.
Come al solito . . .	sono pregati di allacciare le cinture di sicurezza e di non fumare.

This word-search puzzle may be a bit tough! However, all of the words except one are part of the vocabulary you just learned.

customs ______________________ customs officer ______________________

truck ______________________ clock ______________________

seat ______________________ cabin ______________________

crew ______________________ runway ______________________

tray ______________________ window ______________________

q	a	z	w	s	x	e	d	c	r	f	v	t	s	g	b	p	l	m	o	k	n	i
y	h	n	u	j	m	i	d	o	g	a	n	i	e	r	e	q	a	z	w	s	x	e
k	o	l	p	q	a	z	o	w	s	x	e	d	d	c	r	d	c	r	f	v	t	g
g	f	o	r	o	l	o	g	i	o	v	t	g	i	b	y	b	y	h	n	i	k	o
y	h	n	u	j	m	i	a	k	l	p	o	q	l	a	f	q	a	z	w	s	x	e
d	c	a	m	i	o	n	n	r	f	v	r	t	e	q	u	i	p	a	g	g	i	o
g	a	b	y	h	n	u	a	j	m	c	k	o	p	l	s	q	a	z	w	s	x	e
q	b	a	z	w	s	x	e	d	c	r	f	v	y	h	o	n	u	j	m	k	l	o
p	i	s	t	a	q	a	z	w	x	s	e	d	i	l	e	f	v	t	g	b	y	a
h	n	n	u	j	m	i	k	l	v	a	s	s	o	i	o	p	o	q	a	z	w	r
s	a	x	e	d	c	r	f	v	t	g	b	y	h	r	n	i	k	m	l	o	p	l
q	a	z	w	s	x	e	d	f	i	n	e	s	t	r	i	n	o	c	r	f	v	q
t	g	b	y	h	n	u	j	m	q	a	z	w	s	a	x	e	d	r	t	g	b	v

ANSWERS

Word search

dogana doganiere camion orologio sedile cabina equipaggio pista vassoio finestrino

(grah-MMAH-tee-kah)

Un po' di grammatica

Some Grammar

As with English, knowing how to say "me, him, her," and so on, is essential in Italian. These words are called direct object pronouns. Study the following examples.

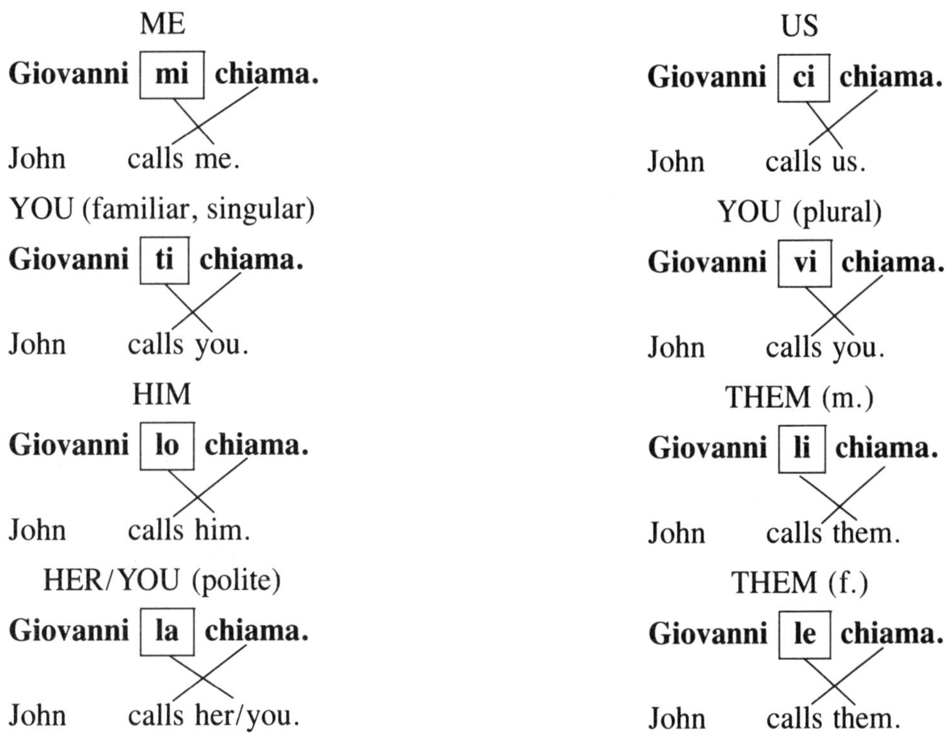

ME
Giovanni mi chiama.
John calls me.
YOU (familiar, singular)
Giovanni ti chiama.
John calls you.
HIM
Giovanni lo chiama.
John calls him.
HER/YOU (polite)
Giovanni la chiama.
John calls her/you.
US
Giovanni ci chiama.
John calls us.
YOU (plural)
Giovanni vi chiama.
John calls you.
THEM (m.)
Giovanni li chiama.
John calls them.
THEM (f.)
Giovanni le chiama.
John calls them.

Notice that these pronouns are put right before the verb, even in the negative:

Giovanni *non mi* chiama.

The forms **lo, la, li, le** also mean "it" and "them" according to gender.

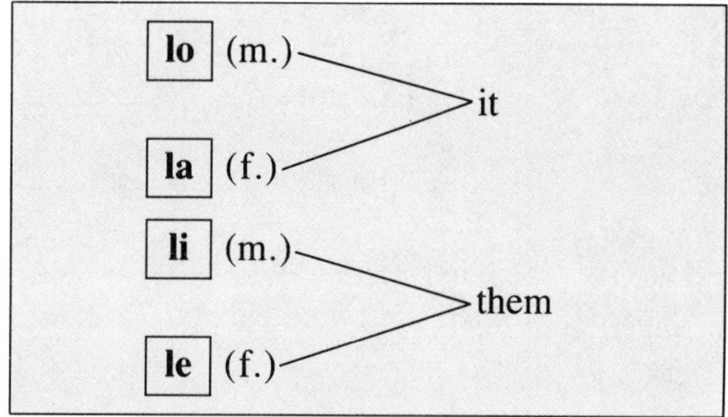

Here are some examples.

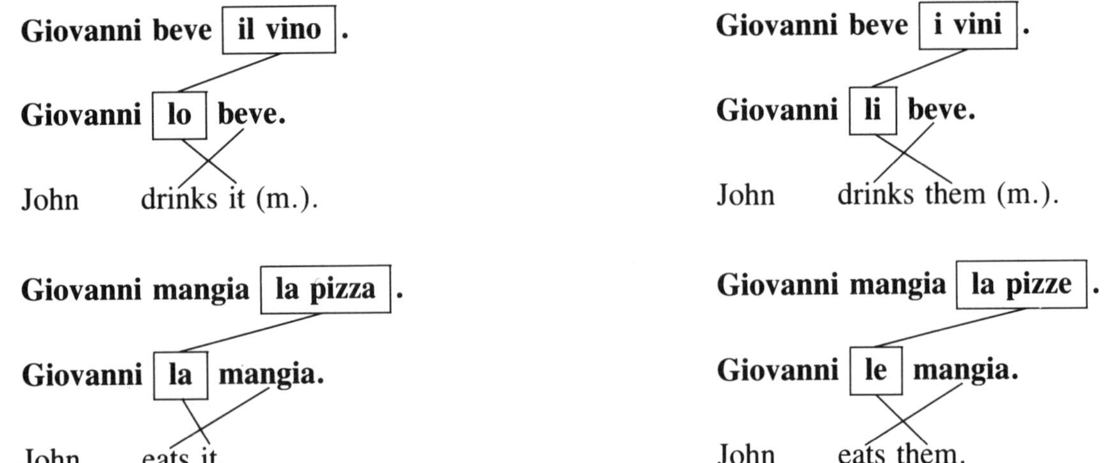

Perhaps a chart will be useful to you if you forget later on.

DIRECT OBJECT PRONOUNS		
mi	me	**S**
ti	you (familiar)	**U**
lo	him, it (m.)	**M**
la	her, you (polite), it (f.)	**M**
ci	us	**A**
vi	you (plural)	**R**
li	them (m.)	**Y**
le	them (f.)	

See if you can select the right pronoun for each blank. **lo, la, li, le ??**

Il signor Smith chiama *la signorina*. Il signor Smith ________ chiama.

Maria prende *il vino rosso*. Maria ________ prende.

La ragazza compra *la penna*. La ragazza ________ compra.

La ragazza compra *le penne*. La ragazza ________ compra.

Giovanni chiama *la sua amica*. Giovanni ________ chiama.

ANSWERS

Pronouns la (chiama.) lo (prende.) la (compra.) le (compra.) la (chiama.)

The answers to the following questions are scrambled. Try to rearrange the words so they make sense. If you have forgotten the meaning of some of the words, look for them in the glossary.

Chiede il passaporto il doganiere? ____________________
passaporto / il / doganiere / il / chiede / Sì

Porta la pizza, l'assistente di volo? ____________________
la / Sì / l'assistente / porta

Compra gli stivali, il ragazzo? ____________________
No / non / ragazzo / il / compra / li

Chi ha la carta d'imbarco? ____________________
signor / Smith / Il / ha / la

Chi ci chiama? ____________________
vi / chiama / Giovanni

(chee-TTAH)

IN CITTÀ

On the Town

Of course, you will want to do some sightseeing on your trip, and the following passage contains some useful information. Read it carefully and then select the appropriate answers to the questions.

(PREE-mah)
La famiglia Smith è a Firenze. Prima vanno a vedere la Piazza del Duomo. Hanno una
First

(foh-toh-GRAH-fee-kah) (foh-toh-grah-FEE-eh) (pah-LAH-tsoh)(VEH-kkyoh)
macchina fotografica e fanno molte fotografie. Poi vanno a vedere il Palazzo Vecchio.
camera photos

(kahr-toh-LEE-neh)(ree-KOHR-dee) (moh-noo-MEHN-tee)
Comprano molte cartoline e ricordi. Vanno a vedere tanti monumenti e
postcards souvenirs monuments

(eh-dee-FEE-chee)(fah-MOH-see) (neh-cheh-SSAH-ree-oh)
edifici famosi. Per andare in giro è necessario camminare molto.
buildings famous around necessary

Dov'è la famiglia Smith?

- ☐ È a Roma.
- ☐ È a Venezia.
- ☐ È a Firenze.

Dove vanno prima?

- ☐ Vanno a vedere la Piazza del Duomo.
- ☐ Vanno a vedere il Vaticano.
- ☐ Vanno a vedere un edificio famoso.

ANSWERS

Comprehension È a Firenze. Vanno a vedere la Piazza del Duomo.

Sentences Sì, il doganiere chiede il passaporto. Sì, l'assistente la porta. No, il ragazzo non li compra. Il signor Smith la ha. Giovanni vi chiama.

Con che fanno molte fotografie?

- ☐ Con un'aereo.
- ☐ Con un vassoio.
- ☐ Con una macchina fotografica.

Che cosa comprano?

- ☐ Comprano molti edifici.
- ☐ Comprano molte cartoline e ricordi.
- ☐ Comprano molti monumenti.

Che cosa vanno a vedere?

- ☐ Tanti monumenti e edifici famosi.
- ☐ La pista dell'aeroporto.
- ☐ La città di Firenze.

Per andare in giro, che cosa è necessario fare?

- ☐ È necessario bere tanto vino.
- ☐ È necessario mangiare la pizza.
- ☐ È necessario camminare.

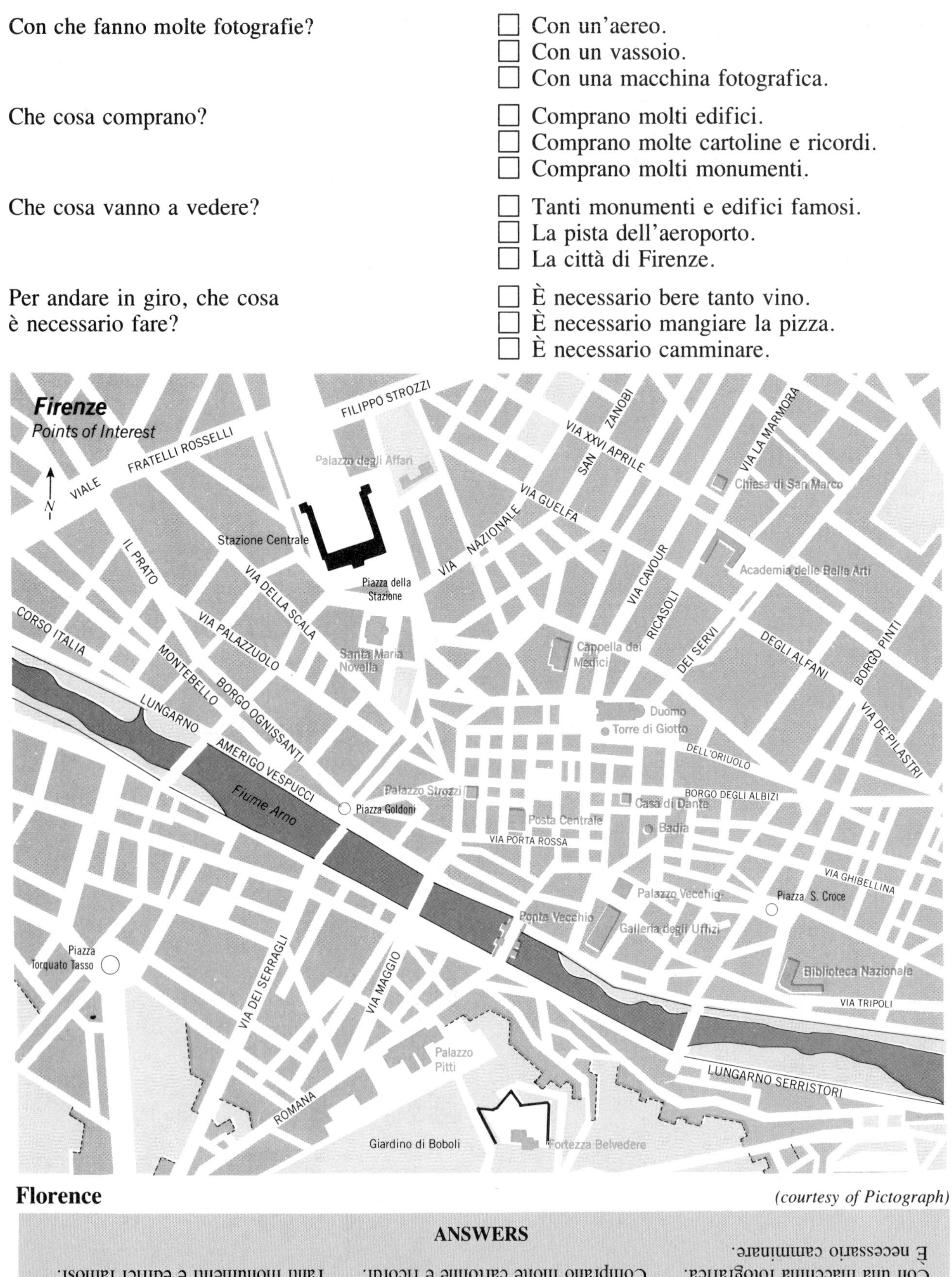

Florence *(courtesy of Pictograph)*

ANSWERS

Con una macchina fotografica. Comprano molte cartoline e ricordi. Tanti monumenti e edifici famosi. È necessario camminare.

ENTERTAINMENT

(dee-vehr-tee-MEHN-tee)
I Divertimenti

12 Il teatro / Il cinema / Le feste

(teh-AH-troh) (CHEE-nee-mah) (FEH-steh)

Theater / Movies / Holidays

AL TEATRO

At the Theater

Surely you will want to attend the opera during your stay in Italy. Read the Smith's dialogue aloud several times, until you can reconstruct it without looking back.

MARK	**Dove andiamo stasera?**	Where are we going tonight?
MARY	*(see-KOO-rah) (DRAH-mmah)* **Non sono sicura. C'è un dramma** *(een-teh-reh-SSAHN-teh)* **molto interessante di Pirandello al teatro.**	I'm not sure. There is a very interesting drama/play by Pirandello at the theater.
MARK	*(PYAH-cheh)* **Il teatro non mi piace.**	I don't like the theater.
MARY	*(OH-peh-rah)* **Allora andiamo all'opera. Stasera c'è *La Traviata* di Verdi. Che** *(MOO-zee-kah) (meh-loh-DEE-eh)* **musica! Che melodie!**	Then let's go to the opera. Tonight there's *La Traviata* by Verdi. What music! What melodies!

MARK **Che noia!** *(NOH-yah)* — What a bore!

MARY **Mark, se non mi porti all'opera, domani non vengo con te al cinema, così non puoi vedere la tua attrice preferita, Sofia Loren.** *(ah-TTREE-cheh) (preh-feh-REE-tah)* — Mark, if you do not take me to the opera, I won't come with you tomorrow to the movies, so you can't see your favorite actress, Sophia Loren.

MARK **Va bene, tesoro! Ma se comincio a russare non ti arrabbiare.** *(teh-SOH-roh) (koh-MEEN-choh) (roo-SSAH-reh) (ah-rrah-BBYAH-reh)* — Okay dear! But if I start to snore don't get angry.

MARY **Va bene. Sbrighiamoci! Sono già le sette e mezzo e lo spettacolo comincia alle otto.** *(zbree-GYAH-moh-chee) (speh-TTAH-koh-loh)* — Okay. Let's hurry up! It's already 7:30 and the show begins at 8:00.

MARK **Sofia, mia bella Sofia, a domani!** — Sophia, my beautiful Sophia, until tomorrow!

See how similar to English these words are.

il dramma
drama

la melodia
melody

il teatro
theater

Now try to complete Mary's part of the dialogue.

MARK **Dove andiamo stasera?**

MARY **Non** ____________________. **C'è** ____________________

____.

MARK **Il teatro non mi piace.**

MARY **Allora** ____.

ENTERTAINMENT

(dee-vehr-tee-MEHN-tee)
I Divertimenti

12	*(teh-AH-troh)* **Il teatro** / *(CHEE-nee-mah)* **Il cinema** / *(FEH-steh)* **Le feste** Theater / Movies / Holidays

AL TEATRO

At the Theater

Surely you will want to attend the opera during your stay in Italy. Read the Smith's dialogue aloud several times, until you can reconstruct it without looking back.

MARK **Dove andiamo stasera?** — Where are we going tonight?

MARY **Non sono sicura.** *(see-KOO-rah)* **C'è un dramma** *(DRAH-mmah)* **molto interessante** *(een-teh-reh-SSAHN-teh)* **di Pirandello al teatro.** — I'm not sure. There is a very interesting drama/play by Pirandello at the theater.

MARK **Il teatro non mi piace.** *(PYAH-cheh)* — I don't like the theater.

MARY **Allora andiamo all'opera.** *(OH-peh-rah)* **Stasera c'è *La Traviata* di Verdi. Che musica!** *(MOO-zee-kah)* **Che melodie!** *(meh-loh-DEE-eh)* — Then let's go to the opera. Tonight there's *La Traviata* by Verdi. What music! What melodies!

MARK	*(NOH-yah)* **Che noia!**	What a bore!
MARY	**Mark, se non mi porti all'opera, domani non vengo con te al cinema, così non puoi vedere la tua** *(ah-TTREE-cheh)* **attrice** *(preh-feh-REE-tah)* **preferita, Sofia Loren.**	Mark, if you do not take me to the opera, I won't come with you tomorrow to the movies, so you can't see your favorite actress, Sophia Loren.
MARK	**Va bene,** *(teh-SOH-roh)* **tesoro! Ma se** *(koh-MEEN-choh)* **comincio a** *(roo-SSAH-reh)* **russare non ti** *(ah-rrah-BBYAH-reh)* **arrabbiare.**	Okay dear! But if I start to snore don't get angry.
MARY	**Va bene.** *(zbree-GYAH-moh-chee)* **Sbrighiamoci! Sono già le sette e mezzo e lo** *(speh-TTAH-koh-loh)* **spettacolo comincia alle otto.**	Okay. Let's hurry up! It's already 7:30 and the show begins at 8:00.
MARK	**Sofia, mia bella Sofia, a domani!**	Sophia, my beautiful Sophia, until tomorrow!

See how similar to English these words are.

il dramma
drama

la melodia
melody

il teatro
theater

Now try to complete Mary's part of the dialogue.

MARK **Dove andiamo stasera?**

MARY **Non** ______________________. **C'è** ______________________

____.

MARK **Il teatro non mi piace.**

MARY **Allora** ______________________________________.

Stasera ______________________________. **Che** ______________!

Che ____________________!

MARK **Che noia!**

MARY **Mark, se non mi** ______________, **domani non** ____________________

________________, **così non puoi vedere** ____________________.

MARK **Va bene, tesoro! Ma se comincio a russare non ti arrabbiare.**

MARY **Va** ______________. **Sbrighiamoci! Sono** ____________________.

e lo ____.

MARK **Sofia, mia bella Sofia, a domani!**

(ree-KOHR-dah-tee)

Ricordati

Remember

Do you recall how to say "I would like"? This is a very useful expression that you will use frequently.

(johr-NAH-leh)
***Vorrei* un giornale.**
newspaper

You continue.

(MEH-tsoh)
______________ **essere nel mezzo.**
in the middle

______________ **il formaggio.**

(pah-rroo-KKYEH-reh)
______________ **andare dal parrucchiere.**
to the hairdresser's

Mi dai i soldi?

Will You Give the Money to Me?

In the previous unit you learned about direct object pronouns. You will also need to know the usage for "to me, to him, to her," and the like. These are called indirect object pronouns. These four are exactly the same as the direct object pronouns.

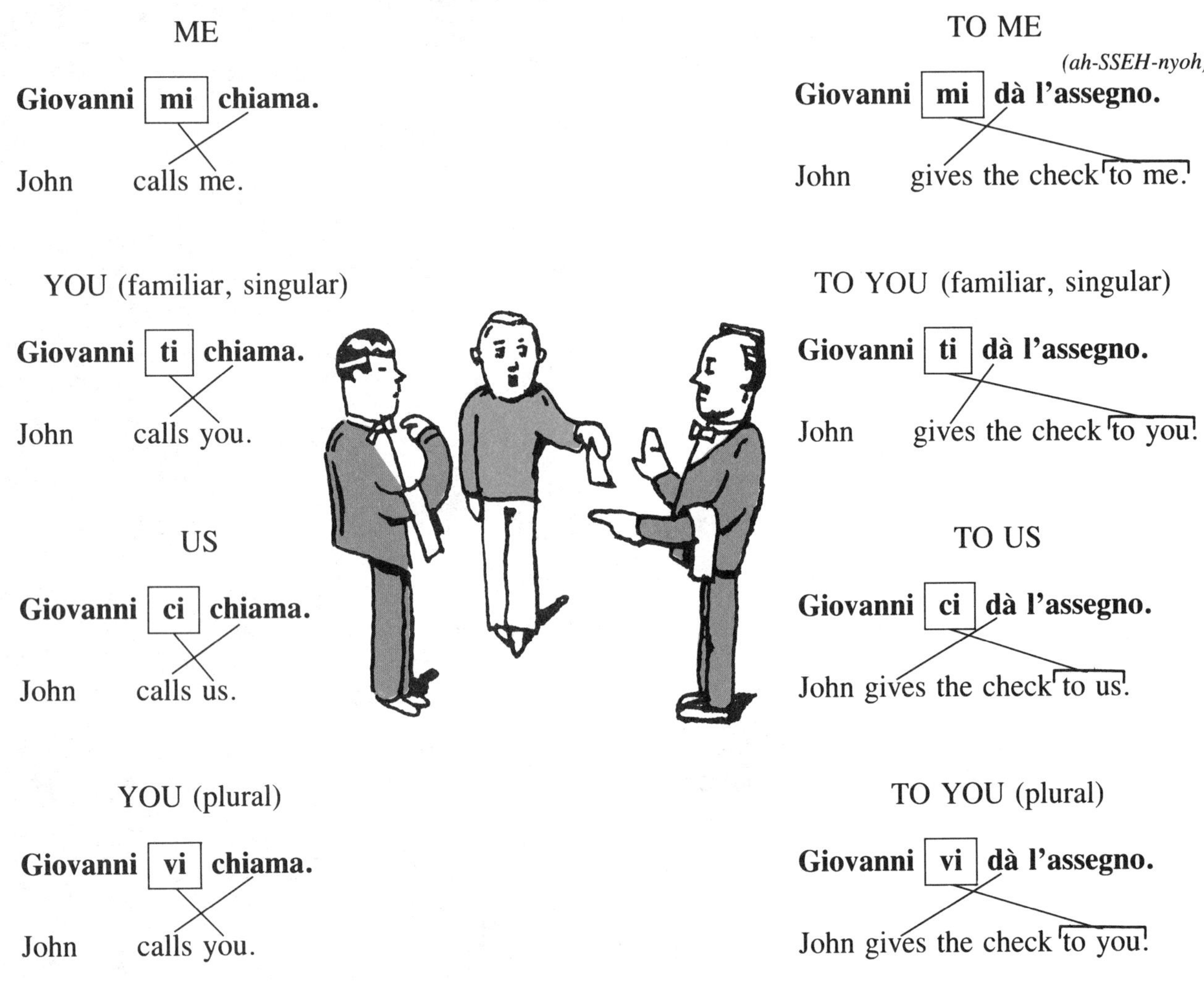

ME
Giovanni mi chiama.
John calls me.
TO ME
(ah-SSEH-nyoh)
Giovanni mi dà l'assegno.
John gives the check to me.
YOU (familiar, singular)
Giovanni ti chiama.
John calls you.
TO YOU (familiar, singular)
Giovanni ti dà l'assegno.
John gives the check to you.
US
Giovanni ci chiama.
John calls us.
TO US
Giovanni ci dà l'assegno.
John gives the check to us.
YOU (plural)
Giovanni vi chiama.
John calls you.
TO YOU (plural)
Giovanni vi dà l'assegno.
John gives the check to you.

This can be summarized in chart form.

		SUMMARY
mi	________ me, to me	
ti	________ you, to you (familiar, singular)	
ci	________ us, to us	
vi	________ you, to you (plural)	

Don't forget to keep these pronouns right before the verb, even in the negative.

Giovanni *non mi* chiama.
Giovanni *non mi* dà la penna.

These examples show how to say "to him, to her, to you (polite, singular), to them."

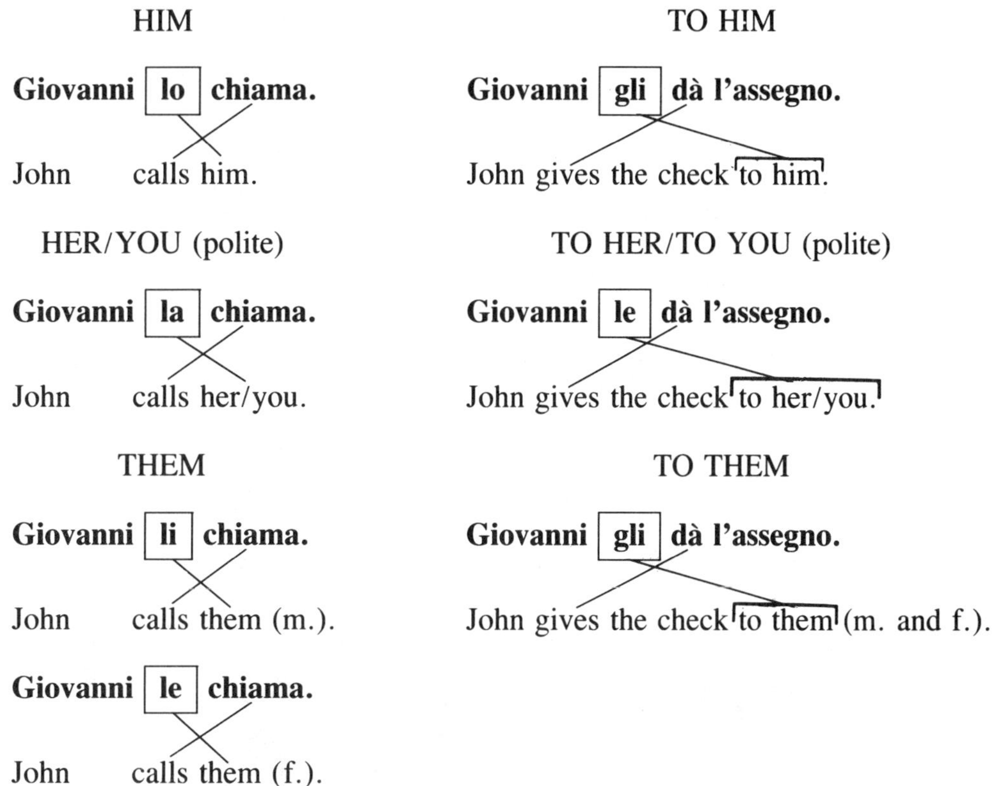

HIM
Giovanni lo chiama.
John calls him.
TO HIM
Giovanni gli dà l'assegno.
John gives the check to him.
HER/YOU (polite)
Giovanni la chiama.
John calls her/you.
TO HER/TO YOU (polite)
Giovanni le dà l'assegno.
John gives the check to her/you.
THEM
Giovanni li chiama.
John calls them (m.).
Giovanni le chiama.
John calls them (f.).
TO THEM
Giovanni gli dà l'assegno.
John gives the check to them (m. and f.).

Notice that there is only one form for "to them," although there is a more formal pronoun for "to them" that does not concern us here. *Gli* is the most commonly used one in spoken Italian. A summary of these pronouns might be helpful.

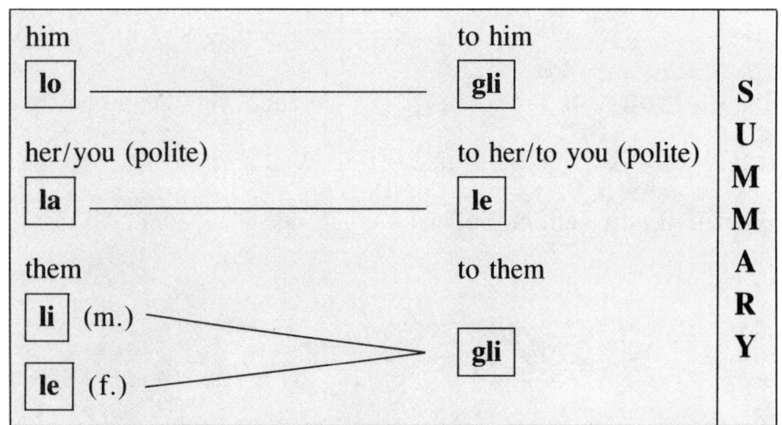

him
lo
to him
gli
her/you (polite)
la
to her/to you (polite)
le
them
li (m.)
le (f.)
to them
gli
SUMMARY

If you have studied these pronouns well, you should have no trouble inserting the proper one in each of the following blanks.

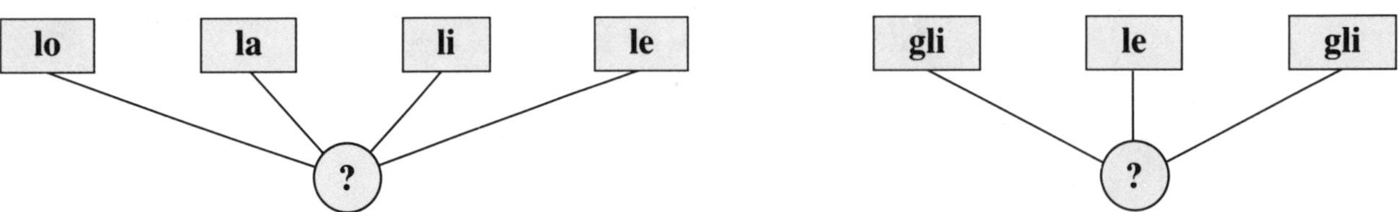

Il turista compra *l'orologio*. Il turista _______________ compra.

Il turista compra *gli orologi*. Il turista _______________ compra.

Il turista dà l'orologio *a suo figlio*. Il turista _______________ dà l'orologio.

Il turista dà l'orologio *a sua figlia*. Il turista _______________ dà l'orologio.

Il turista compra *la cartolina*. Il turista _______________ compra.

Il turista compra *le cartoline*. Il turista _______________ compra.

Il turista dà la cartolina *ai suoi amici*. Il turista _______________ dà la cartolina.

Il turista dà la cartolina *alle sue amiche*. Il turista _______________ dà la cartolina.

AL CINEMA
At the Movies

(Mark and Mary are at the movies the day after having gone to the opera.)

MARK	*(feelm)* **Che bel film! E come è bella Sofia Loren!**	What a beautiful film! And is Sophia Loren ever beautiful!
MARY	*(SEHN-tsah)(soh-ttoh-TEE-toh-lee)* **Senza i sottotitoli non capisco niente.**	Without subtitles I can't understand anything.
MARK	**Non importa. Basta vedere Sofia.**	It doesn't matter. All that's important is to see Sophia.

ANSWERS

Pronouns lo (compra.) li (compra.) gli (dà l'orologio.) le (dà l'orologio.) la (compra.) le (compra.) gli (dà la) gli (dà la)

MARY	**Andiamo via.** *(VEE-ah)* **Non mi piace sedermi nella prima fila.** *(FEE-lah)*	Let's go. I don't like to sit in the first row.
MARK	**Ma il cinema è pieno di gente.** *(PYEH-noh)*	But the movie theater is full of people.
MARY	**Io esco!** *(EHS-koh)*	I'm leaving (I'm going out)!
MARK	**Va bene. Tuo marito ti segue.** *(SEH-gweh)*	Okay. Your husband will follow (*literally:* is following you).

Read the dialogue several times and then try to complete the missing parts. Check your answers after you have attempted to do so from memory.

Che bel f______________! E come è b______________ Sofia Loren!

S______________ i s______________ non capisco niente.

Non i______________. B______________ vedere Sofia.

Andiamo via. Non mi p______________ sedermi nella prima f______________.

Ma il cinema è p______________ di gente. Io e______________!

Va bene. Tuo m______________ ti segue.

Here are two more verbs that you will use often.

(oo-SHEE-reh)
USCIRE
to go out

io	________	**esco** *(EHS-koh)*	**noi**	________	**usciamo** *(oo-SHAH-moh)*
tu	________	**esci** *(EH-shee)*	**voi**	________	**uscite** *(oo-SHEE-teh)*
lui / lei	________	**esce** *(EH-sheh)*	**loro**	________	**escono** *(EHS-koh-noh)*

Now fill in each blank with the correct form of *uscire*.

La signora Smith ______________ alle sei.

La moglie e il marito ______________ insieme.

Io non ______________ mai.

Tu ______________ con Maria.

Noi ______________ **insieme** *(een-SYEH-meh)* (together) per andare al cinema.

Voi non ______________ mai insieme.

ANSWERS

Verbs (to go out) esce (alle sei.) escono (insieme.) esco (mai.) esci (con Maria.) usciamo (insieme) uscite (mai insieme.)

PIACERE to like			
io	*(PYAH-choh)* **piaccio**	noi	*(pyah-CHAH-moh)* **piacciamo**
tu	*(PYAH-chee)* **piaci**	voi	*(pyah-CHEH-teh)* **piacete**
lui / lei	*(PYAH-cheh)* **piace**	loro	*(PYAH-choh-noh)* **piacciono**

This is a troublesome verb. In order to say "I like, you like," and so on, you must say "to be pleasing to."

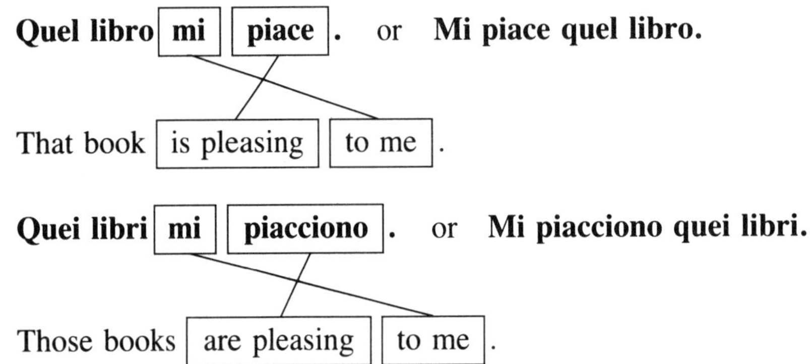

Quel libro mi piace. or **Mi piace quel libro.**
That book is pleasing to me.
Quei libri mi piacciono. or **Mi piacciono quei libri.**
Those books are pleasing to me.

Using the chart and the examples above, try to complete these sentences.

I like Mary. Mary is pleasing to me. **Mi** ______________ **Maria**.

Mary likes me. I am pleasing to Mary. **Io** ______________ **a Maria**.

We like the film. The film is pleasing to us. **Ci** ______________ **il film**.

They like the films. The films are pleasing to them. **Gli** ______________ **i film**.

I like the film. The film is pleasing to me. **Mi** ______________ **il film**.

I don't like the films. The films are not pleasing to me. **Non mi** ______________ **i film**.

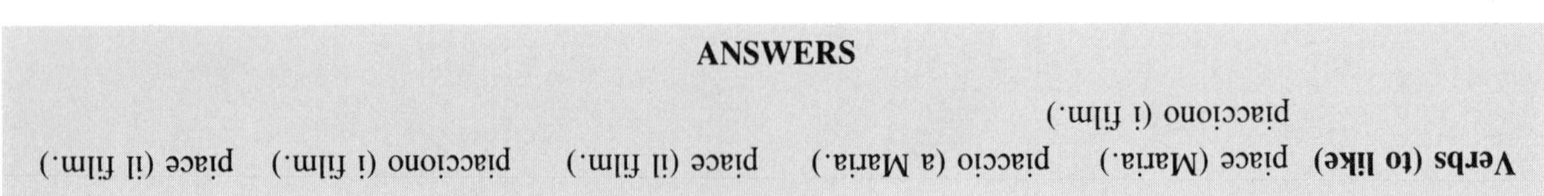
ANSWERS

Verbs (to like) piace (Maria.) piaccio (a Maria.) piace (il film.) piacciono (i film.) piace (il film.) piacciono (i film.)

LE FESTE

Holidays

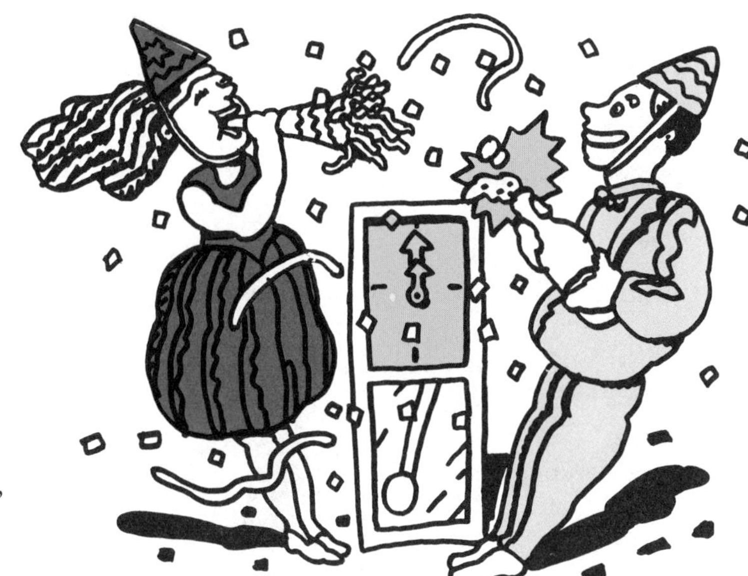

Of course, you will want to join in the festivities, if you are in Italy during a holiday. Read this passage, and then answer the questions that follow.

La prima festa dell'anno è il capodanno. *(kah-poh-DAH-nnoh)* capodanno = New Year's

Poi c'è l'Epifania *(eh-pee-fah-NEE-ah)* Epifania = Epiphany

il sei gennaio. Poi a primavera c'è la Pasqua. *(PAHS-kwah)* Pasqua = Easter

Il quindici agosto c'è il Ferragosto. È una festa particolare in Italia. *(fehr-ah-GOHS-toh)* Ferragosto = Assumption; *(pahr-tee-koh-LAH-reh)* particolare = particular

Naturalmente il venticinque dicembre

c'è il Natale. *(nah-TAH-leh)*

In italiano si dice «Buone feste!»

1. Qual è la prima festa dell'anno?
- ☐ Pasqua.
- ☐ Ferragosto.
- ☐ Capodanno.

2. Che festa c'è il sei gennaio?
- ☐ Ferragosto.
- ☐ Capodanno.
- ☐ Epifania.

3. Che festa c'è in primavera?
- ☐ Pasqua
- ☐ Natale.
- ☐ Ferragosto.

4. Che festa c'é il quindici agosto?
- ☐ Pasqua.
- ☐ Ferragosto.
- ☐ Natale.

5. Che festa c'è il venticinque dicembre?
- ☐ Pasqua.
- ☐ Capodanno..
- ☐ Natale.

6. Che vuol dire «Buone feste»?
- ☐ Hello.
- ☐ Good-bye.
- ☐ Happy holidays.

Let's finish this chapter with an easy one; fill in the blanks with the following words.

birra (beer), **albero, dorme, zia, bandiera** (*bahn-DYEH-rah*) (flag), **biglietti, fila**

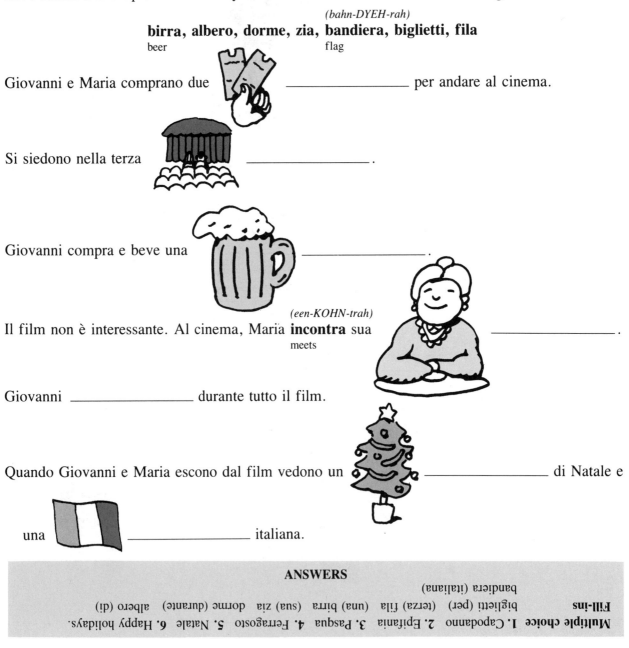

Giovanni e Maria comprano due ______________ per andare al cinema.

Si siedono nella terza ______________.

Giovanni compra e beve una ______________.

Il film non è interessante. Al cinema, Maria **incontra** (*een-KOHN-trah*) (meets) sua ______________.

Giovanni ______________ durante tutto il film.

Quando Giovanni e Maria escono dal film vedono un ______________ di Natale e una ______________ italiana.

ANSWERS

Multiple choice **1.** Capodanno **2.** Epifania **3.** Pasqua **4.** Ferragosto **5.** Natale **6.** Happy holidays.

Fill-ins biglietti (per) (terza) fila (una) birra (sua) zia dorme (durante) albero (di) bandiera (italiana)

13 Gli sport
Sports

ESCURSIONI A PIEDI E IL JOGGING
Hiking and Jogging

(Mark Smith is in great physical condition. He jogs every morning. This morning he is approached by a journalist who is writing an article on sports.)

GIORNALISTA **Buon giorno, signore. Sono un giornalista. Le posso fare alcune domande?**
(johr-nah-LEES-tah) *(ahl-KOO-neh)* *(doh-MAHN-deh)*

Good morning, sir. I am a journalist. Can I ask you some questions?

MARK **Certo. Ma parli lentamente. Sono americano e non capisco tutto.**

Certainly. But speak slowly. I am an American and I don't understand everything.

GIORNALISTA **Lei fa spesso il jogging?**
(SPEH-ssoh)

Do you jog often?

MARK **Sì. Ogni mattina.**
(OH-nyee)

Yes. Every morning.

Incontro sempre un gruppo di turisti che fanno il jogging con me.

I always meet a group of tourists who jog along with me.

Sembrano turisti spagnoli.

They look like Spanish tourists.

(spohr-TEE-veh)
Portano tute sportive
(SKAHR-peh) (KOHR-sah)
e scarpe da corsa.

They wear sweatshirts and running shoes.

GIORNALISTA **Le piacciono altri sport?**

Do you like any other sports?

(neh-AHN-keh) (KAHL-choh)
MARK **No, neanche il calcio.**

No, not even soccer.

(They run into a group of hikers.)

GIORNALISTA **Questi signori hanno un**
(TSAH-ee-noh)
sacco a pelo, uno zaino,
degli utensili da cucina e
(beh-ttoh-LEE-noh)
un bettolino.

These people have a sleeping bag, a backpack, cooking utensils and a canteen.

MARK **Lo so. Sono due giorni che sono qui. Credo che siano turisti francesi.**

I know. They have been here for two days. I think they are French tourists.

GIORNALISTA **Come lo sa?**

How do you know?

(SEE-mee-leh)
MARK **Parlano una lingua molto simile all'italiano.**

They speak a language very similar to Italian.

(The journalist speaks to the hikers and then catches up to Mark.)

(ZBAH-llyah)
GIORNALISTA **Lei si sbaglia, signore. Quei signori sono italiani ma parlano un**
(dyah-LEH-ttoh)
dialetto italiano simile al francese.

You're wrong, sir. They are Italians who speak a dialect similar to French.

MARK **Non li comprendo.**

I don't understand them.

After reading the dialogue over several times, indicate if each of the following is true or false.

1. Il gruppo di turisti fa alcune domande a Mark. ☐ Vero (True) ☐ Falso (False)

2. Mark è americano e non capisce tutto. ☐ Vero ☐ Falso

3. Mark non fa mai il jogging. ☐ Vero ☐ Falso

4. Ogni mattina Mark incontra un gruppo di turisti che fanno il jogging con lui. ☐ Vero ☐ Falso

5. I turisti portano tute sportive e scarpe da corsa. ☐ Vero ☐ Falso

6. A Mark piacciono molti sport. ☐ Vero ☐ Falso

7. I signori che incontrano hanno un sacco a pelo, uno zaino, degli utensili da cucina e un bettolino. ☐ Vero ☐ Falso

8. Quei signori parlano francese. ☐ Vero ☐ Falso

9. Mark vuole parlare ancora. ☐ Vero ☐ Falso

Are you ready for a hiking trip now? Let's see if you can identify this gear.

Che cosa è? È una ________________.

Che cosa è? È un ________________.

Che cosa è? È uno ________________.

Che sono? Sono degli ________________.

Che cosa è? È un ________________.

ANSWERS

True/False

1. Falso **3.** Falso **5.** Vero **7.** Vero **9.** Falso

2. Vero **4.** Vero **6.** Falso **8.** Falso

Identification tuta sportiva sacco a pelo zaino utensili da cucina bettolino

Ricordati

Remember

Nouns like *sport, film,* and *jogging* are all borrowed from English. The singular and plural forms are identical for these nouns.

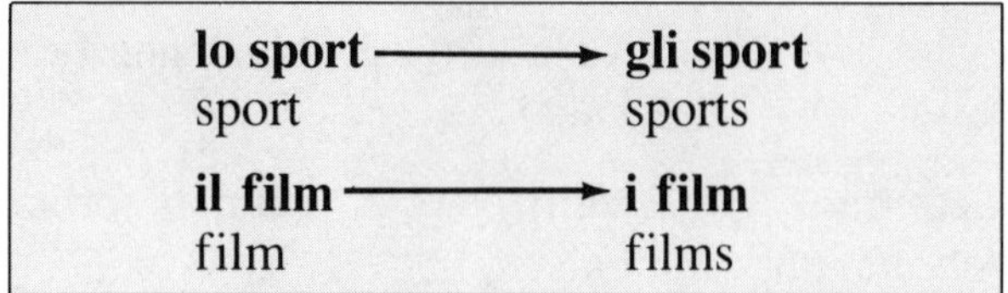

lo sport → **gli sport**
sport — sports

il film → **i film**
film — films

In the first few units you learned about the pronouns "I, you, he, she," and so forth. The pronouns **lui, lei, noi, voi, loro** can also be used as object pronouns.

John calls him.	**Giovanni [lo] chiama.**	*or*	**Giovanni chiama [lui].**
John calls her.	**Giovanni [la] chiama.**	*or*	**Giovanni chiama [lei].**

Instead of **io** the form **me** is used; and instead of **tu** the form **te** is used.

John calls me.	**Giovanni [mi] chiama.**	*or*	**Giovanni chiama [me].**
John calls you.	**Giovanni [ti] chiama.**	*or*	**Giovanni chiama [te].**

Notice that these pronouns come after the verb as in English.

Before the Verb	*After the Verb*
mi	**me**
ti	**te**
lo	**lui**
la	**lei**
ci	**noi**
vi	**voi**
li	**loro**
le	**loro**

The type used *after* verbs is also the *only* one used after prepositions.

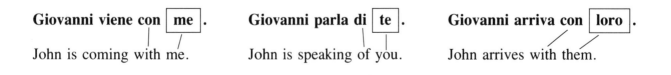

Giovanni viene con [me].	**Giovanni parla di [te].**	**Giovanni arriva con [loro].**
John is coming with me.	John is speaking of you.	John arrives with them.

See if you can replace each pronoun with an equivalent form. Don't get discouraged. These take a while to learn.

1. Il signor Smith *mi* chiama. Il signor Smith chiama ____________.

2. La signora Smith chiama *te*. La signora Smith ____________ chiama.

3. Io *lo* chiamo. Io chiamo ____________.

4. Il giornalista chiama *lei*. Il giornalista ____________ chiama.

5. Il passeggero *ci* chiama. Il passeggero chiama ____________.

6. Il passeggero chiama *voi*. Il passeggero ____________ chiama.

7. L'autista *li* chiama. L'autista chiama ____________.

8. L'autista *le* chiama. L'autista chiama ____________.

(chee-KLEEZ-moh) (NWOH-toh)

IL CICLISMO E IL NUOTO

Bicycling and Swimming

As you learn these words relating to cycling and swimming, you'll see some vocabulary patterns emerging that will help in recalling them.

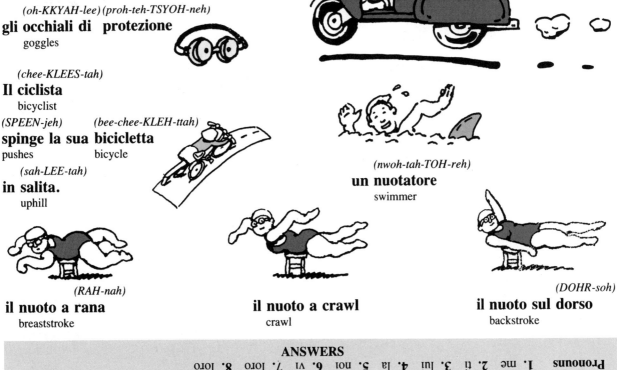

(oh-KKYAH-lee) (proh-teh-TSYOH-neh)
gli occhiali di protezione
goggles

(chee-KLEES-tah)
Il ciclista
bicyclist

(SPEEN-jeh) (bee-chee-KLEH-ttah)
spinge la sua bicicletta
pushes bicycle

(sah-LEE-tah)
in salita.
uphill

(nwoh-tah-TOH-reh)
un nuotatore
swimmer

(RAH-nah)
il nuoto a rana
breaststroke

il nuoto a crawl
crawl

(DOHR-soh)
il nuoto sul dorso
backstroke

ANSWERS

Pronouns **1.** me **2.** ti **3.** lui **4.** la **5.** noi **6.** vi **7.** loro **8.** loro

Add the appropriate word or expression that describes each picture.

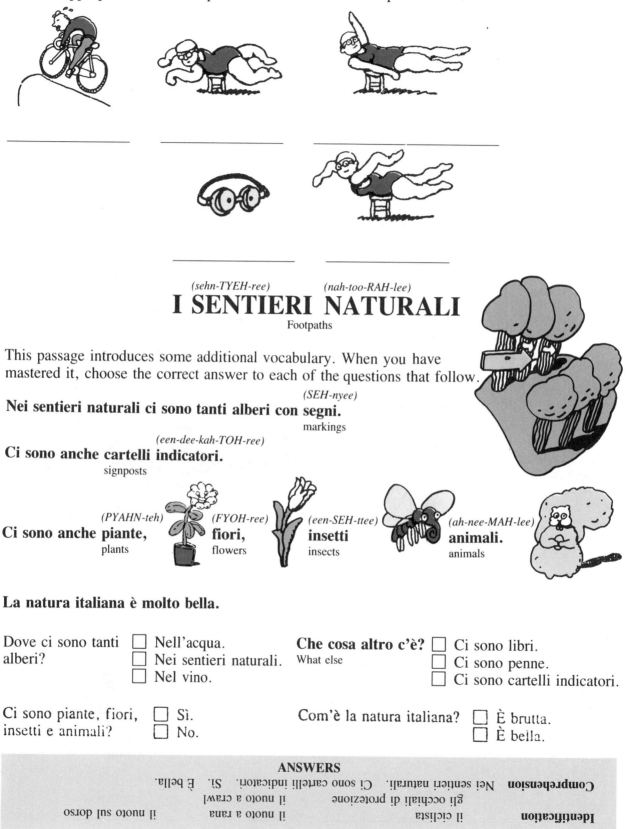

_________________ _________________ _________________

_________________ _________________

I SENTIERI NATURALI
(sehn-TYEH-ree) (nah-too-RAH-lee)

Footpaths

This passage introduces some additional vocabulary. When you have mastered it, choose the correct answer to each of the questions that follow.

Nei sentieri naturali ci sono tanti alberi con segni.
(SEH-nyee) segni = markings

Ci sono anche cartelli indicatori.
(een-dee-kah-TOH-ree) cartelli indicatori = signposts

Ci sono anche piante, *(PYAHN-teh)* plants

fiori, *(FYOH-ree)* flowers

insetti *(een-SEH-ttee)* insects

animali. *(ah-nee-MAH-lee)* animals

La natura italiana è molto bella.

Dove ci sono tanti alberi?
- ☐ Nell'acqua.
- ☐ Nei sentieri naturali.
- ☐ Nel vino.

Che cosa altro c'è? (What else)
- ☐ Ci sono libri.
- ☐ Ci sono penne.
- ☐ Ci sono cartelli indicatori.

Ci sono piante, fiori, insetti e animali?
- ☐ Sì.
- ☐ No.

Com'è la natura italiana?
- ☐ È brutta.
- ☐ È bella.

ANSWERS

Identification il ciclista; il nuoto a rana; il nuoto sul dorso; gli occhiali di protezione; il nuoto a crawl

Comprehension Nei sentieri naturali. Ci sono cartelli indicatori. Sì. È bella.

ORDERING FOOD

(ohr-dee-NYAH-moh) *(mahn-JAH-reh)*
Ordiniamo da mangiare

14 I pasti /I cibi

(PAHS-tee) *(CHEE-bee)*
Meals/Food

Che cosa dire quando ti *piace* qualcosa

What to Say When You *Like* Something

That troublesome verb *piacere* that you learned about in chapter 12 is used when talking about the things you may or may not like to eat.

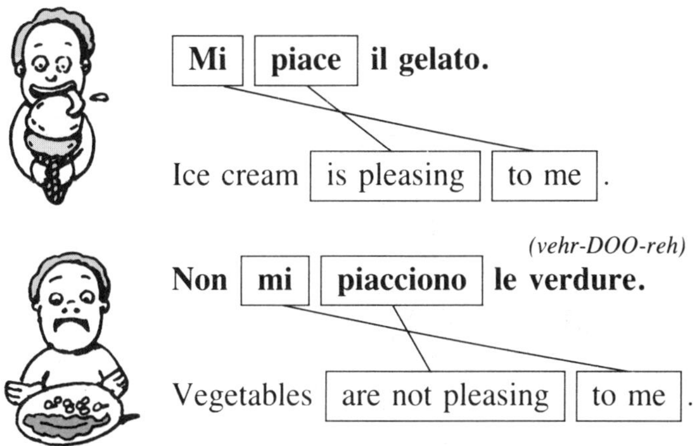

Mi piace il gelato.
Ice cream is pleasing to me.
(vehr-DOO-reh)
Non mi piacciono le verdure.
Vegetables are not pleasing to me.

Now choose either *piace* or *piacciono* to complete these sentences.

Mi ________________ le verdure. Non mi ________________ mangiare. Mi ________________ il gelato. Mi ________________ il nuoto. Non mi ________________ andare in bicicletta. Mi ________________ gli sport. Mi ________________ il calcio. Mi ________________ il tennis e il ciclismo.

ANSWERS

Verbs piacciono (le) piace (mangiare.) piace (il) piace (il) piace (andare) piacciono (gli) piace (il)
piacciono (il)

The verb forms are the same, when used with other pronouns.

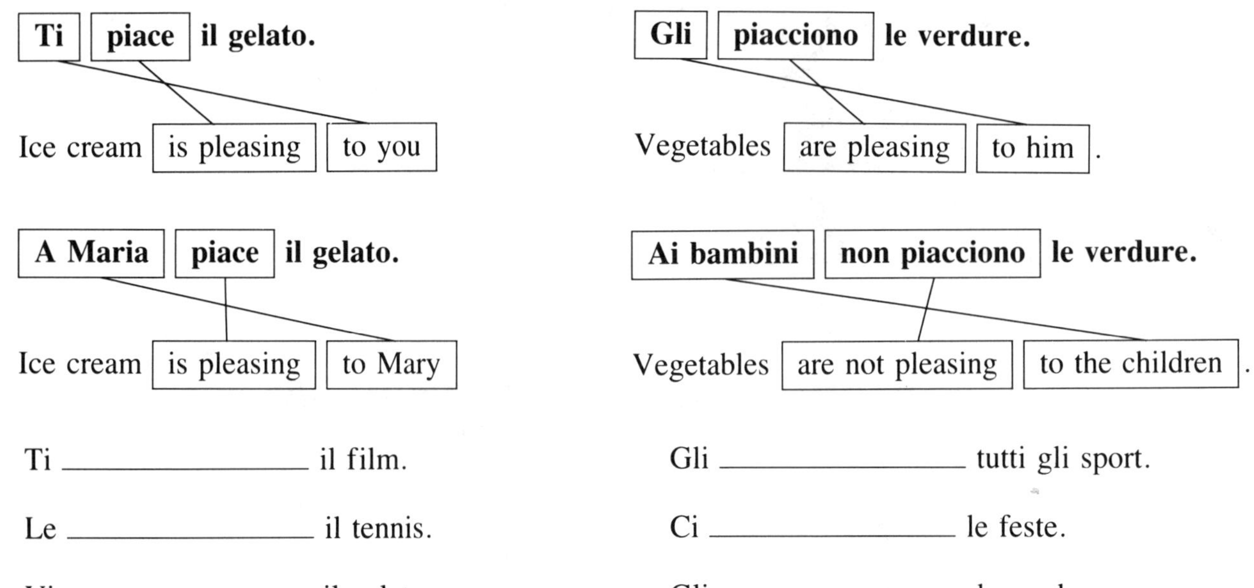

Ti piace il gelato.
Ice cream is pleasing to you
Gli piacciono le verdure.
Vegetables are pleasing to him.
A Maria piace il gelato.
Ice cream is pleasing to Mary
Ai bambini non piacciono le verdure.
Vegetables are not pleasing to the children.

Ti ________________ il film.

Le ________________ il tennis.

Vi ________________ il gelato.

Gli ________________ tutti gli sport.

Ci ________________ le feste.

Gli ________________ le verdure.

Now that we understand *piace* and *piacciono,* let's review nouns.

Notice that nouns ending with an accented vowel do not change in the plural.

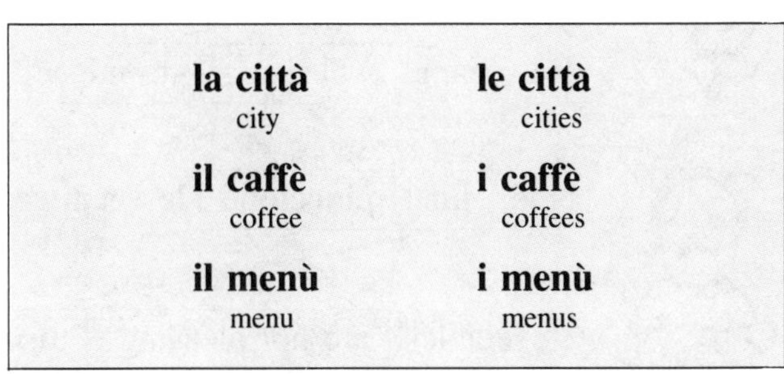

la città city — **le città** cities

il caffè coffee — **i caffè** coffees

il menù menu — **i menù** menus

Nouns ending in **-ista** can be either masculine or feminine.

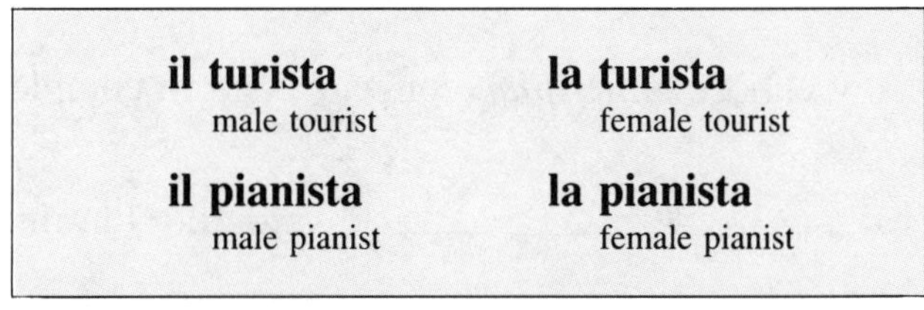

il turista male tourist — **la turista** female tourist

il pianista male pianist — **la pianista** female pianist

Finally, notice this completely irregular noun.

l'uomo man — **gli uomini** *(WOH-mee-nee)* men

ANSWERS

Verbs (Ti) piace (Gli) piacciono (Le) piace (Ci) piacciono (Vi) piace (Gli) piacciono

We want to change these nouns from singular to plural. We've given you the correct article—you add the right noun form.

il gelato → i ____________________, la caramella → le ____________________,

il padre → i ____________________, la madre → le ____________________,

lo sport → gli ____________________, il film → i ____________________,

il caffè → i ____________________, la città → le ____________________,

il menù → i ____________________, l'uomo → gli ____________________.

(koh-lah-TSYOH-neh)

LA (PRIMA) COLAZIONE

Breakfast

(rees-toh-RAHN-teh)
un ristórante
(eh-koh-NOH-mee-koh)
economico

(The Smiths are having breakfast at a local inexpensive restaurant.)

MARK	*(STRAH-noh)* **Che strano! Di solito gli italiani non fanno la prima colazione.**	How strange! Italians normally do not have breakfast.
CAMERIERA	**Buon giorno. Che cosa prendono?**	Good morning. Can I take your orders? (*literally,* what will you take)
MARY	*(TAH-tsah) (kah-ffeh-LLAH-tteh)* **Io vorrei una tazza di caffellate,**	I would like a cup of coffee with milk,

ANSWERS

Nouns gelati caramelle padri madri sport film caffè città menù uomini

(PAH-neh) (tohs-TAH-toh)
il pane tostato con burro — toasted bread with

(mahr-meh-LLAH-tah)
e marmellata, — butter and marmalade,

(bee-KKYEH-reh)
e un bicchiere di — and a glass

(SOO-kkoh)(ah-RAHN-chah)
succo d'arancia. — of orange juice.

MARK **Mamma mia, che fame! Io prendo** — Good grief, what an appetite!

(pah-NEE-noh) (DOHL-cheh)
un panino dolce, un bicchiere di — I'll take a sweet roll,

(poh-moh-DOH-roh)
succo di pomodoro e un — a glass of tomato juice,

(kah-ppoo-CHEE-noh)
cappuccino. — and a cappuccino.

ANNE **Io voglio solo una tazza di tè.** — I only want a cup of tea.

JOHN **E io solo un espresso.** — And I only an espresso coffee.

CAMERIERA **Grazie.** — Thank you.

(The Smiths finish their breakfast.)

(KOHN-toh)
MARK **Cameriera, il conto, per favore.** — Waitress, the bill please!

CAMERIERA **Ecco. Ventimila lire in tutto.** — Here it is. 20,000 lira all together.

(to himself) **Più una mancia.** — Plus a tip.

MARY **Va bene, signorina. Grazie.** — Okay, miss. Thank you.

After you have read the dialogue several times, try to match up the left column with the right one, to get lines from the dialogue. Check your answers.

Di solito gli italiani . . .	una tazza di caffellatte, il pane tostato con burro e marmellata e un bicchiere di succo d'arancia.
Che cosa . . .	una tazza di tè.
Io vorrei . . .	un espresso.
Io voglio solo . . .	non fanno la prima colazione.
E io solo . . .	prendono?
Io prendo . . .	il conto, per favore.
Cameriera, . . .	lire in tutto.
Ventimila . . .	un panino dolce, un bicchiere di succo di pomodoro e un cappuccino.

(TAH-voh-lah)

LA TAVOLA

The Table

When the Smiths dine out, their place settings may look like this one. When you have read and pronounced the vocabulary, try to identify each object without referring to the Italian words.

How many words do you remember? Without looking at the picture, match up the two columns.

1. il coltello	a. wine glass
2. il sale	b. napkin
3. il cucchiaio	c. pepper
4. il bicchiere da vino	d. plate
5. il pepe	e. fork
6. il bicchiere	f. spoon
7. il piatto	g. sugar
8. il piattino	h. cup
9. la forchetta	i. saucer
10. la tazza	j. glass
11. il tovagliolo	k. knife
12. lo zucchero	l. salt

From the following list, choose the appropriate word for each blank.

tazza, bicchiere, forchetta, cucchiaio, cameriere, sale, pepe, zucchero, coltello

Questo panino è molto dolce. C'è molto ________________.

Per mangiare la pizza, ho bisogno di una ________________ e di un ________________.

Ogni mattina io bevo una ________________ di caffè.

(mee-NEHS-trah)
Per mangiare la minestra, ho bisogno di un ________________.
soup

Il ________________ porta il conto.

Questo è un ________________ di acqua.

Mi piace mangiare con tanto ________________ e ________________.

ANSWERS

Matching 1-k, 2-l, 3-f, 4-a, 5-c, 6-j, 7-d, 8-i, 9-e, 10-h, 11-b, 12-g

Fill-ins zucchero forchetta / coltello tazza cucchiaio cameriere bicchiere sale / pepe

(preen-chee-PAH-leh)

IL PASTO PRINCIPALE

The Main Meal

What a feast! But to get a meal like this one, you'll have to learn how to order it.

By filling in the blanks and repeating each sentence several times, you will develop the ability to order the things you want.

Vorrei il ______________________ per antipasto.
(ham and cantaloupe)

Poi, vorrei un ______________________.
(bowl of soup)

Mia moglie/Mio marito prende un ______________________ di spaghetti/ravioli/lasagne.
(plate)

Vorrei anche un piatto di ______________________.
(vegetables)

Poi, vorrei un piatto di ______________________.
(fish)

Mia moglie/Mio marito prende la ______________________.
(roast beef)

Per finire, vorrei ______________________ e il ______________________.
(fruit) (coffee)

Per bere, vorrei una bottiglia di ______________________.
(red wine)

ANSWERS

Ordering Food prosciutto e (il) melone piatto di minestra piatto verdure pesce
carne di manzo la frutta / caffè vino rosso

(CHEH-nah)

LA CENA

The Evening Meal

To conclude the day's dining, read the following passage and then respond to the questions.

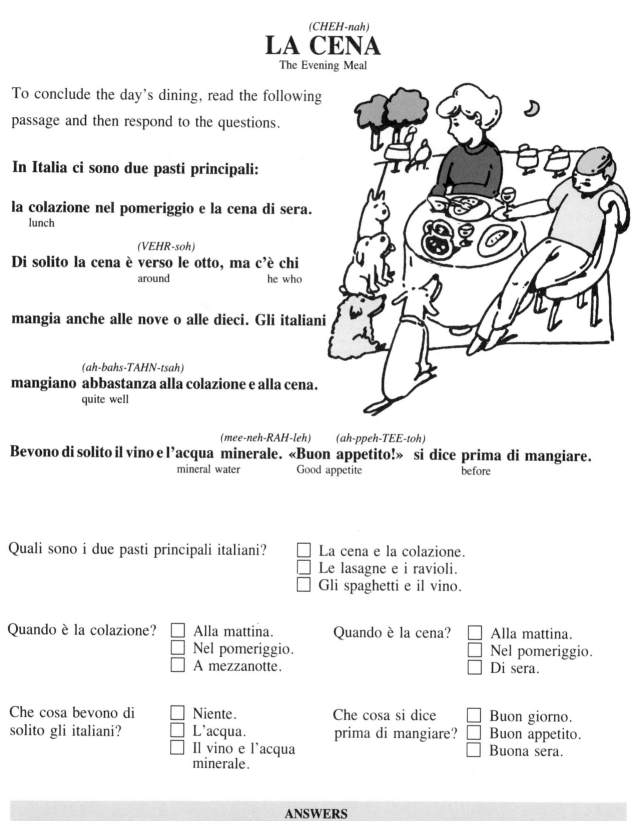

In Italia ci sono due pasti principali:

la colazione nel pomeriggio e la cena di sera.
lunch

(VEHR-soh)
Di solito la cena è verso le otto, ma c'è chi
around — he who

mangia anche alle nove o alle dieci. Gli italiani

(ah-bahs-TAHN-tsah)
mangiano abbastanza alla colazione e alla cena.
quite well

(mee-neh-RAH-leh) *(ah-ppeh-TEE-toh)*
Bevono di solito il vino e l'acqua minerale. «Buon appetito!» si dice prima di mangiare.
mineral water — Good appetite — before

Quali sono i due pasti principali italiani?

- ☐ La cena e la colazione.
- ☐ Le lasagne e i ravioli.
- ☐ Gli spaghetti e il vino.

Quando è la colazione?

- ☐ Alla mattina.
- ☐ Nel pomeriggio.
- ☐ A mezzanotte.

Quando è la cena?

- ☐ Alla mattina.
- ☐ Nel pomeriggio.
- ☐ Di sera.

Che cosa bevono di solito gli italiani?

- ☐ Niente.
- ☐ L'acqua.
- ☐ Il vino e l'acqua minerale.

Che cosa si dice prima di mangiare?

- ☐ Buon giorno.
- ☐ Buon appetito.
- ☐ Buona sera.

ANSWERS

Comprehension La cena e la colazione. Nel pomeriggio. Di sera. Il vino e l'acqua minerale. Buon appetito.

Can you find *ten* words relating to food and eating in this word-search puzzle? After you have circled them, write them on the lines provided.

z	c	b	m	j	g	f	d	w	r	t	u	s	p	i
q	e	r	u	m	a	r	m	e	l	l	a	t	a	b
m	b	c	z	f	h	u	t	i	p	w	r	a	c	m
q	t	e	t	p	a	t	d	g	j	k	m	z	v	r
f	o	r	c	h	e	t	t	a	a	n	e	z	l	p
q	v	a	z	w	s	a	x	e	d	c	s	a	l	e
r	a	f	v	c	t	g	b	y	h	n	u	j	m	p
i	g	k	m	o	l	o	p	q	a	z	w	s	x	e
e	l	d	c	l	r	f	v	t	g	b	y	h	n	i
p	i	a	t	t	o	k	m	o	p	l	q	a	z	w
s	o	x	e	e	d	c	r	f	v	t	g	b	y	h
n	l	u	j	l	m	o	k	l	p	q	a	z	w	s
x	o	e	d	l	c	r	f	v	t	g	b	y	h	n
u	j	m	i	o	l	i	v	e	k	m	p	l	j	b

________________ ________________ ________________

________________ ________________ ________________

________________ ________________ ________________

____

ANSWERS

Word search frutta, marmellata, olive, pepe, sale, forchetta, coltello, piatto, tovagliolo, tazza

15 I ristoranti /Dare la mancia

(rees-toh-RAHN-tee)

Restaurants / Tipping

You will remember that to order food or drink in Italian, all you have to say is:

Vorrei un piatto di spaghetti, per favore.

Vorrei un piatto di ravioli, per favore.

Vorrei una bottiglia di vino rosso, per favore.

To say "I am going to . . ." in Italian, just use the verb in the normal way.

Tomorrow I'm going to eat pizza.⟶Domani **mangio** la pizza.

Tomorrow I'm going to drink wine.⟶Domani **bevo** il vino.

You will find some Italian food selections at the back of this book. Here are some items that you might see on the menu when you dine out.

IL MENÙ

l'antipasto	appetizer
la minestra	soup
(een-sah-LAH-tah) **l'insalata**	salad
le verdure	vegetables
il pesce	fish
la carne	meat
(deh-SSEHRT) **il dessert**	dessert
(beh-VAHN-deh) **le bevande**	drinks
le acciughe	anchovies
(POH-lloh) **il pollo**	chicken
(lah-TTOO-gah) **la lattuga**	lettuce
(ahs-PAH-rah-jee) **gli asparagi**	asparagus
(TROH-tah) **la trota**	trout
la carne di vitello *(vee-TEH-lloh)*	veal
(OO-vah) **l'uva**	grapes
il vino rosso	red wine

(The Smiths have decided to eat at an expensive restaurant.)

CAMERIERE **Buona sera. Vogliono vedere il menù?**

Good evening. Would you (formal, plural) like to see the menu?

MARK **No, grazie. Non voglio vedere i prezzi.**

No, thank you. I do not want to see the prices.

MARY **Non faccia attenzione** *(ah-TEHN-tsyoh-neh)* **a mio marito. Lui scherza** *(SKEHR-tsah)* **sempre.**

Don't pay any attention to my husband. He always jokes around.

CAMERIERE **Abbiamo un antipasto squisito** *(skwee-ZEE-toh)* **di uova** *(WOH-vah)* **con acciughe e molte spezie** *(SPEH-tsee-eh)***.**

We have a delicious appetizer of deviled eggs with anchovies and many spices.

ANNE **Troppo piccante** *(pee-KKAHN-teh)***!**

Too spicy!

MARK **Per il primo piatto, tutti prendiamo la minestra. Poi, io prendo il pollo con le patate** *(pah-TAH-teh)***.**

For the first dish, we will all have soup. Then, I'll have chicken with potatoes.

MARY **E io vorrei la cotoletta** *(koh-toh-LEH-ttah)* **di vitello e l'insalata dí lattuga e pomodori** *(poh-moh-DOH-ree)***.**

And I would like a veal cutlet and the lettuce and tomato salad.

ANNE **Io prendo solo un po' di formaggio con il pane. Faccio la dieta** *(DYEH-tah)***.**

I'll have only a bit of cheese with bread. I'm on a diet.

JOHN **Io vorrei la trota con le patate.**

I would like the trout with potatoes.

MARK **Una bottiglia di vino rosso, e alla fine l'espresso per tutti e un cognac per me e mia moglie.**

A bottle of red wine, and at the end espresso coffee for everyone and a cognac for me and my wife.

CAMERIERE **Grazie.**

Thank you.

(The Smiths have finished the meal and are about to leave.)

MARY	**Mark, lascia una mancia! Questo è un ristorante di lusso.** *(LAH-shah)* *(LOO-ssoh)*	Mark, leave a tip! This is an expensive restaurant.
MARK	**Va bene. Non mangeremo per una settimana!** *(mahn-jeh-REH-moh)*	Okay. We won't eat for a week.

When you have read the dialogue aloud until you are familiar with it, try to complete the missing parts without looking back. Then check your answers.

Buona sera. Vogliono vedere il m______________?

No, grazie. Non v______________ vedere i p______________.

Non faccia a______________ a mio marito. Lui s______________ sempre.

Abbiamo un antipasto s______________ di uova con a______________ e molte s______________.

Troppo p______________!

Per il primo p______________, tutti prendiamo la m______________. Poi, io prendo il p______________ con le p______________.

E io v______________ la c______________ di v______________ e l'______________ dí l______________ e p______________.

Io prendo solo un po' di f______________ con il p______________. Faccio la d______________.

Io vorrei la t______________con le patate.

Una b______________ di vino rosso, e alla f______________ l'espresso per tutti e un cognac per m______________ e mia m______________.

Grazie.

(The Smiths have decided to eat at an expensive restaurant.)

CAMERIERE	**Buona sera. Vogliono vedere il menù?**	Good evening. Would you (formal, plural) like to see the menu?
MARK	**No, grazie. Non voglio vedere i prezzi.**	No, thank you. I do not want to see the prices.
MARY	**Non faccia attenzione** *(ah-TEHN-tsyoh-neh)* **a mio marito. Lui scherza** *(SKEHR-tsah)* **sempre.**	Don't pay any attention to my husband. He always jokes around.
CAMERIERE	**Abbiamo un antipasto squisito** *(skwee-ZEE-toh)* **di uova** *(WOH-vah)* **con acciughe e molte spezie** *(SPEH-tsee-eh)*.	We have a delicious appetizer of deviled eggs with anchovies and many spices.
ANNE	**Troppo piccante!** *(pee-KKAHN-teh)*	Too spicy!
MARK	**Per il primo piatto, tutti prendiamo la minestra. Poi, io prendo il pollo con le patate** *(pah-TAH-teh)*.	For the first dish, we will all have soup. Then, I'll have chicken with potatoes.
MARY	**E io vorrei la cotoletta** *(koh-toh-LEH-ttah)* **di vitello e l'insalata dí lattuga e pomodori** *(poh-moh-DOH-ree)*.	And I would like a veal cutlet and the lettuce and tomato salad.
ANNE	**Io prendo solo un po' di formaggio con il pane. Faccio la dieta** *(DYEH-tah)*.	I'll have only a bit of cheese with bread. I'm on a diet.
JOHN	**Io vorrei la trota con le patate.**	I would like the trout with potatoes.
MARK	**Una bottiglia di vino rosso, e alla fine l'espresso per tutti e un cognac per me e mia moglie.**	A bottle of red wine, and at the end espresso coffee for everyone and a cognac for me and my wife.
CAMERIERE	**Grazie.**	Thank you.

(The Smiths have finished the meal and are about to leave.)

MARY	**Mark, lascia una mancia! Questo è un ristorante di lusso.** *(LAH-shah)* *(LOO-ssoh)*	Mark, leave a tip! This is an expensive restaurant.
MARK	**Va bene. Non mangeremo per una settimana!** *(mahn-jeh-REH-moh)*	Okay. We won't eat for a week.

When you have read the dialogue aloud until you are familiar with it, try to complete the missing parts without looking back. Then check your answers.

Buona sera. Vogliono vedere il m_______________?

No, grazie. Non v_______________ vedere i p_______________.

Non faccia a_______________ a mio marito. Lui s_______________ sempre.

Abbiamo un antipasto s_______________ di uova con a_______________ e molte s_______________.

Troppo p_______________!

Per il primo p_______________, tutti prendiamo la m_______________. Poi, io prendo il p_______________ con le p_______________.

E io v_______________ la c_______________ di v_______________ e l'_______________ dí l_______________ e p_______________.

Io prendo solo un po' di f_______________ con il p_______________. Faccio la d_______________.

Io vorrei la t_______________con le patate.

Una b_______________ di vino rosso, e alla f_______________ l'espresso per tutti e un cognac per m_______________ e mia m_______________.

Grazie.

Il signor Smith . . .

Mr. Smith . . .

You may have noticed that the final *-e* of *signore* is dropped before a name, such as Smith. This is true of all masculine titles ending in *-e*.

il signore	**il signor Smith** Mr. Smith
il professore	**il professor Rossi** Professor Rossi
il dottore	**il dottor Verdi** Dr. Verdi

The article used with titles is dropped when speaking directly to the person.

TALKING ABOUT SOMEONE	TALKING TO SOMEONE
Il signor Smith è americano. Mr. Smith is American.	**Buon giorno, signor Smith.** Good morning, Mr. Smith.
La signora Smith è intelligente. Mrs. Smith is intelligent.	**Buona sera, signora Smith.** Good evening, Mrs. Smith.

(sehn-TEER-see)

Sentirsi (bene, male)

To Feel (Well, Sick)

(toh-LEH-ttah)
toletta
restroom

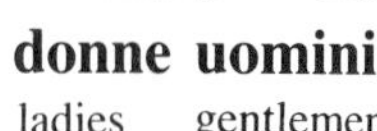

It's easy to tell someone how you are feeling:

Mi sento bene.
Non mi sento bene. Mi sento male.

You continue. Answer the question and fill in the blanks.

Come ti senti? Mi ________________ bene.

Come ti senti? Mi ________________ male.

Here are some additional foods you might want to buy or order. Say them aloud and then repeat them as you look at each picture.

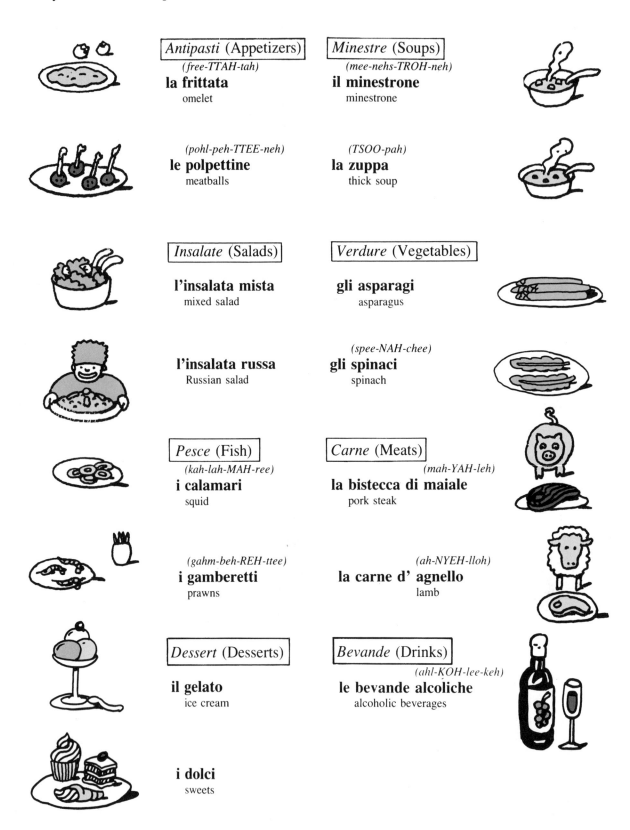

Antipasti (Appetizers)

(free-TTAH-tah)
la frittata
omelet

(pohl-peh-TTEE-neh)
le polpettine
meatballs

Insalate (Salads)

l'insalata mista
mixed salad

l'insalata russa
Russian salad

Pesce (Fish)

(kah-lah-MAH-ree)
i calamari
squid

(gahm-beh-REH-ttee)
i gamberetti
prawns

Dessert (Desserts)

il gelato
ice cream

i dolci
sweets

Minestre (Soups)

(mee-nehs-TROH-neh)
il minestrone
minestrone

(TSOO-pah)
la zuppa
thick soup

Verdure (Vegetables)

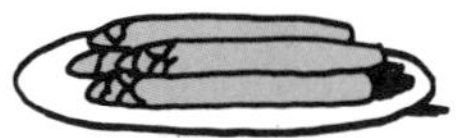

gli asparagi
asparagus

(spee-NAH-chee)
gli spinaci
spinach

Carne (Meats)

(mah-YAH-leh)
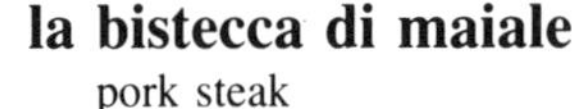
la bistecca di maiale
pork steak

(ah-NYEH-lloh)
la carne d' agnello
lamb

Bevande (Drinks)

(ahl-KOH-lee-keh)
le bevande alcoliche
alcoholic beverages

Now you should be able to zip right through the following brief passage and then select the appropriate answer to each question.

In Italia, si mangia al ristorante, alla trattoria *(trah-ttoh-REE-ah)* [less formal restaurant]**, o al bar dove si mangiano i panini** [sandwiches]**. I pasti italiani consistono** *(kohn-SEES-toh-noh)* [consist] **di un antipasto, un piatto di pasta o di minestra (zuppa, minestrone, e così via), e un piatto di carne o pesce, con patate, verdure, e così via. Poi c'è il dessert, la frutta e il caffè. Naturalmente si beve il vino o l'acqua minerale.**

To wrap up our section on eating out, you fill in the menu; add the Italian words.

Dove si mangiano i panini?

- ☐ A casa.
- ☐ In Francia.
- ☐ Al bar.

Nei pasti italiani, *non* c'è . . .

- ☐ L'antipasto.
- ☐ La frutta.
- ☐ La Coca-Cola.

Che cosa si beve in Italia?

- ☐ La Coca-Cola.
- ☐ Il vino e l'acqua minerale.
- ☐ Il tè.

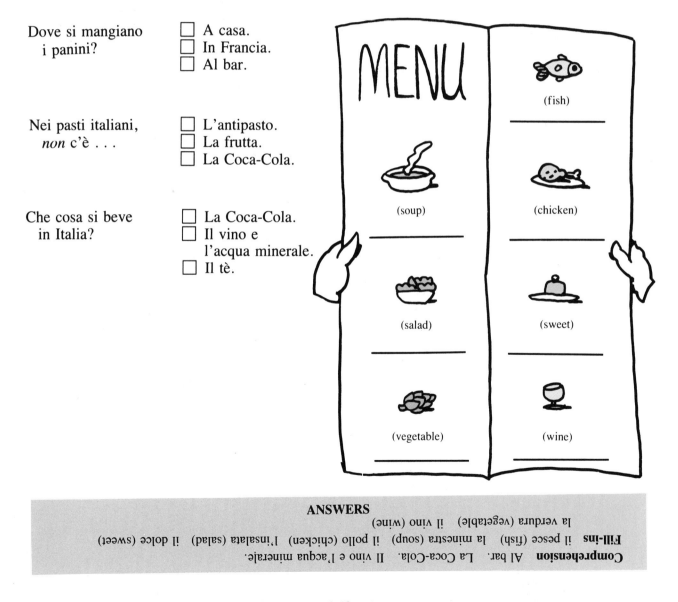

MENU

(fish) ________

(soup) ________

(chicken) ________

(salad) ________

(sweet) ________

(vegetable) ________

(wine) ________

ANSWERS

Comprehension Al bar. La Coca-Cola. Il vino e l'acqua minerale.

Fill-ins il pesce (fish) la minestra (soup) il pollo (chicken) l'insalata (salad) il dolce (sweet) la verdura (vegetable) il vino (wine)

HOW'RE WE DOING?

Come va?

It's time for a breather! This is when you should go back over those sections where you are still having problems. You should also review any vocabulary you may have forgotten and reread the dialogues and comprehension passages. After you have done all that, have some fun with the following activities. If you have forgotten the meaning of any word or expression, you can look it up in the glossary. Are you ready?

First, try unscrambling the letters of the following words. To help you reconstruct the words, English meanings are provided. Each word begins with the letter *p*.

parrimaev ____________ (spring), porzez ____________ (price),

ploita ____________ (pilot), puenmaocit ____________ (tire),

pmoeriiogg ____________ (afternoon), patro ____________ (door),

patrofgolio ____________ (wallet), poien ____________ (full),

pttiao ____________ (plate), ppee ____________ (pepper),

ptniaa ____________ (plant), pscee ____________ (fish),

pstao ____________ (meal), paaatt ____________ (potato), pozaz ____________ (crazy),

praaberazz ____________ (windshield), paaarfnog ____________ (fender),

praautri ____________ (bumper), prahceggoi ____________ (parking),

pssggraeeo ____________ (passenger), ppaassotro ____________ (passport),

pomissor ____________ (next), pgeor ____________ (you're welcome), pean ____________ (bread),

pdrae ____________ (father), pasee ____________ (country), poacc ____________ (package).

ANSWERS

Unscrambling primavera prezzo pilota pneumatico pomeriggio porta portafoglio pieno piatto pepe pianta pesce pasto patata pazzo parabrezza parafango paraurti parcheggio passeggero passaporto prossimo prego pane padre paese pacco

After you have reviewed your verbs, try the following "verb" crossword puzzle.

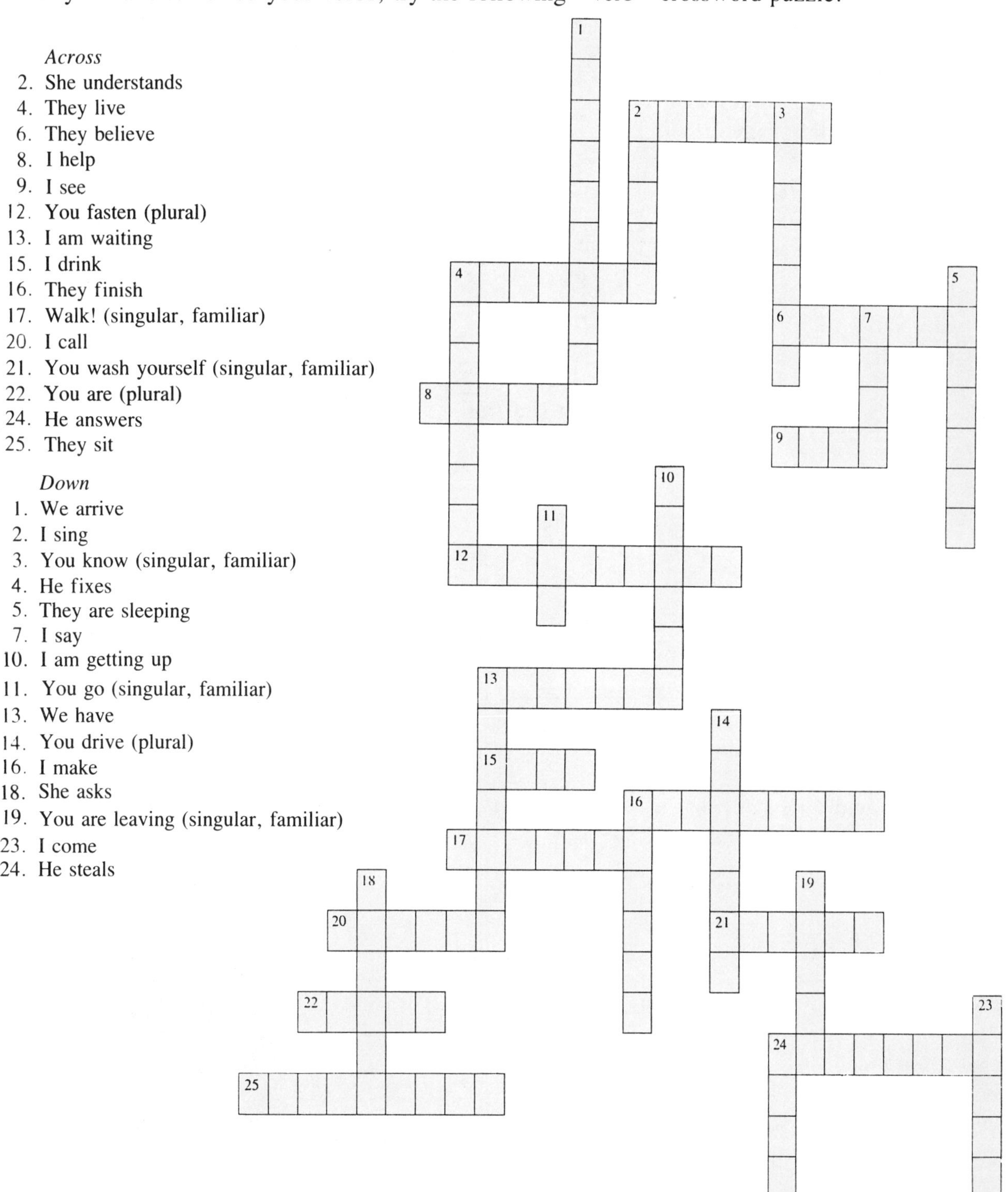

Across

2. She understands
4. They live
6. They believe
8. I help
9. I see
12. You fasten (plural)
13. I am waiting
15. I drink
16. They finish
17. Walk! (singular, familiar)
20. I call
21. You wash yourself (singular, familiar)
22. You are (plural)
24. He answers
25. They sit

Down

1. We arrive
2. I sing
3. You know (singular, familiar)
4. He fixes
5. They are sleeping
7. I say
10. I am getting up
11. You go (singular, familiar)
13. We have
14. You drive (plural)
16. I make
18. She asks
19. You are leaving (singular, familiar)
23. I come
24. He steals

ANSWERS

Crossword Across: 2. capisce **4.** abitano **6.** credono **8.** aiuto **9.** vedo **12.** allacciate **13.** aspetto **15.** bevo **16.** finiscono **17.** cammina **20.** chiamo **21.** ti lavi **22.** siete **24.** risponde. **25.** si siedono **Down: 1.** arriviamo **2.** canto **3.** conosci **4.** aggiusta **5.** dormono **7.** dico **10.** mi alzo **11.** vai **13.** abbiamo **14.** guidate **16.** faccio **18.** chiede **19.** parti **23.** vengo **24.** ruba

This one should be a snap! Read each sentence aloud, and these words will fall right into place.

accanto, acqua, adesso, destra, aereo, albergo, alto, altro, anche, antipasto, appuntamento, autorimessa

1. Maria si siede sempre ____________________ alla sua amica.
2. Vorrei bere un po' di ____________________.
3. L'____________________ di prosciutto è molto buono.
4. La mia macchina è nell'____________________.
5. Domani, il signor Smith ha un ____________________ con me.
6. Gira a ____________________, non a sinistra!
7. ____________________ Gino parla italiano molto bene.
8. Lui non è ____________________; è basso.
9. La signora vuole un ____________________ panino.
10. Devi mangiare ____________________, non dopo.
11. Il pilota è già sull'____________________.
12. Non ho una prenotazione per quell'____________________.

Here we go with plurals! Transpose each "singular" sentence to a "plural" sentence, as we have done with the first one.

il mio amico alto   _i_ mie_i_ amic_i_ alt_i_

la mia amica bella   l____ mi____ amich____ bell____

l'autobus comodo   gl____ autobus comod____

l'albero grande   gl____ alber____ grand____

un bambino bravo   de____ bambin____ brav____

ANSWERS

Fill-ins **1.** accanto **2.** acqua **3.** antipasto **4.** autorimessa **5.** appuntamento **6.** destra **7.** anche **8.** alto **9.** altro **10.** adesso **11.** aereo **12.** albergo

Plurals i miei amici alti le mie amiche belle gli autobus comodi gli alberi grandi dei bambini bravi una bandiera importante   dell___ bandier___ important___

questa bicicletta nuova   quest___ biciclett___ nuov___

questo caffè buono   quest___ caffè buon___

quel cane intelligente   que___ can___ intelligent___

quella cartolina brutta   quell___ cartolin___ brutt___

l'uomo famoso   gl___ uomin___ famos___

la donna gentile   l___ donn___ gentil___

lo zio giovane   gl___ zi___ giovan___

il suo libro interessante   ___ suo___ libr___ interessant___

Find the words that mean the following in the word-search puzzle and circle them. After you find each one, write it in the proper space.

______ gasoline	______ drink	______ ticket
______ bottle	______ room	______ key
______ dashboard	______ spoon	______ yesterday
______ milk	______ every	

a	d	h	k	m	b	p	t	x	c	r	u	s	c	o	t	t	o
t	b	e	n	z	i	n	a	c	u	w	z	a	a	c	f	i	g
l	e	o	r	u	g	x	b	u	f	j	n	r	m	v	z	h	n
c	v	g	k	o	l	s	w	c	h	i	a	v	e	a	d	g	i
g	a	h	l	p	i	t	x	c	q	r	u	p	r	a	f	j	l
z	n	v	m	w	e	r	u	h	o	a	f	j	a	l	z	v	b
m	d	g	d	y	t	l	h	i	e	r	i	d	v	n	e	q	m
l	a	t	t	e	t	a	m	a	s	u	c	n	w	q	h	f	s
a	p	s	o	b	o	t	t	i	g	l	i	a	v	n	w	x	b
y	o	q	x	c	m	e	f	o	r	w	m	q	e	r	i	n	p

ANSWERS

delle bandiere importanti   queste biciclette nuove   questi caffè buoni   quei cani intelligenti
quelle cartoline brutte   gli uomini famosi   le donne gentili   gli zii giovani   i suoi libri interessanti

Word search   benzina   bevanda   biglietto   bottiglia   camera   chiave   cruscotto   cucchiaio   ieri   latte   ogni

Finally, choose the appropriate answer to each question.

Buon giorno, come sta?
- ☐ Bene grazie, e lei?
- ☐ Domani mattina.

Come si chiama, lei?
- ☐ Sono americano.
- ☐ Mi chiamo il signor Smith.

Dove abita, lei?
- ☐ Abito sempre.
- ☐ Abito negli Stati Uniti.

A che ora parte il treno?
- ☐ Parte alle diciassette.
- ☐ Parte ieri.

Che ore sono?
- ☐ È il tre marzo.
- ☐ Sono le tre e venti.

Che data è oggi?
- ☐ È l'una.
- ☐ È il tre novembre.

Che tempo fa?
- ☐ Piove.
- ☐ Domani.

Che cosa prende?
- ☐ Un bicchiere di vino.
- ☐ Vado in Italia.

Perché mangia i ravioli?
- ☐ Perché mi piace.
- ☐ Perché mi piacciono.

Come si sente?
- ☐ Mi sento bene.
- ☐ Mi sento sempre.

How did you do? Don't worry if you made mistakes. Learning a new language is a process of trial and error. It's time to go on!

ANSWERS

Comprehension Bene grazie, e lei? Mi chiamo il signor Smith. Abito negli Stati Uniti. Parte alle diciassette. Sono le tre e venti. È l tre novembre. Piove. Un bicchiere di vino. Perché mi piacciono. Mi sento bene.

AT THE STORE

(ehn-TRYAH-moh) (neh-GOH-tsee)
Entriamo nei negozi

16 Negozi di abbigliamento / Le misure / I colori fondamentali

(ah-bbee-llyah-MEHN-toh) *(mee-ZOO-reh)* *(koh-LOH-ree)*

Clothing Stores / Sizes / Basic Colors

Ti provi i vestiti?

Trying on Clothes?

You can't leave Italy without doing some shopping. Let's hope that you fare better than some of these examples!

(TOH-llyehr-see)
togliersi
to take off

(vehs-TEER-see)
vestirsi
to get dressed

(kah-MEE-chah)
L'uomo si toglie la camicia.
shirt

(MEH-ttehr-see)
mettersi
to put on

(vehs-TEE-toh)
Mi metto il vestito.
dress / suit

(eh-leh-gahn-teh-MEHN-teh)
La donna si veste molto elegantemente.
elegantly

Si metta questa camicia.
Put on this shirt.
Troppo grande!
Too big!
Si metta questo vestito.
Put on this suit.
Troppo grande!
Too big!
No, è perfetto. Le sta proprio bene.
No, it's perfect. It really suits you.

Stare is a verb that you will use while shopping:

STARE to stay, to be			
io	**sto**	**noi**	**stiamo**
tu	*(STAH-ee)* **stai**	**voi**	**state**
lui / lei	**sta**	**loro**	*(STAH-nnoh)* **stanno**

This verb also means "to suit someone" in the expression *stare bene a*:

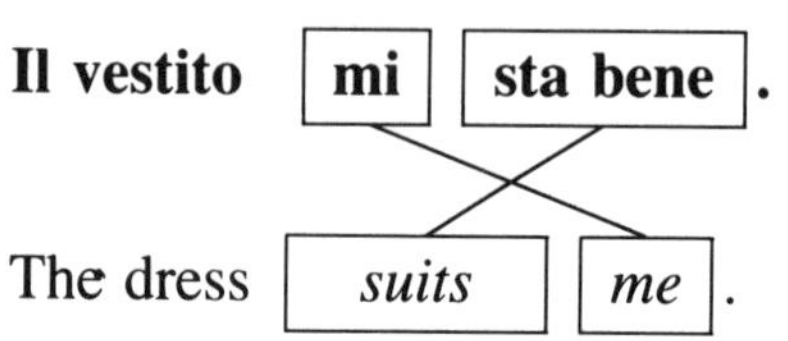

Il vestito **mi** **sta bene**.

The dress *suits* *me*.

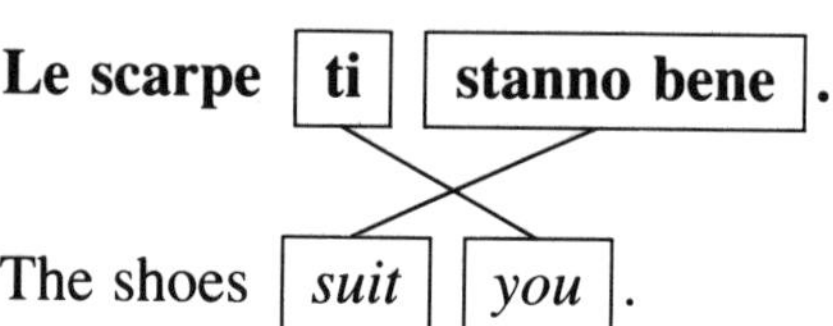

Le scarpe **ti** **stanno bene**.

The shoes *suit* *you*.

(*Literally*, the dress *stays well* on me.)

(*Literally,* the shoes *stay well* on you.)

(mahs-KEE-leh)

L'ABBIGLIAMENTO MASCHILE

Men's Clothes

(Mark and his son are at a clothing store.)

COMMESSO **I signori desiderano?**

Can I help you gentlemen?

MARK **Abbiamo bisogno di un nuovo** *(gwahr-dah-ROH-bah)* **guardaroba. Per mio figlio un paio** *(PAH-yoh)* **di stivali, calzini,** *(kahl-TSEE-nee)* **pantaloni,** *(pahn-tah-LOH-nee)* **guanti,** *(GWAHN-tee)* **e mutande.** *(moo-TAHN-deh)*

We need a new wardrobe. For my son a pair of boots, socks, trousers, gloves, and underwear.

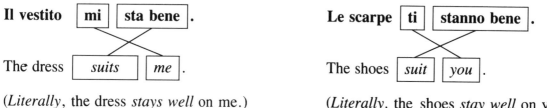

COMMESSO **Bene. E lei?**

Fine. And you?

MARK **Una camicia, una cravatta,** *(krah-VAH-ttah)* **una maglia,** *(MAH-llyah)* **un impermeabile,** *(eem-pehr-meh-AH-bee-leh)* **e un cappello.** *(kah-PPEH-lloh)*

A shirt, a tie, a sweater, a raincoat, and a hat.

(The two Smiths try on their clothes.)

MARK **La camicia mi sta bene, ma il**

The shirt suits me, but not the rest.

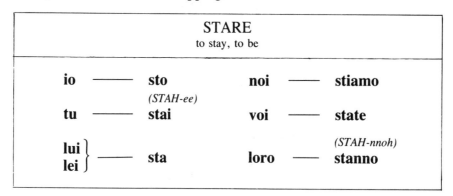

resto no. A mio figlio non sta bene niente.	Nothing suits my son.
COMMESSO **Desiderano qualcos'altro?**	Would you like something else?
(mah-LLYEH-ttah) **Per suo figlio abbiamo una maglietta di** *(MOH-dah) (cheen-TOO-rah) (beh-RREH-ttoh)* **moda, una cintura e un berretto.**	For your son we have a fashionable T-shirt, a belt, and a cap.
JOHN **No, grazie.**	No, thanks.
(JAH-kkah) COMMESSO **Per lei abbiamo una giacca,** *(beh-LLEE-see-moh) (kah-POH-ttoh)* **un bellissimo cappotto e un** *(vehs-TEE-toh) (GREE-doh)* **vestito all'ultimo grido.**	For you we have a sports jacket, a very nice coat, and a suit in the latest style.
MARK **No, grazie.**	No, thanks.
(fah-tsoh-LEH-ttoh) COMMESSO **Neanche un fazzoletto** *(ohm-BREH-lloh)* **o un ombrello?**	Not even a handkerchief or an umbrella?
MARK **No.**	No.
COMMESSO **Ma non ha detto che aveva bisogno di un guardaroba nuovo?**	But didn't you say that you needed a new wardrobe?
(skehr-TSAH-voh)(voh-LEH-voh) MARK **Scherzavo. Volevo solo** *(kah-PEE-vah)* **vedere se lei capiva il mio italiano.**	I was only kidding. I wanted to see if you understood my Italian.
(pah-ROH-lah) (FWOH-ree) COMMESSO **Capisce la parola *fuori*?**	Do you understand the word *out*?
MARK **Capisco. Andiamo, John.**	I understand. Let's go, John.

Ready to try your hand at completing the dialogue? Check your answers when you've finished.

I signori d____________?

Abbiamo b____________ di un n____________ guardaroba. Per mio figlio un

p________ di stivali, c__________, p__________, g__________, e m__________.

Bene. E lei?

Una c__________, una c__________, una m__________, un i__________, e un c__________.

La camicia mi s__________ bene, ma il r__________ no. A mio figlio non s__________ bene niente.

Desiderano qualcos'altro? Per suo figlio abbiamo una m__________ di m__________, una c__________ e un b__________.

No, grazie.

Per lei abbiamo una giacca, un bellissimo c__________ e un vestito all'ultimo g__________.

No, grazie.

Neanche un f__________ o un ombrello?

No.

Ma non ha detto che aveva b__________ di un guardaroba nuovo?

Il mio, il tuo . . .

Mine, Yours . . .

Remember those possessives? You can also use them to say "mine," "yours," and so on.

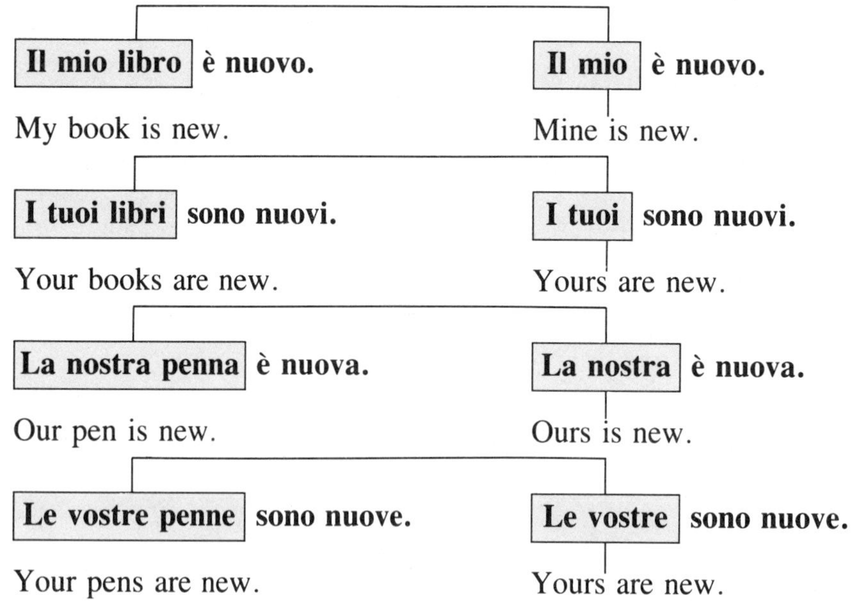

Il mio libro è nuovo.
My book is new.
Il mio è nuovo.
Mine is new.
I tuoi libri sono nuovi.
Your books are new.
I tuoi sono nuovi.
Yours are new.
La nostra penna è nuova.
Our pen is new.
La nostra è nuova.
Ours is new.
Le vostre penne sono nuove.
Your pens are new.
Le vostre sono nuove.
Yours are new.

Got it? All you do is get rid of the noun and keep the form of the possessive.

Questo, quello

This, This One, That, That One

Now that you know about "mine" and "yours," you can apply the same rule to "this, this one" and "these."

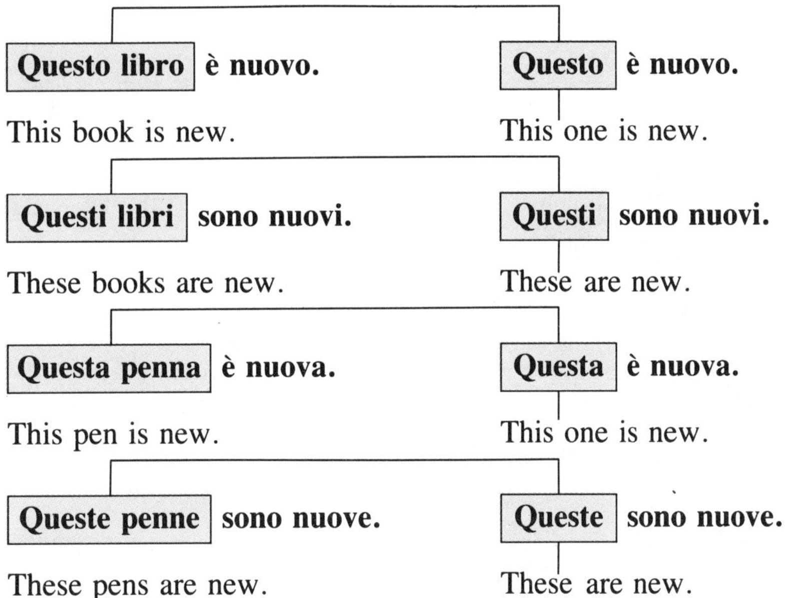

Questo libro è nuovo.
This book is new.
Questo è nuovo.
This one is new.
Questi libri sono nuovi.
These books are new.
Questi sono nuovi.
These are new.
Questa penna è nuova.
This pen is new.
Questa è nuova.
This one is new.
Queste penne sono nuove.
These pens are new.
Queste sono nuove.
These are new.

Now it gets a little trickier. For "that, that one" and "those, the ones" you have to make some adjustments.

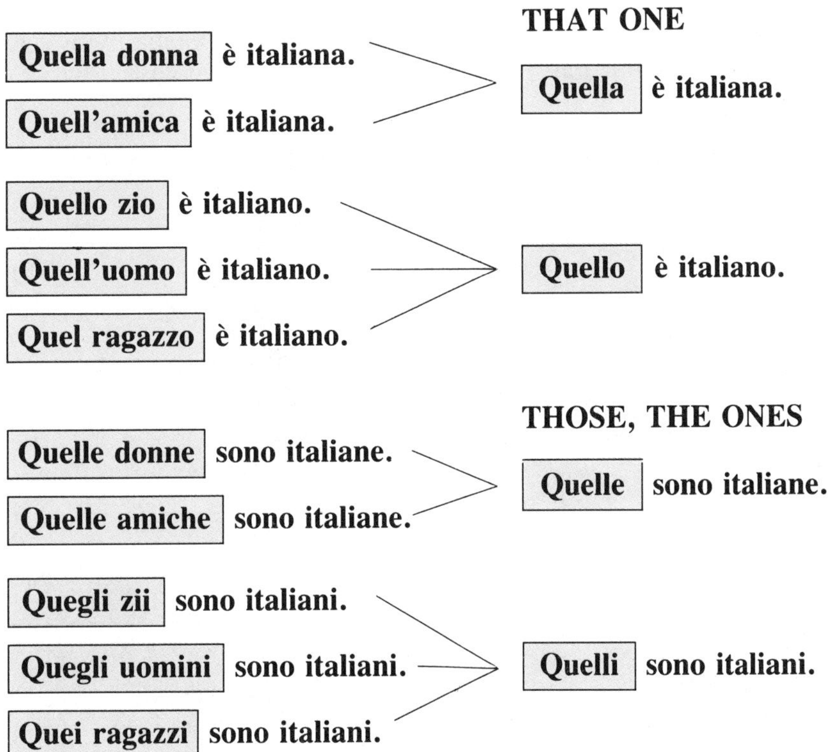

THAT ONE
Quella donna è italiana.
Quell'amica è italiana.
Quella è italiana.
Quello zio è italiano.
Quell'uomo è italiano.
Quel ragazzo è italiano.
Quello è italiano.
THOSE, THE ONES
Quelle donne sono italiane.
Quelle amiche sono italiane.
Quelle sono italiane.
Quegli zii sono italiani.
Quegli uomini sono italiani.
Quei ragazzi sono italiani.
Quelli sono italiani.

Do you think you've got it? Substitute the appropriate possessive for the noun in each of these sentences.

1. La mia penna è nuova. ____________ è nuova.
2. Il suo amico è francese. ____________ è francese.
3. I tuoi libri sono nuovi. ____________ sono nuovi.
4. I suoi calzini sono belli. ____________ sono belli.
5. Questi pantaloni sono belli. ____________ sono belli.
6. Queste mutande sono nuove. ____________ sono nuove.
7. Questa camicia è bianca ____________ è bianca.
8. Quella cravatta è bella. ____________ è bella.
9. Quelle maglie sono belle. ____________ sono belle.
10. Quell'impermeabile è nuovo. ____________ è nuovo.
11. Quel cappello è piccolo. ____________ è piccolo.
12. Quei vestiti sono di moda. ____________ sono di moda.

Misure
Sizes

While you are shopping, you may run into some unexpected problems with sizes, because the metric system is used throughout Italy. Here are some comparisons of sizes of men's clothing.

	MISURA AMERICANA	MISURA ITALIANA
Camicie	14	36
	15	38
	16	40
	17	42
Altre cose Other things	34	44
	36	46
	38	48
	40	50
	42	52
	44	54
	46	56

ANSWERS

Possessives **1.** La mia **2.** Il suo **3.** I tuoi **4.** I suoi **5.** Questi **6.** Queste **7.** Questa **8.** Quella **9.** Quelle **10.** Quello **11.** Quello **12.** Quelli

Now can you complete these sentences? The pictures will give you the necessary clues.

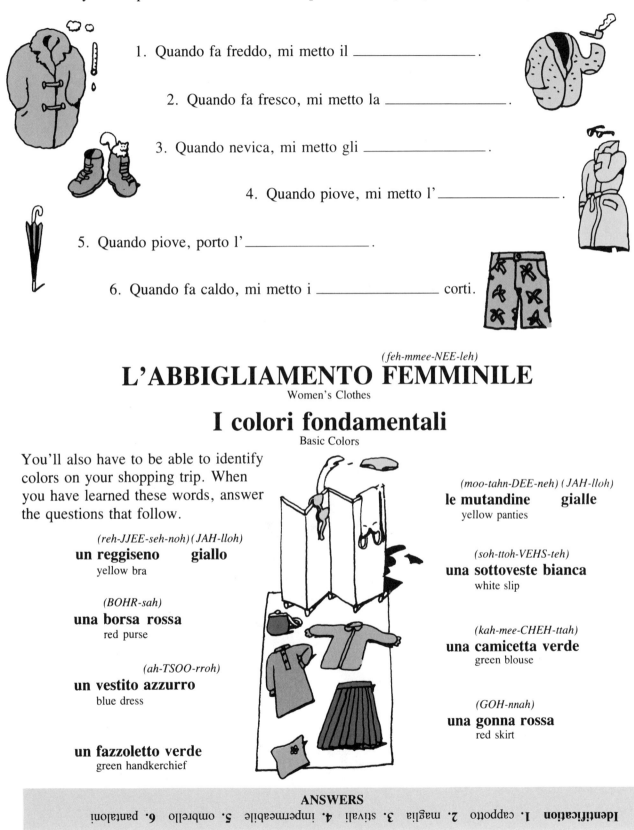

1. Quando fa freddo, mi metto il ______________.

2. Quando fa fresco, mi metto la ______________.

3. Quando nevica, mi metto gli ______________.

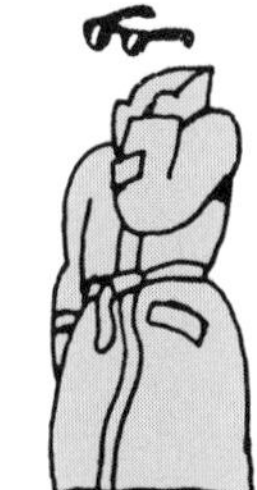

4. Quando piove, mi metto l'______________.

5. Quando piove, porto l'______________.

6. Quando fa caldo, mi metto i ______________ corti.

(feh-mmee-NEE-leh)

L'ABBIGLIAMENTO FEMMINILE

Women's Clothes

I colori fondamentali

Basic Colors

You'll also have to be able to identify colors on your shopping trip. When you have learned these words, answer the questions that follow.

(reh-JJEE-seh-noh) (JAH-lloh)
un reggiseno giallo
yellow bra

(BOHR-sah)
una borsa rossa
red purse

(ah-TSOO-rroh)
un vestito azzurro
blue dress

un fazzoletto verde
green handkerchief

(moo-tahn-DEE-neh) (JAH-lloh)
le mutandine gialle
yellow panties

(soh-ttoh-VEHS-teh)
una sottoveste bianca
white slip

(kah-mee-CHEH-ttah)
una camicetta verde
green blouse

(GOH-nnah)
una gonna rossa
red skirt

ANSWERS

Identification **1.** cappotto **2.** maglia **3.** stivali **4.** impermeabile **5.** ombrello **6.** pantaloni

Di che colore è?
What color is it?

Di che colore è la camicetta? ______________________

Di che colore è il reggiseno? ______________________

Di che colore sono le mutandine? ______________________

Di che colore è il vestito? ______________________

Di che colore il fazzoletto?______________________

Misure
Sizes

And here are some comparisons of women's sizes.

	MISURA AMERICANA	MISURA ITALIANA
Camicette	32	40
	34	42
	36	44
	38	46
	40	48
	42	50
	44	52
Altre cose	8	36
	10	38
	12	40
	14	42
	16	44
	18	46

ANSWERS

Colors (La camicetta è) verde. (Il reggiseno è) giallo. (Le mutandine sono) gialle. (Il vestito è) azzurro. (Il fazzoletto è) verde.

LE SCARPE PER UOMINI E DONNE

Shoes for Men and Women

Misure

Sizes

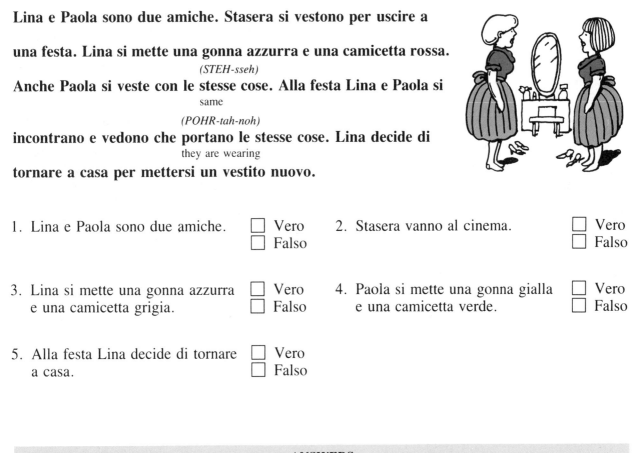

			UOMINI		
Misura americana	7	8	9	10	11
Misura italiana	39	41	43	44	45
			DONNE		
Misura americana	5	6	7	8	9
Misura italiana	35	36	38	38	40

Read the following passage about clothes and then check each statement as true or false.

Lina e Paola sono due amiche. Stasera si vestono per uscire a una festa. Lina si mette una gonna azzurra e una camicetta rossa. Anche Paola si veste con le stesse cose. Alla festa Lina e Paola si incontrano e vedono che portano le stesse cose. Lina decide di tornare a casa per mettersi un vestito nuovo.

stesse *(STEH-sseh)* same; portano *(POHR-tah-noh)* they are wearing

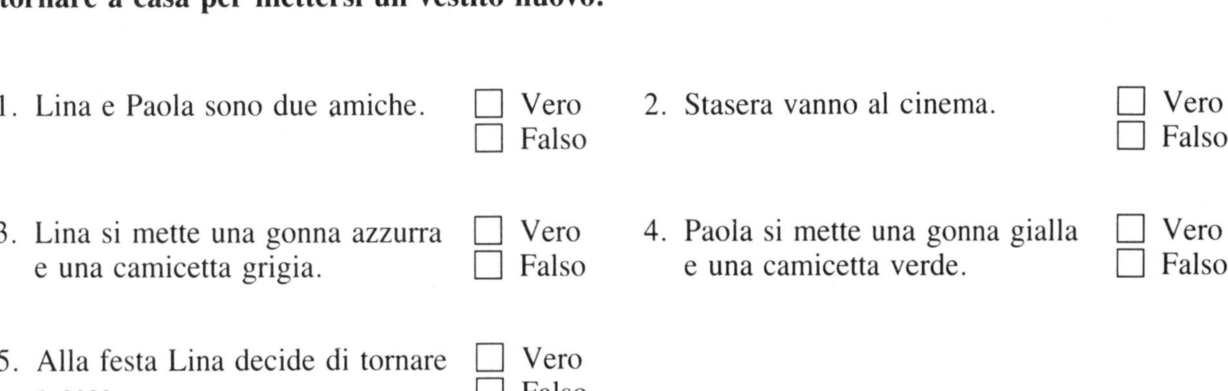

1. Lina e Paola sono due amiche. ☐ Vero ☐ Falso
2. Stasera vanno al cinema. ☐ Vero ☐ Falso
3. Lina si mette una gonna azzurra e una camicetta grigia. ☐ Vero ☐ Falso
4. Paola si mette una gonna gialla e una camicetta verde. ☐ Vero ☐ Falso
5. Alla festa Lina decide di tornare a casa. ☐ Vero ☐ Falso

ANSWERS

True/False **1.** Vero **2.** Falso **3.** Falso **4.** Falso **5.** Vero

17 I negozi di generi alimentari /

(oo-nee-TAH) *(PEH-zoh)*

Unità di peso e di misura

Food Stores / Weights and Measures

Shopping for food can be another pleasant experience, but not unless you know what the shops are! Study the vocabulary carefully.

(lah-tteh-REE-ah)
la latteria
dairy

(mah-cheh-LLAH-yoh)
il macellaio
butcher

(froo-ttee-VEHN-doh-loh)
il fruttivendolo
produce market

(pah-nee-FEE-choh)
il panificio
bread bakery

il latte
milk

la carne
meat

la verdura
vegetables

la frutta
fruit

il pane
bread

(pehs-keh-REE-ah)
la pescheria
fish shop

(kohn-feh-tteh-REE-ah)
la confetteria
candy shop

(pahs-tee-cheh-REE-ah)
la pasticceria
pastry shop

(jeh-lah-teh-REE-ah)
la gelateria
ice cream shop

(eh-noh-TEH-kah)
l'enoteca
wine dealer

il pesce
fish

le caramelle
candy

le paste
pastries

le torte
cakes

il gelato
ice cream

il vino
wine

(doh-MAHN-dah)

Fare una domanda

To Pose a Question

Io faccio una domanda all'uomo.
I pose a question to the man.

Io *gli* faccio una domanda.
I pose a question *to him*.

Dal fruttivendolo

At the Produce Market

Expressions such as "at the market," "at the butcher's," "at the doctor's" or "to the market," "to the butcher's," "to the doctor's" are stated in Italian by the preposition *da* and the appropriate noun.

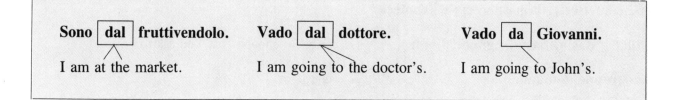

Sono dal fruttivendolo.	**Vado dal dottore.**	**Vado da Giovanni.**
I am at the market.	I am going to the doctor's.	I am going to John's.

Troppe domande!

Too Many Questions!

(Mark Smith and his wife approach a policeman.)

MARK	**Scusi, signore, le vorrei fare una domanda.**	Excuse me, sir, I would like to ask you a question.
VIGILE	**Faccia pure!**	Go ahead!
MARK	**Ho bisogno di un po' di pane. Dov'è il panificio?**	I need some bread. Where is the bread bakery?
VIGILE	**Qui vicino in Via Verdi.**	Nearby on Verdi Street.
MARK	**Dove si compra la carne?**	Where does one buy meat?
VIGILE	**Dal macellaio.**	At the butcher's.
MARK	**E il latte?**	And milk?
VIGILE	**Alla latteria.**	At the dairy.
MARK	**Poi ho bisogno anche di verdura e frutta. Mi sa dire dov'è il fruttivendolo più vicino?**	Then I also need vegetables and fruit. Can you tell me where the nearest market is?
VIGILE	**In Via Nazionale.**	On National Street.

MARK **Ho anche bisogno di un po' di pesce, un pacchetto di caramelle, una torta e due bottiglie di vino. Mi sa dire dove si trovano la pescheria, la confetteria, la pasticceria e l'enoteca?**	I also need a bit of fish, a package of candy, a cake and two bottles of wine. Can you tell me where to find a fish shop, a candy shop, a pastry shop and a wine shop?
VIGILE **Basta, basta, signore! Lei fa troppe domande!**	Enough, enough, sir! You ask too many questions!
MARK **Mamma mia! Che vigile impaziente!**	Heavens! (*literally*, my mom) What an impatient policeman!
MARY **No, Mark, il vigile ha ragione.** *(rah-JOH-neh)* **Tu fai troppe domande.**	No, Mark, the policeman is right. You ask too many questions.

Read the dialogue aloud until you are familiar with the new vocabulary. Then check off each statement as either true or false.

1. Mark fa delle domande a una donna. ☐ Vero ☐ Falso
2. Mark non ha bisogno di pane. ☐ Vero ☐ Falso
3. La carne si compra dal macellaio. ☐ Vero ☐ Falso
4. Il latte si compra alla latteria. ☐ Vero ☐ Falso
5. La verdura si compra in una gelateria. ☐ Vero ☐ Falso
6. Il pesce si compra in una pescheria. ☐ Vero ☐ Falso
7. Il vino si compra in una confetteria. ☐ Vero ☐ Falso
8. Il vigile risponde a tutte le domande. ☐ Vero ☐ Falso

One of the following answers to each question is not correct.

Odd one out

Alla latteria si compra:
il latte
il burro
il vino ____________

Dal macellaio si compra:
la torta
la carne
il pollo ____________

ANSWERS

True/False **1.** Falso **2.** Falso **3.** Vero **4.** Vero **5.** Falso **6.** Vero **7.** Falso **8.** Falso

Odd one out il vino la torta

Dal fruttivendolo si compra:
la verdura
il gelato
la frutta ____________

Alla gelateria si compra:
il pesce
il gelato
le torte di gelato ____________

All'enoteca si compra:
il pane
il vino rosso
il vino bianco ____________

Alla pasticceria si compra:
la torta
le paste
la carne ____________

If you want to make a complaint, here are some suggestions.

Questo pane non è *fresco*!	This bread is not fresh!
Questo panino è *raffermo*!	This roll is stale!
(*MAHR-choh*) **Questo pomodoro è *marcio*!**	This tomato is rotten!
Questo vino è *cattivo*!	This wine is bad tasting!

Si compra, si mangia . . .

One Buys, One Eats . . .

You might have noticed that expressions such as "one buys," and "one eats" are said in Italian by using *si* and the verb. However, be careful! The verb agrees with *what* one buys or eats.

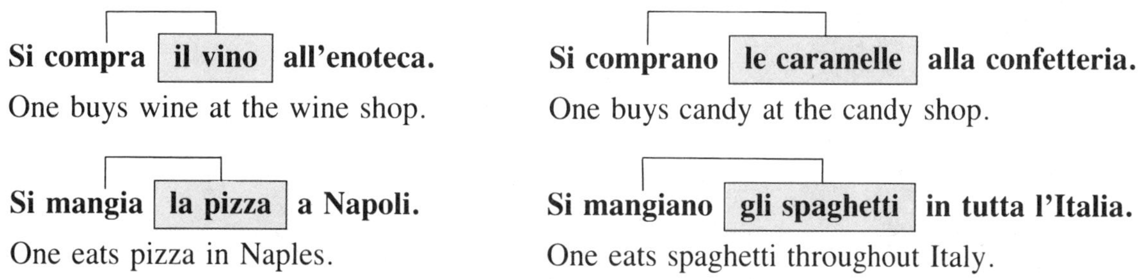

Si compra il vino all'enoteca.
One buys wine at the wine shop.
Si comprano le caramelle alla confetteria.
One buys candy at the candy shop.
Si mangia la pizza a Napoli.
One eats pizza in Naples.
Si mangiano gli spaghetti in tutta l'Italia.
One eats spaghetti throughout Italy.

When you need to compare things, use *più* before the adjective to mean "more." To say "the most," simply use the appropriate definite article before *più*.

Mario è intelligente.	Mario is intelligent.
Gino è *più* intelligente.	Gino is more intelligent.
Pino è *il più* intelligente.	Pino is the most intelligent.
Maria è alta.	Mary is tall.
Gina è *più* alta.	Gina is taller.
Lina è *la più* alta.	Lina is the tallest.

ANSWERS

il gelato il pesce il pane la carne

UNITÀ DI PESO E DI MISURA
Weights and Measures

(peh-ZAH-reh)
pesare
to weigh

(PEH-zoh)
il peso
weight

As we said before, the metric system is used throughout Italy. Here is a chart that gives some metric terms.

(mee-LLEE-meh-troh) **millimetro (mm)**	millimeter	= .039 inch
(chehn-TEE-meh-troh) **centimetro (cm)**	centimeter	= .39 inch
(MEH-troh) **metro (m)**	meter	= 3.28 feet
(kee-LOH-meh-troh) **chilometro (km)**	kilometer	= .62 mile
(chehn-TEE-lee-troh) **centilitro (cl)**	centiliter	= .338 fluid ounce
(LEE-troh) **litro (l)**	liter	= .26 gallon
(mee-llee-GRAH-mmoh) **milligrammo (mg)**	milligram	= .015 grain
(chehn-tee-GRAH-mmoh) **centigrammo (cg)**	centigram	= .154 grain
(GRAH-mmoh) **grammo (g)**	gram	= 15.43 grains
(eh-ttoh-GRAH-mmoh) **ettogrammo (hg)**	hectogram	= 3.52 ounces
(kee-loh-GRAH-mmoh) **chilogrammo (kg)**	kilogram	= 2.2 pounds

(boh-TTEH-gah)
ALLA BOTTEGA DI GENERI ALIMENTARI
At the Grocery Store

These questions are so easy that we haven't given you the answers! If you can't figure out the new words from the pictures, check the glossary.

(sah-poh-NEH-ttah)
Vorrei una saponetta.

Quanto costa ______________________________?

(bah-RAH-ttoh-loh) *(soh-LOO-bee-leh)*
Vorrei un barattolo di caffè solubile.

Quanto costa ______________________________?

(ROH-toh-loh) (ee-JEH-nee-kah)
Vorrei un rotolo di carta igienica.

Quanto costa ______________________________?

(MEH-tsoh) (chee-LYEH-jeh)
Vorrei mezzo chilo di ciliege.

Quanto costa ______________________________?

Vorrei un litro di latte.

Quanto costa ______________________________?

(doh-DZEE-nah)
Vorrei mezza dozzina di limoni.

Quanto costa ______________________________?

Vorrei un barattolo di verdura.

Quanto costa ______________________________?

Vorrei un pacchetto di zucchero.

Quanto costa ______________________________?

Vorrei una dozzina di uova.

Quanto costa ______________________________

(SKAH-toh-lah) (bees-KOH-ttee)
Vorrei una scatola di biscotti.

Quanto costa ______________________________?

Notice that in Italian the article "the" must be used, especially at the beginning of a sentence, to express generalities.

***Gli* italiani mangiano gli spaghetti.**
Italians eat spaghetti.

***L'*italiano è una bella lingua.**
Italian is a beautiful language.

***Lo* zucchero costa molto.**
Sugar costs a lot.

***Il* pane costa molto poco.**
Bread costs very little.

This passage contains more information about shopping in Italy. Read it and then select the appropriate answer to each question.

In Italia la spesa si fa, in genere, ogni giorno.
(spesa = food shopping; genere *(JEH-neh-reh)*: in genere = generally)

Ma come negli Stati Uniti, oggi ci sono anche i supermercati, dove si può comprare il cibo surgelato. Ma il metodo più popolare di fare la spesa è al mercato. Qui si compra sempre "a buon mercato." Il cibo è fresco e buono.
(supermercati *(soo-pehr-mehr-KAH-tee)* = supermarkets; surgelato *(soor-jeh-LAH-toh)* = frozen; metodo *(MEH-toh-doh)* = method; popolare *(poh-poh-LAH-reh)* = popular; mercato *(mehr-KAH-toh)* = open-air market; a buon mercato = cheaply; cibo = food)

Quando si fa, in genere, la spesa in Italia?	☐ Il sabato. ☐ Il venerdì. ☐ Ogni giorno.	Che cosa si può comprare a un supermercato?	☐ Le scarpe. ☐ Il cibo surgelato. ☐ I cappotti.
Oggi ci sono anche . . .	☐ i supermercati. ☐ i negozi. ☐ le ciliege.	Qual è il metodo più popolare di fare la spesa?	☐ Al supermercato. ☐ Alla bottega di generi alimentari. ☐ Al mercato.

Can you unscramble the letters to form the following words?

mrcteao ______ (open-air market)	isbttooc ______ (biscuit/cookie)	alotsca ______ (box)
nzizaod ______ (dozen)	cliiegai ______ (cherry)	brttlaaoo ______ (jar/can)
ettonapas ______ (soap bar)		

ANSWERS

Comprehension Ogni giorno. Il cibo surgelato. I supermercati. Al mercato.

Unscrambling mercato biscotto scatola dozzina ciliegia barattolo saponetta

18 Le farmacie

(fahr-mah-CHEE-eh)

Le farmacie

Drugstores / Pharmacies

Here are some items you might find in an Italian drugstore. Say them aloud as you find them in the showcase.

(dehn-tee-FREE-choh)
il dentifricio
toothpaste

(SPAH-tsoh-lah)
la spazzola
hairbrush

(spah-tsoh-LEE-noh)
lo spazzolino da denti
toothbrush

(speh-KKYEH-ttoh)
lo specchio / lo specchietto
mirror

una scatola di fazzoletti di carta
box of tissues

(PEH-ttee-neh)
il pettine
comb

(roh-SSEH-ttoh)
il rossetto
lipstick / rouge

(LAH-kkah)
la lacca per capelli
hairspray

(KREH-mah) (beh-LLEH-tsah)
la crema (di bellezza)
facial cream

(SPEE-lleh) (see-koo-REH-tsah)
le spille di sicurezza
safety pins

(ZMAHL-toh) (OON-gyeh)
lo smalto per le unghie
nail polish

IN FARMACIA

At the Drugstore

(Mary Smith and Lina Rossi—an Italian friend—are at a drugstore.)

LINA **Che cosa vuoi comprare, Mary?**	What do you want to buy, Mary?
MARY **Non sono sicura.**	I'm not sure.
COMMESSO **Desidera, signora?**	Can I help you, madam?
MARY **Quanto costa la crema?**	How much does cold cream cost?
COMMESSO **Ventimila lire.**	20.000 lira.
MARY **E quel pettine e quella spazzola?**	And that comb and that hairbrush?
COMMESSO **Il pettine duemila e la spazzola cinquemila.**	The comb 2.000 and the hairbrush 5.000.
LINA **Non c'è male, Mary.**	That's not bad, Mary.
MARY **No, grazie.**	No, thanks.
COMMESSO **Forse ha bisogno di uno spazzolino da denti e del dentifricio?**	Maybe you need a toothbrush and some toothpaste?
MARY **No. Vorrei lo smalto per le unghie, il rossetto, il mascara, e la lacca per capelli.**	No. I would like nail polish, lipstick, mascara, and hairspray.
LINA **Ah, ti vuoi mettere il trucco?** *(TROO-kkoh)*	Ah, you want to put on makeup?
MARY **Non è per me. È per mio marito.**	It's not for me. It's for my husband.
LINA **Per tuo marito?**	For your husband?
MARY **Mi ama quando sono bella.**	He loves me when I am beautiful.

After you have read the dialogue several times, check off each statement as either true or false.

1. Mary è sicura di quello che vuole comprare. ☐ Vero ☐ Falso
2. La crema costa ventimila lire. ☐ Vero ☐ Falso
3. Il pettine costa duemila lire. ☐ Vero ☐ Falso
4. La spazzola costa cinquemila lire. ☐ Vero ☐ Falso
5. Mary ha bisogno di uno spazzolino da denti. ☐ Vero ☐ Falso
6. Mary compra lo smalto per le unghie, il rossetto, il mascara, e la lacca per i capelli. ☐ Vero ☐ Falso

Some essential phrases:

Vorrei comprare . . .	*I would like* to buy . . .
Devo comprare . . .	*I have to* buy . . .
È necessario comprare . . .	*It is necessary* to buy . . .

Che, cui

That, Which, Who, Whom

The relative pronoun *che* translates as "that, "which," and "who" when used in sentences like the following.

Il libro **che** è rosso è interessante.
The book, **which** is red, is interesting.

La crema **che** voglio costa troppo.
The cream **that** I want costs too much.

Il ragazzo **che** mangia la pizza è mio fratello.
The boy **who** is eating pizza is my brother.

After a preposition, *cui* is used instead.

Ecco la borsa in **cui** metto il rossetto.
Here is the purse in **which** I put the lipstick.

Questo è il ragazzo a **cui** parlo italiano.
This is the boy to **whom** I speak italian.

ANSWERS

True/False **1.** Falso **2.** Vero **3.** Vero **4.** Vero **5.** Falso **6.** Vero

Now you choose either *che* or *cui.*

Maria compra la spazzola __________ costa cinquemila lire.

L'uomo di __________ parlo è mio marito.

Lina vuole il rossetto __________ costa molto.

Maria dice __________ la sua amica viene domani.

La donna per __________ compro la crema è mia moglie.

Sapere, conoscere

To Know

These verb forms may give you some trouble, so study them well.

	(sah-PEH-reh) SAPERE	(koh-NOH-sheh-reh) CONOSCERE		(sah-PEH-reh) SAPERE	(koh-NOH-sheh-reh) CONOSCERE
io	**so**	(koh-NOHS-koh) **conosco**	**noi**	(sah-PPYAH-moh) **sappiamo**	(koh-noh-SHAH-moh) **conosciamo**
tu	**sai**	(koh-NOH-shee) **conosci**	**voi**	(sah-PEH-teh) **sapete**	(koh-noh-SHEH-teh) **conoscete**
lui / **lei**	**sa**	(koh-NOH-sheh) **conosce**	**loro**	(SAH-nnoh) **sanno**	(koh-NOH-skoh-noh) **conoscono**

What's the difference between these two verbs? Use *conoscere* when you want to say that you know or are acquainted with "someone"; use *sapere* when you want to say you know "something" or "how to do" something. Although there is some overlapping in use, this distinction is all you will need to know for your communicative purposes.

Now choose *sapere* or *conoscere* as the case may be.

Io non ______________________ il signor Smith.

Gina ______________________ parlare italiano molto bene.

Quell'uomo ______________________ lo zio di Carlo.

Noi ______________________ che lui arriva domani.

Tu ______________________ mia moglie?

ANSWERS

Relative pronouns che (costa) cui (parlo) che (costa) che (la sua) cui (compro)

Verbs conosco (il signor) sa (parlare) conosce (lo zio) sappiamo (che lui) conosci (mia moglie?)

I signori Smith non ____________ parlare italiano molto bene.

Il signor Smith non mi ______________________________.

(Mark Smith and his son enter a drugstore.)

MARK **Scusi, signore, lei ha**
(see-gah-REH-tteh) (ah-chen-DEE-noh)
sigarette e un accendino?

Excuse me, sir, do you have cigarettes and a lighter?

COMNESSO **No, lei deve andare da un**
(tah-bah-KKAH-yoh)
tabaccaio.

No. You have to go to a tobacco shop.

(bohm-boh-LEH-ttah)
MARK **Allora mi dia una bomboletta**
(deh-oh-doh-RAHN-teh)(rah-ZOH-yoh)
di deodorante e un rasoio con le
(lah-MEH-tteh) (eh-LEH-ttree-koh)
lamette. Il mio rasoio elettrico non funziona in questo paese!

Then give me a can of deodorant and a razor with blades. My electric razor doesn't work in this country!

COMMESSO **Perché ha bisogno di un**
(kohn-vehr-tee-TOH-reh)
convertitore.

Because you need a converter.

(kohm-plee-kah-TSYOH-nee)
MARK **Quante complicazioni!**

So many complications!

COMMESSO **Senta, signore. Ho la**
(soh-loo-TSYOH-neh) (KREH-sheh-reh)
soluzione. Si faccia crescere la barba come me.

Listen, sir. I have the solution. Let your beard grow like me.

(Mary and Anne now enter.)

MARY **Ciao, Mark. Cosa fai?**

Hi, Mark. What are you doing?

MARK **Compro delle cose.**

I am buying some things.

(ahs-pee-REE-neh)
MARY **Anch'io ho bisogno di aspirine,**
(BEHN-deh) (tehr-MOH-meh-troh)
bende e un termometro.

I too need aspirins, Band-Aids, and a thermometer.

MARK **Ti senti male?**

Do you feel sick?

ANSWERS

sanno (parlare) conosce.

MARY **Mi fa male un po' la testa, e abbiamo bisogno di bende per il nostro viaggio.** *(TEHS-tah)*	My head hurts a bit, and we need Band-Aids for our trip.
COMMESSO **Vuole anche delle spille di sicurezza, un po' di talco e dei pannolini?** *(TAHL-koh)* *(pah-nnoh-LEE-nee)*	Do you want safety pins, a bit of talcum powder, and some diapers?
MARY **Dei pannolini? Non ho un bambino a casa.**	Some diapers? I do not have a baby at home.
COMMESSO **No, ma penso che lei deve essere incinta.** *(een-CHEEN-tah)*	No, but I think that you must be pregnant.
MARY **Per favore! Mi dia subito un' aspirina!**	Please! Give me an aspirin, quick!

When you are familiar with the dialogue, try to reconstruct it below.

Il / non / in / questo / mio / paese / funziona / rasoio

____

convertitore / un / di / bisogno / Perché / ha

____

me / come / crescere / barba / la / Si / faccia

____

Anch'io / termometro / un / e / bende / bisogno / ho / di / aspirine

____

spille / delle / sicurezza / di / anche / Vuole / talco / di / po' / un / e / pannolini / dei

____

lamette / le / con / un / e / rasoio / mi / Allora / dia / bomboletta / una / deodorante / di

____

19 La lavanderia / La lavanderia a secco

(lah-vahn-deh-REE-ah)

Laundry / Dry Cleaner

Laundromats can be found throughout Italy in the major hotels. In general, the service in Italy for laundry and dry cleaning is quite good. However, you should always plan to bring along some wash-and-wear clothes, just in case! And remember, during the weekend of or near August 15, everything closes down in Italy.

(lah-vah-TREE-cheh)
la lavatrice
washer

(ah-shoo-gah-TREE-cheh)
l'asciugatrice
dryer

ALLA LAVANDERIA AUTOMATICA

(ah-oo-toh-MAH-tee-kah)

At the Laundromat

(Anne Smith is at the hotel laundromat where she runs into her Italian friend Lina.)

ANNE **Ciao, Lina. Mi puoi aiutare? E la mia prima volta a una lavanderia italiana.** *(VOHL-tah)*
Hi, Lina. Can you help me? It's my first time at an Italian laundromat.

LINA **Certo. Hai il sapone in polvere, una cesta, un ferro da stiro, e delle mollette?** *(sah-POH-neh) (POHL-veh-reh) (CHES-tah) (FEH-rroh) (STEE-roh) (moh-LLEH-tteh)*
Certainly. Do you have soap powder, a wash basket, an iron, and clothespins?

ANNE **Sì. Ho tutto. Vedo che c'è un' asciugatrice e un tavolo da stiro. Meno male.**
Yes, I have everything. I see that there is a dryer and an ironing board. Thank goodness.

(MEH-tteh-reh) (jeh-TTOH-neh)

LINA **Ora, devi mettere un gettone nella lavatrice e dopo nell'asciugatrice. Ecco. Io ho due gettoni per te.** — Now, you have to put a token in the washer and then in the dryer. Here. I have two tokens for you.

(feh-SSOO-rah) (EH-kkoh-lah)

ANNE **Dov'è la fessura? Ah, eccola!** — Where is the slot? Ah, here it is!

(The machine does not start.)

(NYEHN-teh)

ANNE **Perché sembra che niente** *(foon-TSYOH-nah)* **funziona?** — Why does nothing seem to work?

LINA **Perché tu non sai fare.** — Because you don't know how to do things.

(Lina gives the machine a kick and the machine starts.)

(MOH-doh)

LINA **Questo è il modo di fare le cose all'italiana!** — This is the way to do things the Italian way!

(The machine begins to overflow with suds.)

(soo-CHEH-deh)

ANNE **Mamma mia, che cosa succede?** — Oh dear! What's happening?

(preh-oh-kkoo-PAH-reh)

LINA **Non ti preoccupare. C'è troppo** *(PAH-nnee)* **sapone. I tuoi panni non sono più** *(SPOHR-kee)* **sporchi!** — Don't worry, there is too much soap. Your clothes are no longer dirty.

Read the dialogue several times out loud and then fill in the missing parts from memory. Afterwards, check your answers.

Ciao, Lina. Mi p____________ a____________? È la mia prima v____________ a una l____________ italiana.

Certo. Hai il s____________ in p____________, una c____________, un f____________ da stiro, e delle m____________?

Sì. Ho tutto. Vedo che c'è un'a____________ e un t____________ da stiro. Meno male.

Ora, devi m______________ un g______________ nella

l______________ e dopo nell'a______________. Ecco. Io ho due gettoni per te.

Dov'è la f______________? Ah, eccola!

Perché s______________ niente f______________?

Perché tu non s______________ fare.

Questo è il m______________ di fare le cose all'italiana!

Ci, ne

There, Some of

Notice that *ci* means "there" and that *ne* means "some of." Like the pronouns you learned earlier, these occur right before the verb.

Mark va *in Italia* domani.	**Mark *ci* va domani.**
Mark is going to Italy tomorrow.	Mark is going *there* tomorrow.

Io metto il rossetto *nella borsa*.	**Io *ci* metto il rossetto.**
I put the lipstick in the purse.	I put the lipstick *there*.

Voglio *del pane*.	***Ne*** voglio.
I want some bread.	I want *some* (of it).

Mangio *degli spaghetti*.	***Ne* mangio.**
I am eating some spaghetti.	I am eating *some* (of it).

Got it? Now it's your turn; you choose *ci* or *ne*.

Anne mette il gettone *nella fessura*. Anne ______ mette il gettone.

Lina ha *delle mollette*. Lina ______ ha. Anne ha *cinque gettoni*. Anne ______ ha cinque.

ANSWERS

Pronouns ci (mette) ne (ha.) ne (ha cinque.)

Lina mette il sapone *nella lavatrice*. Lina ______ mette il sapone.

Anne mette un gettone *nell'asciugatrice*. Anne ______ mette un gettone.

Lina ha bisogno *di un ferro da stiro*. Lina ______ ha bisogno.

Anne non ha bisogno *di un tavolo da stiro*. Anne non ______ ha bisogno.

(sehr-VEE-tsee)

SERVIZI DI LAVANDERIA ALL'ALBERGO

Hotel Laundry Services

Here are some common expressions you may use when you use the laundry services of the hotel where you are staying.

Avete un servizio di lavanderia? — Do you have a laundry service?

(PAH-nnee)
Devo far lavare dei panni. — I have some clothes to be washed.

(koo-CHEE-reh) (boh-TTOH-neh)
Mi puó cucire questo bottone? — Can you sew on this button?

(rah-mmehn-DAH-reh)
Mi può rammendare la manica? — Can you mend the sleeve?

(stee-RAH-reh)
Mi può stirare questa camicia? — Can you iron this shirt?

(AH-mee-doh)
C'è troppo amido nelle mie mutande! — There's too much starch in my undershorts!

Dov'è la lavanderia a secco? — Where is the dry cleaner?

Mi può portare questo vestito alla lavanderia? — Can you take this suit to the cleaners?

(TOH-llyeh-reh) (MAH-kkyah)
Può togliere questa macchia? — Can you take out this spot?

You might want to look over the words and expressions you have learned in this unit before you try to unscramble the following.

lvaandriea ______________________ (laundry) lvaandriea a cceso ______________________ (dry cleaner)

lvaartiec ______________________ (washer) ecirtaguiasc ______________________ (dryer)

ANSWERS

ci (mette il) ci (mette un) ne (ha bisogno.) ne (ha bisogno.)

Unscrambling lavanderia lavanderia a secco lavatrice asciugatrice

spaone in plovree ____________ (soap powder) sceta ____________ (wash basket) tolgieer ____________ (to take out)

rrfeo da stoir ____________ (iron) lltteeom ____________ (clothespins) mcchaia ____________ (spot)

mtteere ____________ (to put) ttgeone ____________ (token) fsseuar ____________ (slot)

pnnai ____________ (clothes) ccuier ____________ (to sew) bttnooe ____________ (button)

rmmaenared ____________ (to mend) arestir ____________ (to iron) miado ____________ (starch)

(lah-mehn-TEH-leh)

Lamentele

Complaints

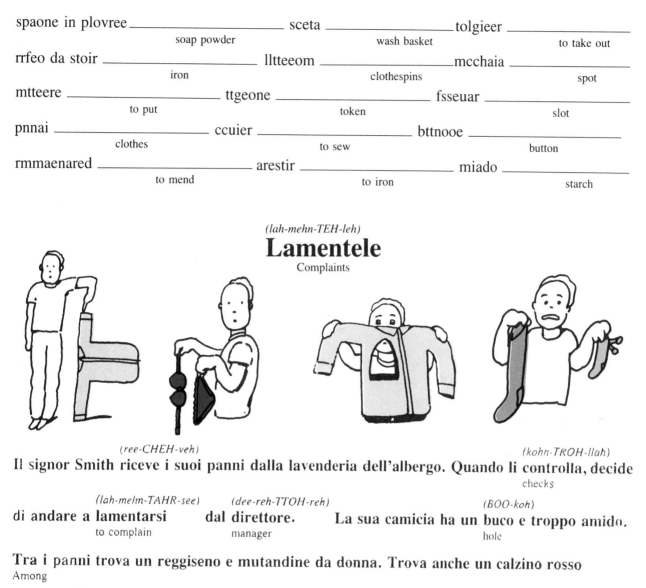

Il signor Smith riceve *(ree-CHEH-veh)* **i suoi panni dalla lavenderia dell'albergo. Quando li controlla** *(kohn-TROH-llah)* checks**, decide di andare a lamentarsi** *(lah-mehn-TAHR-see)* to complain **dal direttore** *(dee-reh-TTOH-reh)* manager**. La sua camicia ha un buco** *(BOO-koh)* hole **e troppo amido.**

Tra Among **i panni trova un reggiseno e mutandine da donna. Trova anche un calzino rosso e uno verde.**

Wouldn't you know that Mark would have these kinds of laundry problems? Answer the true-and-false after you have read the passage.

1. Il signor Smith non ha lamentele. ☐ Vero ☐ Falso
2. Il signor Smith riceve i suoi panni dalla lavanderia a secco. ☐ Vero ☐ Falso
3. Il signor Smith si lamenta con il direttore. ☐ Vero ☐ Falso
4. La sua camicia ha un buco. ☐ Vero ☐ Falso
5. Trova panni da donna. ☐ Vero ☐ Falso
6. Trova due calzini gialli. ☐ Vero ☐ Falso

ANSWERS

sapone in polvere cesta togliere ferro da stiro mollette macchia mettere gettone fessura panni
cucire bottone rammendare stirare amido

True/False 1. Falso **2.** Falso **3.** Vero **4.** Vero **5.** Vero **6.** Falso

20	*(pah-rroo-KKYEH-reh)* *(bahr-BYEH-reh)*
	Dal parrucchiere / Dal barbiere
	At the Hairdresser, Beauty Shop / At the Barber

DAL PARRUCCHIERE

At the Beauty Shop / Hairdresser

(Mary and Anne decide to go to a beauty shop.)

PARRUCCHIERE **Desiderano?** — Can I help you?

(SHAHM-poh)
MARY **Per mia figlia, uno shampoo, un** — For my daughter, a shampoo,

(trah-ttah-MEHN-toh) (FAH-chah)
trattamento alla faccia, — a facial massage,

(mah-nee-KOO-reh) *(PYEH-gah)*
una manicure, e una messa in piega. — a manicure, and a (hair) set.

Io vorrei solo una
(pehr-mah-NEHN-teh)
permanente. — I would like only a permanent.

(kah-PEH-llee)
Attenzione ai miei capelli! — Be careful with my hair!

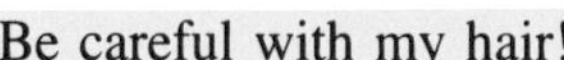

Hanno un bel colore! — It is a beautiful color!

PARRUCCHIERE **Va bene. Prima** — Okay. First you have

(lah-VAH-reh)
bisogna lavare i capelli — to have your hair washed

(SOH-ttoh)
e poi andare sotto — and then you have to go

(KAHS-koh)
il casco. — under the hair dryer.

(after they have been under the hair dryer for a while:)

PARRUCCHIERE **Venga, signora! I capelli sono asciutti. Prima le devo spazzolare i capelli e poi le faccio la permanente. Un momento che prendo una spazzola e alcuni bigodini.**

(ah-SHOO-ttee) *(spah-tsoh-LAH-reh)* *(SPAH-tsoh-lah)* *(bee-goh-DEE-nee)*

Come, madam! Your hair is dry. First I have to brush your hair and then I'll give you a permanent. Hold on a moment; I'm going to get a brush and some curlers.

(as the beautician is about to finish:)

PARRUCCHIERE **Signora, si guardi nello specchio! Lei è veramente bella!**

(veh-rah-MEHN-teh)

Madam, you can look at yourself in the mirror.

You are truly beautiful!

MARY **Mamma mia! I miei capelli sono biondi!**

(BYOHN-dee)

Good heavens!

My hair is blonde!

When you have the dialogue down cold, match up the phrases in the left column with those in the right column. Then, check your answers.

Per mia figlia . . .	solo una permanente.
Io vorrei . . .	lavare i capelli e poi andare sotto il casco.
Attenzione . . .	sono biondi!
Hanno un bel . . .	guardi nello specchio!
Prima bisogna . . .	spazzolare i capelli e poi le faccio la permanente.
I capelli . . .	prendo una spazzola e alcuni bigodini.
Prima le devo . . .	ai miei capelli!
Un momento che . . .	sono asciutti.
Signora, si . . .	colore!
I miei capelli . . .	uno shampoo, un trattamento alla faccia, una manicure, e una messa in piega.

Here are some more useful expressions for you.

(shah-KKWAH-reh)
Mi può sciacquare i capelli? — Can you give me a rinse?

(tah-LLYAH-reh)
Mi può tagliare i capelli? — Can you give me a haircut?

Non voglio la lacca, per favore. No hair spray, please.

(frahn-JEH-ttah)
Mi fa la frangetta? Can you give me some bangs?

One last word about those pesky object pronouns! What happens when the two types, direct and indirect (remember?), are used together? Watch!

Giovanni *mi* dà *il libro*.
John gives the book to me.

Maria ti dà *la penna*.
Mary gives the pen to you.

Lui *ci* dà *i libri*.
He gives the books to us.

Giovanni *me lo* dà.
John gives *it to me*.

Maria *te la* dà.
Mary gives *it to you*.

Lui *ce li* dà.
He gives *them to us*.

Confused? Don't worry. You probably won't need to know how to use the two types together. However, someone may use them when speaking to you. Just be aware that they both come before the verb and that minor changes are made: *mi* becomes *me*; *ti* becomes *te*; and so on.

DAL BARBIERE

At the Barber

Il signor Smith decide di andare dal barbiere per farsi tagliare i capelli e la barba.
to have his hair cut

Al signor Smith non piace farsi la barba.
to shave himself

(LOON-gah) (bah-ZEH-tteh) (BAH-ffee)
Ha la barba lunga, le basette, e i baffi.
long sideburns moustache

Decide di farsi tagliare tutto!
to have everything cut

Il barbiere è un uomo simpatico.

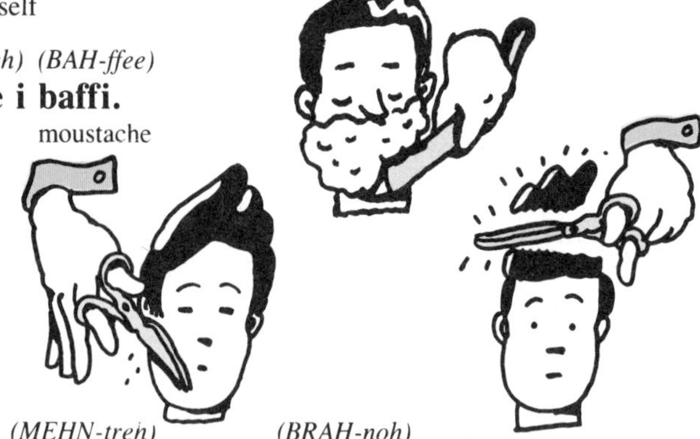

(MEHN-treh) (BRAH-noh)
Comincia a tagliare i capelli del signor Smith, mentre canta un brano d'opera.
while *excerpt*

È molto veloce *(veh-LOH-cheh)* [quick] **con le forbici** *(FOHR-bee-chee)* [scissors] **e la macchinetta** *(mah-kkee-NEH-ttah)* [clippers]**. Con il rasoio** *(rah-ZOH-yoh)* [straight razor]**, comincia a fare la barba del signor Smith. Ma il barbiere pensa** *(PEHN-sah)* **solo a cantare. Taglia la barba del signor Smith e gli taglia tutti i capelli! Adesso il signor Smith è calvo** *(KAHL-voh)* [bald]**!**

Il barbiere dice al signor Smith: «Non si preoccupi! Lei non deve più pettinarsi *(peh-ttee-NAHR-see)*[You do not have to comb yourself anymore!]**!»**

Are these passages getting easier for you? If not, go over this one again, and look up the words you don't recognize. Then select the correct answer to each question.

Dove decide di andare il signor Smith?

- ☐ Dal parrucchiere.
- ☐ Dal barbiere.
- ☐ Dal fruttivendolo.

Perché va a farsi tagliare la barba?

- ☐ Perché è calvo.
- ☐ Perché è simpatico.
- ☐ Perché non gli piace farsi la barba.

Ha i baffi?

- ☐ Sì.
- ☐ No.

Che cosa fa il barbiere al signor Smith?

- ☐ Gli taglia tutti i capelli.
- ☐ Lo pettina.
- ☐ Gli fa la permanente.

ANSWERS

Comprehension Dal barbiere. Perché non gli piace farsi la barba. Sì. Gli taglia tutti i capelli.

Review the words and expressions introduced in this unit, and then give this crossword puzzle a try.

Across
2. Curlers
4. To comb oneself
6. Hair dryer
8. Hair

Down
1. Blond
2. Sideburns
3. Moustache
4. Permanent
5. Razor
7. Bald
9. To wash

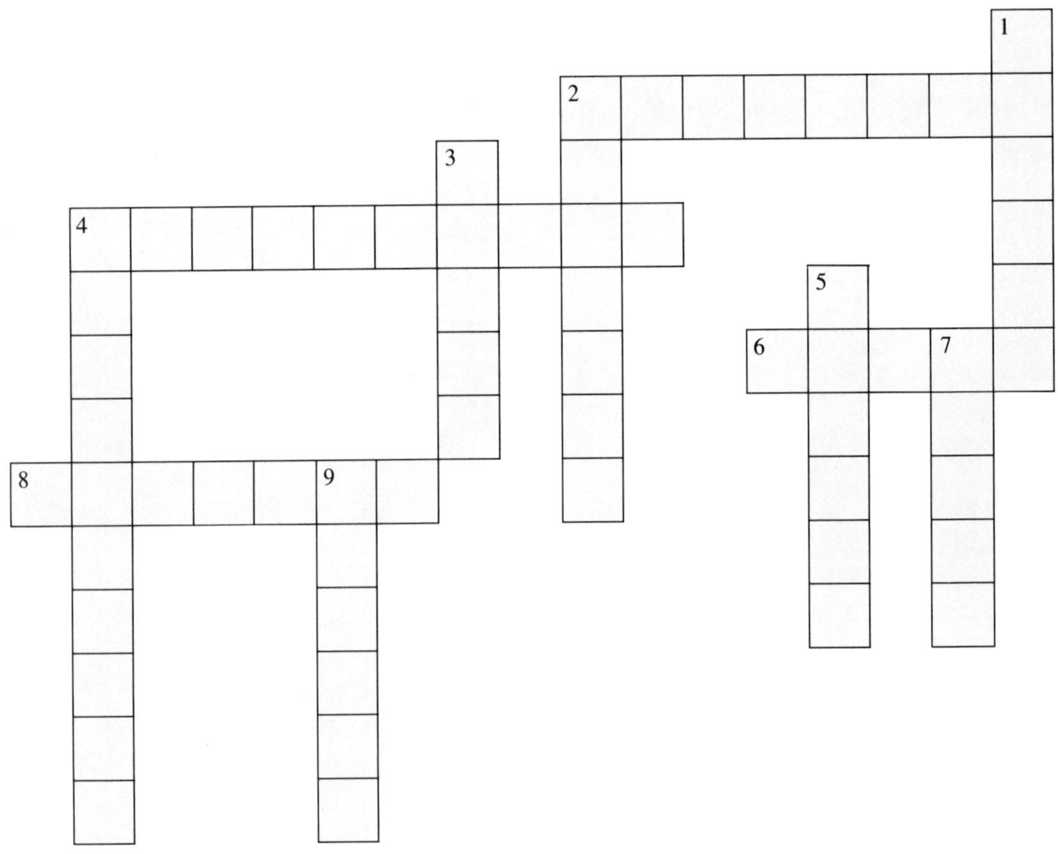

ANSWERS

Crossword Across: 2. bigodini **4.** pettinarsi **6.** casco **8.** capelli
Down: 1. biondo **2.** basette **3.** baffi **4.** permanente **5.** rasoio **7.** calvo **9.** lavare

21 Il chiosco / La cartoleria

(KYOHS-koh) (kahr-toh-leh-REE-ah)

Kiosk / Stationery Store

AL CHIOSCO

At the Kiosk

Naturally by this time, you know what to do with this dialogue.

(While walking through Rome, Anne and John Smith stop at a kiosk.)

(VEHN-deh) (johr-NAH-lee) JOHN **Scusi, lei vende i giornali in lingua inglese?**	Excuse me, do you sell English language newspapers?
PROPRIETARIO DI CHIOSCO **No signore. Lei è turista? Ho delle riviste americane.** *(ree-VEES-teh)*	No, sir. Are you a tourist? I have some American magazines.
(peh-ROH) JOHN **No, grazie. Però vorrei comprare delle cartoline e dei francobolli.** *(kahr-toh-LEE-neh) (frahn-koh-BOH-llee)*	No, thank you. However, I would like to buy some postcards and stamps.
PROPRIETARIO DI CHIOSCO **Ecco, signore.**	Here you are, sir.
ANNE **Io vorrei comprare delle sigarette per la mia amica in America e dei fiammiferi.** *(fyah-MMEE-feh-ree)*	I would like to buy some cigarettes for my friend in America and some matches.
PROPRIETARIO DI CHIOSCO **Ecco, signorina.**	Here you are, miss.
ANNE **Grazie. Quanto le devo?**	Thank you. How much do I owe you?

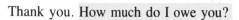

JOHN *(looking through wallet)* (*LAH-shah*) **Lascia** (*PEHR-deh-reh*) **perdere, Anne.** — Forget it, Anne.

ANNE **Perché?** — Why?

JOHN **Perché non abbiamo soldi con noi!** — Because we do not have any money with us!

Now you do the dialogue. Don't forget to check your answers.

JOHN **Scusi,** ______________________________?

PROPRIETARIO DI CHIOSCO **No signore. Lei è turista? Ho delle riviste americane.**

JOHN **No,** ______________________________.

PROPRIETARIO DI CHIOSCO **Ecco, signore.**

ANNE **Io** ______________________________.

PROPRIETARIO DI CHIOSCO **Ecco, signorina.**

ANNE **Grazie.** ______________________________?

JOHN **Lascia perdere, Anne.**

ANNE **Perché?**

JOHN **Perché** ______________________________!

You may have noticed that *molto* has several meanings. Here are some of them.

Marco mangia *molti* spaghetti.	**Gina ha *molti* amici.**	**La ragazza è *molto* bella.**
Mark eats *a lot of* spaghetti.	Gina has *many* friends.	The girl is *very* beautiful.

It is usually an adjective and therefore agrees with the noun it is describing. However, when it means "very," it is *not* an adjective and it is not followed by a noun, so it does not agree with the following word.

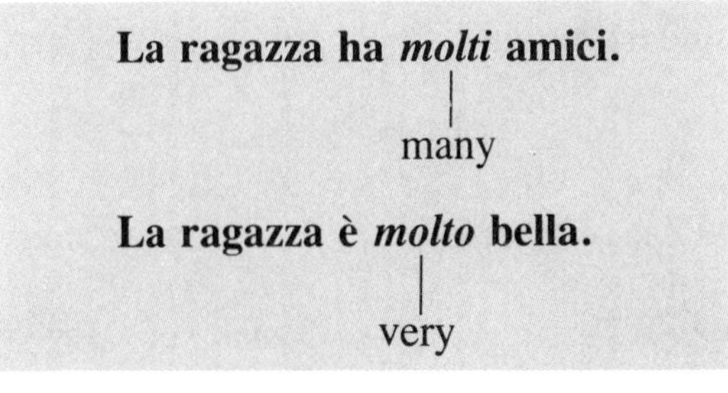

La ragazza ha molti amici.
many
La ragazza è molto bella.
very

ALLA CARTOLERIA

At the Stationery Store

You may have to visit a stationery store so you can write home. If so, you'll need to know these words.

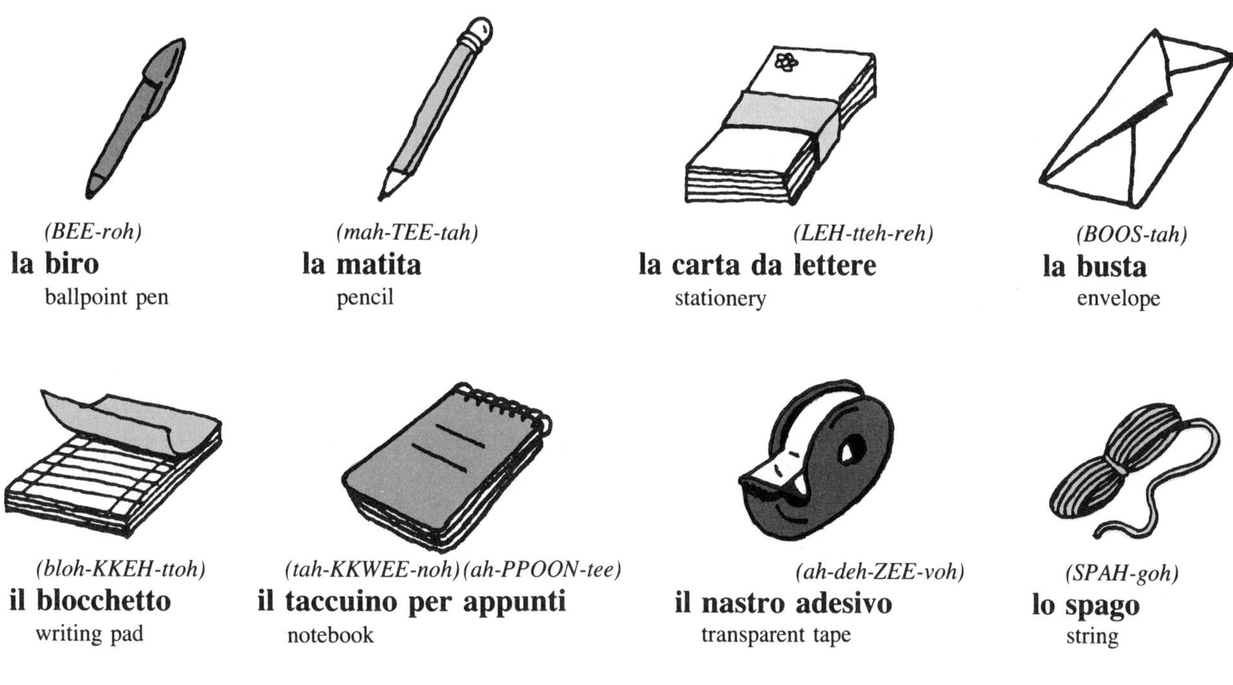

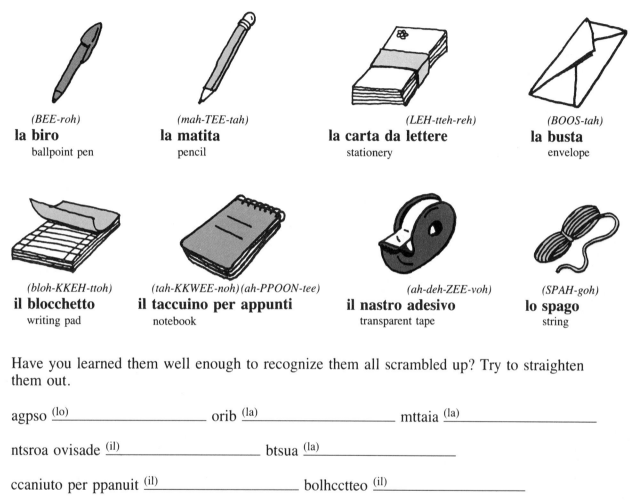

(BEE-roh)
la biro
ballpoint pen

(mah-TEE-tah)
la matita
pencil

(LEH-tteh-reh)
la carta da lettere
stationery

(BOOS-tah)
la busta
envelope

(bloh-KKEH-ttoh)
il blocchetto
writing pad

(tah-KKWEE-noh) (ah-PPOON-tee)
il taccuino per appunti
notebook

(ah-deh-ZEE-voh)
il nastro adesivo
transparent tape

(SPAH-goh)
lo spago
string

Have you learned them well enough to recognize them all scrambled up? Try to straighten them out.

agpso (lo) ________________ orib (la) ________________ mttaia (la) ________________

ntsroa ovisade (il) ________________ btsua (la) ________________

ccaniuto per ppanuit (il) ________________ bolhcctteo (il) ________________

tcraa da ttleeer (la) ________________

You're doing so well that you should have no trouble with this passage and the questions that follow.

Due signore entrano *(EHN-trah-noh)* (enter) **in una cartoleria. La prima signora compra un blocchetto di carta** (paper)**, una biro, una busta, e dei francobolli perché vuole scrivere una lettera. L'altra signora compra un taccuino per appunti, il nastro adesivo e lo spago. La prima signora è una turista**

ANSWERS

Unscrambling spago biro matita nastro adesivo busta taccuino per appunti blocchetto carta da lettere

americana, e l'altra è una turista francese. Le due signore fanno conoscenza e poi vanno al bar a prendere un espresso.

1. Chi entra in una cartoleria?
   - ☐ Due donne francesi.
   - ☐ Due donne americane.
   - ☐ Una francese e un'americana.

2. Chi compra la biro?
   - ☐ La donna francese.
   - ☐ La donna americana.
   - ☐ Nessuno.

3. Chi compra lo spago?
   - ☐ La donna francese.
   - ☐ La donna americana.
   - ☐ Nessuno.

4. Chi compra la matita?
   - ☐ La donna francese.
   - ☐ La donna americana.
   - ☐ Nessuno.

5. Dove vanno le due signore?
   - ☐ Al cinema.
   - ☐ Al chiosco.
   - ☐ Al bar.

You deserve an easy one, now! After reviewing the new words and expressions in this unit, you'll see some of them in the word-search puzzle. Write them out as you find them.

________	________	________
kiosk	newspaper	magazine
________	________	________
stamp	ballpoint pen	pencil

a	a	a	a	a	a	c	h	i	o	s	c	o	b	b	b	b	b	b	b
b	b	b	b	b	b	b	b	b	b	b	b	b	b	b	r	d	d	d	d
i	c	v	g	i	o	r	n	a	l	e	c	c	c	y	i	y	y	y	y
r	p	p	p	p	p	p	p	p	p	p	p	p	p	p	v	j	j	j	j
o	t	u	v	b	n	m	m	m	m	m	m	m	m	m	i	m	m	m	m
r	r	r	r	r	r	r	r	r	r	r	r	r	r	r	s	a	e	r	t
b	b	b	m	a	t	i	t	a	a	a	a	a	a	a	t	a	a	a	a
f	r	a	n	c	o	b	o	l	l	o	x	x	x	x	a	u	u	u	u

ANSWERS

Comprehension 1. Una francese e un'americana. **2.** La donna americana. **3.** La donna francese. **4.** Nessuno. **5.** Al bar.

Word search chiosco giornale rivista francobollo biro matita

22 *(joh-yeh-LLYEH-reh)* Il gioielliere / *(oh-roh-loh-JAH-yoh)* L'orologiaio

Jeweler / Watchmaker

IL GIOIELLIERE

The Jeweler

(brah-chah-LEH-ttoh)
il braccialetto
bracelet

(SPEE-llah)
la spilla
brooch

(koh-LLAH-nah)
la collana
necklace

(kah-TEH-nah)
la catena
chain

(ah-NEH-lloh)
l' anello
ring

(oh-reh-KKEE-noh)
l' orecchino
earrings

l'orecchino
(pehn-DEHN-teh)
pendente
pendant earrings

(As Mark and his wife are shopping at a jewelry store near the Ponte Vecchio in Florence, a tall, handsome man comes into the store.)

GIOIELLIERE **Desidera, signore?**	Can I help you, sir?
UOMO **Sì. Vorrei comprare qualcosa per mia moglie. Un braccialetto o un anello d'oro.**	Yes, I would like to buy something for my wife. A bracelet or a gold ring.

GIOIELLIERE **Ecco un braccialetto** *(ahr-JEHN-toh)* **d'argento e un anello d'oro.** — Here is a silver bracelet and a gold ring.

UOMO **Li prendo tutti e due.** — I'll take them both.

GIOIELLIERE **Vuole vedere qualcos'altro?** — Do you want to see something else?

UOMO **Sì. Una spilla e gli orecchini.** — Yes. A brooch and earrings.

GIOIELLIERE **Pendenti?** — Pendants?

UOMO **Sì. E poi vorrei anche una collana e una catena.** — Yes. And then I would also like a necklace and a chain.

GIOIELLIERE **D'oro?** — Gold?

UOMO **Naturalmente.** *(takes out a gun)* **E adesso mi dia tutti i soldi che ha!** — Naturally. And now give me all the money you've got!

When you're sure you have mastered this dialogue, go ahead and reconstruct it—but be sure to check it when you're finished.

Desidera, signore?

Sì. Vorrei comprare q_______________ per mia moglie. Un b_______________ o un anello d'_______________.

Ecco un braccialetto d'_______________ e un a_______________ d'oro.

Li p_______________ tutti e due.

Vuole vedere qualcos'altro?

Sì. Una s_______________ e gli o_______________.

P_______________?

Sì. E poi vorrei anche una c_______________ e una c_______________.

D'oro?

Naturalmente. E adesso mi dia tutti i s_______________ che ha!

(PYEH-treh) (preh-TSYOH-seh)
PIETRE PREZIOSE
Precious Stones

(zmeh-RAHL-doh)
lo smeraldo

(roo-BEE-noh)
il rubino

(PLAH-tee-noh)
il platino

(toh-PAH-tsee-oh)
il topazio

(DZAH-ffee-roh)
lo zaffiro

(PEHR-lah)
la perla

l' argento
silver

(dyah-MAHN-teh)
il diamante

l' oro
gold

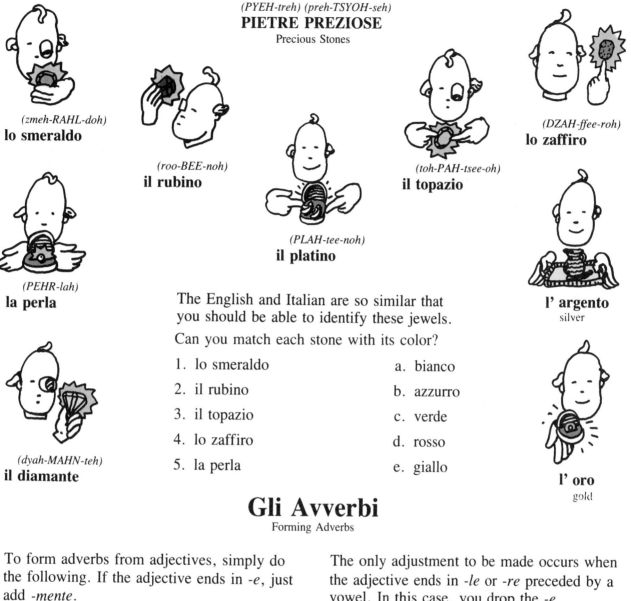

The English and Italian are so similar that you should be able to identify these jewels.

Can you match each stone with its color?

1. lo smeraldo	a. bianco
2. il rubino	b. azzurro
3. il topazio	c. verde
4. lo zaffiro	d. rosso
5. la perla	e. giallo

Gli Avverbi
Forming Adverbs

To form adverbs from adjectives, simply do the following. If the adjective ends in *-e*, just add *-mente*.

elegante elegant	**elegante*mente*** elegant*ly*
intelligente intelligent	**intelligente*mente*** intelligent*ly*

The only adjustment to be made occurs when the adjective ends in *-le* or *-re* preceded by a vowel. In this case, you drop the *-e*.

(proh-BAH-bee-leh) **probab*ile*** probable	**probabil*mente*** probab*ly*
popol*are* popular	**popolar*mente*** popular*ly*

If the adjective ends in *-o*, change the *-o* to *-a* and add *-mente*.

sicuro sure	**(sicura)**	**sicura*mente*** sure*ly*	**lento** slow	**(lenta)**	**lenta*mente*** slow*ly*

ANSWERS

Matching 1-c, 2-d, 3-e, 4-b, 5-a

L'OROLOGIAIO

The Watchmaker

(ZVEH-llyah)
la sveglia
alarm clock

(POHL-soh)
l' orologio da polso
wrist watch

l' orologiaio
watchmaker

(oh-roh-loh-jeh-REE-ah)
l' orologeria
watchmaker's shop

If you have to get your watch fixed, here are some useful expressions.

(ah-jjoos-TAH-reh) **Mi può aggiustare il mio orologio?**	Can you fix my watch?
(ah-VAHN-tee) **Il mio orologio va avanti.**	My watch is fast.
(een-DYEH-troh) **Il mio orologio va indietro.**	My watch is slow.
Il mio orologio non va.	My watch has stopped.
(kah-ree-KAH-reh) **Devo caricare il mio orologio.**	I have to wind my watch.

Here we go with another passage; test yourself by completing the statements.

Il mio orologio non va bene. Un giorno va avanti e un'altro va indietro. Oggi non va e non lo posso caricare. Allora lo porto dall'orologiaio e l'orologiaio lo aggiusta. Il giorno dopo l'orologio va avanti! Forse devo comprare un orologio nuovo.

L'uomo dice che il suo orologio non ____________________.

Un giorno l'orologio va ____________________ e un'altro va ____________________.

Oggi non va e l'uomo non lo può ____________________.

Allora l'uomo porta l'orologio dall'____________________

e l'orologiaio lo ____________________.

Ma il giorno dopo l'orologio va ____________________!

L'uomo dice che deve comprare un orologio ____________________.

ANSWERS

Comprehension (non) va bene. (va) avanti (e) / (va) indietro. (può) caricare. (dall') orologiaio (e) / (lo) aggiusta. (va) avanti! (orologio) nuovo.

23 Il negozio di articoli da regalo / Il negozio di musica / Il negozio di fotografie

(ahr-TEE-koh-lee) (reh-GAH-loh) (MOO-zee-kah) (foh-toh-grah-FEE-eh)

Gift Shop / Music Store / Photography Shop

AL NEGOZIO DI ARTICOLI DA REGALO

At the Gift Shop

You certainly won't want to go home without some Italian presents! Here is what to look for.

(sehr-VEE-tsee-oh)
il servizio da tè
tea service

(PEH-lleh)
la pelle
leather

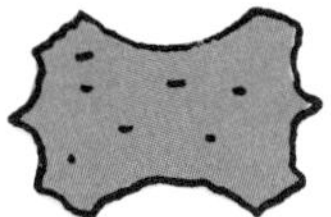

(reh-GAH-loh)
il regalo
present

(BOHR-sah)
la borsa
purse

(ah-NEH-lloh)
l'anello
ring

(bohr-SEH-ttah)
la borsetta
small purse

(KYAH-veh)
la chiave
key

(proh-FOO-moh)
il profumo
perfume

(pohr-tah-FOH-llyoh)
il portafoglio
wallet

(SHAHR-pah)
la sciarpa
scarf

(CHOHN-doh-loh)
il ciondolo
charm

(ree-cheh-VOO-tah)
la ricevuta
receipt

(KWAH-droh)
il quadro
painting

Are you ready for the dialogue? Follow it up with the true-false questions.

(Mary Smith and her son John go into a gift shop.)

COMMESSA	**Desiderano?**	Can I help you?
MARY	**Sì. Vorrei portare dei regali ai miei amici in America. Mi può aiutare?**	Yes. I would like to bring my friends in America some gifts. Can you help me?
COMMESSA	**Volentieri. Forse un po' di profumo, una borsetta, o una sciarpa?**	Gladly. Maybe some perfume, a small purse, or a scarf?
MARY	**No. Voglio qualcosa per uomo.**	No. I want something for men.
JOHN	**Sì. Abbiamo molti zii in America.**	Yes. We have many uncles in America.
COMMESSA	**Allora un portafoglio o un quadro?**	Then a wallet or a painting?
JOHN	**No. Costano troppo.**	No. They cost too much.
COMMESSA	**Lei può portare un regalo gratis ai suoi zii.**	You can bring a free gift to your uncles.
JOHN	**Ah, sì? Che?**	Yes? What?
COMMESSA	**I miei saluti!**	My greetings!

1. Mary vuole comprare dei regali per i suoi amici. ☐ Vero ☐ Falso
2. Mary compra il profumo. ☐ Vero ☐ Falso
3. Mary vuole una sciarpa. ☐ Vero ☐ Falso
4. Mary vuole qualcosa per uomo. ☐ Vero ☐ Falso
5. Il portafoglio e il quadro costano poco. ☐ Vero ☐ Falso
6. Il commesso dà un regalo gratis a John. ☐ Vero ☐ Falso

ANSWERS

True/False **1.** Vero **2.** Falso **3.** Falso **4.** Vero **5.** Falso **6.** Falso

AL NEGOZIO DI MUSICA

At the Music Store

We haven't given you all the translations for this new vocabulary, but you should be able to figure them out.

(RAH-dee-oh)
la radio

(jee-rah-DEES-kee)
il giradischi
record player

(reh-jees-trah-TOH-reh)
il registratore
tape recorder

(teh-leh-vee-ZOH-reh)
il televisore

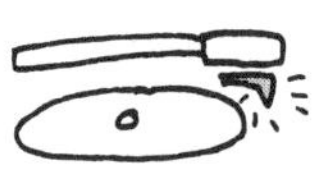

(poon-TEE-nah)
la puntina
needle

(moo-zee-kah-SSEH-ttah)
la musicassetta

(náhs-troh) (mah-nyéh-tee-koh)
il nastro magnetico
tape

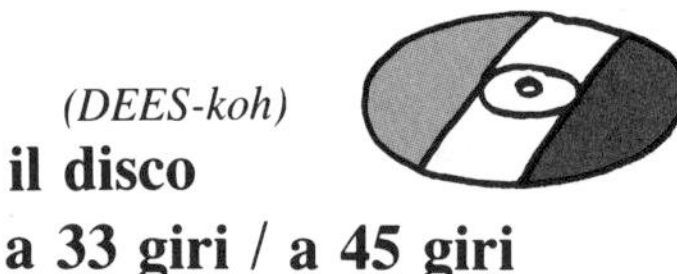

(DEES-koh)
il disco
a 33 giri / a 45 giri

Did you get them all? Then go ahead with the following paragraph.

(KLAH-ssee-kah)
Il signor Smith ama la musica classica.
loves
Cerca un negozio di musica in tutta la città.

Finalmente ne trova uno. Ascolta i dischi
Finally
per tre ore! Suo figlio, invece, ama solo la

musica «folk». Anche il figlio entra nel negozio.

(kee-TAH-rrah)
Lui compra una chitarra e si mette a cantare.
starts to

(eem-bah-rah-TSAH-toh)
Imbarazzato, il signor Smith torna all'albergo.
Embarrassed

Now you can probably rearrange these sentences without even looking back.

classica / ama / Smith / Il / la / signor / musica

____

tutta / in / città / la / Cerca / negozio / musica / di / un

____

trova / Finalmente / uno / ne

____

figlio / Suo / ama / solo / invece / folk / musica / la

____

chitarra / Lui / una / compra / cantare / a / mette / e / si

____

IL NEGOZIO DI FOTOGRAFIE

At the Photography Shop

Once again we have left out some translations—but you will recognize the words or the pictures.

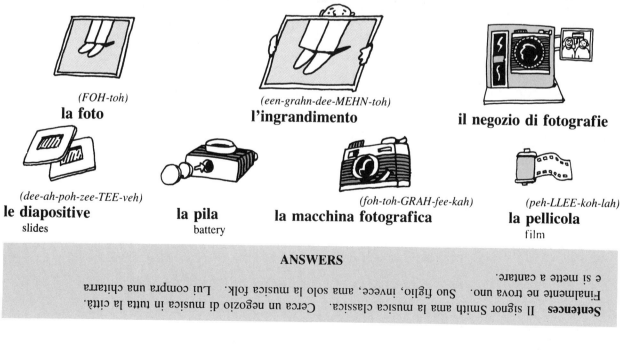

(FOH-toh)
la foto

(een-grahn-dee-MEHN-toh)
l'ingrandimento

il negozio di fotografie

(dee-ah-poh-zee-TEE-veh)
le diapositive
slides

la pila
battery

(foh-toh-GRAH-fee-kah)
la macchina fotografica

(peh-LLEE-koh-lah)
la pellicola
film

ANSWERS

Sentences Il signor Smith ama la musica classica. Cerca un negozio di musica in tutta la città. Finalmente ne trova uno. Suo figlio, invece, ama solo la musica folk. Lui compra una chitarra e si mette a cantare.

(Mark is picking up the photos he had brought in to be developed.)

MARK	**Sono pronte le mie foto?**	Are my prints ready?
COMMESSO	**Sì, eccole.** *(EH-kkoh-leh)*	Yes, here they are.
MARK	**Mamma mia, come sono brutto!**	Heavens, how ugly I am!
COMMESSO	**No, signore. Lei ha torto.**	No, sir. You are wrong.
MARK	**Lei è molto gentile. Senta, la mia macchina fotografica non funziona. La può aggiustare?**	You're very kind. Listen, my camera doesn't work. Can you fix it?

COMMESSO	**Certo.**	Certainly.
MARK	**Ecco un'altra pellicola. Questa volta voglio le diapositive.**	Here is another roll of film. This time I want slides.
COMMESSO	**Va bene, signore. Grazie e arrivederla.**	Okay, sir. Thank you and good-bye.
MARK	**Arrivederla.**	Good-bye.

Be sure you thoroughly understand the dialogue before going on to the completion exercise below (and check your answers!).

Sono pronte le mie f_______________?

Sì, eccole.

Mamma mia, come sono b_______________!

No, signore. Lei ha t_______________.

Lei è molto g_______________. S_______________, la mia m_______________ f_______________ non funziona. La può a_______________?

Certo.

Ecco un'altra p_______________. Questa volta voglio le d_______________.

Va bene, signore. Grazie e arrivederla.

A_______________.

Before you leave this chapter, go over the new vocabulary again; then practice it by unscrambling these words.

qdruao ____________________ (painting) grleao ____________________ (gift)

dioar ____________________ (radio) chidisragi ____________________ (record player)

rgiestraerot ____________________ (tape recorder) tlveeirose ____________________ (television set)

msuicassatte ____________________ (cassette) dscoi ____________________ (record)

plleicoal ____________________ (film)

ANSWERS

Unscrambling quadro regalo radio giradischi registratore televisore musicassetta disco pellicola

24 Riparazioni: L'optometrista / Il calzolaio

(ree-pah-rah-TSYOH-nee) (ohp-toh-meh-TREES-tah) (kahl-tsoh-LAHyoh)

Repair Services: Optometrist / Shoemaker

This dialogue contains words and expressions that you might find helpful if you break your glasses in Italy.

DALL'OPTOMETRISTA

At the Optometrist

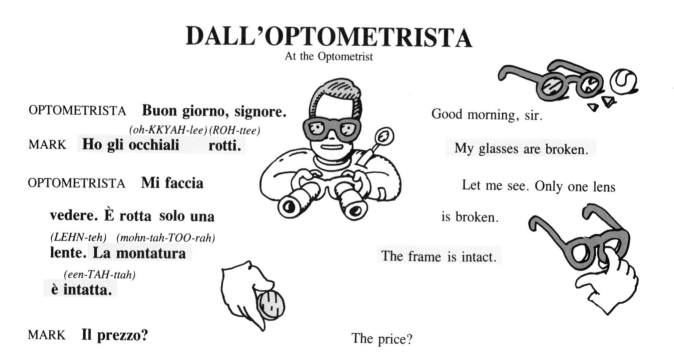

OPTOMETRISTA **Buon giorno, signore.** — Good morning, sir.

(oh-KKYAH-lee) (ROH-ttee)

MARK **Ho gli occhiali rotti.** — My glasses are broken.

OPTOMETRISTA **Mi faccia vedere. È rotta solo una** *(LEHN-teh)* **lente. La** *(mohn-tah-TOO-rah)* **montatura** *(een-TAH-ttah)* **è intatta.** — Let me see. Only one lens is broken. The frame is intact.

MARK **Il prezzo?** — The price?

OPTOMETRISTA **Cinquantamila lire.**	50.000 lira.
MARK **Cinquantamila lire!**	50.000 lira!
Per solo una lente?	For just one lens?
OPTOMETRISTA **Va bene. Per lei solo venticinquemila lire.**	Okay. For you only 25.000 lira.
MARK **Li posso ritirare martedì?**	Can I get them Tuesday?
OPTOMETRISTA **No, ma venga giovedì.**	No, but come back Thursday.
MARK **Sì. Grazie e arrivederci**	Yes. Thank you and good-bye.

Now here are some lines from the dialogue. Matching them won't be difficult.

Ho gli . . .	una lente?
È rotta solo . . .	venga gìovedì.
La montatura . . .	occhiali rotti.
Per solo . . .	ritirare martedì?
Li posso . . .	una lente.
No, ma . . .	è intatta.

DAL CALZOLAIO

At the Shoemaker

(kahl-tsoh-LAH-yoh)
il calzolaio
shoemaker

(STREEN-geh)
le stringhe
shoelaces

(SAHN-dah-loh)
il sandalo
sandal

le scarpe
shoes

See how quickly you can read this paragraph. Then go over it until it all comes easily, and answer the questions that follow.

La signora Smith porta le sue scarpe (shoes) **e i suoi sandali** *(SAHN-dah-lee)* **dal calzolaio. I sandali hanno bisogno di un tacco** *(TAH-kkoh)* (heel) **nuovo e le scarpe hanno bisogno di stringhe** *(STREEN-geh)* (shoelaces)**. Va dal calzolaio in Via Veneto. È un uomo molto simpatico. La signora Smith gli chiede se può aggiustare le sue scarpe e i suoi sandali. Il calzolaio dice che saranno** *(sah-RAH-nnoh)* (they will be) **pronti tra due giorni. Quando la signora Smith va a prendere le scarpe e i sandali vede un cartello** (sign) **sulla porta: "Chiuso** *(KYOO-zoh)* **per le ferie** *(FEH-ree-eh)***."** (Closed for the holidays.)

Dove va la signora Smith?

- ☐ Dall'optometrista.
- ☐ Dal gioielliere.
- ☐ Dal calzolaio.

Di che cosa hanno bisogno i sandali?

- ☐ Di un colore nuovo.
- ☐ Di un tacco nuovo.
- ☐ Di niente.

Di che cosa hanno bisogno le scarpe?

- ☐ Di stringhe.
- ☐ Di un tacco nuovo.
- ☐ Di niente.

Dov'è il calzolaio?

- ☐ In Via Nazionale.
- ☐ In Via Veneto.
- ☐ A casa.

Quando saranno pronti i sandali e le scarpe?

- ☐ Domani.
- ☐ Tra una settimana.
- ☐ Tra due giorni.

Che cosa vede sulla porta la signora Smith?

- ☐ Vede un cartello.
- ☐ Vede una foto.
- ☐ Vede una lettera.

ANSWERS

Comprehension Dal calzolaio. Di un tacco nuovo Di stringhe. In Via Veneto. Tra due giorni. Vede un cartello.

ESSENTIAL SERVICES

(eh-ssehn-TSYAH-lee)
Servizi Essenziali

(BAHN-keh)
25 Le banche
Banks (Banking)

(vah-LOH-reh)
VALORE DEL DENARO
Denominations

Notice that Italian denominations are high in comparison to American ones. In fact, a 1.000 lira note is worth less than *one* American dollar. There are also coins for 10, 50, and 100 lire. Be aware that if your expected change is less than 50 lira you might get a token or even a piece of candy! These are probably worth more than the actual change you would otherwise get. You can get good exchange rates at most banks and hotels. And many stores give a good exchange rate as well.

(Courtesy of Ernst Klett Verlag, Stuttgart)

(KAHM-byoh)

LE BANCHE, IL CAMBIO, E GLI

(ah-SSEH-nyee)

ASSEGNI TURISTICI

Banks, Money Exchange, and Traveler's Checks

Gente e cose

People and Things

(deh-NAH-roh)
il denaro
money

l'assegno turistico
traveler's check

(kohn-TAHN-tee)
i contanti
cash

(PREHS-tee-toh)
il prestito
loan

la banca
bank

(eem-pyeh-GAH-toh)
l'impiegato di banca
bank employee

(dee -reh-TTOH-reh)
il direttore
manager

(kah-SSYEH-rah)
la cassiera (f)
(kah-SSYEH-reh)
il cassiere (m)
teller

(spohr-TEH-lloh)
lo sportello
teller's window

il conto
account

il biglietto di banca
bank note

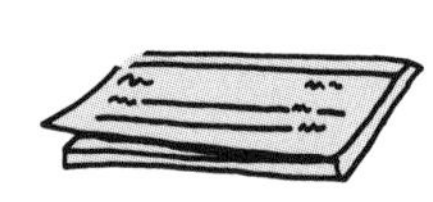

(lee-BREH-ttoh)
il libretto di assegni
checkbook

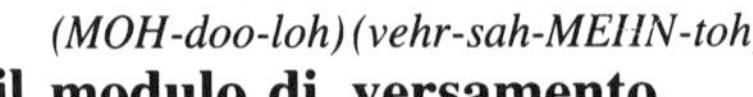

(MOH-doo-loh) (vehr-sah-MEHN-toh)
il modulo di versamento
deposit slip

il modulo di
(preh-leh-vah-MEHN-toh)
prelevamento
withdrawal slip

Come si fa . . .

How to . . .

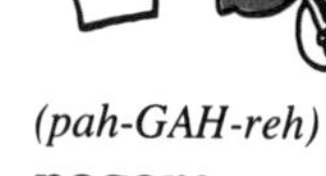
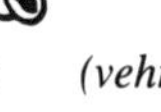

(*kahm-BYAH-reh*)
il cambio / cambiare
to exchange

(*vah-LOO-tah*)
la valuta
exchange rate

(*pah-GAH-reh*)
pagare
to pay

(*vehr-SAH-reh*) (*deh-poh-zee-TAH-reh*)
versare / depositare
to deposit

(*preh-leh-VAH-reh*)
prelevare
to withdraw

(*een-kah-SSAH-reh*)
incassare un assegno
to cash a check

aprire un conto
to open an account

(*feer-MAH-reh*)
firmare
to sign

After all of that vocabulary, see how much of it you can remember. Match each word or expression to each picture by checking off the appropriate box.

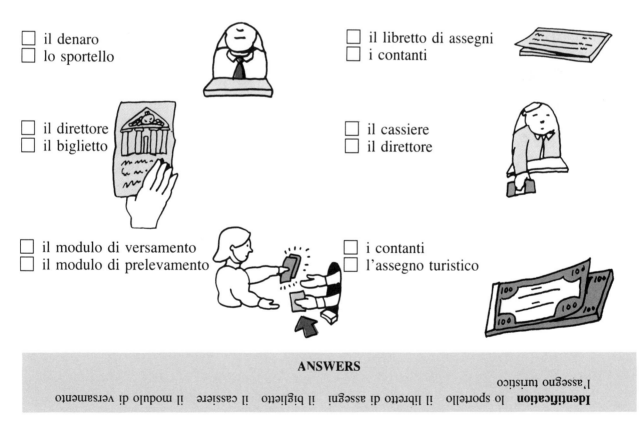

☐ il denaro
☐ lo sportello

☐ il libretto di assegni
☐ i contanti

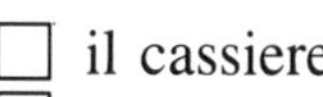

☐ il direttore
☐ il biglietto

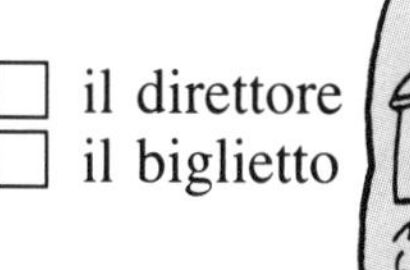
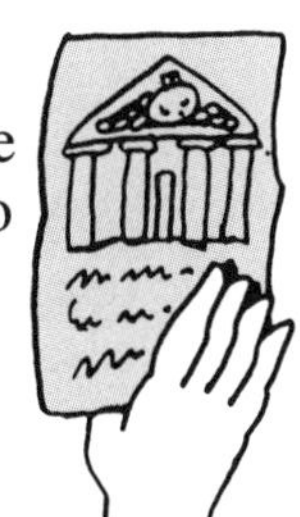

☐ il cassiere
☐ il direttore

☐ il modulo di versamento
☐ il modulo di prelevamento

☐ i contanti
☐ l'assegno turistico

ANSWERS

Identification lo sportello il libretto di assegni il biglietto il cassiere il modulo di versamento l'assegno turistico

Did you get them all? Let's try once more:

1. Io vorrei ________________ dieci dollari americani.
exchange

2. Io vorrei ________________ centomila lire (100.000 lira).
withdraw

3. Io vorrei ________________ un assegno.
cash

4. Io vorrei ________________ 50,000 lire.
deposit

(Mark Smith enters a bank; there are several people ahead of him.)

CASSIERE **Desidera?**	May I help you?
UOMI **Vorrei incassare un assegno ma è finito il mio libretto d'assegni.**	I want to cash a check, but my checkbook is used up.
CASSIERE **Per favore compili questo modulo di prelevamento, lo firmi, e ritorni.** *(kohm-PEE-lee)*	Please fill out this withdrawal slip, sign it, and come back.
UN GIOVANE **Vorrei chiedere un imprestito.** *(eem-PREHS-tee-toh)*	I would like to apply for a loan.

ANSWERS

Verbs 1. cambiare **2.** prelevare **3.** incassare **4.** versare / depositare

CASSIERE **Per favore, attenda là il direttore. Lui si occupa degli impréstiti.** *(OH-koo-pah)*	Please wait over there for the manager. He takes care of loans.
DONNA **È possibile aprire un conto e fare un versamento?**	May I open an account and make a deposit?
CASSIERE **Deve andare da un altro impiegato, al prossimo sportello.**	You must see another bank employee for that, at the next teller's window.

(Finally Mark approaches the teller.)

MARK **Buon giorno, signora. Ho bisogno di cambiare questo assegno turistico di cento dollari americani in lire italiane.**	Good day, sir. I need to exchange this $100 American traveler's check for Italian lira.
CASSIERE **Molto bene. Vuole i soldi in banconote alte o basse?**	Very well. Do you want the money in large or small bills?
MARK **Alte, per favore.**	Large, please.
CASSIERE **Ecco, signore. Per favore firmi questa ricevuta.** *(ree-cheh-VOO-tah)*	Here you are, sir. Please sign this receipt.
MARK **Grazie e arrivederci.**	Thank you and good-bye.

After you have become familiar with the dialogue, try to complete the following sentences from it.

Vorrei incassare un ________________ ma è finito il mio ________________ d'assegni.

Vorrei chiedere un ________________.

È possibile aprire _____ __________ e fare un ________________?

Ho bisogno di ________________questo assegno ________________ di ________________

________________ americani in ______ ________. Per favore firmi questa ____________.

If you got all that, then this paragraph and the questions that follow will be a breeze!

Il signor Smith entra in una banca con sua moglie. Chiede al cassiere di cambiare cento dollari americani. Il cassiere gli chiede di riempire un modulo e di firmare il suo nome. Il signor Smith non vuole firmare il suo nome e allora decide di non cambiare più i cento dollari.

Chi entra in una banca?

- ☐ Il signor Smith e suo figlio.
- ☐ Il signor Smith e sua moglie.
- ☐ Il cassiere.

Che cosa chiede al cassiere?

- ☐ Gli chiede come sta.
- ☐ Gli chiede di versare un assegno.
- ☐ Gli chiede di cambiare dollari americani.

Quanti dollari vuole cambiare?

- ☐ Cento.
- ☐ Duecento.
- ☐ Trecento.

Che cosa gli chiede il cassiere?

- ☐ Di bere il caffè.
- ☐ Di prelevare i soldi.
- ☐ Di firmare il suo nome.

Che cosa decide di fare il signor Smith?

- ☐ Di cambiare i soldi.
- ☐ Di non cambiare i soldi.
- ☐ Di chiamare il direttore.

ANSWERS

Comprehension Il signor Smith e sua moglie. Gli chiede di cambiare dollari americani. Cento. Di firmare il suo nome. Di non cambiare i soldi.

This crossword puzzle is a final check on how much you have learned about money and banking.

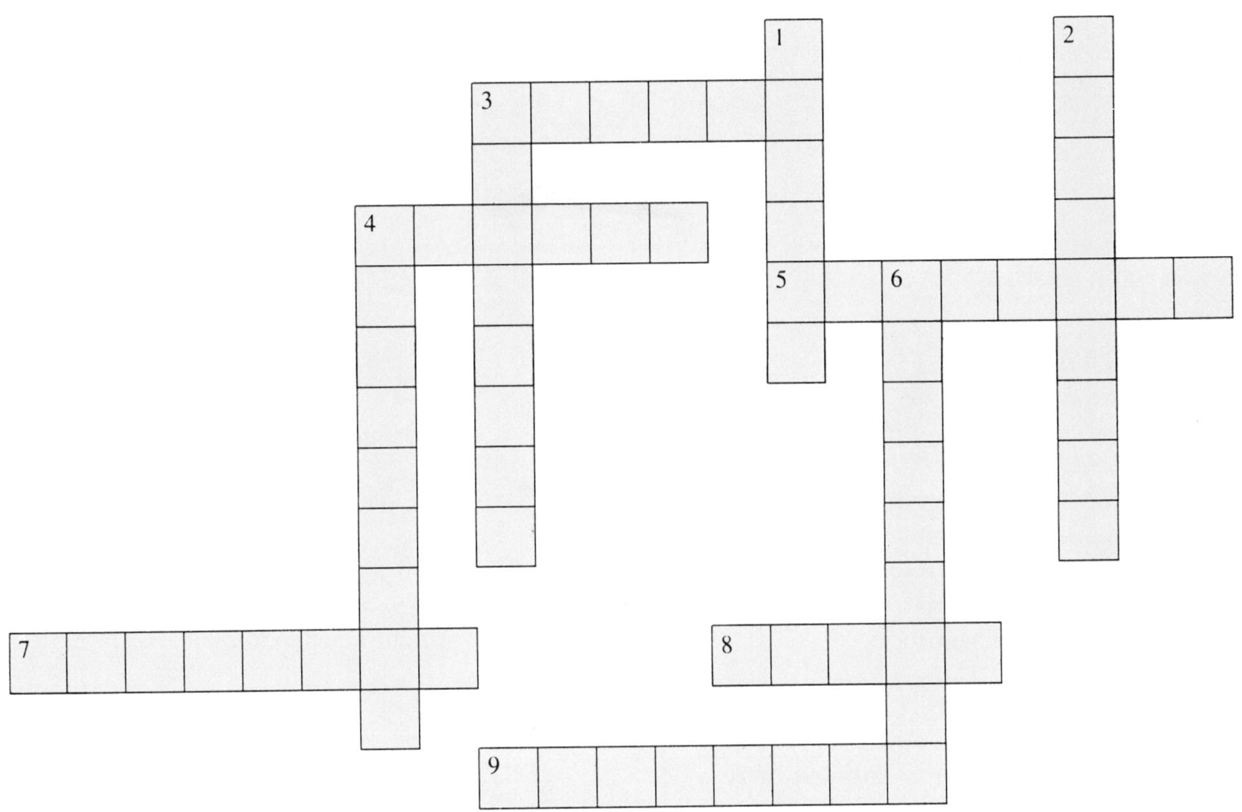

Across

3. Exchange
4. Money
5. Checkbook
7. Teller (f.)
8. Account
9. Deposit

Down

1. Slip
2. Teller's window
3. Cash
4. Manager
6. Bank note

ANSWERS

Crossword Across: 3. cambio **4.** denaro **5.** libretto **7.** cassiera **8.** conto **9.** deposito

Down: 1. modulo **2.** sportello **3.** contanti **4.** direttore **6.** biglietto

26 Servizio postale
(pohs-TAH-leh)

Postal Service

There are some new words in this dialogue. If you need help, check the vocabulary on the next page.

LINA	**Che cosa fai?**	What are you doing?
	(JOH-koh) (pohs-TEE-noh)	
PINO	**Gioco a postino.**	I'm playing postman.
LINA	**E le lettere dove sono?**	And where are the letters?
	(kah-SSEH-tteh)	
PINO	**Nelle cassette per le lettere delle case dei nostri vicini.**	In our neighbors' mailboxes.
	(PREH-zoh)	
LINA	**E dove hai preso le lettere?**	And where did you get the letters?
	(bah-OO-leh) *(TYEH-nee)* *(ah-TTOHR-noh)*	
PINO	**Dal baule nella tua camera dove tieni quel pacchetto di lettere con un bel nastro rosa attorno.**	From the trunk in your room where you keep that package of letters with a beautiful pink ribbon around them.
	(ah-MOH-reh)	
LINA	**Mamma mia! Sono le mie lettere d'amore!**	Heavens! They are my love letters!

Are you sure you've got it? Then go ahead and fix up these sentences.

a / Gioco / postino

E / dove / lettere / sono / le

ANSWERS

Sentences Gioco a postino. E le lettere dove sono?

le / per / cassette / lettere / Nelle / case / delle / dei / vicini / nostri

---

dove / E / hai preso / lettere / le

---

tieni / dove / Dal / camera / baule / tua / nella / pacchetto / quel / di / bel / lettere / un / con / attorno / nastro / rosa

---

d'amore / Sono / lettere / mie / le

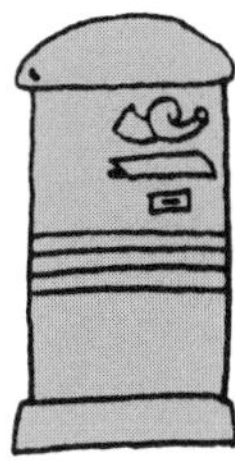

la cassetta per le lettere
mailbox

il postino
mailman

(teh-leh-GRAH-mmah)
il telegramma
telegram

la posta / le lettere / le cartoline
mail letters cards

lo sportello
office window

il pacco / il pacchetto
package

ANSWERS

Nelle cassette per le lettere delle case dei nostri vicini. E dove hai preso le lettere?
Dal baule nella tua camera dove tieni quel pacchetto di lettere con un bel nastro rosa attorno.
Sono le mie lettere d'amore!

You learned the last dialogue so quickly that we have another for you!

(John wants to mail a package to the U.S. Anne goes with him to the post office.)

JOHN	**È molto lontano l'ufficio postale?**	Is the post office very far?
ANNE	**No, è vicino all'albergo,**	No, it's near the hotel,
	ma c'è sempre tanta gente.	but there's always a lot of people.
	Gli italiani non sempre fanno *(KOH-dah) (ohr-dee-NAH-tah)* **la coda ordinata,** *(zbree-GYAH-moh-chee)* **allora sbrighiamoci!**	Italians don't always line up in an orderly way, so let's hurry.

(They reach the post office and find that it isn't busy.)

JOHN	**Meno male che non c'è nessuno.**	Thank heavens that no one is here.
ANNE	**John, ecco lo sportello per i pacchi.**	John, here is the parcel post window.
JOHN	**Ecco signore. Voglio mandare** *(mahn-DAH-reh)* **questo pacco negli Stati Uniti.**	Here you are, sir. I want to send this package to the U.S.
CLERK	*(weighs the package)* *(ah-ffrahn-kah-TOO-rah)* **L'affrancatura per questo pacco è di tremila lire. Vada allo sportello per i francobolli.**	The postage for this package is 3,000 lira. Go to the stamp window.

(John buys stamps and Anne goes to the postcard window.)

ANNE **Quattro cartoline, per favore.**	Four postcards, please.
CLERK **Ecco signorina.**	Here you are, miss.
ANNE **Quanto è l'affrancatura per via** *(ah-EH-reh-ah)* *(rah-kkoh-mahn-DAH-tah)* **aerea e per posta raccomandata?**	What's the postage for airmail and for registered mail?
CLERK **Mi dispiace, signorina, ma non la posso più servire. In questo momento comincia lo sciopero!** *(SHOH-peh-roh)*	I'm sorry, miss, but I cannot serve you anymore. We are on strike as of this moment! (*literally,* at this moment the strike begins)

When you have read the dialogue several times, check off each statement as either true or false.

1. L'ufficio postale è molto lontano. ☐ Vero ☐ Falso
2. Gli italiani fanno sempre la coda ordinata. ☐ Vero ☐ Falso
3. Oggi non c'è tanta gente all'ufficio postale. ☐ Vero ☐ Falso
4. L'affrancatura per il pacco di John è di tremila lire. ☐ Vero ☐ Falso
5. Anne compra tre cartoline. ☐ Vero ☐ Falso
6. Lo sciopero comincia domani. ☐ Vero ☐ Falso

Ricordati

Remember

Here are a few useful expressions. Can you understand them?

(speh-DEE-reh)
mandare/spedire una lettera

depositare la valigia

ANSWERS

True/False 1. Falso **2.** Falso **3.** Vero **4.** Vero **5.** Falso **6.** Falso

spedire un telegramma

la commessa

You may have noticed that the adjective *buono* is used both before and after the noun. When it is used before the noun, you must make a few adjustments.

> The form *buon* is used before a singular masculine noun beginning with any vowel or consonant, except *z*, and before *s* plus a consonant.
>
> **Buon giorno.**
> **Buon appetito.**
>
> And in front of a feminine singular noun beginning with any vowel, the appropriate form is *buon'*.
>
> **Buon'amica.**

Let's take a breather and do an easy one! Fill in the blanks as suggested by the pictures.

Maria scrive una ____________________.

Giovanni spedisce dei ____________________ in Italia.

La signora ha bisogno di un ____________________.

Gina mette le lettere nella ____________________.

ANSWERS

Identification lettera (letter) pacchi (packages) francobollo (stamp) cassetta per le lettere (mailbox)

I verbi ancora una volta!

Verbs Again!

Notice that verbs ending in *-care* and *-gare* require an *h* when the verb ending starts with an *i*.

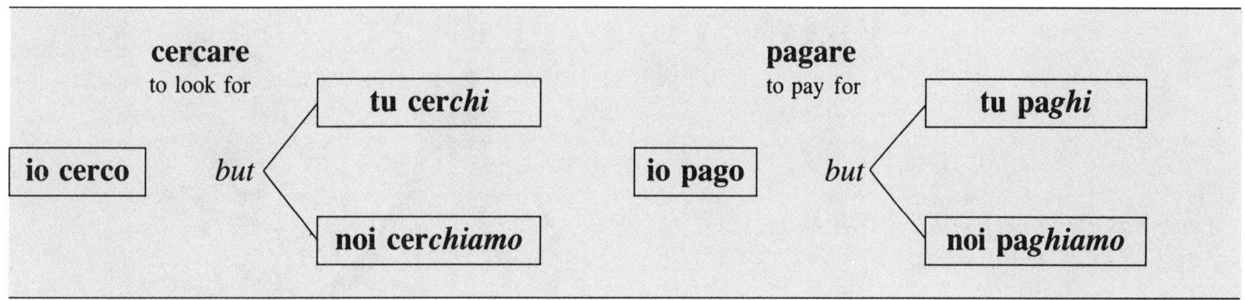

That's not so hard to remember, is it? Now let's wind up the post office chapter by adding the missing letters to the following words.

il post____no, la ____assetta per le l____tter____, la post____, il t____l____gramma,

lo sportel____o, l'____ffrancatur____

ANSWERS

Fill-ins il postino; la cassetta per le lettere; la posta; il telegramma; lo sportello; l'affrancatura

27 Il servizio telefonico

(sehr-VEE-tsee-oh) (teh-leh-FOH-nee-koh)

Telephone Service

PRONTO . . . PRONTO

Hello . . . Hello

(John has become friendly with Paola, a girl he met at the bank last week. He is in a phone booth and Anne is outside.)

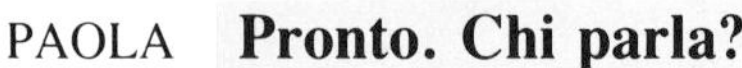

PAOLA **Pronto. Chi parla?** — Hello. Who is it?

JOHN **Ciao, Paola. Sono John.** — Hi, Paola. It's John. (*literally,* I am John)

PAOLA **Dove sei?** — Where are you?

(kah-BEE-nah) (teh-leh-FOH-nee-kah)

JOHN **In una cabina telefonica vicino alla casa tua. Vuoi uscire con me stasera?** — At a phone booth near your home. Do you want to come out with me tonight?

PAOLA **Dove?** — Where?

JOHN **Al cinema.** — To the movies.

PAOLA **No. Non mi piace il cinema.** — No. I don't like the movies.

(bah-LLAH-reh)

JOHN **Allora andiamo a ballare?** — Then shall we go out dancing?

PAOLA **No. Non so ballare.** — No. I don't know how to dance.

JOHN **Andiamo a un ristorante?** — Shall we go to a restaurant?

PAOLA **No. Sono a dieta.** — No. I'm on a diet.

ANNE *(who has been waiting to use the phone)* **Ti dico io dove devi andare, John! A un'altra cabina!** — I'll tell you where to go, John! To another booth!

Are you sure you have completely mastered the dialogue? Maybe you should read it once more, before answering the true-false.

1. John è in una cabina telefonica. ☐ Vero ☐ Falso
2. John chiede a Paola di andare al bar. ☐ Vero ☐ Falso
3. A Paola piace il cinema. ☐ Vero ☐ Falso
4. Paola non sa ballare. ☐ Vero ☐ Falso
5. Paola decide di andare al ristorante. ☐ Vero ☐ Falso
6. Anne ha molta pazienza. ☐ Vero ☐ Falso

(teh-leh-foh-NAH-tah) *(een-tehr-oor-BAH-nah)*

TELEFONATA LOCALE O INTERURBANA?

Local or Long Distance?

The telephone system of another country always seems to have its mysteries. Here are some words and expressions that you might need.

il telefono	telephone
(teh-leh-foh-NAH-reh) **telefonare**	to phone
formare il numero	to dial
la cabina telefonica	phone booth
(chehn-trah-lee-NEES-tah) **il/la centralinista**	operator
(jeh-TTOH-neh) **il gettone**	token (needed for public phones)
Pronto	Hello
la guida telefonica	phone book
la telefonata interurbana	long distance call

ANSWERS

True/False 1. Vero **2.** Falso **3.** Falso **4.** Vero **5.** Falso **6.** Falso

When you have learned them thoroughly, write the appropriate word or expression in the blanks.

In Italia, bisogna avere un ____________________ per usare il telefono pubblico.

Quando si risponde al telefono si dice «____________________».

I numeri di telefono si trovano nella ____________________.

Una telefonata a una persona lontana si chiama uno ____________________.

In una ____________________ si trova il telefono pubblico.

Prima di parlare al telefono, bisogna ____________________.

Lina forma il numero del macellaio. Un uomo risponde. Lina dice all'uomo che vuole comprare un pollo. Gli dice che è molto urgente la situazione perché stasera arrivano i suoi zii dall'America. Vuole preparare *(preh-pah-RAH-reh)* to prepare **una bella cena. L'uomo ascolta con pazienza. Poi dice:**

«Scusi, signora, ma lei ha il numero sbagliato *(zbah-LLYAH-toh)* the wrong number**. Io sono un fioraio** *(fyoh-RAH-yoh)* florist**.»**

You're doing great! Now prove to yourself how much you have learned:

L'uomo ascolta con ____________.

Un ____________ risponde.

Gli dice che è ____________ ____________ la situazione ____________

____________ ____________ i suoi zii dall'America.

Io sono un ____________.

ANSWERS

Fill-ins (un) gettone (dice) «Pronto». (nella) guida telefonica. (chiama una) interurbana. (una) cabina telefonica (bisogna) formare il numero.

28	*(dehn-TEES-tee)* *(doh-TTOH-ree)* *(ohs-peh-DAH-lee)*

I dentisti, i dottori, gli ospedali

Dentists, Doctors, Hospitals

(RAH-pee-dah) *(oh-KKYAH-tah)*

UNA RAPIDA OCCHIATA

A Once-Over

We're getting close to the end! But you really *should* learn the parts of the body.

MARIO **Chi incomincia, tu o io?** — Who'll start, you or I?

GINO **Tu chiedi a me prima.** — You ask me first.

MARIO **Bene. Che sono questi?** — Good. What do you have here?

(kah-PEH-llee)
GINO **I capelli.** — The hair.

MARIO **E nel mezzo agli occhi?** — And between the eyes?

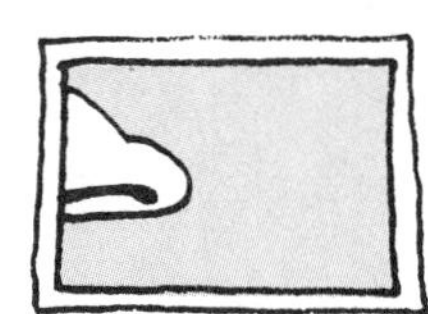

GINO **Il naso.** — The nose.

MARIO **Tra il naso e la bocca** — Between the nose and the mouth,

molti uomini hanno — many men wear

(BAH-ffee)
GINO **i baffi.** — a moustache.

(oh-REH-kkee)
MARIO **Hai due orecchi** — You have two ears

(GWAHN-cheh)
GINO **e due guance,** — and two cheeks,

(FAH-chah)
MARIO **ma solo una faccia** — but only one face

GINO **e una testa.** — and only one head.

MARIO **Quando si ride, si vedono** — When you laugh, one sees

(DEHN-tee)
GINO **i denti** — the teeth

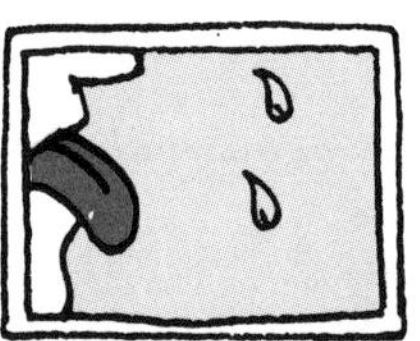

MARIO **e quando si va dal medico,** — and when you go to the doctor, you

(LEEN-gwah)
GINO **gli si fa vedere la lingua, aah.** — show him your tongue, aah.

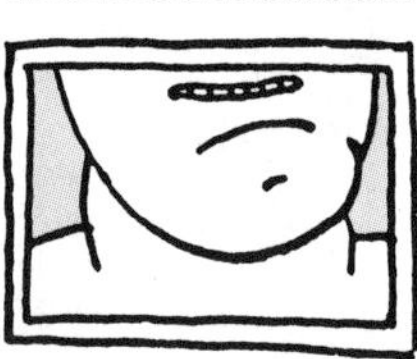

MARIO **Questo è** — This is

(MEHN-toh)
GINO **il mento** — the chin

MARIO **e quello è** — and that is

(KOH-lloh)
GINO **il collo.** — the neck.

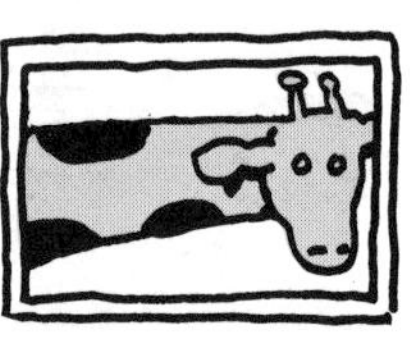

MARIO **Ecco due** — Here are two

(SPAH-lleh)
GINO **spalle** — shoulders

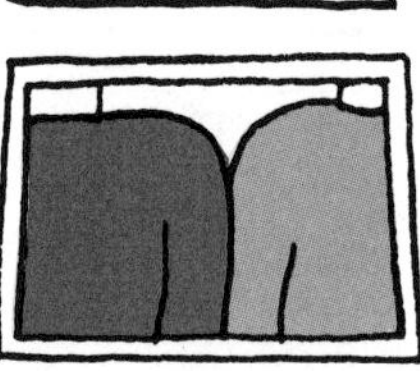

MARIO **e due** — and two

(GOH-mee-tee)
GINO **gomiti—** — elbows—

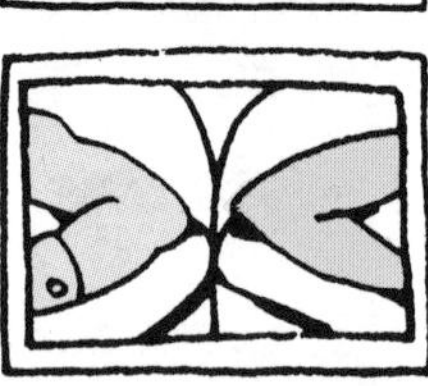

MARIO **due** — two

GINO **mani** — hands

MARIO **e dieci** | and ten

GINO **dita.** | fingers.

MARIO **Ora tocca a me.** | Now it's *my* turn.

GINO **Questa è** | This is

(SKYEH-nah)
MARIO **la schiena,** | the back,

GINO **e qui davanti** | and here in front

(PEH-ttoh)
MARIO **c'è il petto,** | is the chest,

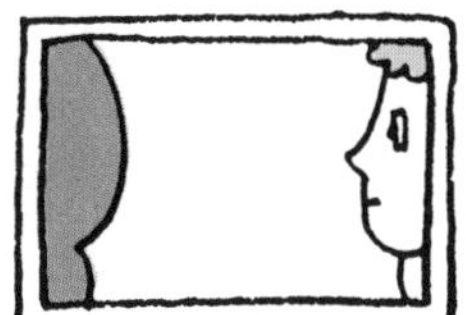

GINO **e lì dietro c'è** | and there in back is

(seh-DEH-reh)
MARIO **il sedere.** | the fanny.

GINO **E da qui a qui ci sono due** | And from here to here you have two

(KOH-sheh)
MARIO **cosce** | thighs

GINO **con due** | with the two

(jee-NOH-kkee)
MARIO **ginocchi.** | knees.

GINO **E più in giù ci sono i due** | And farther down the two

(pohl-PAH-chee)
MARIO **polpacci,** | calves,

(kah-VEE-lyeh)
GINO **le due caviglie e** | to the two ankles, are

(PYEH-dee)
MARIO **i piedi** | the feet

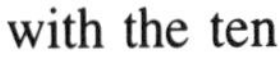

GINO **con dieci** | with the ten

MARIO **dita.** | toes.

Now try this difficult association exercise. Which part of the human body would you associate with the following?

l'anello ________________, lo shampoo ________________, il mascara ________________,

la sigaretta ________________, il profumo ________________, gli occhiali ________________,

la radio ________________, l'intelligenza *(een-teh-llee-JEHN-tsah)* ________________, il dentifricio ________________,

la collana ________________, il guanto ________________, la scarpa ________________,

la camicia ________________.

Ricordati

Remember

Remember that the verb *sentirsi* allows you to say that you are not feeling well.

Mi sento male.	I feel bad.

You can also use *fare male*.

Mi fa male la testa.	My head hurts.

A list of common ailments might come in handy, just in case! Consider this a basic survival list.

(STOH-mah-koh) **Mi fa male lo stomaco.**	My stomach hurts.
(GOH-lah) **Mi fa male la gola.**	My throat hurts.
Mi fa male un dente.	My tooth hurts.
(rah-ffreh-DDOH-reh) **Ho un raffreddore.**	I have a cold.
(FEH-bbreh) **Ho la febbre.**	I have a temperature/fever.
(TOH-sseh) **Ho la tosse.**	I have a cough.
(voh-mee-TAH-reh) **Mi viene da vomitare.**	I feel like vomiting.
(SAHN-gweh) **Mi esce il sangue dal naso.**	My nose is bleeding.

ANSWERS

Association (l'anello) il dito (lo shampoo) i capelli / la testa (il mascara) gli occhi (la sigaretta) la bocca (il profumo) il naso (gli occhiali) gli occhi (la radio) gli orecchi (l'intelligenza) la testa (il dentifricio) i denti (la collana) il collo (il guanto) la mano (la scarpa) il piede (la camicia) il braccio

Now pretend you are at the doctor's. Write out the suggested parts. When you have finished composing your dialogue, read it out loud several times.

DOCTOR	**Buon giorno. Si sente male?**	Good day. Are you not feeling well?
YOU	______________________, **dottore.**	Good day, doctor. I feel bad.
	________________________ **male.**	
DOCTOR	**Che cosa le fa male?**	What hurts?
YOU	______________________________	I have a cough. My throat hurts, and I have
	______________________________	a fever.
	______________________________	
DOCTOR	**Forse ha un raffreddore. Ha altri** *(SEEN-toh-mee)* **sintomi?**	Maybe you have a cold. Do you have any other symptoms?
YOU	______________________________	Yes. My stomach hurts. I feel like vomiting,
	______________________________	and my nose is bleeding.
	______________________________	
DOCTOR	**Lei ha probabilmente** *(een-floo-EHN-tsah)* **l'influenza.**	You probably have the flu.
YOU	**Che cosa devo fare?**	What should I do?
DOCTOR	**Deve andare a letto e bere vino.**	You have to go to bed and drink wine.
YOU	_____________________________?	Drink wine?
DOCTOR	**Sì. È la cura** *(KOO-rah)* **migliore.** *(mee-LLYOH-reh)*	Yes. It's the best cure.

Splendid! We knew you could do it!

ANSWERS

Dialogue with doctor Buon giorno, dottore. Mi sento male. Ho la tosse. Mi fa male la gola, e ho la febbre. Sì. Mi fa male lo stomaco. Mi viene da vomitare, e mi esce il sangue dal naso. Bere vino?

APRA LA BOCCA!

Open Wide!

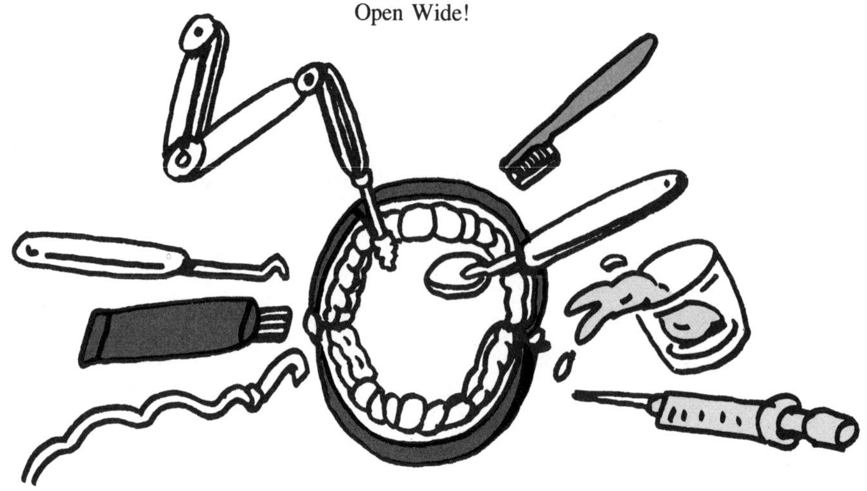

You might, of course, need to go to a dentist. If so the following list may prove useful to you.

Mi fa male un dente.	My tooth hurts.
(kah-VAH-reh) **Mi deve cavare un dente?**	Do you have to take a tooth out?
(eem-pyohm-bah-TOO-rah) **Ho bisogno di un'impiombatura?**	Do I need a filling?
(dehn-TYEH-rah) **Ho bisogno di una dentiera nuova.**	I need new dentures.

You did so well with the last assignment—let's try another.

YOU	______________________________.	Doctor, my tooth hurts.
DENTISTA	**Non si preoccupi. Apra**	Don't worry. Open your mouth.
	(kah-REE-eh) **la bocca. Lei ha una carie.**	You have a cavity.
YOU	____________________?	Do you have to take a tooth out?
DENTISTA	**No. Non è male.**	No. It's not bad.
YOU	______________________________?	Do I need a filling?
DENTISTA	*(poon-TOO-rah)* **Sì. Prima le faccio una puntura.**	Yes. First I'll give you a shot.
YOU	______________________________.	No thanks, doctor. I'll come tomorrow.

ANSWERS

Dialogue with dentist Dottore, mi fa male un dente. Mi deve cavare un dente? Ho bisogno di un'impiombatura? No, grazie, dottore. Vengo domani.

DENTISTA **Lei ha paura delle punture? Non si preoccupi. Signore/Signora, dove va?** — You're afraid of needles? Don't worry. Sir/Madam, where are you going?

YOU ____________, **dottore.** ____________ **volo** ____________ **tra** ____________**!** — Good day, doctor. My flight is leaving in two hours!

APRA LA BOCCA E FACCIA AAAAAAH . . .

Say Aaaaaah . . .

You probably won't need to use these terms, but see if you can translate them.

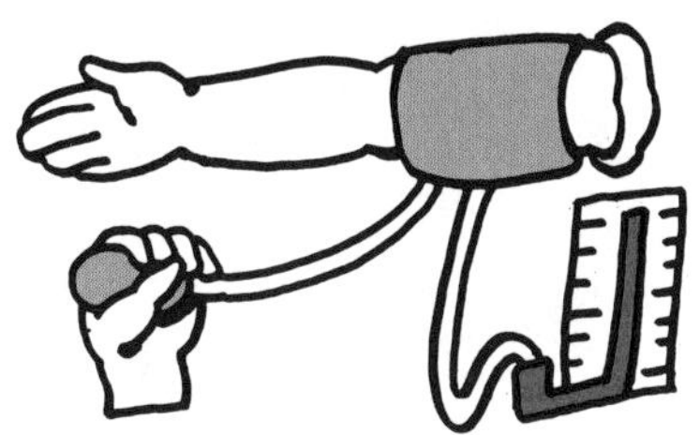

la carta medica (MEH-dee-kah)

la pressione (preh-SSYOH-neh) **sanguigna** (sahn-GWEE-nyah)

il termometro (tehr-MOH-meh-troh)

la sigla del dottore/medico (MEH-dee-koh)

(Mark Smith is not feeling well, so he goes to the doctor.)

MARK **Buon giorno, dottore. Mi sento molto male.** — Hello, doctor. I feel really bad.

DOTTORE **Dove le fa male?** — Where does it hurt?

MARK **In gola.** — In my throat.

DOTTORE **Apra la bocca e faccia aaaaaah.** — Open your mouth and say aaaaaah.

MARK **Che c'è di male, dottore?** — What's wrong, doctor?

DOTTORE **Lei ha le tonsille** (tohn-SEE-lleh) **infiammate.** (een-fyah-MMAH-teh) — Your tonsils are inflamed.

(The doctor takes out his surgical instruments.)

ANSWERS

Buon giorno / Arrivederla, dottore. Il mio volo parte tra due ore!

MARK **Che cosa fa, dottore?** — What are you doing, doctor?

(TOH-lyehr-leh)

DOTTORE **Dobbiamo toglierle adesso.** — We should take them out now.

È il metodo più sicuro. — It's the best way.

MARK *(as he is running out of the office)*

Mamma mia, quel dottore è pazzo! — Heavens, that doctor is crazy!

Now wasn't that easy? You're nearly there!

1. Mark si sente molto bene. ☐ Vero ☐ Falso
2. Gli fa male la gola. ☐ Vero ☐ Falso
3. Il dottore dice di aprire la bocca. ☐ Vero ☐ Falso
4. Mark ha un raffreddore. ☐ Vero ☐ Falso
5. Mark si fa togliere le tonsille. ☐ Vero ☐ Falso

(proh-toh-KOH-lloh) *(ohs-peh-DAH-leh)*

PROTOCOLLO D'OSPEDALE

Hospital Protocol

(proh-feh-SSOH-reh)

In Italy the head physician of a hospital is called: **il professore.**

(ah-ssees-TEHN-tee)

The other doctors are called: **gli assistenti.**

Then come the nurses (male and female):

(een-fehr-MYEH-reh) *(een-fehr-MYEH-rah)*

l'infermiere (m) / **l'infermiera** (f).

Try this paragraph—bet you get it the first time!

(een-FAHR-toh) *(kahr-DEE-ah-koh)* *(SOO-bee-toh)*

Al signor Dini prende un infarto cardiaco. Sua moglie chiama subito

heart attack — right away

(ah-oo-toh-ahm-boo-LAHN-tsah)

un' autoambulanza. Per strada l'autoambulanza si ferma. Non ha più benzina!

ambulance — On the way — stops

(fohr-TOO-nah)

Per fortuna passa un'altra autoambulanza che porta il signor Dini all'ospedale.

Fortunately — comes by

ANSWERS

True/False **1.** Falso **2.** Vero **3.** Vero **4.** Falso **5.** Falso

And now the questions:

Che cosa prende al signor Dini?	☐ Un infarto cardiaco. ☐ Un raffreddore.
Che cosa chiama subito sua moglie?	☐ Un medico. ☐ Un'autoambulanza.
Che cosa fa l'autoambulanza per strada?	☐ Va velocemente. ☐ Si ferma.
Perché si ferma?	☐ Perché non ha più benzina. ☐ Perché c'è troppo traffico.
Come arriva all'ospedale il signor Dini?	☐ A piedi. ☐ Con un'altra autoambulanza.

Terrific!

(bahr-tseh-LLEH-ttah)

UNA BARZELLETTA

A Joke

(JOH-vah-neh)
Un giovane va dal dottore. Il giovane dice, «Dottore, vorrei . . .»
young man

(SPOH-llyee)
«Si spogli!» dice subito il dottore.
undress

«Ma dottore . . .» dice ancora il giovane.

«Si spogli!» insiste il dottore. Il giovane si spoglia.
insists

(eh-zah-mee-NAHR-loh)
Quando il dottore va per esaminarlo, il giovane ripete,
goes to examine him

(KYEH-dehr-leh)
«Dottore, io non mi sento male! Io sono qui per chiederle,
I am here to ask you

(ah-bboh-NAHR-see)
se vuole abbonarsi alla rivista *L'Espresso*!»
subscribe

ANSWERS

Comprehension Un infarto cardiaco. Un'autoambulanza. Si ferma. Perché non ha più benzina. Con un'altra autoambulanza.

Do you remember the parts of the body? See how many words and expressions you can match. Don't look back until you have finished—then review those you missed.

1. il piede	a. face
2. la gamba	b. hair
3. il dito	c. eyes
4. la mano	d. mouth
5. il braccio	e. foot
6. il collo	f. leg
7. la faccia	g. finger
8. la bocca	h. ears
9. gli occhi	i. neck
10. i capelli	j. arm
11. gli orecchi	k. hand
12. Mi fa male lo stomaco.	l. I feel like vomiting.
13. Mi fa male la gola.	m. My stomach hurts.
14. Ho la febbre.	n. My head hurts.
15. Ho la tosse.	o. My throat hurts.
16. Mi viene da vomitare.	p. I have a cough.
17. Mi fa male la testa.	q. I have a fever.
18. cavare un dente	r. nurse
19. l'impiombatura	s. to take out a tooth
20. la carie	t. needle
21. la puntura	u. thermometer
22. il termometro	v. head physician
23. il professore	w. cavity
24. l'infermiere	x. ambulance
25. l'autoambulanza	y. heart attack
26. l'infarto cardiaco	z. filling

ANSWERS

Matching **1**-e, **2**-f, **3**-g, **4**-k, **5**-j, **6**-i, **7**-a, **8**-d, **9**-c, **10**-b, **11**-h, **12**-m, **13**-o, **14**-q, **15**-p, **16**-l, **17**-n, **18**-s, **19**-z, **20**-w, **21**-t, **22**-u, **23**-v, **24**-r, **25**-x, **26**-y

29 In cerca di soccorso/aiuto (ah-YOO-toh)

Getting Help

UNA BARZELLETTA

A Joke

GIUDICE **Allora, signora, ha rotto** (ROH-ttoh) **l'ombrello sulla testa di suo marito?** — So, madam, you broke your umbrella over your husband's head?

DONNA **Un errore!** — It was an accident! (*literally*, an error)

GIUDICE **Un errore?** — An accident (error)?

DONNA **Non volevo** (voh-LEH-voh) **rompere** (ROHM-peh-reh) **l'ombrello!** — I didn't want to break the umbrella!

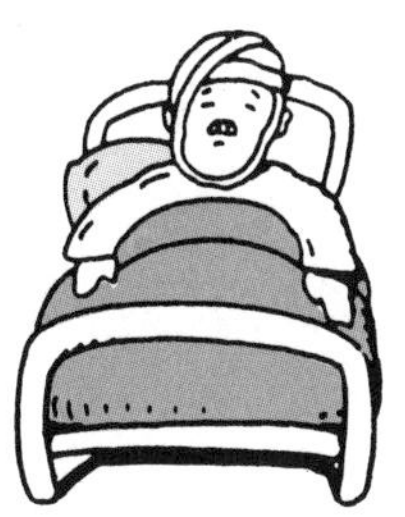

SE HAI BISOGNO DI UN'AUTOAMBULANZA

If You Need an Ambulance

(Mark has fallen down the stairs. In the foyer of the hotel, Mary seeks help.)

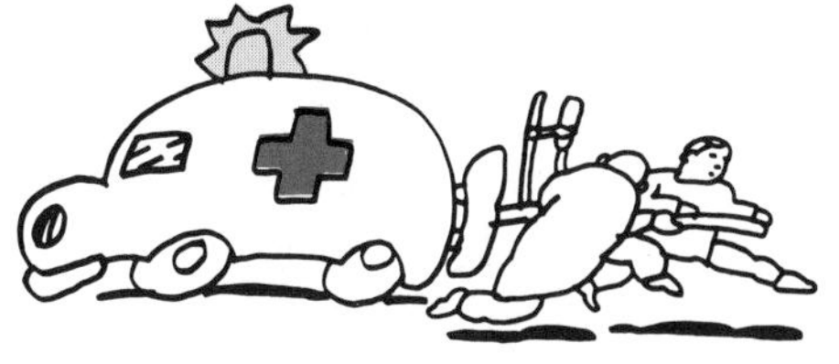

MARY **Signore, aiuto! Mio marito ha rotto una gamba. Che devo fare?** — Help, sir! My husband has broken a leg. What am I to do?

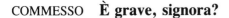

COMMESSO **È grave, signora?** — Is it serious, madam?

MARY **Sì, molto. E a pensare che la nostra partenza per l'America è domani.**	Yes, very. And to think that tomorrow is our departure for America.
COMMESSO **Non si preoccupi. Adesso chiamo l'autoambulanza.**	Don't worry. I'm calling the ambulance now.
MARY **Come si fa?**	What does one do?
COMMESSO **Si chiama il centralinista e si chiede aiuto.**	You call the operator and ask for help.

(At this point, Mark walks into the room.)

MARY **Mark, che fai?**	Mark, what are you doing?
MARK *(to the clerk)* **Non è necessario telefonare all'autoambulanza. Non ho niente. Ora so che mia moglie mi ama ancora!**	It is not necessary to call the ambulance. I'm okay. (*literally*, I have nothing) Now I know that my wife still loves me.

No cheating now—complete the missing parts from memory. Afterwards, check your answers in the dialogue.

Signore, a_______________! Mio marito ha rotto una g_______________.

Che d_______________ fare?

È g_______________, signora?

Sì, molto. E a pensare che la nostra p_______________ per l'America è domani.

Non si preoccupi. Adesso, chiamo l'a _______________.

Come si fa?

Si chiama il c_______________ e si chiede aiuto.

Mark, che fai?

Non è necessario t_______________ all'autoambulanza. Non ho niente.

Ora so che mia moglie mi ama a_______________!

(poh-lee-TSEE-ah)

CHIAMA LA POLIZIA!

Call the Police!

One last dialogue—with a few questions following.

(The Smiths are packing their bags.)

MARK	**Mary! Non trovo il mio portafoglio!**	Mary! I can't find my wallet!
MARY	**Forse è in una valigia.**	Maybe it's in a suitcase.
MARK	**No, non è sotto il cuscino** *(koo-SHEE-noh)* **dove lo metto ogni sera. Chiama la polizia!**	No, it is not under the pillow where I put it every night. Call the police!
MARY	**Come devo fare?**	What should I do?
MARK	**Telefona** *(teh-LEH-foh-nah)* **al centralinista e chiedi l'aiuto della polizia.**	Phone the operator and ask for police help.

(A policeman arrives.)

MARK	**Signore, qualcuno ha rubato** *(roo-BAH-toh)* **il mio portafoglio!**	Sir, someone stole my wallet!
POLIZIA	**Si calmi, signore!**	Calm down, sir!
MARK	**Io lo metto sempre sotto il cuscino! E adesso non c'è!**	I always put it under the pillow! And now it's not there!
POLIZIA	**C'è in una valigia?**	Is it in a suitcase?
MARK	**No.**	No.
POLIZIA	**Nella borsa di sua moglie?**	In your wife's purse?
MARY	**No, non c'è.**	No, it's not there.
POLIZIA	**Guardi nella sua tasca.** *(TAS-kah)*	Look in your pocket.
MARK	**Ah, eccolo!** *(EH-kkoh-loh)* **Meno male!**	Ah, here it is! Thank heavens!

(oo-GWAH-lee)

POLIZIA *(to himself)* **I turisti sono tutti uguali!** Tourists are all alike!

MARK **Grazie e arrivederla.** Good-bye and thank you.

POLIZIA **Arrivederla.** Good-bye.

(later at the airport)

THE SMITHS **Arrivederci, Italia, e grazie per una bella vacanza!** Good-bye, Italy, and thanks for a great vacation!

Chi non trova il portafoglio?
- ☐ Mary.
- ☐ Mark.
- ☐ Anne.

È in una valigia, il portafoglio?
- ☐ Sì.
- ☐ No.

Dove mette il portafoglio?
- ☐ Nella valigia.
- ☐ Nella borsa.
- ☐ Sotto il cuscino.

Per chiedere l'aiuto della polizia, chi si deve chiamare?
- ☐ Il centralinista.
- ☐ Il commesso.
- ☐ Il direttore dell'albergo.

Dov'è il portafoglio?
- ☐ Sotto il cuscino.
- ☐ In una valigia.
- ☐ Nella tasca di Mark.

Aren't you pleased with yourself?

(dees-GRAH-tsyah)

IN CASO DI UN INCIDENTE/UNA DISGRAZIA

Handling an Accident

Here are some common accidents.

(ree-cheh-VOO-toh)

Aiuto! Ho ricevuto una scossa elettrica!
electrical cord

Fuoco!
fire

ANSWERS

Comprehension Mark. No. Sotto il cuscino. Il centralinista. Nella tasca di Mark.

Ahi! Mi sono tagliata il dito!
(*tah-LLYAH-tah*) tagliata = cut

Attenzione ai bambini!

Ahi! C'è troppa acqua!

If you have an accident follow the normal procedures for any emergency situation. Take care of first-aid needs right away. Then call for the appropriate help. Always have a phone token with you in order to be able to use the public phones in Italy. You will find Italians extremely helpful in emergency situations. So ask for anybody's help and remember the key word:

AIUTO!

Help!

Here are the expressions you might need in an emergency:

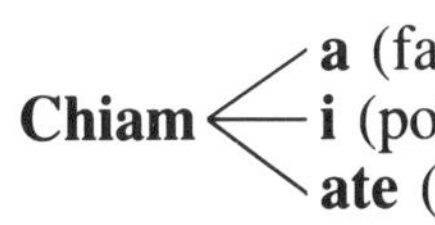

Chiam < **a** (familiar) / **i** (polite) / **ate** (plural) **la polizia!** Call the police!

Chiama/Chiami/Chiamate il soccorso medico! Call for medical help!

Chiama/Chiami/Chiamate i vigili del fuoco! (*FWOH-koh*) Call the fire department!

Chiama/Chiami/Chiamate il medico! Call the doctor!

Chiama/Chiami/Chiamate l'autoambulanza! Call the ambulance!

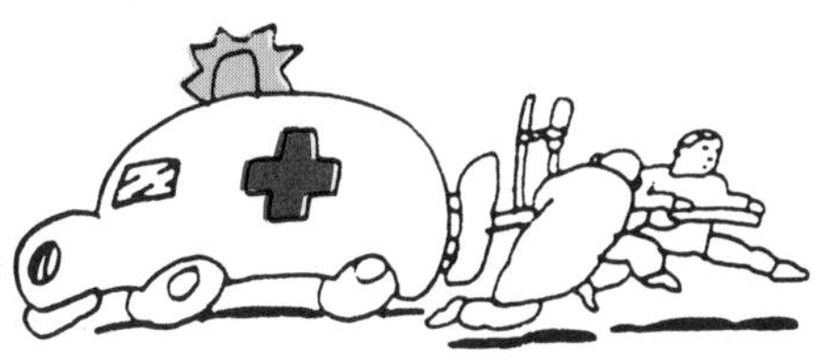

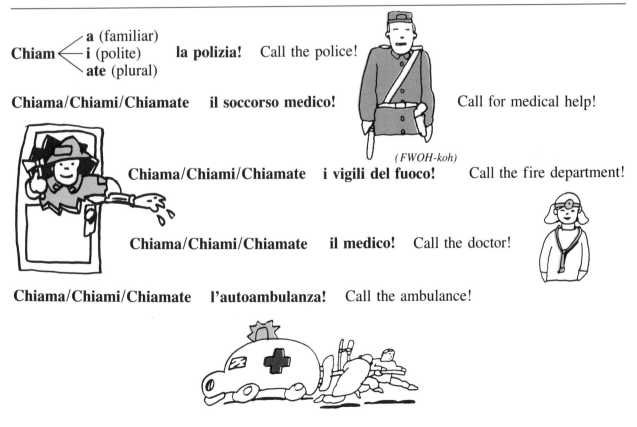

BEFORE YOU LEAVE

Prima di partire

Now we come to the final step in the learning process, and the most important one. You might view it as a final exam. What will you do and say in the following situations? You may want to look over the sections of the book that correspond to each of the following seven situations, before you get started. Ready? Then let's go!

Situazione 1: Fare la conoscenza della gente

Situation 1: Getting to Know People

A. It is daytime and you meet someone.
What do you say in order to start a conversation?

1. ☐ Buon giorno.
2. ☐ Arrivederci.
3. ☐ Prego.

B. You have just run into a friend.
What do you say?

1. ☐ Grazie.
2. ☐ Ciao.
3. ☐ Buona sera.

C. It is evening. How do you greet a stranger?

1. ☐ Ciao.
2. ☐ Buon giorno.
3. ☐ Buona sera.

D. How do you say good-bye to a stranger?

1. ☐ Arrivederci.
2. ☐ Arrivederla.
3. ☐ Ciao.

E. How do you say good-bye to a friend?

1. ☐ Arrivederci/Ciao.
2. ☐ Arrivederla.

F. Someone asks you how you are. Which of the following is *not* possible as an answer?

1. ☐ Non c'è male, grazie.
2. ☐ Molto bene, grazie.
3. ☐ Buon giorno, grazie.

G. How would you ask a friend how he/she feels?

1. ☐ Come stai?
2. ☐ Come sta?
3. ☐ Dove vai?

H. How would you ask a stranger how he/she feels?

1. ☐ Come stai?
2. ☐ Come sta?
3. ☐ Dove vai?

I. Someone has just said "grazie." As a possible answer, you might say . . .

1. ☐ Bene.
2. ☐ Prego.
3. ☐ Arrivederci.

ANSWERS

Multiple choice **Situation 1:** A-1, B-2, C-3, D-2, E-1, F-3, G-1, H-2, I-2.

Situazione 2: L'arrivo

Situation 2: Arrival

You do not have a reservation at the hotel. What do you say?

1. ☐ Come sta, signore?
2. ☐ Scusi, signore, non ho la prenotazione.
3. ☐ Buon giorno, signore, come si chiama?

You want to say you really need a room. You might say . . .

1. ☐ Per favore, ho bisogno urgente di una camera.
2. ☐ Per favore, non voglio il bagno.

You want to inquire about price and what is included. So you might say . . .

1. ☐ Mi può dire come si chiama, lei?
2. ☐ Mi può dire dov'è il bagno?
3. ☐ Mi può dire quanto costa la camera e quali sono i servizi?

Under "Nome" one might find:

1. ☐ Ottantamila lire al giorno.
2. ☐ Mark Smith.
3. ☐ Tre.

Under "Indirizzo" one might find:

1. ☐ Ottantamila lire al giorno.
2. ☐ Tre.
3. ☐ Via Washington, 25, Washington, D.C., U.S.A.

Under "Numero di camera" one might find:

1. ☐ Ottantamila lire al giorno.
2. ☐ Tre.
3. ☐ Via Verdi, 3, Roma.

Under "Data" one might find:

1. ☐ Ottantamila lire al giorno.
2. ☐ Via Verdi, 3, Roma.
3. ☐ (Il) 30 luglio.

Under "Prezzo" one might find:

1. ☐ Ottantamila lire al giorno.
2. ☐ Mark Smith.
3. ☐ (Il) 3 agosto.

Under "Firma" one might find:

1. ☐ Ventidue.
2. ☐ Mark Smith.
3. ☐ (Il) 5 agosto.

ANSWERS

Situation 2: 2, 1, 3, 2, 3, 2, 3, 1, 2.

Situazione 3: I punti d'interesse

Situation 3: Seeing the Sights

You are on foot and want to find a certain street. You might ask a passerby:

1. ☐ Scusi, come sta?
2. ☐ Scusi, dove si trova Via . . .?
3. ☐ Scusi, lei abita in Via . . .?

The passerby might say:

1. ☐ A sinistra, a destra, dritto . . .
2. ☐ Domani, ieri, oggi . . .
3. ☐ Il semaforo, l'ufficio postale, la banca . . .

You have boarded a bus. You want to ask where to get off. You might say:

1. ☐ Scusi, quanto costa il biglietto?
2. ☐ Scusi, dove devo scendere per Via Verdi?
3. ☐ Scusi, come si chiama lei?

You have flagged down a taxi; but before getting in you want to know how much it would cost to get to Via Verdi. You might say:

1. ☐ Scusi, quanto è lontana Via Verdi?
2. ☐ Scusi, lei sa dov'è Via Verdi?
3. ☐ Scusi, quanto costa per andare a Via Verdi?

You have forgotten your watch. You stop a passerby to ask what time it is. You might say:

1. ☐ Scusi, mi sa dire che ora è?
2. ☐ Scusi, ha un orologio?
3. ☐ Scusi, che tempo fa?

The passerby would *not* answer:

1. ☐ Sono le due e venticinque.
2. ☐ È domani.
3. ☐ È l'una e mezzo.

You are at a train station and want to buy a ticket. You might say:

1. ☐ Scusi, quanto costa un biglietto per Firenze?
2. ☐ Scusi, dov'è Firenze?
3. ☐ Scusi, che ore sono?

The clerk answers that there is no room left on the train. He/She might say something like:

1. ☐ Mi dispiace, ma lei è pazzo.
2. ☐ Mi dispiace, ma lei non parla italiano.
3. ☐ Mi dispiace, ma non c'è posto.

You want to say that you are an American and that you speak only a little Italian. You might say:

1. ☐ Sono americano(a) e parlo solo un po' d'italiano.
2. ☐ Parlo americano e non sono italiano(a).
3. ☐ Non sono italiano(a); sono americano(a).

ANSWERS

Situation 3: 2, 1, 2, 3, 1, 2, 1, 3, 1

If someone were to ask what nationality you are, he/she would *not* say:

1. ☐ Lei è canadese?
2. ☐ Lei è intelligente?
3. ☐ Lei è americano(a)?

You want to rent a car cheaply. You might ask the clerk:

1. ☐ Vorrei noleggiare una macchina che non costa molto.
2. ☐ Vorrei noleggiare una macchina che costa molto.
3. ☐ Vorrei noleggiare una macchina nuova.

You want to fill up your car. You might say to the attendant:

1. ☐ Per favore, una macchina nuova.
2. ☐ Per favore, il pieno.
3. ☐ Per favore, costa troppo.

You have just been in a car accident and wish to ask how the other motorist is. You might say:

1. ☐ Buon giorno, come sta?
2. ☐ Si sente male?
3. ☐ Come si chiama?

A service station attendant might tell you that your car needs repairs. He would *not* say:

1. ☐ La sua macchina è bella.
2. ☐ La sua macchina ha bisogno di freni nuovi.
3. ☐ La sua macchina ha bisogno di un motore nuovo.

You ask an employee at a camping site if there are certain services. You would *not* say:

1. ☐ C'è l'acqua?
2. ☐ Ci sono posti per far giocare i bambini?
3. ☐ C'è il cinema?

When asked how much the charges are, a clerk might respond:

1. ☐ Duecentomila lire.
2. ☐ Duecento dollari americani.
3. ☐ Duecento ore.

If someone were to ask you about the weather back home, you would *not* say:

1. ☐ Fa bel tempo.
2. ☐ Piove sempre.
3. ☐ Nevica.
4. ☐ È vicino.

As an answer to ''Che data è oggi?'' you would *not* hear:

1. ☐ È il trenta marzo.
2. ☐ È il secondo giorno.
3. ☐ È il tre maggio.

At the airport you might hear this over the loudspeaker.

1. ☐ Il volo numero 303 per New York è interessante.
2. ☐ Il volo numero 303 per New York non arriva.
3. ☐ Il volo numero 303 per New York parte alle tre e mezzo.

ANSWERS

2, 1, 2, 2, 1, 3, 1, 4, 2, 3

To ask an airline employee at what time your flight leaves, you might say:

1. ☐ Scusi, a che ora parte il mio volo?
2. ☐ Scusi, quando arriva il mio volo?
3. ☐ Scusi, dov'è l'aeroporto?

Where would you find this sign?

1. ☐ All'aeroporto.
2. ☐ Al capolinea. *(kah-poh-LEE-neh-ah)* bus terminal
3. ☐ Alla stazione ferroviaria.

Where would you find this sign?

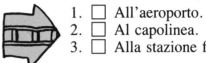

1. ☐ All'aeroporto.
2. ☐ Al capolinea.
3. ☐ Alla stazione ferroviaria.

Look at this plan of the city.

1. To which spot would you go to buy *aspirine*? ______________________
2. To which spot would you go to buy *francobolli*? ______________________
3. To which spot would you go to exchange *denaro*? ______________________
4. To which spot would you go to buy *un anello*? ______________________
5. To which spot would you go to buy *le sigarette*? ______________________
6. To which spot would you go to buy *il burro*? ______________________
7. To which spot would you go to get *la tua barba* shaved off? ______________________
8. To which spot would you go to get *una permanente*? ______________________
9. To which spot would you go to buy *una camicia*? ______________________

ANSWERS

1, 1, 3.

Identifying **1.** la farmacia **2.** l'ufficio postale **3.** la banca **4.** il gioielliere **5.** la tabaccheria **6.** (il negozio di) generi alimentari **7.** il barbiere **8.** il parrucchiere **9.** (il negozio di) abbigliamento

10. To which spot would you go to buy *un quadro*? ______________________

11. To which spot would you go to buy *un giornale*? ______________________

12. To which spot would you go to buy *delle buste*? ______________________

13. To which spot would you go to get *il tuo vestito* cleaned? ______________________

Situazione 4: I divertimenti

Situation 4: Entertainment

You are at a ticket agency. The clerk would *not* ask you:

1. ☐ Lei vuole un biglietto per l'opera?
2. ☐ Lei vuole un biglietto per il cinema?
3. ☐ Lei vuole un biglietto per l'aereo?

If someone were to ask you what your favorite sport was, you would *not* say:

1. ☐ Mi piace il tennis.
2. ☐ Mi piace il nuoto.
3. ☐ Mi piace il calcio.
4. ☐ Mi piace l'italiano.

Situazione 5: Ordiniamo da mangiare

Situation 5: Ordering Food

Use this menu to answer some of the Dining Out questions.

MENÙ

Antipasto:	**Prosciutto e melone.**	**Dessert:**	**Gelato** **Torta**
Primo piatto:	**Minestra al brodo** **Spaghetti** **Risotto alla milanese** **Tortellini alla bolognese**	**Bevande:**	**Vino rosso** **Vino bianco** **Acqua minerale** **Caffè**
Secondo piatto:	**Cotoletta** **Bistecca alla fiorentina** **Pesce**		

A. You want to ask someone what kinds of restaurants are available. You might say:

1. ☐ Si mangia bene in Italia?
2. ☐ Come sono i ristoranti?
3. ☐ Che tipo di ristoranti ci sono?

B. As a possible answer you would *not* hear:

1. ☐ Ci sono solo ristoranti locali.
2. ☐ Ci sono solo i bar.
3. ☐ Ci sono solo trattorie.
4. ☐ Ci sono solo forchette.

ANSWERS

Multiple choice Situation 4: 3, 4. **Situation 5: A**-3, **B**-4.

10. (il negozio di) articoli da regalo **11.** il chiosco **12.** la cartoleria **13.** la lavanderia.

C. When a waiter asks you to order he might say:
1. ☐ Mangia?
2. ☐ Desidera?
3. ☐ Paga?

D. To see the menu you would say:
1. ☐ Posso vedere il cucchiaio?
2. ☐ Posso vedere il menù?
3. ☐ Posso vedere il direttore?

E. Which of the following is not connected with eating?
1. ☐ La colazione.
2. ☐ Il pranzo.
3. ☐ La benzina.
4. ☐ La cena.

F. If you chose *Prosicutto e melone* you would *not* need:
1. ☐ Una forchetta.
2. ☐ Un bicchiere.
3. ☐ Un coltello.

G. If you chose *minestra al brodo* you would need:
1. ☐ Un cucchiaio.
2. ☐ Un coltello.
3. ☐ Una tazza.

H. Spaghetti, risotto, and tortellini are all types of:
1. ☐ Zucchero.
2. ☐ Pasta.
3. ☐ Carne.

I. If you want to order something from the *secondo piatto* section you might say:
1. ☐ Vorrei della frutta.
2. ☐ Vorrei un po' di sale e pepe.
3. ☐ Vorrei della carne e un po' di pesce.

J. To eat *gelato* or *torta* you would need:
1. ☐ Un coltello.
2. ☐ Una tazza.
3. ☐ Un piatto.

K. You drink *vino* or *acqua minerale* in:
1. ☐ Un bicchiere.
2. ☐ Una tazza.
3. ☐ Una bottiglia.

L. You drink *caffè* in:
1. ☐ Un bicchiere.
2. ☐ Una tazza.
3. ☐ Una bottiglia.

ANSWERS

C. 2. D-2. E-3, F-2 G-1, H-2, I-3, J-3, K-1, L-2.

Situazione 6: Entriamo nei negozi

Situation 6: At the Store

Which of the following would you *not* say in a clothing store?

1. ☐ Scusi, quanto costa questa camicia?
2. ☐ Scusi, quanto costa la benzina?
3. ☐ Vorrei dei calzini e delle cravatte.

Which of the following lists has nothing to do with clothing?

1. ☐ Un vestito azzurro, una giacca rossa, una camicia bianca.
2. ☐ Due calzini, tre cravatte, un paio di mutande.
3. ☐ L'italiano, il tedesco, lo spagnolo.

You would *not* hear which of the following in a supermarket?

1. ☐ Quanto costa la frutta?
2. ☐ Dove sono le ciliege?
3. ☐ Quanto costa la carta?
4. ☐ La carne costa molto oggi.
5. ☐ Il pesce è fresco.
6. ☐ Non abbiamo più pasta.

You would *not* say this at a pharmacy.

1. ☐ Quanto costa l'aspirina?
2. ☐ Dov'è la garza?
3. ☐ Dove sono i francobolli?

You are at the laundry. You would *not* see this there.

1. ☐ Il ferro da stiro.
2. ☐ Il casco.
3. ☐ Il sapone in polvere.

You are at a barbershop. You might say:

1. ☐ Per favore, mi dia un pacco di sigarette.
2. ☐ Per favore, mi tagli i capelli.
3. ☐ Per favore, mi dia un biglietto.

The hairdresser would *not* ask you:

1. ☐ Vuole la messa in piega?
2. ☐ Vuole un biscotto?
3. ☐ Vuole una permanente?
4. ☐ Vuole uno shampoo?

ANSWERS

Situation 6: 2, 3, 3, 3, 2, 2, 2.

Match up the following:

1. Quanto costa un tacco per questa scarpa?
2. Ho bisogno di un orologio nuovo.
3. Quanto costa questa rivista?
4. Quanto costano queste foto?
5. Quanto costano queste cartoline?
6. Lei ha dei ricordi d'Italia?
7. Quanto costa questo disco?

a. Negozio di articoli da regalo
b. Calzolaio
c. Orologiaio
d. Negozio di musica
e. Chiosco
f. Negozio di fotografia
g. Ufficio postale

Situazione 7: Servizi essenziali

Situation 7: Essential Services

You are at a bank and wish to exchange a traveler's check. You might say . . .

1. ☐ Scusi, che ore sono?
2. ☐ Scusi, mi può cambiare questo assegno turistico?
3. ☐ Scusi, devo riempire questo modulo?

Now you want to deposit some money. You might say . . .

1. ☐ Vorrei versare questo denaro.
2. ☐ Vorrei pagare il biglietto.
3. ☐ Vorrei firmare il modulo.

A bank employee would *not* ask . . .

1. ☐ Per favore, firmi il suo nome su questo modulo.
2. ☐ Per favore, mangi la pizza.
3. ☐ Per favore, compili questo modulo.

You want to buy stamps at a post office. You might say . . .

1. ☐ Per favore, vorrei comprare delle cartoline.
2. ☐ Per favore, vorrei comprare delle buste.
3. ☐ Per favore, vorrei comprare dei francobolli.

Which of the following would you *not* say in a post office?

1. ☐ Vorrei spedire la lettera per via aerea.
2. ☐ Vorrei spedire la lettera per via raccomandata.
3. ☐ Vorrei spedire la lettera per valigia.

ANSWERS

Matching 1-b, 2-c, 3-e, 4-f, 5-g, 6-a, 7-d. **Multiple choice Situation 7:** 2, 1, 2, 3, 3

You answer a phone call with . . .

1. ☐ Pronto.
2. ☐ Buon giorno.
3. ☐ Ciao.

You want to say "Who is it?" You would say . . .

1. ☐ Come si chiama?
2. ☐ Chi parla?
3. ☐ Perché chiama, lei?

You want to make a long distance call. You would say . . .

1. ☐ Vorrei pagare il conto telefonico.
2. ☐ Vorrei fare una telefonata interurbana.
3. ☐ Vorrei il suo numero di telefono.

You want to ask someone how to dial a number. You would say . . .

1. ☐ Scusi, come si forma il numero?
2. ☐ Scusi, come si fa il telefono?
3. ☐ Scusi, dov'è il telefono?

Which of the following would *not* be used to seek help?

1. ☐ Chiama l'autoambulanza!
2. ☐ Chiama la polizia!
3. ☐ Chiama i vigili del fuoco!
4. ☐ Chiama il soccorso medico!
5. ☐ Chiama il cugino!

You would *not* say one of the following to a doctor.

1. ☐ Dottore, mi sente male.
2. ☐ Dottore, lei è pazzo.
3. ☐ Dottore mi sente bene.
4. ☐ Dottore, ho la febbre.

Choose the appropriate box for each of the pictures.

A. 1. ☐ È un telegramma.
   2. ☐ È una cartolina.
   3. ☐ È una lettera.

ANSWERS

1, 2, 2, 1, 5, 2. A-1

B. 1. ☐ Si chiama per i dolori allo stomaco.
2. ☐ Si chiama per un incidente stradale.
3. ☐ Si chiama per comprare i biglietti.

C. 1. ☐ Si beve con il latte.
2. ☐ Si beve con lo zucchero.
3. ☐ Non si beve perché è veleno.

D. 1. ☐ Si trova davanti a un negozio di generi alimentari.
2. ☐ Si trova nella camera dell'albergo.
3. ☐ Si trova in una cartoleria.

E. 1. ☐ Si prende per il raffreddore.
2. ☐ Si prende per la strada.
3. ☐ Si prende per il telefono.

ANSWERS

B-2, C-3, D-3, E-1.

VOCABULARY CARDS

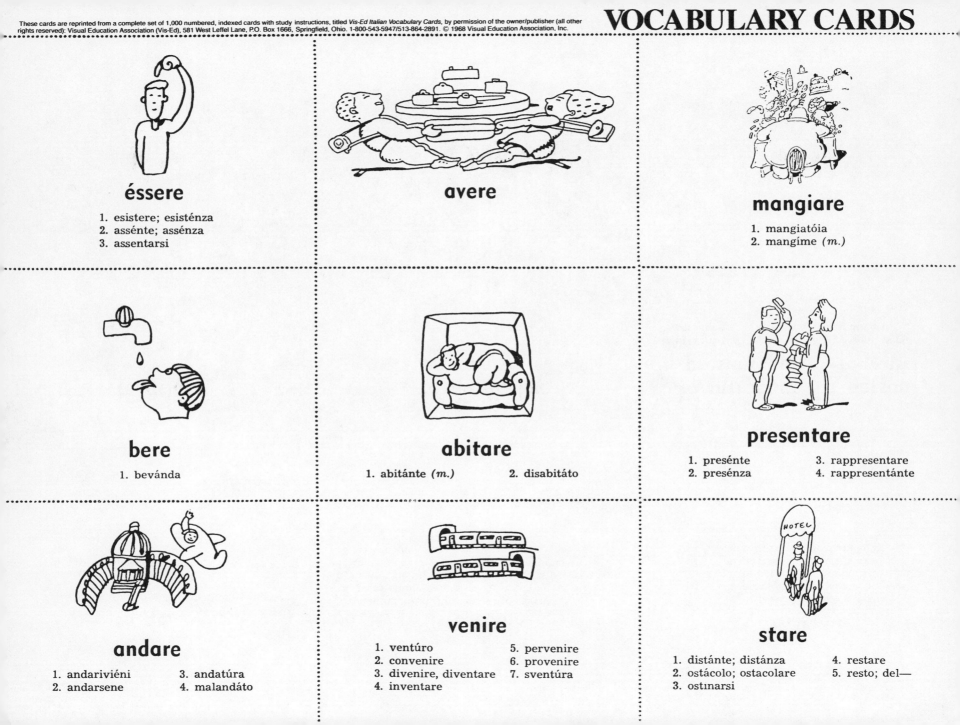

éssere

1. esistere; esisténza
2. asénte; asénza
3. assentarsi

avere

mangiare

1. mangiatóia
2. mangíme *(m.)*

bere

1. bevánda

abitare

1. abitánte *(m.)*
2. disabitáto

presentare

1. presénte
2. presénza
3. rappresentare
4. rappresentánte

andare

1. andariviéni
2. andarsene
3. andatúra
4. malandáto

venire

1. ventúro
2. convenire
3. divenire, diventare
4. inventare
5. pervenire
6. provenire
7. sventúra

stare

1. distánte; distánza
2. ostácolo; ostacolare
3. ostınarsi
4. restare
5. resto; del—

to go

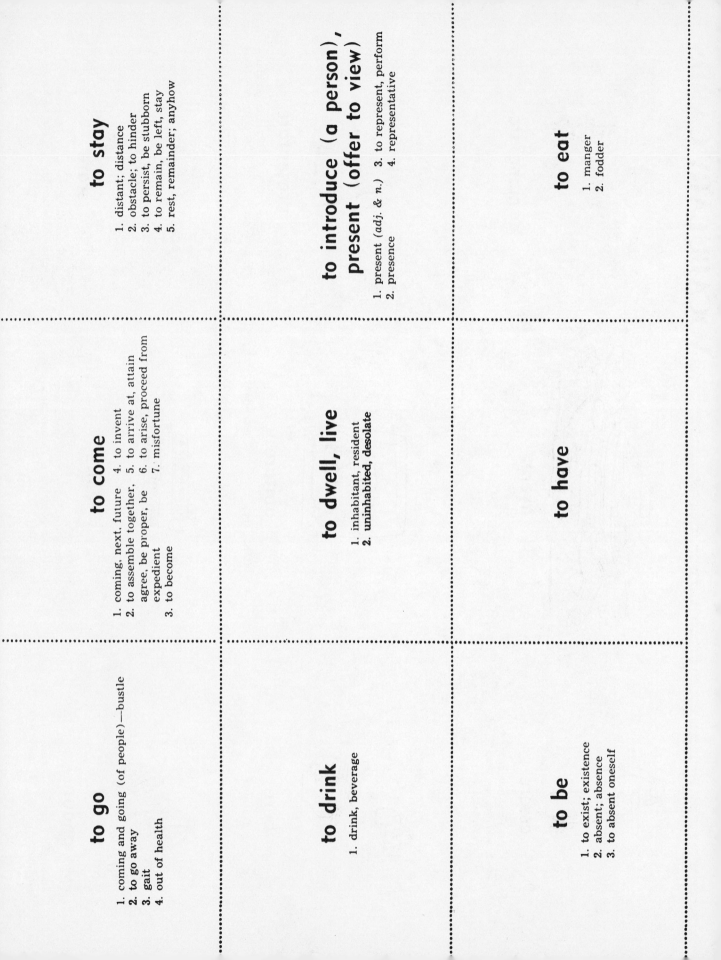

1. coming and going (of people)—bustle
2. to go away
3. gait
4. out of health

to come

1. coming, next, future
2. to assemble together, agree, be proper, be expedient
3. to become
4. to invent
5. to arrive at, attain
6. to arise, proceed from
7. misfortune

to stay

1. distant; distance
2. obstacle; to hinder
3. to persist, be stubborn
4. to remain, be left, stay
5. rest, remainder; anyhow

to drink

1. drink, beverage

to dwell, live

1. inhabitant, resident
2. uninhabited, desolate

to introduce (a person), present (offer to view)

1. present *(adj. & n.)*
2. presence
3. to represent, perform
4. representative

to be

1. to exist; existence
2. absent; absence
3. to absent oneself

to have

to eat

1. manger
2. fodder

partire

1. parténza

mandare

1. comandare
2. domandare
3. dománda
4. raccommandare
5. rimandare

volare

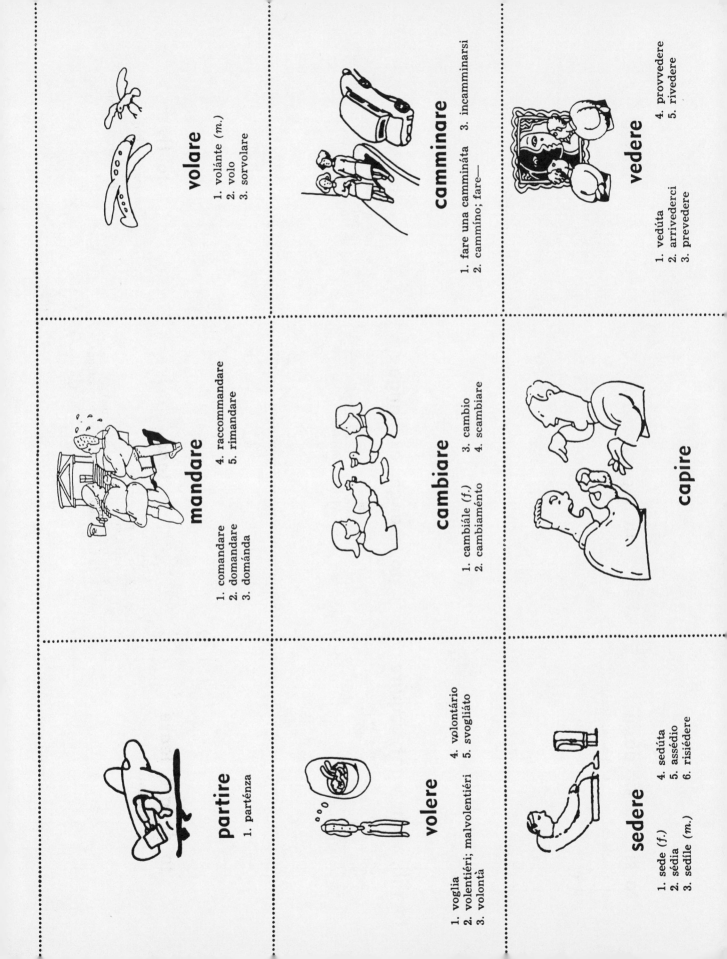

1. volánte (*m.*)
2. volo
3. sorvolare

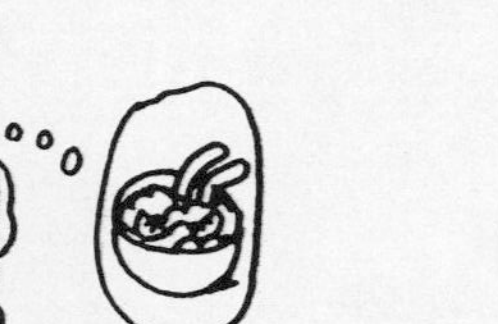

volere

1. voglia
2. volentiéri; malvolentiéri
3. volontà
4. volontário
5. svogliáto

cambiare

1. cambiále (*f.*)
2. cambiaménto
3. cambio
4. scambiare

camminare

1. fare una cammináta
2. cammíno; fare—
3. incamminarsi

sedere

1. sede (*f.*)
2. sédia
3. sedíle (*m.*)
4. sedúta
5. assédio
6. risiédere

capire

vedere

1. vedúta
2. arrivederci
3. prevedere
4. provvedere
5. rivedere

to sit; to sit down

1. seat, residence
2. chair
3. seat, bench
4. session, sitting
5. siege
6. to reside

to understand

to see

1. view
2. till we meet again! good-bye!
3. to foresee
4. to provide, take care of
5. to review, to see again; to meet again

to will, wish, want, require

1. desire, wish, intention, craving
2. willingly, gladly; unwillingly
3. will, willingness
4. voluntary; volunteer
5. loath, negligent

to change, exchange

1. promissory note
2. change
3. exchange, rate of exchange
4. to exchange, mistake

to walk

1. to take a walk
2. walk, path, route, journey; to go places
3. to set out, start on one's way

to depart, leave

1. departure

to send

1. to command, order
2. to ask, ask for, demand
3. question
4. to recommend, register (letter)
5. to send again or back, refer to, postpone

to fly

1. flying; steering-wheel
2. flight
3. to fly over, rise above

cercare

1. ricérca
2. ricercáto

chiédere

1. inchiésta
2. richiédere; richiésta
3. squisíto

véndere

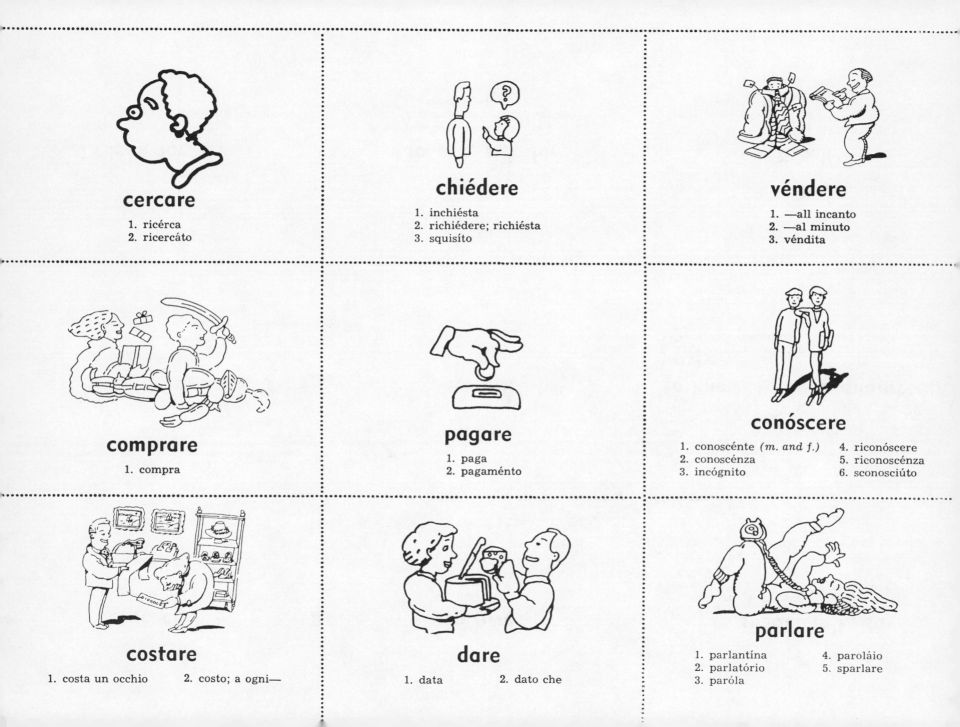

1. —all incanto
2. —al minuto
3. véndita

comprare

1. compra

pagare

1. paga
2. pagaménto

conóscere

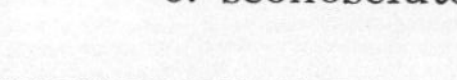

1. conoscénte (*m. and f.*)
2. conoscénza
3. incógnito
4. riconóscere
5. riconoscénza
6. sconosciúto

costare

1. costa un occhio
2. costo; a ogni—

dare

1. data
2. dato che

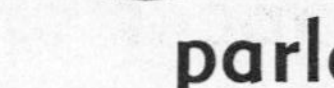

parlare

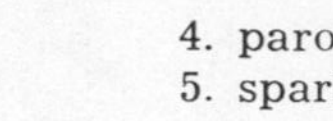

1. parlantína
2. parlatório
3. paróla
4. paroláio
5. sparlare

to cost

1. it is exceedingly expensive
2. cost; at any cost, by all means

to give

1. date
2. granted that

to speak, talk, say

1. indiscreet loquacity
2. parlor
3. word
4. prater
5. to speak evil of

to buy

1. purchase

to pay

1. pay
2. payment

to know, to be acquainted

1. acquaintance
2. knowledge; acquaintance
3. incognito, unknown
4. to recognize
5. gratitude
6. unknown; stranger

to look for, try

1. research, demand
2. exquisite, rare, overly refined (in manners)

to ask, ask for

1. search, inquiry, inquest
2. to request; request, demand
3. exquisite, excellent

to sell

1. to sell by auction
2. to sell by retail
3. sale

dire

1. dettare; dettáto
2. benedire
3. contradire
4. maledire
5. predicare; prédica
6. predire

dormire

1. dormicchiare
2. dormiglióne *(m.)*
3. dormivéglia
4. addormementarsi

firmare

1. firma

méttere

1. amméttere
2. comméttere; commissióne
3. diméttersi
4. introméttersi
5. ométtere

piacere

1. per—
2. piacévole
3. compiacere
4. dispiacere *(m.)*
5. mi dispiace *(di)*

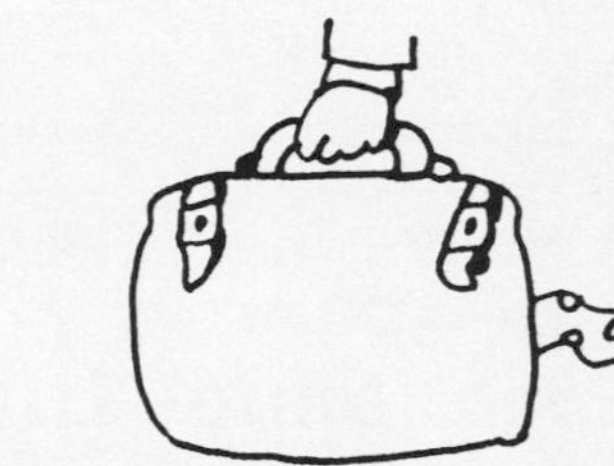

portare

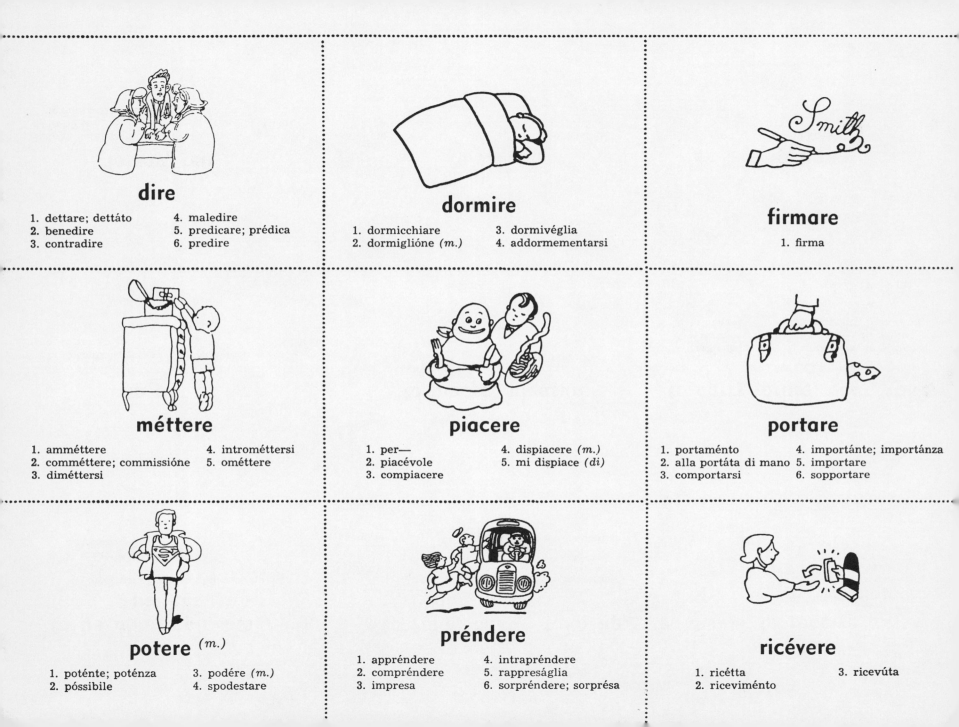

1. portaménto
2. alla portáta di mano
3. comportarsi
4. importánte; importánza
5. importare
6. sopportare

potere *(m.)*

1. poténte; poténza
2. póssibile
3. podére *(m.)*
4. spodestare

préndere

1. appréndere
2. compréndere
3. impresa
4. intrapréndere
5. rappreságlia
6. sorpréndere; sorprésa

ricévere

1. ricétta
2. ricevиménto
3. ricevúta

to be able, can, may; power

1. powerful; power, might, potency
2. possible
3. farm, estate
4. to dispossess

to take, catch, take up, get, fetch

1. to learn, apprehend, hear
2. to comprehend, consist of, include, understand
3. undertaking, enterprise
4. to undertake
5. reprisal
6. to surprise; surprise

to receive

1. prescription, recipe
2. reception
3. receipt

to put

1. to admit
2. to commit; errand
3. to resign
4. to meddle
5. to omit

to please; pleasure

1. please
2. pleasant, pleasing, agreeable, nice
3. to please; to condescend
4. to displease; displeasure
5. I am sorry (to)

to carry, bring, bear, take, wear

1. carriage, gait
2. within reach
3. to behave
4. important; importance
5. to matter, to import
6. to support, bear

to say, tell

1. to dictate; dictation
2. to bless
3. to contradict
4. to curse
5. to preach; sermon
6. to predict

to sleep

1. to doze
2. late riser, slow fellow
3. drowsy state
4. to fall asleep

to sign

1. signature

rispóndere

1. rispósta
2. responsábile

aprire

1. all'apérto
2. apertúra

preposizioni

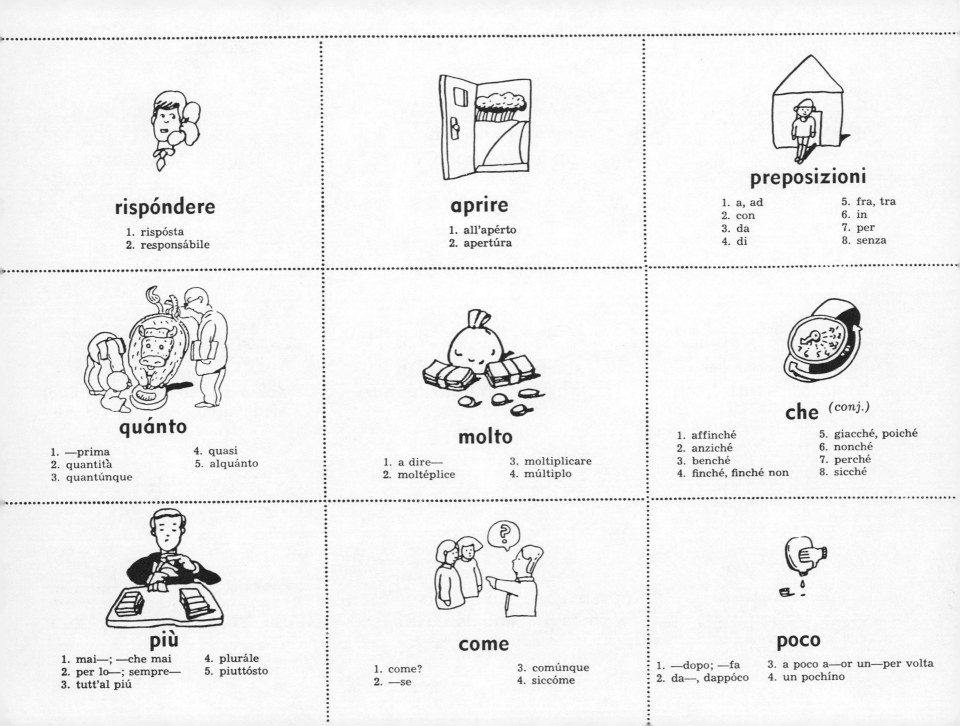

1. a, ad
2. con
3. da
4. di
5. fra, tra
6. in
7. per
8. senza

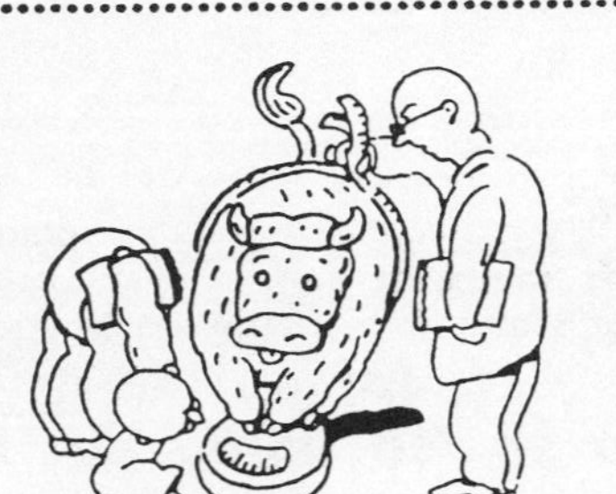

quánto

1. —prima
2. quantità
3. quantúnque
4. quasi
5. alquánto

molto

1. a dire—
2. moltéplice
3. moltiplicare
4. múltiplo

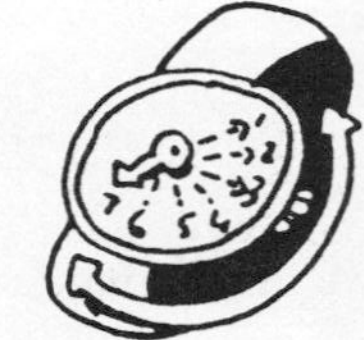

che *(conj.)*

1. affinché
2. anziché
3. benché
4. finché, finché non
5. giacché, poiché
6. nonché
7. perché
8. sicché

più

1. mai—; —che mai
2. per lo—; sempre—
3. tutt'al piú
4. plurále
5. piuttósto

come

1. come?
2. —se
3. comúnque
4. siccóme

poco

1. —dopo; —fa
2. da—, dappóco
3. a poco a—or un—per volta
4. un pochíno

more, any more, plus, many

1. certainly not; more than ever
2. for the most part, ordinarily; more and more
3. at the most
4. plural
5. rather

as, just as, how, like, as to, as well as, such as

1. what did you say?
2. as if
3. no matter how
4. as, since, just as

little, few

1. soon afterward; a little while ago
2. of little value, worthless
3. little by little
4. a little bit

how much, how many, how long, as much as, as many as, as far as

1. as soon as possible
2. quantity
3. although
4. almost, as if
5. rather, somewhat

much, many; very, quite, a great deal, a lot

1. at the maximum
2. multiple *(adj.)*
3. to multiply
4. multiple *(n.)*

that, than, so that, while

1. so that, in order that
2. rather than
3. although
4. as long as, until
5. since
6. as well as
7. why, because
8. so that

to answer, reply

1. answer
2. responsible

to open, open up

1. in the open
2. opening

prepositions

1. to, at, in, into, on, toward
2. with, by
3. from, by, of, to, with, on, since, at or to the house (shop, office, etc.) of
4. of, for, from, to, in, about, with
5. between, among, within
6. in, into, during, on, at, to, for
7. for, because, of, by, to, through, across, over, on account of
8. without

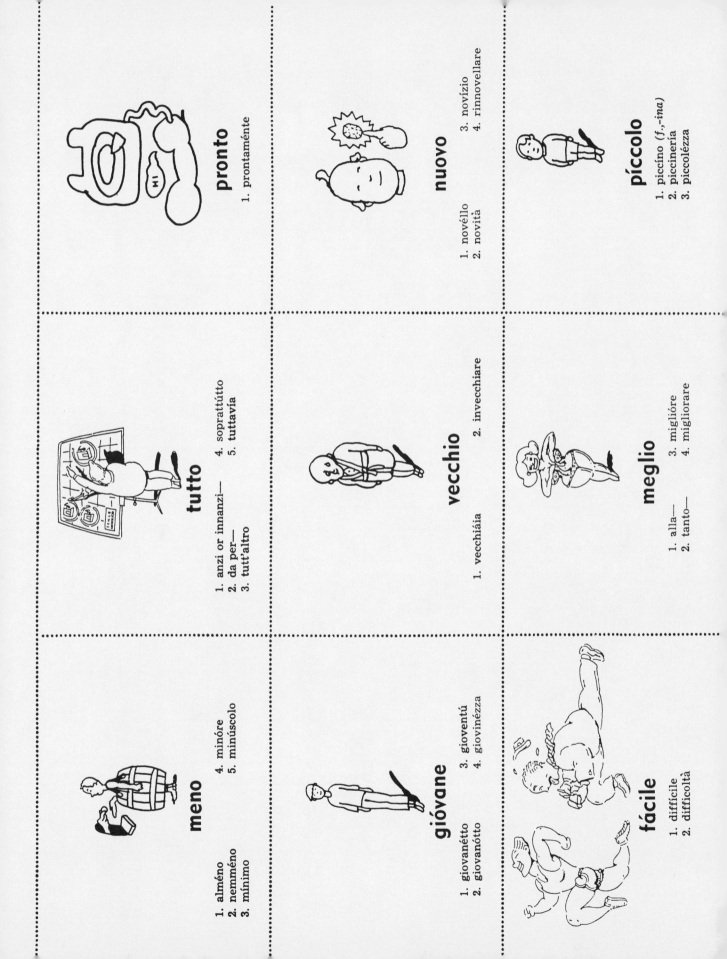

meno

1. alméno
2. nemméno
3. mínimo
4. minóre
5. minúscolo

tutto

1. anzi or innanzi—
2. da per—
3. tutt'altro
4. soprattútto
5. tuttavía

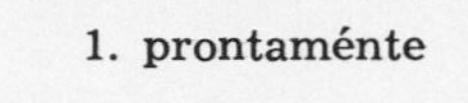

pronto

1. prontaménte

gióvane

1. giovanétto
2. giovanótto
3. gioventú
4. giovinézza

vecchio

1. vecchiáia
2. invecchiare

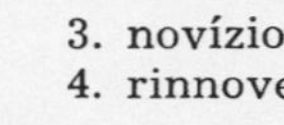

nuovo

1. novéllo
2. novità
3. novízio
4. rinnovellare

fácile

1. diffícile
2. difficoltà

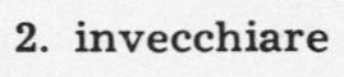

meglio

1. alla—
2. tanto—
3. miglióre
4. migliorare

píccolo

1. piccíno *(f.,-ina)*
2. piccinería
3. piccolézza

easy

1. difficult, hard
2. difficulty

better *(adv.)*, rather

1. as well as one can (or could)
2. so much the better
3. better, best
4. to improve

small, little

1. tiny, little boy or girl
2. pettiness
3. smallness, trifle

young, young man or woman

1. boy
2. young man
3. youth
4. youthfulness, young people

old

1. old age
2. to grow old

new

1. new, fresh
2. novelty, news
3. novice
4. to renew, refresh

less, fewer

1. at least
2. not even
3. least, minimum, very small
4. less, smaller, minor, younger
5. small (letters), paltry, tiny

all, whole, entire, every

1. first of all
2. everywhere
3. quite on the contrary
4. above all
5. nevertheless, still, yet

ready, prompt

1. promptly, quickly, hello (on phone)

grande

1. grandézza
2. grandióso
3. ingrandire

caro

1. carézza; accarezzare
2. rincarare; rincarire

freddo

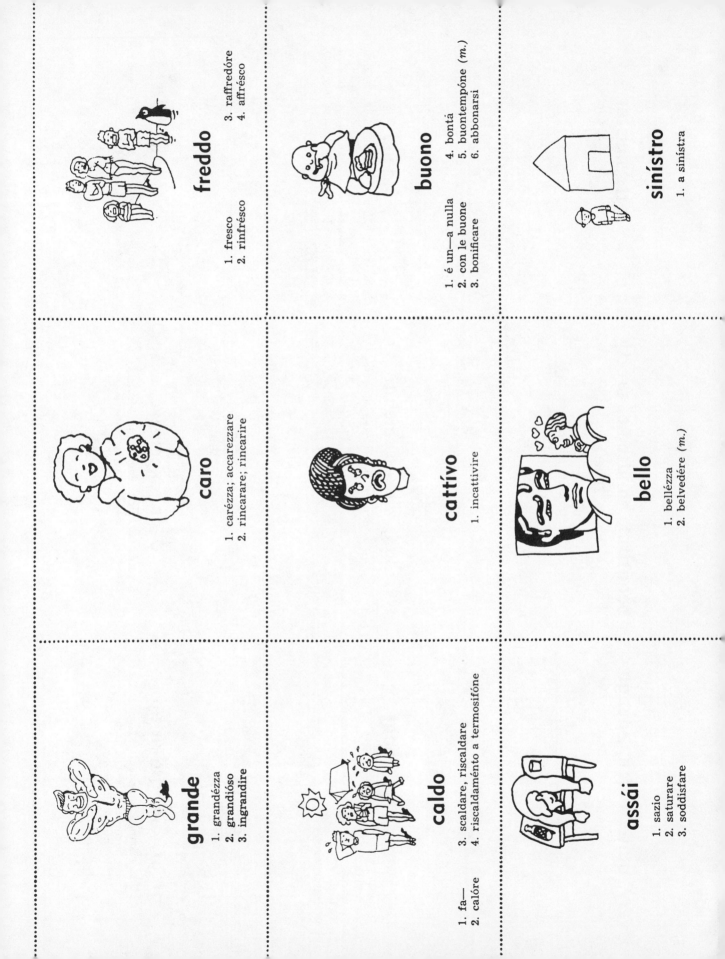

1. fresco
2. rinfrésco
3. raffredóre
4. affrésco

caldo

1. fa—
2. calóre
3. scaldare, riscaldare
4. riscaldaménto a termosifóne

cattívo

1. incattivire

buono

1. é un—a nulla
2. con le buone
3. bonificare
4. bontá
5. buontempóne (*m.*)
6. abbonarsi

assái

1. sazio
2. saturare
3. soddisfare

bello

1. bellézza
2. belvedére (*m.*)

siníst ro

1. a sinístra

very, quite, much, enough

1. satiated
2. to saturate
3. to satisfy, please

beautiful, handsome, pretty, fine

1. beauty
2. look-out tower, terrace

left, sinister

1. at, on, to the left

warm, hot; heat

1. It's warm
2. warmth, heat
3. to warm, warm up; to warm oneself, to get excited
4. central heating

bad, wicked, mean

1. to grow bad, wicked

good

1. he is a good for nothing
2. with kindness
3. to reclaim (by drainage or irrigation)
4. goodness, kindness
5. gay fellow
6. to subscribe (to a magazine, etc.)

great, big, grown up

1. greatness, grandeur
2. grandiose, imposing, grand
3. to enlarge; to increase

dear, expensive

1. caress; to caress, cherish (an idea)
2. to raise, or rise, in price; to rise in price

cold *(adj. & n.)*

1. cool
2. refreshment
3. a cold, severe chill
4. fresco

destro

1. a destra
2. destrézza
3. addestrare

avverbi di tempo

1. adésso
2. dománi
3. dopo
4. ieri
5. intánto
6. mai
7. mentre
8. oggi
9. poi
10. quándo
11. súbito
12. sempre

avverbi di luogo

1. davanti (*a*), dinnanzi a
2. ci, vi; ivi
3. dove, ove; dovunque
4. giú, su
5. là, li; qua, qui
6. laggiú, lassú; quaggiú, quassú
7. ne
8. presso (*a*)
9. sotto

indirízzo

1. indirizzare

via

1. viaggiare
2. viággio
3. viale (*m.*)
4. avviare
5. inviare
6. rinviare

strada

1. stradále (*m.*)
2. autostráda

città

1. cittadíno
2. civíle
3. civiltà

paese (*m.*)

1. paesággio
2. compaesáno

bottéga

city

1. citizen
2. civil, civilized; civilian
3. civilization

country, land, village

1. landscape
2. countryman, compatriot

shop, store

address, direction

1. to address, direct

way, road, street; away

1. to travel
2. trip, journey, voyage
3. boulevard
4. to give a start to; to set out, start on one's way, career
5. to send
6. to postpone, send back or again

road, street, way

1. road *(adj.)*, long stretch of road
2. speedway

right, dextrous

1. at, to the right
2. dexterity
3. to drill, train; to perfect oneself

adverbs of time

1. now
2. tomorrow
3. afterward, later, then
4. yesterday
5. meanwhile
6. ever, never
7. while
8. today
9. then, after, afterward
10. when, whenever
11. at once, immediately
12. always

adverbs of place

1. before, in front of
2. here, there, in it; there
3. where; everywhere, wherever
4. down, up
5. there; here
6. down there, up there; down here, up here
7. from there, thence, of there, from it, from here
8. near, by
9. under

negózio

1. negoziare
2. negoziánte *(m.)*
3. negoziatóre

mercáto

1. a buon—
2. mercánte *(m.)*
3. merce
4. merciáio *(f.,-iaia)*
5. commércio
6. smerciare

banca

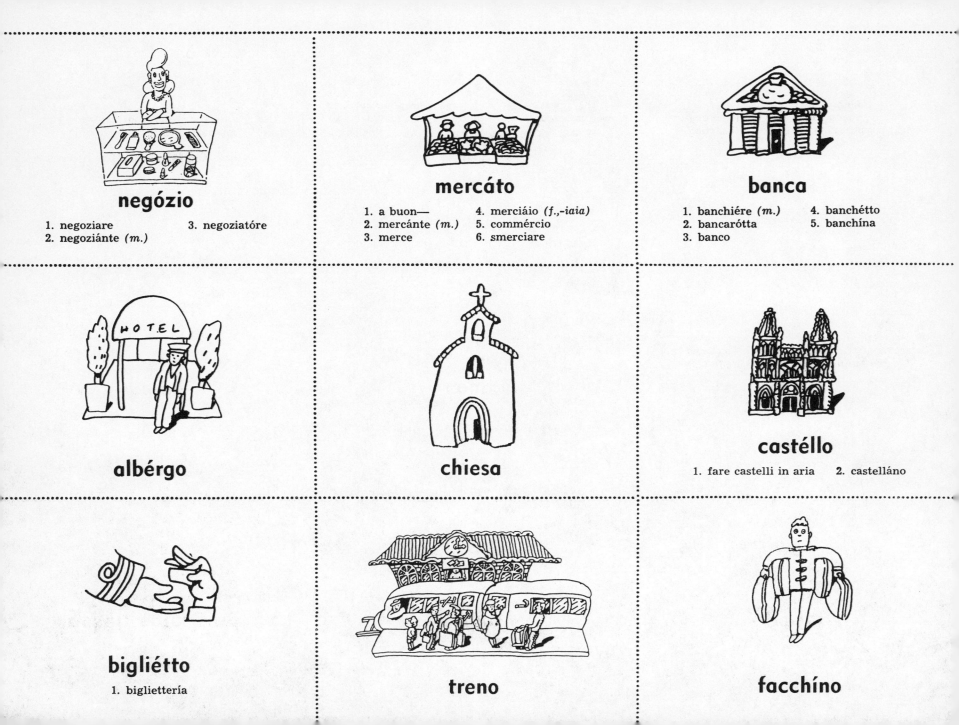

1. banchiére *(m.)*
2. bancarótta
3. banco
4. banchétto
5. banchína

albérgo

chiesa

castéllo

1. fare castelli in aria
2. castelláno

bigliétto

1. bigliettería

treno

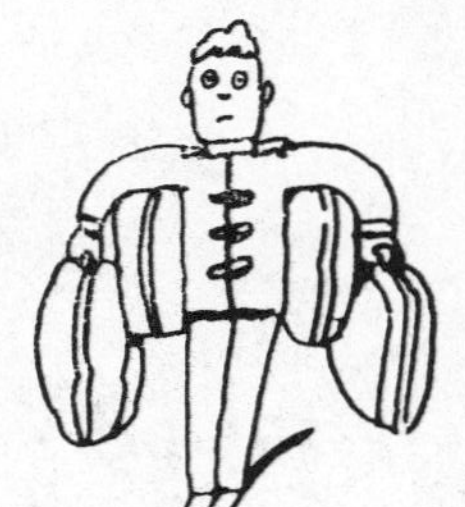

facchíno

ticket, note, card

1. ticket-office

train

porter

hotel

church

castle

1. to build castles in Spain (in the air)
2. governor, inhabitant, or owner of a castle

store, shop

1. to negotiate, trade, transact
2. dealer, merchant
3. negotiator

market

1. cheap
2. merchant, business man
3. merchandise, goods
4. haberdasher
5. commerce, trade
6. to sell

bank

1. banker
2. bankruptcy
3. counter, desk, bank
4. banquet
5. pier, quay

bagáglio

valígia

1. svaligiare

denáro

dogána

prezzo

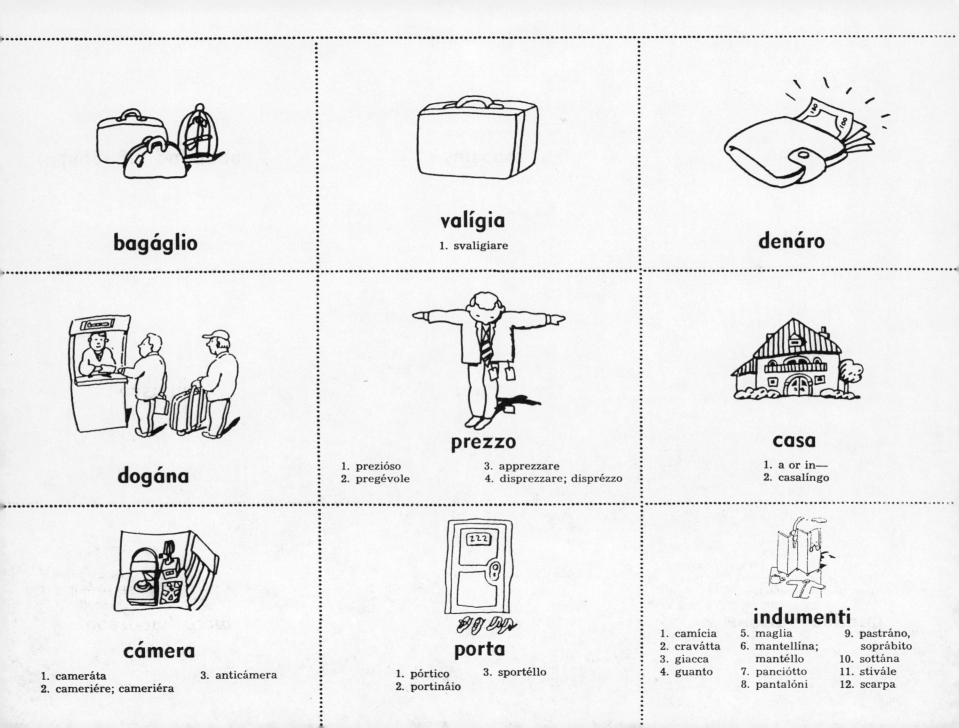

1. prezióso
2. pregévole
3. apprezzare
4. disprezzare; disprézzo

casa

1. a or in—
2. casalíngo

cámera

1. cameráta
2. cameriére; cameriéra
3. anticámera

porta

1. pórtico
2. portináio
3. sportéllo

indumenti

1. camícia
2. cravátta
3. giacca
4. guanto
5. maglia
6. mantellína; mantéllo
7. panciótto
8. pantalóni
9. pastráno, soprábito
10. sottána
11. stiвále
12. scarpa

bedroom, room

1. dormitory; boys sleeping in one room
2. waiter, steward, butler; maid, stewardess
3. antechamber

door

1. porch, arcade
2. doorkeeper
3. door (of a car), window (of an office)

wearing apparel

1. shirt
2. necktie
3. coat
4. glove
5. sweater
6. mantelet; cape, cloak
7. vest
8. trousers
9. overcoat
10. skirt, cassock
11. boot
12. shoe

customs

price

1. precious
2. valuable
3. to appreciate, value
4. to despise; contempt

house, home

1. at home
2. domestic, homely

luggage, baggage

suitcase

1. to unpack, pillage, steal

money

borsa

1. —di studio
2. borsaiuólo
3. rimborsare
4. sborsare

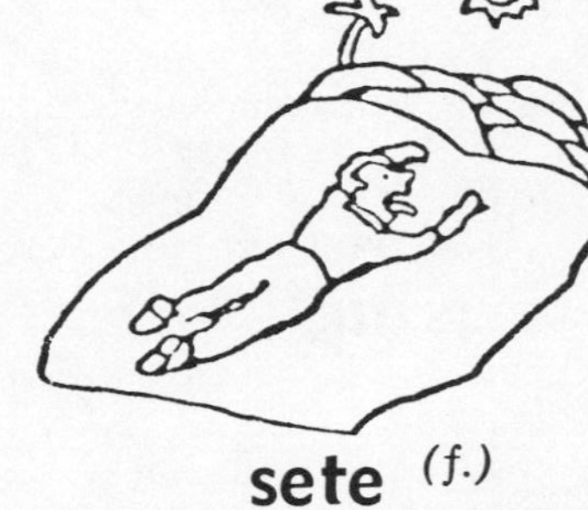

sete (*f.*)

1. avere—
2. morire di—
3. assetáto
4. dissetare

fame (*f.*)

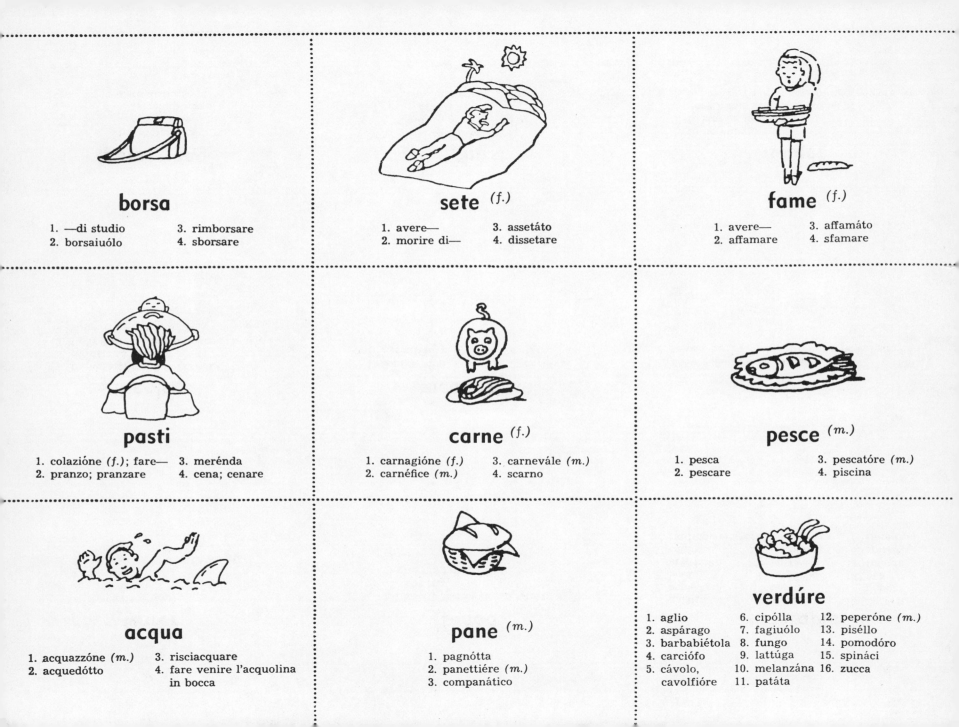

1. avere—
2. affamare
3. affamáto
4. sfamare

pasti

1. colazióne (*f.*); fare—
2. pranzo; pranzare
3. merénda
4. cena; cenare

carne (*f.*)

1. carnagióne (*f.*)
2. carnéfice (*m.*)
3. carneväle (*m.*)
4. scarno

pesce (*m.*)

1. pesca
2. pescare
3. pescatóre (*m.*)
4. piscina

acqua

1. acquazzóne (*m.*)
2. acquedótto
3. risciacquare
4. fare venire l'acquolina in bocca

pane (*m.*)

1. pagnótta
2. panettiére (*m.*)
3. companático

verdúre

1. aglio
2. aspárago
3. barbabiétola
4. carciófo
5. cávolo, cavolfióre
6. cipólla
7. fagiuólo
8. fungo
9. lattúga
10. melanzána
11. patáta
12. peperóne (*m.*)
13. piséllo
14. pomodóro
15. spináci
16. zucca

water

1. shower (of rain)
2. aqueduct
3. to rinse
4. to make one's mouth water

bread

1. small loaf of bread, bun
2. baker
3. accompaniments of foods

vegetables

1. garlic
2. asparagus
3. beets
4. artichoke
5. cabbage, cauliflower
6. onion
7. bean
8. mushroom
9. lettuce
10. eggplant
11. potato
12. (green) pepper
13. pea
14. tomato
15. spinach
16. pumpkin

meals

1. breakfast; to have breakfast
2. dinner; to dine
3. light (afternoon) luncheon, snack
4. supper; to have supper

meat, flesh

1. complexion
2. executioner
3. carnival
4. thin, lean

fish

1. fishing, fishery
2. to fish
3. fisher
4. swimming pool, fish pond

purse, bag

1. scholarship
2. purse-lifter
3. to reimburse
4. to disburse

thirst

1. to be thirsty
2. to be very thirsty
3. thirsty
4. to quench the thirst

hunger

1. to be hungry
2. to starve, famish
3. very hungry, very desirous of
4. to satisfy (one's own) hunger, desire, etc.

frutta

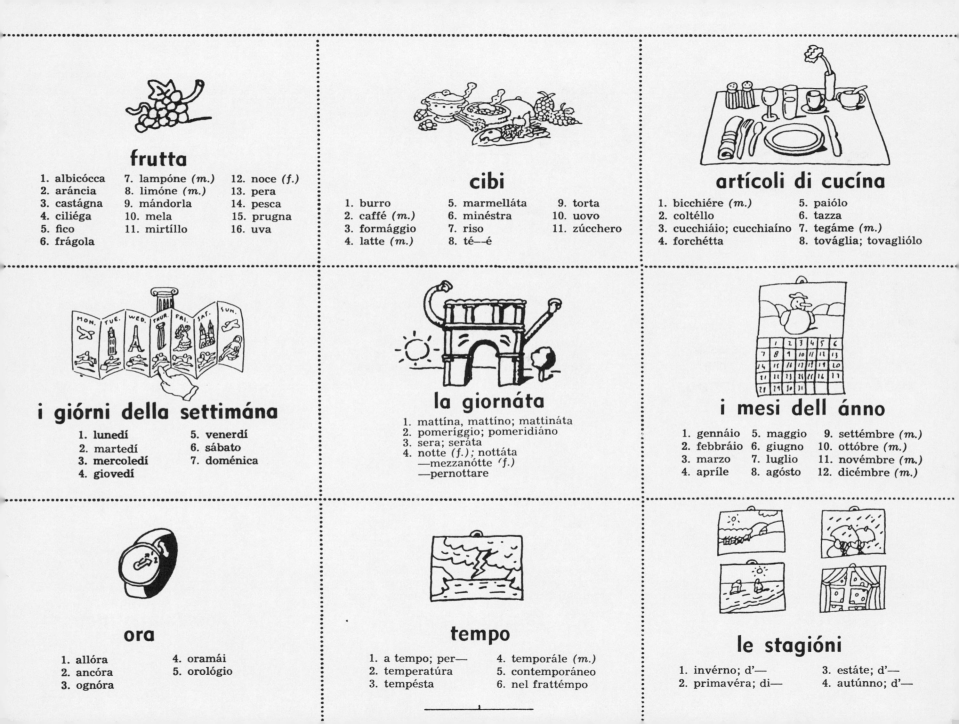

1. albicócca
2. aráncia
3. castágna
4. ciliéga
5. fico
6. frágola
7. lampóne *(m.)*
8. limóne *(m.)*
9. mándorla
10. mela
11. mirtíllo
12. noce *(f.)*
13. pera
14. pesca
15. prugna
16. uva

cibi

1. burro
2. caffé *(m.)*
3. formággio
4. latte *(m.)*
5. marmelláta
6. minéstra
7. riso
8. té—é
9. torta
10. uovo
11. zúcchero

artícoli di cucína

1. bicchiére *(m.)*
2. coltéllo
3. cucchiáio; cucchiaíno
4. forchétta
5. paiólo
6. tazza
7. tegáme *(m.)*
8. tovåglia; tovagliólo

i giórni della settimána

1. **lunedí**
2. martedí
3. **mercoledí**
4. **giovedí**
5. **venerdí**
6. **sábato**
7. **doménica**

la giornáta

1. mattína, mattíno; mattináta
2. pomeríggio; pomeridiáno
3. sera; seráta
4. notte *(f.)*; nottáta
   —mezzanótte *(f.)*
   —pernottare

i mesi dell ánno

1. gennáio
2. febbráio
3. marzo
4. apríle
5. maggio
6. giugno
7. luglio
8. agósto
9. settémbre *(m.)*
10. ottóbre *(m.)*
11. novémbre *(m.)*
12. dicémbre *(m.)*

ora

1. allóra
2. ancóra
3. ognóra
4. oramái
5. orológio

tempo

1. a tempo; per—
2. temperatúra
3. tempésta
4. temporále *(m.)*
5. contemporáneo
6. nel frattémpo

le stagióni

1. invérno; d'—
2. primavéra; di—
3. estáte; d'—
4. autúnno; d'—

hour, time; now

1. then, at that time
2. again, still, yet, more, too, even
3. always
4. by now, henceforth
5. watch, clock

time, weather

1. on time; early
2. temperature
3. tempest, storm
4. storm; temporal
5. contemporary
6. in the meantime

the season

1. winter; in winter
2. spring; in spring
3. summer; in summer
4. fall, autumn; in the fall

the days of the week

1. Monday
2. Tuesday
3. Wednesday
4. Thursday
5. Friday
6. Saturday
7. Sunday

the day

1. morning; morning (in its duration)
2. afternoon; afternoon *(adj.)*
3. evening; evening (in its duration)
4. night; night (in its duration)
   —midnight
   —to spend the night, lodge

the months of the year

1. January
2. February
3. March
4. April
5. May
6. June
7. July
8. August
9. September
10. October
11. November
12. December

fruits

1. apricot
2. orange
3. chestnut
4. cherry
5. fig
6. strawberry
7. raspberry
8. lemon
9. almond
10. apple
11. blueberry
12. nut
13. pear
14. peach
15. plum, prune
16. grapes

foods

1. butter
2. coffee
3. cheese
4. milk
5. jam, marmalade
6. soup
7. rice
8. tea
9. cake
10. egg
11. sugar

kitchen items

1. glass
2. knife
3. spoon; teaspoon
4. fork
5. kettle
6. cup
7. pan
8. tablecloth; napkin

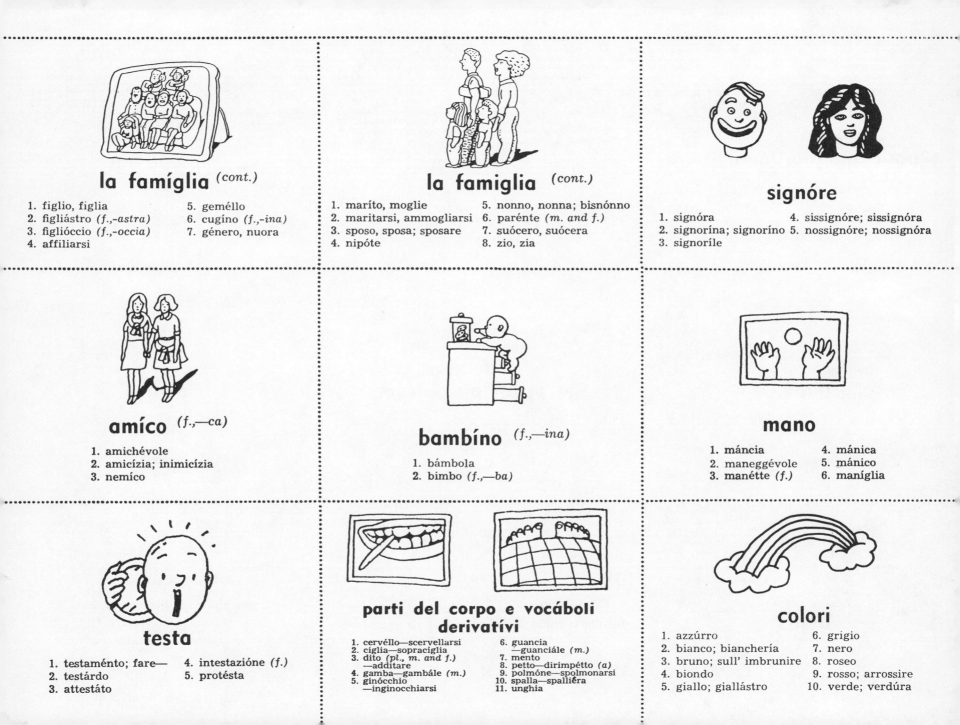

la famíglia (cont.)

1. figlio, figlia
2. figliástro (*f.,-astra*)
3. figlióccio (*f.,-occia*)
4. affiliarsi
5. geméllo
6. cugíno (*f.,-ina*)
7. género, nuora

la famiglia (cont.)

1. maríto, moglie
2. maritarsi, ammogliarsi
3. sposo, sposa; sposare
4. nipóte
5. nonno, nonna; bisnónno
6. parénte (*m. and f.*)
7. suócero, suócera
8. zio, zia

signóre

1. signóra
2. signorína; signoríno
3. signoríle
4. sissignóre; sissignóra
5. nossignóre; nossignóra

amíco (*f.,—ca*)

1. amichévole
2. amicízia; inimicízia
3. nemíco

bambíno (*f.,—ina*)

1. bámbola
2. bimbo (*f.,—ba*)

mano

1. máncia
2. maneggévole
3. manétte (*f.*)
4. mánica
5. mánico
6. maníglia

testa

1. testaménto; fare—
2. testárdo
3. attestáto
4. intestazióne (*f.*)
5. protésta

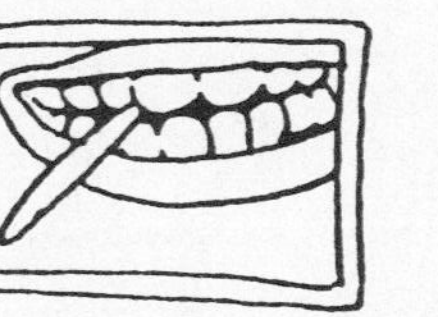

parti del corpo e vocáboli derivatívi

1. cervéllo—scervellarsi
2. ciglia—sopracíglia
3. dito (*pl., m. and f.*) —additare
4. gamba—gambále (*m.*)
5. ginócchio —inginocchiarsi
6. guancia —guanciále (*m.*)
7. mento
8. petto—dirimpétto (*a*)
9. polmóne—spolmonarsi
10. spalla—spalliéra
11. unghia

colori

1. azzúrro
2. bianco; biancheria
3. bruno; sull' imbrunire
4. biondo
5. giallo; gialIástro
6. grigio
7. nero
8. roseo
9. rosso; arrossire
10. verde; verdúra

head

1. testament, will; to make a will
2. stubborn
3. certificate, token, evidence
4. title, inscription
5. protest

parts of the body & derivatives

1. brain
   —to cudgel one's brain
2. eye-lashes
   —eyebrows
3. finger
   —to point out
4. knee
   —to kneel
6. cheek
   —pillow
7. chin
8. chest
   —opposite
9. lung
   —to become breathless with talking
10. shoulder
   —back (of a chair)

colors

1. blue
2. white; linen
3. dark; at dusk
4. blond
5. yellow; yellowish
6. gray
7. black
8. rosy
9. red; to blush
10. green; green vegetables, greenery

friend

1. friendly
2. friendship; enmity
3. enemy

baby, child, little boy or girl

1. doll
2. baby, child, little boy or girl

hand

1. tip
2. easy to handle
3. handcuffs
4. sleeve
5. handle (of a knife, shovel, etc.)
6. handle (of a door, drawer, etc.)

the family *(cont.)*

1. son, daughter
2. step-son, step-daughter
3. god-child
4. to associate oneself (with)
5. twin
6. cousin
7. son-in-law, daughter-in-law

the family *(cont.)*

1. husband, wife
2. to get married
3. bridegroom, bride; to marry, get married
4. nephew, niece
5. grandfather, grandmother; great-grandfather
6. relative
7. father-in-law, mother-in-law
8. uncle, aunt

gentleman, lord, sir, man, Mr.

1. lady, madam, Mrs., wife
2. young lady, miss; master
3. noble, refined
4. yes, sir; yes, madam
5. no, sir; no, madam